THE STUDIA PHILONICA ANNUAL
Studies in Hellenistic Judaism

Society of Biblical Literature

THE STUDIA PHILONICA ANNUAL
Studies in Hellenistic Judaism

Editors
David T. Runia
Gregory E. Sterling

THE STUDIA PHILONICA ANNUAL
Studies in Hellenistic Judaism

Volume XX

2008

EDITORS:
David T. Runia
Gregory E. Sterling

ASSOCIATE EDITOR
David Winston

BOOK REVIEW EDITOR
Ronald Cox

Society of Biblical Literature
Atlanta

THE STUDIA PHILONICA ANNUAL
Studies in Hellenistic Judaism

The financial support of
C. J. de Vogel Foundation, Utrecht
Queen's College, University of Melbourne
University of Notre Dame
Pepperdine University
is gratefully acknowledged

The cover photo, *Ezra Reads the Law*, is from a wall painting in the Dura Europos synagogue and used with permission from Zev Radovan (www.BibleLandPictures.com).

THE STUDIA PHILONICA ANNUAL
STUDIES IN HELLENISTIC JUDAISM

Contributions should be sent to the Editor, Prof. Gregory E. Sterling, Dean of the Graduate School, 408 Main Building, University of Notre Dame, Notre Dame, IN 46556, USA; email: sterling@nd.edu. Please send books for review to the Book Review Editor, Dr. Ronald Cox, Religion Division, Pepperdine University, 24255 Pacific Coast Highway, Malibu, CA 90263-4352, email rcox@pepperdine.edu.

Contributors are requested to observe the "Instructions to Contributors" located at the end of the volume. These can also be consulted on the Annual's website: http://www.nd.edu/~philojud. Articles which do not conform to these instructions cannot be accepted for inclusion.

The Studia Philonica Monograph series accepts monographs in the area of Hellenistic Judaism, with special emphasis on Philo and his *Umwelt*. Proposals for books in this series should be sent to Prof. Gregory E. Sterling, Dean of the Graduate School, 408 Main Building, University of Notre Dame, Notre Dame IN 46556, USA; email sterling.1@nd.edu

CONTENTS*

ARTICLES

Burton L. MACK, Argumentation in Philo's *De Sacrificiis* 1

James M. SCOTT, Dionysus in Philo of Alexandria: A Study of *De vita
contemplativa* 33

Ilaria L. E. RAMELLI, Philosophical Allegoresis of Scripture in Philo and
its Legacy in Gregory of Nyssa 55

Cyril O'REGAN, Hegel's Retrieval of Philo: Constitution of a Christian
Heretic 101

SPECIAL SECTION: PHILO'S *DE ABRAHAMO*

Gregory E. STERLING, Philo's *De Abrahamo*: Introduction 129

David T. RUNIA, The Place of *De Abrahamo* in Philo's *oeuvre* 133

James R. ROYSE, The Text of Philo's *De Abrahamo* 151

BIBLIOGRAPHY SECTION

D. T. RUNIA, E. BIRNBAUM, K. A. FOX, A. C. GELJON, H. M. KEIZER,
J. P. MARTÍN, M. R. NIEHOFF, J. RIAUD, G. SCHIMANOWSKI, T. SELAND,
Philo of Alexandria: An Annotated Bibliography 2005 167

SUPPLEMENT: A Provisional Bibliography 2006–2008 198

BOOK REVIEW SECTION

George W. E. NICKELSBURG, *Jewish Literature Between the Bible and the
Mishnah: A Historical and Literary Introduction*
Reviewed by Randall D. CHESNUTT 211

Terence L. DONALDSON, *Judaism and the Gentiles: Jewish Patterns of
Universalism (to 135 C.E.)*
Reviewed by Ellen BIRNBAUM 213

Naomi G. COHEN, *Philo's Scriptures. Citations from the Prophets and Writings:
Evidence for a* Haftarah *Cycle in Second Temple Judaism*
Reviewed by Jutta LEONHARDT-BALZER 221

Francesca CALABI, *God's Acting, Man's Acting: Tradition and Philosophy in
Philo of Alexandria*
Reviewed by John DILLON 224

Ronald Cox, *By the Same Word: Creation and Salvation in Hellenistic Judaism and Early Christianity*
Reviewed by Thomas H. Tobin S.J. 227

Torrey Seland, *Strangers in the Light: Philonic Perspectives on Christian Identity in 1 Peter*
Reviewed by Kenneth L. Schenck 230

William Loader, *The Septuagint, Sexuality, and the New Testament: Case Studies on the Impact of the LXX in Philo and the New Testament*
Reviewed by L. Ann Jervis 234

John Barclay, *Against Apion*. Flavius Josephus, Translation & Commentary: Volume 10
Reviewed by Gregory E. Sterling 236

M. Bonazzi, C. Lévy, and C. Steel (eds.), *A Platonic Pythagoras: Platonism and Pythagoreanism in the Imperial Age*
Reviewed by David T. Runia 242

News and Notes 245

Notes on Contributors 248

Instructions to Contributors 252

* The editors wish to thank the typesetter Gonni Runia once again for her tireless and meticulous work on this volume. They also wish to thank Tamar Primoratz (Melbourne) for her assistance with the bibliography, and Kindalee DeLong for the assistance she has given in maintaining the Annual's website.

The Studia Philonica Annual 20 (2008) 1–32

ARGUMENTATION IN PHILO'S *DE SACRIFICIIS**

BURTON L. MACK

Challenge: The Scripture as Chreia

Scholars are not clear about the organizing principles for a Philonic unit of composition. We call it a treatise when we think of its title. We call it a commentary when we notice its *lemmata*. And we call it ethical philosophy when we have its content in mind. The embarrassments begin when the student asks us to go on and say more about a Philonic composition. We cannot outline its progression of thought as a treatise. We are unable to say what its hermeneutic is or achieves as a commentary. And we falter when talking about the system of thought which must be there, we assume, in order to support such ethical statements. Perhaps then we should call it a unit of elaboration.

The challenge to work this out was handed to me at the Philo Seminar of SNTS at its 1983 meeting. Such an assignment was a natural response to my paper on *Sacr.* 1–10 in which I sought to demonstrate a pattern of rhetorical logic and composition in the first *lemma* of the treatise.[1] The pattern itself was taken right out of the rhetors' *progymnasmata*. But the discovery of the pattern's logic and of its significance for literary composition in the Greco-Roman period was made at Claremont where I and others had been working on the *chreia*. The pattern behind the elaboration of the *chreia* in Hermogenes' *Progymnasmata* was found to have played an important role in education during our period. The pattern is simple in outline but

---

* Editorial Note: This article was prepared by one of the founding figures of the *Studia Philonica*, the forerunner of the current publication. The paper was a sequel to the work mentioned in the note below. Professor Mack never published this piece and recently "discovered it." The article was part of Professor Mack's attempt to develop a programmatic method for reading the Philonic corpus. The article is important not only for the history of scholarship that it provides, but for the careful analysis of an important Philonic treatise.

[1] B. L. Mack, "Decoding the Scripture: Philo and the Rules of Rhetoric," in *Nourished with Peace: Studies in Hellenistic Judaism in Memory of Samuel Sandmel* (ed. F. Greenspahn, E. Hilgert, and B. Mack; Scholars Press Homage Series; Chico, CA: Scholars Press, 1984), 80–115.

powerful in the logic of persuasion. It virtually compresses the complex and exhaustive theories of argumentation available in the tradition of the rhetorical *techne* into a short, ordered list of items required for any "complete argument." It could be used to develop a little argument in support of traditional aphoristic materials, or compose a small paragraph on a theme or thesis. That much became clear from a study of the rhetorical handbooks. The further question which interested us was whether it could be used for other literary compositions as well.

My paper on *Sacr.* 1–10 was able to show that this elaboration pattern was in evidence as a kind of outline for the development of the argument in a small unit of Philonic commentary. The scriptural *lemma* was found to be treated as an enigmatic *chreia*. The first moves away from it, in order to establish restatements of the text's intention, were found to correspond to rhetorical procedures for setting up a case or thesis. The subsequent discussion was found to follow the rhetorical pattern of supporting argumentation. It could be shown that extremely precise considerations had determined the selection of terms, analogies, major metaphors, and contrasts employed in the elaboration, and that the section as a whole composed a period which did make sense given the rules of persuasion common to rhetorical practice. With this discovery a pattern of logic surfaced which appeared to suggest some answers to our questions about Philo's hermeneutic, commentary composition, and system of thought. The next obvious question was whether the elaboration pattern had influenced the construction of other *lemmata*, and whether it could be traced throughout the treatise as a whole.

This paper is a response to that challenge. The discussions in the earlier paper are presupposed. There the elaboration pattern is given, described, and discussed. A theory of persuasion using aphoristic maxims, comparisons and contrasts, analogies, examples, and the citation of authorities is presented. The exegesis of *Sacr.* 1–10 given in that paper is schematic, showing how the elaboration pattern can help to identify the rhetorical moves crucial to the development of the argument. Not every statement in the section (*Sacr.* 1–10) required comment, many belonging to stylistic ornamentation, emphases of points particularly interesting to Philo, or rhetorical embellishments. But everything could be accounted for as functional rhetorically in some way to the main line of argument. And certain characteristics of the Philonic elaboration could be noted.

These characteristics may be summarized. Decoding the encoded text (scripture as *chreia*) did not occur all at once in the first moves. At first only one or two "signs" in the text were translated into new symbols. Decoding of the entire text occurred step by step throughout the elaboration. Themes also were introduced which then were developed more fully in the course of the elaboration. A penchant for contrastive comparisons and dialectical inversions was discovered. And the period as a whole was found to have a double rhetorical function: 1) to demonstrate that the proposed interpretation of the text was the right one and 2) to persuade the reader of the logic, truth, and significance of the thesis developed.

The questions which remained unsolved at the end of that paper had to do with 1) the function of the scriptural text as authority, and 2) the source and authority for the system of values assumed in the use of rhetorical elaboration itself. If the scripture can be called Philo's "field of play," it is still the case that he takes it quite seriously. And if the terms "bad" and "good" are at first empty ciphers for Philo, not necessarily committing him to Greek systems of value, they are nevertheless exactly those terms about which Philo always appears to be most concerned. If we extend our investigation now to a larger unit of Philonic composition, the question is whether more clarity can be obtained on these fronts. This presumes, of course, that the larger unit continues to follow the pattern of elaboration!

The reader will recall that the pattern of elaboration consists of the following items:

1) *Prooimion,* or a brief work of praise for the author
2) The *Chreia* cited or paraphrased
3) The *Rationale*
4) A statement of the *Converse,* or a Contrast
5) An *Analogy*
6) An *Example*
7) A *Witness,* or citation of an Authority
8) *Epilog* as Conclusion and / or Exhortation.

We will seek now to demonstrate that this pattern of rhetorical argumentation has determined Philo's treatment of the scriptural text in the composition of the commentary-treatise as a whole.

Foray: The Commentary as Elaboration

De Sacrificiis is a treatise of 139 paragraphs on the theme of "The Sacrifices of Abel and Cain." It is a commentary upon Gen 4:2–4a, which is divided into four *lemmata* as follows:

I   *Sacr.* 1–10 on Gen 4:2a:
"He added to this that she brought forth his brother Abel."

II *Sacr.* 11–51 on Gen 4:2b:
"And Abel become a shepherd of the sheep;
but Cain was a tiller of the land."

III *Sacr.* 52–87 on Gen 4:3:
"And it came to pass after some days that Cain brought
of the fruits of the earth as a sacrifice to the Lord."

IV *Sacr* 88–139 on Gen 4:4a:
"And Abel brought also himself of the first-born of his
sheep and of their fats."

In the earlier study, the first section of ten paragraphs was found to contain two complete elaborations, each of which, however, had the first four items of the pattern in common. From that point on, first one and then the other of the two themes being contrasted (relative to Cain/relative to Abel) were given separate supporting argumentations. This bit of duplication and complexity in the employment of the pattern can be understood as a creative and clever use of the author's logical and compositional skills. It alerts us to the possibility that there may be other ways to arrange combinations of the pattern. Professional teachers of rhetoric would have approved. They spoke frequently about the danger of imitating models woodenly, and the need to develop one's own inventive style. One sought always to erase the outlines of the rhetorical model by stylistic embellishments and clever rhetorical moves.

But especially in the case of a lengthy theme-treatise with only four major *lemmata*, one sees at once that, should the elaboration pattern continue to provide the sub-structural model for argumentation, ingenuity will be called for to develop interlocking combinations of the sequences. This turns out to be exactly what Philo achieved.

There are seven major elaborations in sequence which give outline to the treatise. Section I (*Sacr.* 1–10) has one elaboration; Section II (*Sacr.* 11–51) has two; Section III (*Sacr.* 52–87) has three; and Section IV (*Sacr.* 88–139) has one. These follow the order of the scriptural *lemmata* cited with subdivisions of a given *lemma* providing for the additional major elaborations in Sections II and III. But there are thirteen minor elaborations occurring within this overall outline. This can happen because the citation of another scriptural text as Example or authoritative Witness can always be taken as a fresh point of departure for another full elaboration. It can also happen because a text can be divided into more than one phrase or topic for investigation, a portion of the text being introduced at a convenient seam in the major argumentation as a sub point calling for its own complete elaboration. There are also many mini-elaboration sequences providing the logic for speeches, paragraphs, and even smaller sets of sentences. The surprising thing is that almost every unit of rhetorical argumentation in the treatise is structured along the lines of the *chreia*-elaboration-pattern.

There are, however, several places in which the pattern has been modified a bit by introducing rhetorical proofs (and terms) which belong to the forensic speech model, rather than to the essentially deliberative speech model of the elaboration pattern. This has occurred because Philo has chosen to introduce other scriptural texts on sacrifice as "legal" texts, in order to show that the description of Cain's sacrifice in Gen 4:3 was "bad" (not according to the "law"), and that Abel's was approved. But as we shall see, the forensic categories are playfully superimposed on what remains an essentially didactic elaboration. The discussion of "accusations," "oaths," "witnesses," and determination of the applicable "law," as well as "definitions" of the "crime" in order to determine the *status qualitas* of the deed (who, when, how, why, what?)—all occur in the first sections of the elaboration pattern. These sections correspond to the *Narratio* of the rhetorical speech outline. They are 1) the Paraphrastic recitation of the Scriptural text (*Chreia*) as an Account of the deed (*diegema*); 2) the *Ratio* and Rationale which establish the case for or against the party; and 3) the *Converse/Contrast* consideration which helps define the quality of the deed. The elaboration pattern allows for such discussion at these points because it is a reduction of the traditional (forensic) speech outline. But the reduction has taken place in the interest of deliberative (or didactic) persuasion, as I argued in the earlier paper. And Philo's forensic rhetoric in Sections III and IV of the treatise should not fool us. In every case the forensic considerations are merely rhetorical moves to reposition ethical discussions, or to position new texts (the "legal" texts on Sacrifice) for more extensive (didactic) elaboration.

Other modifications of the simple eight-fold outline of the elaboration pattern also occur. One is that a *series* of examples may be given at the appropriate place for an Example. And with a series, other possibilities for making points are given. Gradation, ranking, and subtle comparisons and contrasts can be worked out. Here it is frequently the case that Philo works to mediate the extreme contrast of the absolutely "bad" and the perfectly "good" by means of a series of graded examples, all of whom are "on the way toward" perfection. The favorite triad is that of Jacob (the one who toils to make some progress), Abraham (who experiences the transforming vision), and either Isaac or Moses (who are examples of perfection).

There is also one case in which the Exhortation called for at the end of the elaboration pattern is taken as the occasion for developing two lengthy, full-blown speeches. Both "Pleasure" and "Virtue" address the soul in *Sacr.* 20–25 and 26–44. Virtue's speech follows the outline of the rhetorical

speech, and functions subtly as an elaboration of the preceding citation of
Dt 21:15–17. That citation had been introduced to serve the function of the
authoritative Witness within the larger elaboration of the lemma. Toward
the end of Virtue's speech the themes of that larger preceding elaboration
are expressly taken up, and another Analogy (toil), other Examples (Jacob,
Abraham, Isaac!), and another telling scriptural Witness (Gen 33:11) are
given. What we have is an elaboration within an elaboration, interlocked by
attributing a double function to a scriptural citation. This device, using a
scriptural text to serve two rhetorical functions in the elaboration pattern
(usually as 1) Example, or Witness and 2) subordinate *Chreia*), actually
occurs quite frequently in Philo.

But this is not the only means available for interlocking sequential
elaborations. We learned in the earlier paper that motifs could become
"themes" by developing their connotations and arenas of application as the
elaboration progressed. We now need to consider the possibility that certain motifs belonging to the theme of "sacrifice" as Philo wants to construe
it may reoccur throughout the treatise as sub-themes. There are in fact a
cluster of terms related to the notions of "separation," "subtraction," and
"division" on the one hand, and "addition," "referral," and "offering" on
the other, which appear to surface in every major elaboration in one way or
the other. Our thesis is that these notions are being developed intentionally,
and that this thematic development creates a unity to the treatise as a
whole.

It is being proposed, then, that the elaboration pattern is the major
compositional device for the treatise *De Sacrificiis*. The scriptural unit, Gen
4:2–4a, provides the *chreia* which is to be interpreted and elaborated. It is
divided into four *lemmata* which, however, may be further divided in order
to obtain the sequence of seven major elaboration sequences. Smaller units
occur as sub-elaborations on other scriptural texts introduced as Examples
or Authoritative Citations within the larger major elaboration outlines.
Interlocking occurs which relates sub-elaborations to major elaborations.
And the development of themes throughout gives the sequence unity. A
"stacking up" of Analogies, Examples, Scriptural Citations, and Rationales
occurs which gives the impression that the lesson derived from the text
pertains in all of the orders of reality appealed to by the elaboration
pattern—logic, nature, society, human experience, cultural and literary
tradition. If that impression can be sustained, a persuasive argumentation
will have been achieved.

We turn now to the task of demonstrating the pattern at work in the
treatise as a whole. It will not be possible in a brief essay to discuss all of
the many rhetorical turns the treatise takes, nor to elucidate even the way in

which each major item in the elaboration outline functions to further the rhetorical argumentation. What we can do is to outline the treatise in such a way as to identify the patterns of elaboration which structure the argument. The earlier paper on *Sacr.* 1–10 may be taken as a study of the way in which the elaboration pattern actually functions as argumentation. There it was clear that the persuasive power of, e.g., an Analogy was merely assumed by Philo in accordance with the rhetorical theory which underlay the elaboration pattern itself. That theory was accepted and relied upon by Philo, hardly ever appealed to in order to explain what he was doing. A thorough rhetorical analysis of the treatise would have to spell out the interrelationships of the elaboration steps in order to determine the specific point at which, e.g., an Example was found to be appropriate to the further development and support of the thematic interpretation intended for the major *lemma* (*chreia*) under consideration. Specific points of comparison and contrast, appeal to one or another of the "chief objectives" (teleka kephalaia), felicitous or infelicitous rhetorical ploys, diairetic schemata for definition and ranking—all and much more would need to be considered in order to see how Philo's argumentation actually works in given moments. To provide such an analysis would require a full commentary on the treatise.

Nevertheless, knowing in general how the elaboration pattern works to interpret, teach, and persuade, some sense can be made of the treatise merely by following the outline we shall give. That is because, if our thesis is correct, the elaboration outline will have collected up the major points or "proofs" which Philo is making. The problem with such an outline is that it is difficult to indicate the gradual decoding of the "signs" of the text as we go along. That is because it is frequently the case that the Analogies, Examples, and Citations brought in to help with the decoding and elaboration are also replete with metaphors and encoded images. It is all but impossible to devise a clean and readable system of sigla to indicate the complex relationships a given point or term will have to the text and the other items in the elaboration pattern.

What we have done is to cite, paraphrase, or state in nuce the content of the item in question. In some cases brief, explanatory remarks have been given in parentheses, but only in order to follow the moves from item to item in the elaboration pattern.

In most cases we have used the simple outline of eight items which comprise the elaboration pattern in Hermogenes (see above, and cf. the earlier paper). But in other cases it has been thought helpful to subsume the elaboration pattern under the outline of the four main parts of the rhetorical speech (*Prooimion; Narratio; Argumentatio; Conclusio*). This has been done for two reasons. One is that, as we saw in the earlier paper on *Sacr.* 1–10, the

Narratio ("*Chreia*," *Ratio,* and *Contrast*) can support at least two (contrastive)
argumentation sequences without being repeated. At the end a *Conclusio*
can be given which sums up both argumentations and forms a period with
the original *Prooimion* and/or *Narratio.*

The other reason is that, again as we saw in the earlier paper, the first
moves away from the scriptural text as *chreia* are frequently quite complex
and require more than a single statement of *Rationale.* This is because the
scripture is "encoded" in a way which *chreiai* usually are not. We mentioned in the earlier paper, however, that for theses taken from *chreia*-like
material two moves were frequently necessary even in Greco-Roman
elaborations. The first would be the *Ratio* as a reasonable restatement of the
point of the *chreia* in thesis form. Then a *Rationale* would be given to
support the logic of the restatement itself. (See *ad Herennium* II, xviii, 28; IV,
xliii, 56.) These moves belong in general to the *ratiocinatio* of the *narratio*
section of a speech. It is quite possible that Philo was knowledgable about
these more advanced theories, and that he was able easily to incorporate
more difficult rhetorical procedures into the simpler elaboration pattern
when necessary. It has been found helpful, in any case, to be more
discriminating in analyzing the ways in which Philo finds to restate the
scriptural text as thesis for elaboration. Instead of a single term (Rationale),
we have used three terms: Paraphrase, Ratio, and Rationale. *Paraphrase* is
used in those cases where Philo finds it possible to rephrase the text itself as
thesis. *Ratio* is used to indicate statements which translate "signs" in the
text into statements of what they indicate or mean. Rationale is used to
indicate statements which support the Ratio of the text by indicating the
Ratio's sense or logic, or explaining why the text expressed the Ratio in
some particular way.

Thus we arrive at the following outline. The mixture of Greek, Latin,
and English designations is awkward. It is the result of an attempt to use
the more familiar term where possible and, in any case, to describe the
function as clearly and simply as possible. Numbers are given to highlight
correspondence with the simpler elaboration pattern of eight items referred
to above.

1) Prooimion
2) Narratio
        Text as *Chreia*
        Paraphrase
        Ratio
3) Rationale
4) Converse/Contrast
        Argumentatio

5) Analogy
6) Example
7) Authoritative Witness/Citation
8) Epilog
      Conclusio
      Exhortation

Mapping: The Treatise as Argumentation

We are now ready to analyze the argumentation of the treatise according to the elaboration outline. The items of the outline will be given as headings (underlined). A system of indentation will be used to set off minor and sub-elaborations within the larger patterns. Arabic numbers in the margin refer to paragraphs in the treatise.

I First Lemma. *Sacr.* 1–10 (Gen 4:2)

Prooimion
   (Missing)

Narratio
   Text as Chreia
      "And 'He' 'added' to this that 'she' 'brought forth' 'Abel' his brother."

Ratio
   The addition of one thing implies the subtraction of another.

Rationale
   If we must say that "Abel" was "added," we must imagine that "Cain" was "subtracted."

Contrast
   There are two opposite and contending views.
      ("Abel" is the dogma that God is the cause of all things; "Cain" is the opinion that the human mind possesses all things.)

First Argumentatio (on "subtracting" "Cain")

Analogy
   Birth (as moment of "separation")

Example (Gen 25:21–24)
   Rebekah's conception of two contending natures

Witness (God's words to Rebekah; Gen 25:23)
"Two nations" are in your womb; Two "peoples" shall be separated
from your womb."

Conclusio
(God's remedy for the soul is to separate the evil from the good.)

Second Argumentatio (on "adding" "Abel")

Analogy
Death (as moment of "addition" to the people of God)

Example (Gen 25:8)
Abraham's death as translation

Example (Gen 49:33)
Jacob's death as "addition" to his fathers

Example (Gen 35:29)
Isaac's death as "addition" to "a genus."
(This is an example of the highest "addition," i.e., complete
abandonment of the body as perfection of the soul.)

Analogy
There are two stages in *Paideia*:
1) to be a pupil under a teacher;
2) to have complete knowledge (of God).

Example (Dt 5:31; 34:5; Ex. 7:1; Dt 34:6)
Moses' death as translation to a position beside God

Epilogue
The text (Gen 4:2) is about the transformation of the soul to
holiness.

II Second Lemma. *Sacr.* 11–51 (Gen 4:2)

A. The First Elaboration
(There are two elaboration cycles, each dealing with a separate issue
presented by the text. The first is about the sequence of the mention of
the names; the second is about the meaning of the term "shepherd.")

Narratio
Text as Chreia
"And Abel became a 'shepherd of sheep,' but Cain was a 'tiller of
the ground.'"

Quaestio
> Why is Abel mentioned before Cain when occupations are under discussion?
> (Chronologically Cain comes before Abel.)

Prooimion (Inserted into the *Narratio* section)
> Moses does not deal in the rhetoric of probabilities, but sets out the truth.

(*Narratio* continues)
Ratio
> Chronologically vice (Cain) precedes virtue (Abel);

Contrast
> But in terms of honor it is the opposite.
> (Virtue "precedes" vice; so the "occupations" will have to do with the theme of virtue and vice.)

Argumentatio
Analogy
> The stages in the Life of Man
>> (A common topos, usually distinguishing from three to seven stages; Philo divides life into two stages here: the time of the passions/the age of maturity. Interwoven is another common topos: the storm at sea and the haven of rest.)

Example (Gen 25:33)
> Esau and Jacob
>> (Chronologically Esau is the elder, but he sold his birthright to Jacob who symbolizes the "athlete" of virtue who contends successfully for the prize. The prize is Sophia.)

Legal Witness (Dt 21:15–17)
> "If a man have two wives, one loved and the other hated, and each bear a son to him, and the son of her that is hated is the first born . . . to him belong the rights of the first born."
> (This "law" picks up on the theme of the inversion of primogenator which has been at work in the Cain-Abel, Esau-Jacob cases, and introduces the theme of the "wives" who can symbolize vice and virtue. In order to use this text, however, Philo has to explain that the "hated" wife is virtue, not vice, because at first we "think" virtue unlovely.)

Exhortations
  1) The Speech of the Courtesan Pleasure
     (In her train are the vices.)
  2) The Speech of guiless Virtue
     (The speech is deliberative, complete with prooimion, narratio,
     rebuttal, argumentation, and exhortation. There is a fine section
     on the necessity of toil in the paideia of virtue which follows the
     elaboration pattern and may be compared to Hermogenes'
     elaboration of Isocrates' saying about the two stages of paideia:
     first work, then reward.)

Epilog
     After hearing this the mind turns away from Pleasure and
     cleaves to Virtue.

B. The Second Elaboration

Narratio
     (At this point the argumentation returns to the text in order to
     take up another issue. The first elaboration has been about the
     question of sequence; now the significance of the occupation
     "shepherd" will be explored. The Narratio in pars 11–14 is as-
     sumed, so that it is necessary now only to restate the new thesis
     before going on to the supporting argumentation.)

  Ratio
     When the mind turns from vice to virtue it "becomes a 'shep-
     herd' of the sheep."

Argumentatio
  Analogy
     The charioteer and the Helmsman

  Example (Gen 30·36)
     Jacob as shepherd of Labon's sheep
        (This section is a mini-elaboration on the thesis that Jacob agreed
        to "shepherd" the ignorant soul, not the wickedly defiant soul.
        This sets up for the next example.)

  Example (Gen 47:3)
     Jacob's sons as "shepherds" in Pharaoh's Egypt

  Example (Ex 3:1)
     Moses, who led his sheep into the wilderness

Witness (Gen 46:34) (The text also serves as *chreia*)
"Every 'shepherd' of the sheep is an 'abomination' to 'the Egyptians'."

> *Mini Elaboration*
> > *Ratio* (assumed)
> > "Shepherd" is symbol for the Logos.
> > *Rationale* of Thesis
> > The Logos is our pilot to virtue.
> > *Contrast*
> > The Logos is an abomination to those who love the passions.
> > *Analogy* (negative)
> > Foolish children who hate their teachers
> > *Example* (positive) and *Witness*
> > Moses will "sacrifice" to God the "abominations" of Egypt (Ex 8:26).
> > *Epilog*
> > (Which means that Moses offers virtues to God)

Conclusio
So Abel is called "shepherd" because he is the one who "refers" all good things to God.

C. The Third Major Elaboration

(There should be a discussion here of Cain as "tiller of the soil" to complete the contrast Philo announced in pars 11–14. Philo acknowledges that this is the case, but explains that he has discussed this symbolism already in earlier books. A full elaboration is not given in any existing treatise, but in *Agr* 21–22 a "tiller of the soil" is one oriented to bodily pleasures. The lack of a further discussion of Cain at this point will not destroy the contrastive balance of positive and negative perspectives because the next *lemma* will take up the "charges" against Cain and carry the elaboration forward.)

III THIRD LEMMA. *Sacr.* 52–87 (Gen 4:3)

Narratio
> *Text as Chreia*
> > "And it came to pass 'after some days' that Cain brought of the 'fruits' of the earth as an offering to God."

Text as Forensic Charge
>   There are two charges against the self-lover:
>> 1) He offered "after some days," not "at once."
>> 2) He offered "fruits" instead of "first fruits."

A. Elaboration of the First Charge

Narratio (The immediately preceding text as *chreia* is assumed.)

>   *Rationale*
>   Good deeds should be done eagerly, without delay.

>   *Contrast*
>   Slackness and hesitation should be avoided.

>   *The Law* (Dt 23:21)
>   "If you vow a vow, delay not to pay it."

First Argumentatio (against delay)
>   *Analogy* as a *General Class*
>   (The analogy proper is missing, because the ratio has uncovered a "forensic" instead of a "deliberative" issue. In place of the analogy, "cases" of delay will be offered.)
>> 1. Those who forget.
>> 2. Those with pride.
>> 3. Those who consider themselves worthy.

>   *Authoritative Exhortation*
>   (To each of these three classes there is cited a scriptural "counter argument." It functions in the elaboration pattern as an authoritative citation as well as an exhortation.)
>> 1. "When thou has eaten... take heed lest thou... forget the Lord thy God." (Dt 8:12–14).
>> 2. "Say not 'my strength...'" (Dt 8:17f.)
>> 3. "Not for thy righteousness... that he might establish the covenant..." (Dt 9:5)

Epilog as Transitional Statement.
>   The covenant is a symbol of God's gifts. If we destroy the reasons for delay we shall run and leap to meet our Master.

Second Argumentatio (for speed)
>   *Example* (Gen 18:6)
>   Abraham's eagerness and speed in response to the visitation of the three.

Mini-Elaboration
  Ratio
    The three are God and his two powers.
  Rationale
    They are the "measure" of all things.
  Contrast
    They themselves are not measurable.
  Analogy
    Making bread (the three measures kneaded and blended in the soul).
  Example
    Initiation into the mysteries
  Exhortation
    Let us eagerly keep the Passover.

Example (Gen 27:20)
  Jacob who found quickly what the Lord God set before him

Mini-Elaboration
  Rationale
    Learning about creation takes time.
  Contrast
    The knowledge of God occurs quickly.
  Analogy
    Paideia vs *Sophia* from God
  Example
    God's creation of the world by a word
  Witness (Num 11:23)
    "My word shall overtake thee."
  Witness (Ex 17:6)
    "Here I stand before thou wast."
  Epilog
    God's children then do not delay to do what is good.

Example
  Israel fleeing from Pharaoh.

Conclusio
  "So then every imagination which counts that all things are its own possession (Cain) and honors itself before God—and such a mind is shown by the words 'to sacrifice after some days'—may know that it stands in danger to be brought to the judgment bar for impiety."

B. Elaboration of the Second Charge

Narratio

(The *Narratio* in §52 is assumed; here the "charge" becomes a "*quaestio*.")

Quaestio

Why does Cain offer "fruits," not "first fruits"?

Ratio

To honor creation before God

The Law (Ex 23:19)

The law states to bring "the firstlings of the first fruits of the land into the house of the Lord God."

Rationale

It is right (*dikaion*) that we acknowledge as belonging to God all the movements of the soul that come first either in order or in value.

Argumentatio

Examples (of first things)
1) The parts of the soul (first in order)
2) The virtues (first in value)

Analogies (of first things offered as eucharistia)
1) The lyre
2) The vowels in language

Exhoration (Lev 2:14)

"Wherefore if you bring an offering..."
(But this *text* also serves as a new *chreia* for constructive elaboration, the charge against Cain now sustained.)

C. Four Elaboration Cycles on the Text on First Fruits (Lev. 2:14)

First Cycle: "The New"

Ratio

The first "division" (i.e., definitional characteristic) of the offering of first fruits is "the new."

Rationale

To realize the instantaneous power of God is to receive new, fresh thoughts about God.

Contrast
Those who cling to old, fabled traditions

Analogy
Paideia

Witness (Lev 19:32)
"Thou shalt rise up away from the head of the hoary and thou shalt honor the head of the elder."

Example (Num 11:16)
Moses, the friend of God, "knew the elders."

Conclusio
1) The relative value of *paideia*
(A fine paragraph on the value of *paideia* for civic virtue, mentioning the opinions of sages and philosophers, as well as the *encomia* of historians and poets)
2) The ultimate value of God's Sophia
(The famous passage on the "sudden beam of self-inspired wisdom" which shines on the eye of the soul and makes *paideia* inconsequential)

Exhortation
(Summing up the conclusion, based on a *witness* from scripture,—Lev 26:10)

Second Cycle: "The Roasted"

Ratio
The second "division" of the offering of first fruits (= the soul) is "roasted."

Rationale
The soul is to be tested by the Logos.

Analogy
As gold in the furnace; as corn in the fire

Examples (Gen 25:29)
Jacob who "seethes" and Esau who "faints."

Conclusio
The Logos hardens the good man and undoes the man of vice and passion.

Third Cycle: "Slicing"

Ratio
The Logos itself must be divided.

Rationale
Order is better than disorder.

Analogies
Rhetorical classification of "topics" then invention of a harmonious speech. Like archery and garment making.

Example (Ex 36:10)
Moses weaving a whole out of golden threads

Witness (Lev 1:6)
The victim to be burnt shall be "divided."

Exhortation
Thus must we train our reason to think clearly (on the model of rhetorical *diairesis, heuresis,* and *ergasia*), and thus exercise the soul.

Fourth Cycle: "Pounding"

Ratio
The last "division" of the soul "offering first fruits" is "pounding."

Rationale
After *diairesis* one needs to be immersed in reflection characterized by diatribe and criticism.

Analogy
Exercise (*ergazesthai*) which leads to solid knowledge

Example (Num 9:8)
Those who fed with manna.

Exhortation
If you acknowledge these four things you will bring (an acceptable) offering of first fruits.
(The exhortation is based on all four cycles of elaboration of Lev 2:4. It also serves as conclusion to the entire argumentation in the third lemma.)

IV FOURTH LEMMA. *Sacr.* 88–139 (Gen 4:4)

A. Elaboration of Gen 4:4.

Narratio
> *Text as Narratio Brevis*
>> We are told that Abel offered of the firstlings of the sheep and of their fat.

Statement of the Status qualitas
> This was done according to the sacred ordinance.
>
> (It was *nomimon* (lawful). This move is clever. It requires now a citation of that law Abel fulfilled. If Philo can find a more suggestive text than the one at hand, his elaboration of "Abel's" sacrifice will allow for a much fuller thematic development.)

Statement of the Law (Ex 13:11–13)
> "It shall be 'when' the Lord thy God has brought thee into the land of the Canaanites, as 'he swore' to thy fathers, and 'shall give' it unto thee, 'thou shalt separate' everything 'that opens the womb' that is 'male unto the Lord;' everything that opens the womb 'from thy herds among thy cattle,' all that are born to thee, the males to the Lord. All that opens the womb of an ass, thou shalt 'exchange' for a sheep; but if thou dost not exchange it, thou shalt redeem it."

Ratio (re: *status qualitas*)
> "That which opens the womb" (in the legal text) equals "the first born" (in the *narratio brevis*); thus Abel's gift complied with the law.
>
> (At this point Ex 13:11–13 becomes the text to be elaborated. Only at the end of the *lemma* will Abel and Gen 4:4 be mentioned expressly again in the *conclusio*. But the relation between Gen 4:4 and Ex 13:11–13 which has been established means that the elaboration of Ex 13:11–13 is intended to serve at the same time as an elaboration of Gen 4:4. This in fact has been achieved by dividing Ex 13:11–13 into a set of signs, and assigning to each one a function within the elaboration pattern. Thus it can be seen that Ex 13:11–13 has been treated as sufficient resource for the derivation of all elaboration components necessary to support Gen 4:4. But since each argument for the elaboration of Gen 4:4 must be derived from Ex 13:11–13 by decoding, each textual reference to Ex 13:11–13 can become the occasion for a complete mini-elaboration as well. Thus each citation from Ex 13:11–13

serves a double function: it is an argument in support of Gen 4:4 as well as a *chreia* inviting its own elaboration.)

B. Elaboration of Ex 13:11–13

Narratio

Quaestio/Text as Chreia
But the "when" and the "how" need still to be determined.
(Here it is that the shift takes place from the basically forensic issue to deliberative questions. "Time" and "manner" belong to the list of facts to be determined in a forensic case, of course. So it seems as if Philo is still following the outline of a legal argument. But all of that was playful maneuver in order to get the new text situated for a lengthy deliberative elaboration. The "when" and the "how" will be discussed as elaboration of the *law-text*, not of the *narratio brevis* which recounts Abel's deed!)

Rationale
The "when" is the time when the logos is aswirl in the "land of the Canaanites"; the "how" is by the guidance of God's "oath."

Prooimion (Inserted into the *Narratio* by taking up the clue on God as speaker given in the text.)
(This section on the words "God swore" continues the fiction of forensic argumentation, addressing the questions of the validity of the *oath*, and the problem of a "second witness." But it actually is taken as opportunity to lay out a theology of God and his word on the one hand, and a rationale for Moses' use of anthropomorphic characterization of God on the other. It consists of a series of rhetorical syllogisms, none of which are logically convincing, but, taken together, function as an *encomium* appropriate as a *proem* to the elaboration of the text to follow.)
1. An oath is an appeal to God on a disputed matter. But with God nothing is disputed. His oaths, therefore, are signs of the truth.
2. An oath calls on God to be a witness. But God needs no witness. For there is no other god to be his peer.
3. One who bears witness is superior to the one for whom the witness is made. For the latter needs help, the former helps. There is nothing superior to God, the Cause.
4. Men use an oath to win belief when others deem them untrustworthy. But God is trustworthy completely, and in his

speech. So all his words are oaths. It is therefore God who assures his own oath.

5. Moses anthropomorphizes because human minds cannot imagine God otherwise. But "God is not as man" (Num 23:19). So God's "oath" is merely an "aid." (And the text requires decoding!)

(*Narratio* continues)

    Ratio (The conditions requisite to "Abel's" offering)

"If 'God gives' such and such to thee, 'thou shalt separate' them."

    Mini-Elaboration: Text as *chreia* (Ex 13:11)

      Ratio

        Unless God gives, you don't have.

      Rationale

        All things are God's.

      Contrast

        All things outside of you;

        All things inside of you.

      Analogy

        Onomasticon of natural elements in simple diairetic schema.

      Conclusio

        Whatever you bring as an offering, it will be God's possession, not yours.

    Contrast

      "Thou shalt separate"

    Mini-Elaboration

      Text as Chreia (Ex 13:11)

      Rationale

        It is necessary to distinguish what is to be given.

      Contrast

        The whole is not to be given.

      Analogy

        Physis itself is distinct from her numberless gifts.

        So God as the Uncreated is distinct from creation.

      Conclusion-Exhortation

        Separate all created things from your conception of God.

Argumentatio

    Analogy (giving birth)

      "of all that openeth the womb, the males to the Lord."

Mini-Elaboration
   Text as Chreia (Ex 13:12)
   Ratio
      Nature has provided both "womb" (in the body) and
      "mind" (in the soul) with generative powers.
   Contrast
      Things generated are "male" and "female."
   Analogy
      As with physical generation, so with the psyche: the "fe-
      males" are emasculating (= vice and passion); the "males"
      are strengthening (= *eupatheia*).
   Conclusion
      Only the *hegemonikon* is to be offered to the Lord.

Analogy (herding cattle)
   "from thy herd amongst thy cattle"

   Mini-Elaboration
      Text as Chreia (Ex 13:12)
      Ratio
         "Cattle" refers to the senses (*aistheseis*).
      Contrast
         Wild and tame
      Analogy
         As with cattle, so with the soul, a "herdsman" is needed to
         rule and tame.
      Rationale
         The mind (*nous*) can tame unruly senses.
      Analogy
         Anarchy and order in the polis
      Conclusion
         The orderly rule of the mind must be acknowledged as
         occurring "according to God" (*kata theon*).

Example (Israel's offering of cakes)
   "And it shall be that when ye eat of the bread of the land, ye
   shall set apart a portion marked out for the Lord: a loaf as the
   first offering of your mixture, ye shall set it apart as a portion. As
   ye do with a portion from the threshing-floor, so shall ye set it
   apart."

Mini-Elaboration
  Text as Chreia (Num 14:19–20)
  Ratio
    The "mixture" refers to ourselves.
  Rationale and Contrast
    The self is compounded of opposites. The primary division is soul and body.
  Analogy
    Threshing separates grain from chaff. As with threshing, so with us: the best is to be dedicated to God.
  Contrast
    Powers pure from evil are not to be divided into parts.
  Example
    Isaac as a whole burnt offering.
  Witness (Num 28:2)
    "My gifts, my offerings, my fruits ye shall observe to offer me at my feasts."
  Conclusion
    Only the Sage can celebrate joyously the feast of perfect virtue.

Example ("Exchange ")

Mini-Elaboration
  Prooimion
    Moses has laid out the teaching of the soul and its parts. He now proceeds to teach us about the necessity of toil in order for us to achieve a male offspring.
  Text as Chreia (Ex 13:13)
    (The text is not cited but the sentence in view is "exchanging" an ass for a sheep, or "redeeming" it.)
  Rationale
    We should exchange all toil for progress.
  Ratio
    The ass is symbol of toil; the sheep of progress (via etymology).
  Contrast
    Profitable toil is to be exchanged for progress; unprofitable toil is to be redeemed, i.e., given up.
  Analogies of profitable toil
    Paideia, arts and trades, life of virtue

Analogies of giving up unprofitable toil
Beheaded animals, unsuccessful athletes, unproductive merchants
Examples of Redemption

Mini-mini-elaboration
Prooimion
Moses is the one who tells us.
Paraphrase
The Levites were a ransom for all others.
Text as Chreia (Num 3:12–13)
"And behold I have taken the Levites from the midst of the sons of Israel, in place of every firstborn that opens the womb from among the sons of Israel. They shall be their ransom and the Levites shall be mine, for every firstborn is mine. On the day when I smote every firstborn in the land of Egypt, I hallowed to myself every firstborn in Israel."
Ratio
Levite refers to the *logos.*
First Rationale
God took the *Logos* from the *hegemonikon* of the soul and assigned it to himself as worthy of the inheritance of the firstborn.
Contrast
Jacob and Reuben are symbols of arriving at virtue by toil and progress. Israel and Levi are symbols of perfect divine service by means of God's redemption (i.e., severance from the created world).
Second Rationale
The perfectly virtuous are the redeemers for others.
Examples of Redeemers
1. The Sage as ransom for the city (a long passage on physicians; Sodom and Abraham; the good man a protector of household and city.)
2. The Levites in the Cities of Refuge (a long argumentation on why the involuntary homicide finds refuge with the Levites.)

Witness
"On the day that I smote all the firstborn in Egypt, I sanctified to myself all the firstborn in Israel."

Mini-elaboration
> *Text as Chreia* (Num 3:13)
> *Rationale*
>> This is not about a single past event, but about the
>> sanctification of the soul.
> *Ratio*
>> For the exodus of evil works is the entrance of virtue.
> *Contrast*
>> The opposite is also true.
> *Example* (Gen 28:30)
>> Hardly has Jacob gone out, when Esau is in our mind.
>> Nevertheless Jacob will return and win the inheritance.

Conclusio

1. That is why Abel offers the "fat", i.e., all the richness of the soul, and all that protects and gives joy.
2. The *hegemonikon* cannot be offered until it is cleansed.
3. When it is, a whole burnt offering is to be given to the sacrificial fire.
4. So "a soul wholly complete in all its parts, should be given in its entirety as a burnt-offering to God."

Borders: The Pattern of Persuasion and Piety

We may ask now about what it is that Philo has achieved. In order to do this, observations of a general nature on his use of the elaboration pattern may be given as follows:

The *Scripture* is consistently taken as *Chreia* for elaboration by regarding it as encoded. This is achieved primarily by parcelling out its linguistic elements and viewing them as "figures," i.e., as metaphors referring to another system of signs.

The *Ratio* begins the process of decoding, usually by making explicit the term of reference needed to understand the metaphor in the scriptural text. Orders of reference are usually taken from Greek systems of thought. There is, however, no one system (e.g., Stoic), nor one order of reality (e.g., psychology), which comes into play consistently and automatically at this point. Any order will do to get started (even mathematics!). This means that, if there is a privileged system of thought to which the decoding is directed, first order terms of reference will themselves have to be decoded further in a process of metaphoric reductions.

The *Rationale* and *Converse* can be used to move the process of decoding along toward that preferred level of discourse, usually an ethical discourse about the soul. But these slots in the elaboration pattern are also and primarily the place where assertions occur. This means that the isolated terms and images of the scriptural text, now decoded in the *Ratio*, are placed in relation to other terms and images. Sentences can now be formed; definitions can be given by using comparison and contrast; and all manner of diairectic and dialectic schemata can be used to position a primary term from the text somewhere within the system of ethical psychology to which it is said to refer.

The *Analogies* are taken, by and large, from the arena of Hellenistic commonplaces. These reflect Greek views of the natural and social orders of things.

But the *Examples* are invariably taken from the Scriptures, as are the *Authoritative Witnesses*. That the examples all come from the scripture is significant. It means that if one is being educated in Philo's school, one's "history" continues to be the Jewish epic, not that of the Greeks. That the *Authoritative Citations* are all taken from the Scripture is significant as well. It means that a way has been found to set the Five Books of Moses over against Greek literary traditions as the major source for maxims, oracles, aphoristic wisdom, and laws.

We are very close to a discovery of sorts at this point. One need not argue that the process of elaboration was the only way in which the Five Books as Jewish literary tradition were attributed with that privileged authority we now call canon. The process of canonization cannot be understood without acknowledging the importance of subcultural literary traditions for social identity in the Greco-Roman period. And the Books of Moses were clearly understood as Epic, Torah, and Constitution for Judaism (e.g., in Ben Sira) before being taken up for allegorical commentary. But the special way in which the elaboration pattern could direct that literary-critical activity common to the Greco-Roman period as a whole should not be discounted as a significant factor in the literary canonization of the Five Books. By filling in the slots of the pattern as Philo did, the "authority" of the scriptures contra other literatures was made precise in specifically rhetorical ways.

One can see, as well, that this way of filling out the pattern has as its result the illusion of "scripture interpreting scripture." Express employment of Greek categories and logic are necessary in order to move the discourse along. And Greek *ratiocinatio* is in evidence particularly in the *narratio* section of the pattern, and in the *analogies*. But these moves are invariably playful. They deal, moreover, almost exclusively in the logic of analogy (with its alignments of similarities and differences among things), thus functioning merely to set up the possibilities for the alignments of scriptural text with scriptural text.

The various texts are isolated at first, then assigned rhetorical functions (*chreia*, example, maxim, oracle, law). But the overall impression achieved is that the Five Books are sufficient source and authority for Jewish *paideia*, and that all of scripture witnesses to the same "truth."

In order to determine that "truth," scholars have usually assumed that it must be some system of Greek thought. This is a natural assumption, given Philo's practice of decoding the scriptural figure by reference to Greek philosophical categories. As those accustomed to Western intellectual tradition, it seems natural also to conclude that the alternative to metaphoric or poetic discourse must be rational, conceptual and discursive. But we should proceed more cautiously with Philo.

Caution is called for as soon as one sees that words which function as technical terms within systems of Greek thought are used by Philo in a bewildering variety of ways. An example would be the use of the term *logos*, which, in Philo, is used to link several orders of reality including the divine, cosmic, mythological, religious, and anthropological. He also uses it in the context of discussions which are focused upon physical, ethical, epistemological, and linguistic anthropologies. If we add to this phenomenon of linguistic misusage the observation that there is no precision in the use of terms for a particular reference (e.g., the *"hegemonikon"*), the problem is compounded. One looks in vain for consistency in the choice of terms to name or define a particular phenomenon. Instead, the full range of broadly synonymous terms comes into play even when, technically, alternative terms are competitive within the context of Greek school traditions. Some of this imprecision may be due to the amalgamation of Greek systems in the middle Platonism of the time. Some may be due to Philo's employment of pre-Philonic exegetical traditions. But that the fuzziness is allowed to stand at the level of Philonic composition in just the way it is indicates something else. It indicates that Philo understands the language of reference used to decode the scriptural metaphors as metaphoric itself. If we put quotation marks around the terms taken as figural within the Scriptural text, we should also put quotation marks around the terms of reference. The logic of analogy and elaboration is not intended to bring the reader to rest upon a single conceptual grasp of a system of truth which ends the quest. Instead, the process of moving logically from one set of signs to another creates a space in the middle of the two terms of the metaphoric equation. It is within this space that the "truth" resides. And it can't be seen once for all. As soon as one equation is constructed between the two systems of signs (scripture and Greek philosophy), the logic of analogy is broken by pointing out the limitations of similarities and differences. This sets things up for another metaphoric equation, and so on.

Another way to view this process is given with the observation that Philo frequently interlocks sets of equations in such a way as to create escalated ranking. He almost invariably does this with the patriarchial triad of examples. Another favorite device is to play on the sequence given with the Greek notion of *paideia*: first labor, then reward (virtue). The reader will have noted the many places in the treatise where this schema was used. The lovely compositions on the subject of *paideia*, toil, and the achievement of wisdom support our contention that Philo is drawing upon just that tradition of Greek education we have theorized. Some of this material is very close to the elaboration on *paideia* in Hermogenes which we have used to demonstrate the pattern. And Philo no doubt has in mind the actual institutions of education when writing about *paideia*, just as he has Greek philosophical traditions in mind when referring to concepts taken from them. But the way in which he *uses* the *paideia* schema of staged progress is hardly as a protreptic for the gymnasium. It also is a metaphor for some noetic-psychological process which he wants the reader to glimpse in that space between the two systems of signs.

The process Philo wants his readers to "see" is both a notion and an experience. As a notion it is extremely difficult to spell out. Philo does have some terms for it: "progress," "practice," "toil," and so forth. But it is with process as an experience that Philo has achieved something remarkable. This is the way in which the process of following the elaboration becomes an intellectual exercise which corresponds to the psychological experiences intended as the "truth" to which scripture calls.

Working with isolated terms and images from Scripture on the one hand, and with Greek systems of thought on the other, the logic of correlation (metaphoric equations) is all but destined to produce reductions into stable systems of signs in synchronic relationships. World-view or philosophical system should be the result. But Philo has played on the aspect of difference (the lack of complete correlation or symmetry) between the two terms of every metaphoric equation. He does this in order to "move" the discourse ahead to yet another set of terms. Frequently it is the case that, in the process of moving through a sequence of related metaphoric equations, the reference of an original term can no longer hold at the end. Thus, in a single paragraph, "wisdom" can refer to the highest stage of the *paideia* schema, then placed on the lowest of the two stages when the highest is reserved for the divine Wisdom. This process of subversion is achieved by a playful manipulation of the space between two equations which at first glance appear to be similar and correlatable. By moving the reader through sequence after sequence of this kind of intellectual play, Philo has approximated the "truth" which he claims for Moses and his Books. That "truth" is the possibility of a certain noetic-psychological experience. It begins by reflection upon the world, but it proceeds in the interest of catching a glimpse of that which is not world, i.e., God. The experience is both procedural and progressive, but only in the sense that, in the repeated and repeatable moments where the glimpses occur, the notion of a perfect and everlasting vision of God is imaginable as "goal" of the "journey." But as soon as this thought is thought (or image is exampled), Philo tucks it away again, first under the rhetoric of the "stages" on the way, and finally under the exhortation to persist in the process of reflection. Thus it is that a marvelous co-mingling of the noetic and the psychological, of the ideal and the practical, of the divine and the human is achieved without eroding the conceptual differentiations. The process of reflection which follows the pattern of elaboration is both an intellectual and a psychological process.

And then it turns out that this process is also what the "content" of the scriptural text is about: i.e., "Sacrifice." As process, sacrifice consists of making the proper *selection* of the object to be offered *from* among one's produce, then *giving* the object back *to* the unified and unifying source from which all objects ultimately derive. This enactment of a partial and delayed "take and give" in the interest of imitating a universal (divine) "give and take" describes the pattern of reflection which Philo demands of his readers. Thus the true sacrifice is a process of making the proper "distinctions" on the one hand and of "seeing" the proper "referent" on the other. The goal is imagined as a fully reciprocal exchange of gifts in which that which is "returned" is just that which must be imagined as given, namely the glimpse or vision of God as one's true self.

Philo, then, is no Greek philosopher. He is, however, not for that reason an intellectual weakling. His mind is clear, and his powers of imagination and logical reasoning are strong and under control. But he has put these intellectual powers to the service of a profound conception of Jewish piety. At the last "stage" of the "process" there occurs a kind of intellectual mysticism which erases all distinctions, to be sure. But this also is carefully rationalized, and marks merely the ideal "feast of the sage" who has bothered to elaborate the text of Moses—perfectly and instantaneously.

We, of course, are unable to describe that moment. Merely to suggest the ultimate identity of text, elaboration, intellection, psychologization, and religious being in Philo's image of the ideal sacrifice is eerie. We must fall back, then on a discourse which keeps things in their place. Philo would understand why. He himself has written a whole treatise "about" the process and the vision. If we want, then, to follow the argument of the treatise as a whole, knowing that it is, of course, all about the same thing ultimately, what notion can we follow? There is actually only one which we can use. It is the "theme" of the story or experience of the "soul" which binds everything together. To lift it out of Philo's text as that which comes to be seen in the space between the two systems of signs may do violence to the experience of reading the treatise, of course. It makes "objective" that which is intended to be experienced in the "soul" of the reader. But it may not be a complete deconstruction of Philo's thought and logic. He himself has provided the story line, and he has developed it carefully in considered sequences by means of his elaborations on the text. We conclude, then, by paraphrasing this elaboration on the story of the soul in order to suggest that it, not some philosophical system, is the *tertium comparationis* for Philo's exegetical commentaries.

Quest: The Theme as the Knowledge of God

A. Sacr. 1–10 (Gen 4:2) The Soul's Problem and Remedy

The soul has within it two contending natures. The soul is also capable of holding two opposing views of the Cause and Ruler of all things. One view is that the human mind is master of all. The other is that God is the only creator and master, even of the mind. The first view is wrong, and leads to evil. The second view is right, but in order for it to prevail the soul must experience a separation of the two contending natures and be made perfectly holy and good. There appears to be two kinds or stages of being made perfect. One is to be instructed and trained; the other is to experience some kind of spiritual transformation.

B. Sacr. 11–51 (Gen 4:2) The Instruction which is Necessary for the Soul.

The issue is drawn for the soul in that it experiences the passions first in the course of life, and so is in danger of falling into vice. But virtue, though at first unrecognized, and then thought unattractive, can be achieved if one submits to the discipline of instruction, eschews pleasure, works at the task of practicing good, and sustains pain and testing.

The instruction which guarantees virtue has to do with Reason. If the mind of the soul accepts Reason it can rule all of the parts and functions of the soul and lead it to virtue. The Reason in view is, apparently, the acknowledgment that God is the sole creator and ruler of all things. This means that the only mind which can rule the passions is the mind which knows that God is its own creator and ruler. It is this acknowledgment which brings to an end the foolish attempt of the mind to attribute everything to its own powers. It is also this acknowledgment which unites the life of virtue with religious devotion.

C. Sacr. 52–87 (Gen 4:3) *The Insight which the Soul must Receive.*

Passions and pleasure, then, are not the only hindrances to Reason. Pride, self-love, and preoccupations which cause one to forget divine blessings are contrary to the piety Reason demands. A certain "eagerness" should characterize one's deeds of virtue. This eagerness has as its condition a soul which is completely devoted to God and determined by a knowledge of God won not by instruction, but by insight. This insight should be attributed to God as a divine revelation.

But it appears that even this special experience which completely unites the soul momentarily must not be taken for granted. The insight is the divine Reason available to the soul. It must be allowed to test and harden the soul. And it should be tested itself by critical analysis and reflection. In the process the soul finds itself attributing all things to God, even its own knowledge of God. This attribution is the highest form of piety.

D. Sacr. 88–139 (Gen 4:4) *The Ensuing Sacrificial Labor of the Soul.*

The problem now is to conceive of God without attributing human images to him. In keeping with the knowledge that God is the creator and ruler of all things, there are two rubrics. One is that God is not man, nor like man. The other is that God is to be distinguished from creation. All things are his gifts and possessions. We must not, therefore, think of God either in terms of human images or created phenomena. That is the problem.

If, however, we analyze the insight by which this knowledge of God's dissimilarity is experienced, we are able to imagine God in appropriate ways. We recall that the human soul is a mixture, unruly until governed by a *hegemonikon*. In this respect the *hegemonikon* is like God, even if God is not like anything human. But the *hegemonikon* or mind must be cleansed, separated from the foolish opinions of self-worth, in order to acknowledge its creation by God. This occurs by insight which cannot be attributed to the mind's own power, but to God himself. With this insight a new principle is introduced as the ruler of the soul. This principle can be called divine Wisdom, Power, or Reason. Since it is not a human possession, yet is experienced by the soul, the divine Reason is an appropriate image for our conception of God.

We may even imagine that those who are completely ruled by the divine Wisdom or Reason are not only translated into the nature of God, but function as mediators of God's power within the world. This would give us a way to imagine God in human form without attributing human form to God. And the image is important. For if we can't imagine God in himself, we can be instructed by imagining men who have achieved perfect transformation of their minds by the divine Reason. Nevertheless, these are ideals of perfection rarely achieved. For the most of us we will do well to set before us the image of the ones who toil faithfully on the path of progress toward that ideal.

Goal: Intellection as the Sacrifice of the Soul

According to Philo, the value of the books of Moses is just that this labor is made possible for us. The stories represent those who encountered the powers, oracles, and commands of God in a world of his creation and rule. Encoded as human history, the task of decoding their experiences as moments in the soul's quest for the knowledge of God provides us with instructive images. In the present treatise the theme of sacrificial offering has been explored as a major symbol for this quest. Terminology related to "sacrifice" and "offering" have been found most appropriate to explore the problem of the knowledge of God as creator and ruler. Thus "separation," "dividing," "distinguishing," and "translating," as well as "subtracting," "taking away," "smiting," and "killing" are all terms for sacrifice which can be used to explore the ways in which the soul prepares for, participates in, and experiences its severence from the wrong opinions about itself and the world. The terms for offering, on the other hand—"adding," "attributing," "referring," "repaying," and so forth—all can be used to imagine the same moment as insight into the soul's proper acknowledgement of God as the source of its life and knowledge. A marvelous reciprocity results in which, to use the terms of sacrifice, the true offering to God is of one's own self, a self which is thereby acknowledged as a gift from God. That is the lesson we can learn from Abel.

Claremont

The Studia Philonica Annual 20 (2008) 33–54

DIONYSUS IN PHILO OF ALEXANDRIA
A STUDY OF *DE VITA CONTEMPLATIVA*

JAMES M. SCOTT

Philo frequently uses the language of the Greek mystery cults in his writings.[1] To name just one example, he refers to the translators of the Septuagint as "hierophants" (ἱεροφάνται).[2] According to Hesychius (s.v. ἱεροφάντης), a hierophant is the cultic title for "the mystagogue, he who

---

[1] Cf., e.g., Celia Deutsch, "The Therapeutae: Text Work, Ritual and Mystical Experience," in *Paradise Now: Essays on Early Jewish and Christian Mysticism* (ed. April D. DeConick; SBLSS 11; Atlanta, GA: Society of Biblical Literature, 2006, 287–312; Christoph Riedweg, *Mysterienterminologie bei Platon, Philon und Klemens von Alexandria* (Untersuchungen zur antiken Literatur und Geschichte 26; Berlin/New York: de Gruyter, 1987), 70–115. Citations of Philo's works in the following study are from the Loeb edition.

[2] Cf. Philo, *Mos.* 2.40, referring to the reputed accuracy of the Greek translation of the Torah (cf. *Let. Aris.* 310): "The clearest proof of this is that, if Chaldeans have learned Greek, or Greeks Chaldean, and read both versions, the Chaldean and the translation, they regard them with awe and reverence as sisters, or rather one and the same, both in matter and words, and speak of the authors not as translators but as *hierophants* and prophets (ἱεροφάντας καὶ προφήτας), whose sincerity and singleness of thought has enabled them to go hand in hand with the purest of spirits, the spirit of Moses." The point of this passage is not apologetic, as if Philo had somehow become uncomfortable with or embarrassed about the Greek of the Septuagint, possibly as a result of some theological conflict to which Philo is responding (cf. Benjamin B. Wright III, "Translation as Scripture: The Septuagint in Aristeas and Philo," in *Septuagint Research: Issues and Challenges in the Study of the Greek Jewish Scriptures* [eds. Wolfgang Kraus and R. Glenn Wooden; SBLSCS 53; Atlanta, GA: Society of Biblical Literature, 2006], 47–61, esp. 59–61); rather, Philo is merely reinforcing what the *Letter of Aristeas* already asserts: "The outcome was such that in seventy-two days the business of translation was completed, *just as if a result was achieved by some deliberate design*" (§ 307). On the legend of the Septuagint, see further Abraham Wasserstein and David J. Wasserstein, *The Legend of the Septuagint From Classical Antiquity to Today* (Cambridge: Cambridge University Press, 2006); Sylvie Honigman, *Septuagint and Homeric Scholarship in Alexandria: A Study in the Narrative of the* Letter of Aristeas (London/New York: Routledge, 2003); Nina L. Collins, *The Library in Alexandria and the Bible in Greek* (VTSup 82; Leiden: Brill, 2000); Giuseppe Veltri, *Eine Tora für den König Talmai. Untersuchungen zum Übersetzungsverständnis in den jüdisch-hellenistischen und rabbinischen Literatur* (TSAJ 41; Tübingen: Mohr-Siebeck, 1994); idem, *Libraries, Translations, and "Canonic" Texts: The Septuagint, Aquila and Ben Sira in the Jewish and Christian Traditions* (JSJSup 109; Leiden: Brill, 2006).

shows/explains the sacred objects" (ὁ μυσταγωγός, ὁ τὰ ἱερὰ δεικνύων), that is, one who instructs persons before initiation into religious mysteries or before participation in the sacraments, the showing of the sacred objects being the rite of initiation itself.[3]

One of the most popular and widespread mystery cults in antiquity was that of Dionysus.[4] As we shall see, Philo refers to Dionysus and his cult several times in his writings. For our purposes, however, the most interesting and extensive of these is found in *De vita contemplativa*, which will therefore be the main focus of the present study.

---

[3] On Philo's use of ἱεροφάνται, see Riedweg, *Mysterienterminologie*, 97, 114; H. A. Wolfson, *Philo: Foundations of Religious Philosophy in Judaism, Christianity, and Islam*, Structure and Growth of Philosophic Systems from Plato to Spinoza (2 vols.; rev. ed.; Cambridge, MA 1947 [1982]), 1.43: "God [*Somn.* 1.26, 164], Moses [*Spec.* 1.8, 41; 2.32, 201; 4.34, 176; *Virt.* 11, 75; 32, 174], the seventy elders of Moses [*Sobr.* 4.20], the high priest [*Spec.* 3.24, 135] and Jeremiah [*Cher.* 14, 49] are each described by him by the term Hierophant (ἱεροφάντης), the technical term which designated the highest officer of the heathen mysteries and the demonstrator of its knowledge." On Dionysiac ἱεροφάνται, see Franz Cumont, "La grande Inscription bachique du Metropolitan Museum. II. Commentaire religieux de l'inscription," *AJA* 37 (1933): 232–63, esp. 243–44; Albert Henrichs, "Die Maenaden von Milet," *ZPE* 4 (1969): 223–41, esp. 229 with n. 21. Note that Euripides (*Bacchae* 551) refers to the female followers of Dionysus as προφῆται.

[4] The literature on Dionysus and his cult is extensive. For recent overviews, see Richard Seaford, *Dionysos* (Gods and Heroes of the Ancient World; London/New York: Routledge, 2006); Fritz Graf and Sarah Iles Johnston, *Ritual Texts for the Afterlife: Orpheus and the Bacchic Gold Tablets* (London/New York: Routledge, 2007). On the popularity and widespread distribution of the Dionysiac cult, see Albert Henrichs, "Changing Dionysiac Identities," in *Jewish and Christian Self-Definition, Vol. 3: Self-Definition in the Greco-Roman World* (eds. Ben F. Meyer and E. P. Sanders; Philadelphia, PA: Fortress, 1982), 137–60, esp. 137: "The following three qualities in particular make Dionysus and his worship ideal pagan candidates for such comparison [i.e., a comparative study of Judaeo Christian versus pagan self-definition and religious identity]. First, Dionysus appealed to fundamental human interests which were shared by men and women alike; secondly, his cult had a very long history which produced an abundant documentation in Greek and Roman literature, art, and cult inscriptions from the late Bronze Age well into late antiquity; lastly, at all periods of its recorded history, the cult of Dionysus attracted large numbers of followers who were extremely well organized locally or regionally and who shared universal symbols which gave verbal and visual expression to their faith. Students of Dionysus and his cult cannot complain about any lack of evidence. The sheer quantity of the extant documentation, and its distribution over almost two millennia, over widely different geographical areas and over a variety of media, are equally overwhelming. If one wants to illustrate consistent trends or new departures in the ancient conception and worship of Dionysus, it is necessary to avoid vague generalizations as well as mere accumulation of data, and to aim for a reasonable balance, which is difficult to achieve."

Overview of De vita contemplativa

There has been a great deal of controversy about Philo's treatise on the Therapeutae, *De vita contemplativa*, since he is virtually the only source on them.[5] The Therapeutae are portrayed as an ideal Jewish religious community wholly devoted to meditation and worship,[6] whom Philo calls "philosophers" (2; cf. 28, 35, 67, 68, 89).[7] Our interest in the Therapeutae here is not in how they may be like the Essenes or the Qumran community,[8] or whether they correspond to an actual group at all.[9] Instead, our focus on the group is precisely where Philo himself puts it: their similarity to adherents of the Greek mysteries and particularly the Dionysiac mysteries. The language of the Greek mysteries suffuses Philo's description of the Therapeutae. Indeed, the term θεραπευταί itself is also used in the mysteries.[10]

---

[5] Church fathers who refer to the Therapeutae seem dependent on Philo's information about them. Cf., e.g., Eusebius, *HE* 2.17.

[6] The Therapeutae's name itself derives from θεραπεύω, meaning "to heal" or "to worship" (*Contempl.* 2). For the translation of θεραπευταί as "devotees [of God]," see Joan E. Taylor and Philip R. Davies, "The So-called Therapeutae of 'De vita contemplativa,'" *HTR* 91 (1998): 3–24, esp. 4–10; Joan E. Taylor, *Jewish Women Philosophers of First-Century Alexandria: Philo's "Therapeutae" Reconsidered* (Oxford: Oxford University Press, 2003), 55–68.

[7] Cf. *Contempl.* 14 (the Therapeutae are portrayed as superior to Greek philosophers in the way that they dispose of their possessions), 26 ("many when asleep and dreaming give utterance to the glorious verities of their holy philosophy").

[8] Although Philo does open the treatise (*Contempl.* 1) with a reference to the Essenes, who represent the *vita activa*, in contrast to the Therapeutae, whom he will now adduce as examples of the *vita contemplativa*. On the issue of the relationship between the Therapeutae and the Essenes and/or the Qumran community, see, e.g., C. T. R. Hayward, 'Therapeutae,' in *Encyclopedia of the Dead Sea Scrolls* (eds. Lawrence H. Schiffman and James C. VanderKam; 2 vols.; Oxford: Oxford University Press, 2000), 2.943–46; Geza Vermes and Martin D. Goodman, *The Essenes According to the Classical Sources* (Oxford Centre Textbooks 1; Sheffield: JSOT Press, 1989), 15–17, 75–99; Taylor and Davies, "The So-called Therapeutae," 3–24; Taylor, *Jewish Women Philosophers*, 68–73; Martin Hengel, *Judentum und Hellenismus. Studien zu ihrer Begegnung unter besonderer Berücksichtigung Palästinas bis zur Mitte des 2.Jh.s v.Chr.* (2nd ed.; WUNT 10; Tübingen: Mohr-Siebeck, 1973), 452 with n. 810.

[9] Cf., e.g., Mary Ann Beavis, "Philo's Therapeutai: Philosopher's Dream or Utopian Construction?" *JSP* 14 (2004): 30–42; Troels Engberg-Pedersen, "Philo's *De Vita Contemplativa* as a Philosopher's Dream," *JSJ* 30 (1999): 40–64; Taylor, *Jewish Women Philosophers*, 7–11; Peter Richardson and Valerie Heuchan, "Jewish Voluntary Associations in Egypt and the Roles of Women," in *Voluntary Associations in the Graeco-Roman World* (ed. John S. Kloppenborg and Stephen G. Wilson; London/New York: Routledge, 1996), 226–51, esp. 239–46.

[10] Cf. Walter Burkert, *Antike Mysterien. Funktion und Gehalt* (4th ed.; Munich: Beck, 2003), 43; Taylor, *Jewish Women Philosophers*, 55–68; Celia Deutsch, "The Therapeutae," 289–90.

Moreover, comparisons of the Therapeutae with Dionysiacs frame the whole account. Thus, towards the beginning of the treatise, Philo writes:

> (11) But it is well that the Therapeutae, a people always taught from the first to use their sight, should desire the vision of the Existent and soar above the sun of our senses and never leave their place in this company which carries them on to perfect happiness. (12) And those who set themselves to this service, not just following custom nor on the advice and admonition of others but carried away by a heaven-sent passion of love, remain rapt and enthused like Bacchantes or Corybantes until they see the object of their desire (ἀλλ' ὑπ' ἔρωτος ἁρπασθέντες οὐρανίου, καθάπερ οἱ βακχευόμενοι καὶ κορυβαντιῶντες, ἐνθουσιάζουσι μέχρις ἂν τὸ ποθούμενον ἴδωσιν).

Likewise, towards the end of *De vita contemplativa*, Philo refers again to the Dionysiac mysteries, this time in the context of the communal meal and the divine service that takes place after it (evidently as a substitute for the symposium after a Greek banquet):

> (85) Then when each choir has separately done its own part in the feast, having drunk as in the Bacchic rites of the strong wine of God's love (καθάπερ ἐν ταῖς βακχείαις ἀκράτου σπάσαντες τοῦ θεοφιλοῦς) they mix and both together become a single choir, a copy of the choir set up of old beside the Red Sea in honor of the wonders there wrought [Exod 15:1–21]. [...] (89) Thus they continue until dawn, drunk with this drunkenness in which there is no shame, then not with heavy heads or drowsy eyes but more alert and wakeful than when they came to the banquet, they stand with their faces and whole body turned to the east and when they see the sun rising they stretch their hands up to heaven and pray for bright days and knowledge of truth and the power of keen sighted thinking.

Obviously, these similarly worded passages deliberately frame the intervening discussion. This suggests that to understand the precise framing function of these passages, we need to gain an overview of Philo's description of the Therapeutae as a whole. As we shall see, the comparison that the Alexandrian makes between the Therapeutae and the Dionysiacs is actually a study in contrasts as well.

The Therapeutae are said to be of a kind found "in many places of the inhabited world," but their main locus is in the vicinity of Alexandria, especially on a hill above Lake Mareotis characterized by a healthful, temperate climate (21–23).[11] In this relatively isolated and secure location, the premises consist of several communal buildings for worship and meals (32, 36), as well as modest individual houses (24, 38), each containing a consecrated

---

[11] Alexandria was built on a ridge of land lying between the Mediterranean Sea to the northwest and Lake Mareotis to the south. On the geographical location of the Mareotic community, see further Taylor, *Jewish Women Philosophers*, 75–93.

room called a "sanctuary" or *monasterion* (25). What the Therapeutae did in these rooms is worth particular note:

> ... and closeted in this [consecrated room] they are initiated into the mysteries of the sanctified life (ἐν ᾧ μονούμενοι τὰ τοῦ σεμνοῦ βίου μυστήρια τελοῦνται). They take nothing into it, either drink or food or any other of the things necessary for the needs of the body, but laws and oracles delivered through the mouth of the prophets, and psalms and anything else which fosters and perfects knowledge and piety.

Here we have an image of the Therapeutae as separatists who, although living communally, practice their contemplative lives of study and meditation for the most part in splendid solitude.[12] The language of initiation into the mysteries that is used here further underscores the theme of the Greek mysteries that we are tracking in *De vita contemplativa*.

The daily lives of the Therapeutae were quite regimented. Six days of the week they spent in their closets (30), praying twice daily, at dawn—turning toward the rising sun—and at sunset (27, 89), and, in between, completely devoting themselves to spiritual exercise, including scripture reading (25), accompanied by allegorical interpretation and the composition of hymns and psalms (28–29).[13] Only after sunset would they eat or drink (34), and some would not eat until after the six days elapsed (35). They abstained from meat and wine (73–74), drinking only water (37, 73).[14] Every seventh day they met together for a very orderly general assembly, sitting in order of their seniority (30, 67, 75), listening to the most learned senior member of the group deliver an allegorical homily (31–33), and eating a modest amount of extremely simple fare (36–37). After seven sets of seven days, the chief feast takes place (65),[15] which is also referred to as a "sacred banquet" (71).

---

[12] Although the Therapeutae consist of both men and women, they not only remain celibate (68), but the sexes live and worship apart from each other (32–33, 69).

[13] Cf. *Contempl.* 28: "They read the holy scriptures and seek wisdom from their ancestral philosophy by taking it as an allegory."

[14] Cf. *Contempl.* 74: "Abstinence from wine is enjoined by right reason as for a priest when sacrificing, so to these for their lifetime."

[15] On the solar calendar of the Therapeutae, which has a remarkable resemblance in some ways with that of *1 Enoch* and the *Book of Jubilees*, see Taylor, *Jewish Women Philosophers*, 154–70, who argues that this feast refers not to the annual Feast of Weeks/Pentecost, but rather to "the week-of-weeks Sabbath" that occurs every seven weeks. Cf. also Deutsch, "The Therapeutae," 306–7.

Comparison between the Therapeutae and Dionysiacs

Philo's description of the Therapeutae should certainly be seen in light of the references to the Greek mysteries elsewhere in his writings, which includes the use of τελετή ("initiation") and related words with respect to Judaism.[16] Here, however, the specific focus is on a comparison between the Therapeutae and the Dionysiac mysteries, as the aforementioned framing passages demonstrate. Since every comparison is simultaneously a contrast, we will do well also to consider the major contrast that Philo makes in *De vita contemplativa* between the Therapeutae and the Dionysiacs.[17] Thus, when Philo emphasizes the modesty and simplicity of the Therapeutae in various material respects, as well as their sober, orderly lives of quiet contemplation, he does so in stark contrast to the drunken debauchery that frequently attends the ritualized drinking at symposia and the material luxuriousness that is often associated with the celebration of the Dionysiac mysteries. At the same time, he wishes to stress the philosophical luxuriousness of the Therapeutae.

On the one hand, Philo emphasizes the modesty and simplicity of the Therapeutae in various material respects.[18] Once they had divested themselves of their major property and possessions in order to retreat to the contemplative life (13–20), including slaves (70), the Therapeutae retained only the barest essentials of the humblest sort: dwellings (24, 38), food and drink (37, 73–74, 81–82), dining couches (69), and clothing (one garment for summer and another for winter [38], as well as a white robe for festivals

---

[16] Cf. Riedweg, *Mysterienterminologie*, 70–115, which unfortunately devotes very little attention to *De vita contemplativa* in particular. On Philo's view of Judaism as a mystery religion, see further Louis H. Feldman, *Jew and Gentile in the Ancient World: Attitudes and Interactions from Alexander to Justinian* (Princeton: Princeton University Press, 1993), 66–67, 126–28; Markus N, A. Bockmuehl, *Revelation and Mystery in Ancient Judaism and Pauline Christianity* (WUNT 2.36; Tübingen: Mohr-Siebeck, 1990), 76–81.

[17] Cf. David M. Hay, "Foils for the Therapeutae: References to Other Texts and Persons in Philo's *De vita contemplativa*," in *Studies in Honor of Peter Borgen* (ed. David E. Aune et al.; Leiden: Brill, 2003), 330–48.

[18] A related point is that the Therapeutae represent an inclusive community of free persons, both young and old, male and female; there is no hint of slavery or exclusivism among those belonging to the community (*Contempl.* 30–31, 70–72). We may compare these characteristics to those of Dionysiac associations. Cf. Albert Henrichs, "Changing Dionysiac Identities," 149: "Dionysus has been described as 'a democratic god' who imposed no limit of age or status and who invited worship by young and old, freemen and slaves alike. Dionysiac inscriptions confirm for the imperial period that Roman citizens, freedmen and slaves were often members of the same Dionysiac mystery cults which were invariably of local and private character."

[66]).[19] This abnegation of worldly goods is coupled, as we have seen above, with abstinence from marriage and wine and a generally ascetic lifestyle of quiet contemplation. For the Therapeutae, simplicity and vanity are strict opposites: simplicity is the source of truth, whereas vanity is the source of falsehood (39). The festivals of the Therapeutae are marked by self-control and silent attention to allegorical exposition of the scriptures by the president before the meal (75–78), with hymns to God concluding the service (80).[20] After the banquet of leavened bread (81), they sing further hymns to God until sunrise (83–89). On the other hand, however, there is one respect in which some Therapeutae do indulge in luxury: "Others so luxuriate and delight in the banquet of truths which wisdom richly and lavishly supplies that ... only after six days do they bring themselves to taste such sustenance as is absolutely necessary" (35). This indulgence in the luxuriousness of a metaphorical banquet of truths goes along with the notion that when they sing songs after their communal meal, the Therapeutae drink "as in the Bacchic rites of the strong wine of God's love" (85 [cited above]). Thus, the group's singing of hymns after the meal functionally takes the place of the drinking-bouts of a symposium.

[19] *De vita contemplativa* 38, describes the Therapeutae's two types of clothing as "a thick coat of shaggy skin [= woolen cloak] in winter and in summer a vest or linen shirt" (χλαῖνα μὲν ἀπὸ λασίου δορᾶς παχεία χειμῶνος, ἐξωμὶς δὲ θέρους ἢ ὀθόνη). Herodotus (2.81) describes the Egyptian custom of wearing two garments—a linen tunic (κιθῶνας λινέους) and a white woolen cloak (εἰρίνεα εἵματα λευκά) on top of it—and then defines as "Orphic and Bacchic" a proscription against burial in woolen garments, alluding to a *hieros logos* that explains the reason for this. Also otherwise, Book 2 of Herodotus has a great interest in the relationship between Egypt and cult of Dionysus and the *hieroi logoi* that provide an explanation for it (cf. 2.42, 47–49). See further Albert Henrichs, "*Hieroi Logoi and Hierai Bibloi*: The (Un)written Margins of the Sacred in Ancient Greece," *HSCP* 101 (2003): 207–66. On the interpretation of "Orphic and Bacchic" in Herodotus 2.81 as a hendiadys that refers to one and the same religious group, see Graf and Johnston, *Ritual Texts*, 159; also 50–51, 175. On the clothing of the Therapeutae, see Taylor, *Jewish Women Philosophers*, 287–302.

[20] Noach Hacham draws attention to a similar contrast between the deportment of worshipers in the Dionysiac cult and that of Alexandrian Jews who celebrate their deliverance from death: "Dancing, an activity common in Dionysian ritual, is also mentioned in conjunction with the Jews' parties ([3 Macc] 6:32, 35). Once again they stand in contrast to the Dionysian practice of losing self-control, for these dances signify joy and peace (6:32) and are accompanied by thanksgiving and psalms (6:35)." Cf. Noach Hacham, "3 Maccabees: An Anti-Dionysian Polemic," in *Ancient Fiction: The Matrix of Early Christian and Jewish Narrative* (ed. Jo-Ann A. Brant et al.; SBLSS 32; Atlanta, GA: Society of Biblical Literature, 2005), 167–83, esp. 180–81. See also ibid., 181: "Thus, in the description of these details as well, the writer of 3 Maccabees claims that the Jews have what the Dionysian cult has, but in a pure, gentle, Jewish way and not in a vulgar, disgusting way."

All this stands in sharp contrast to the wonted material luxuriousness and indulgence that is often associated with the celebration of the Dionysiac mysteries and the nocturnal carousing that frequently attends symposia after a banquet.[21] Whereas the communal meals of the Therapeutae were sober affairs that abstained from wine (73–74), the convivial meals of other people are characterized by dissolute nocturnal binges (40–47). Moreover, Philo points to "method of banqueting now prevalent everywhere through hankering for the Italian extravagance (πολυτέλεια) and luxury (τρυφή) emulated both by Greek and non-Greeks who make their arrangements for ostentation rather than festivity" (48). Thereupon, Philo provides concrete examples of this luxuriousness, including the exquisite banqueting couches, the finely wrought drinking cups, the handsome servants, and the lavish profusion of food and drink (49–56).

> Luxuriousness is a Dionysiac motif. Hellenistic monarchs positively reveled in this aspect of Dionysus worship.[22] For instance, Demetius I Poliorcetes (336–283 B.C.E.), who is said to have "modeled himself especially on Dionysus," is characterized as "a most agreeable companion for leisure and drinking, and the most sophisticated of kings in luxurious living (τρυφαί)" (Plutarch, *Demetrius* 2–4). The story that Lucian (*Calumniae con temere credendum* 16) relates about a Platonist named Demetius at the court of Ptolemy XII Neos Dionysos (117–51 B.C.E.) provides a characteristic example of the veneration of Dionysus that is connected with the royal banquets of the Ptolemies: Demetrius, who had been denounced for drinking only water and failing to don women's clothing during the Dionysia, was called before the king the very next morning and required in front of everyone, on pain of death if he refused, to drink wine and, after putting on a gossamer dress, to play the cymbal (a favorite musical instrument of the Dionysus cult) and dance to it. The reason given for this demand is that the king would not tolerate that someone would oppose his way of life (βίος), which was bent on luxuriousness (τρυφή).[23] In light of this characteristic

---

[21] On Philo's negative take on the Greek mysteries, see Erich S. Gruen, *Diaspora: Jews amidst Greeks and Romans* (Cambridge, MA: Harvard University Press, 2002), 216.

[22] On Dionysiac *tryphē* as Hellenistic royal ideology, see further Heinz Heinen, "Die Tryphé des Ptolemaios VIII. Euergetes II. Bemerkungen zum ptolemäischen Herrscheri-deals un zu einer römischen Gesandtschaft in Ägypten (140/39 v.Chr.)," in *Althistorische Studien, Hermann Bengston zum 70. Geburtstag dargebracht von Kollegen und Schulern* (ed. H. Heinen; Historia Einzelschriften 40; Wiesbaden: Steiner Verlag, 1983), 116–30; Adrian Stähli, *Die Verweigerung der Lüste. Erotische Gruppen in der antiken Plastik* (Berlin: Reimer, 1999), 248–55; Julien Tondriau, "La tryphè, philosophie royale ptolémaïque," *REA* 50 (1948): 49–54.

[23] Cf. Konrad Vössing, *Mensa Regia. Das Bankett beim hellenistischen König und beim römischen Kaiser* (Beiträge zur Altertumskunde 193; Leipzig: Saur, 2004), 140: "Auffallend ist, daß die 'Dionysien' hier nicht an einen bestimmten Termin gebunden sind. Offenbar war der ganze Hof zu einer Kultgenossenschaft geworden, der man sich anzuschließen hatte. Am Schluß wird deutlich, daß 'die *tryphê* des Königs' hier ein gleichsam verkündetes Programm ist. Da kaum vorstellbar ist, daß diese positive Wertung von Ptolemaios XII.

Dionysiac theme of extravagant luxury in the royal banquets of the Ptolemaic court (Vössing refers to "Dionysos-Imitatio" and the *"thiasos*-Charakter des königlichen Konsums"),[24] we can see how the Therapeutae represent the opposite of societal norms in this respect, particularly in Hellenistic Egypt.[25]

To further illustrate his point, Philo adduces two renowned banquets in which Socrates took part (57–62): Xenophon's *Symposium* (58) and Plato's *Symposium* (59–62). What Philo mentions—and fails to mention—about these symposia is noteworthy. On the one hand, he mentions that the discussion in Plato's *Symposium* was all about "love" (ἔρως) in the sense of pederasty (59). This is evidently meant to contrast with the kind of "love" (ἔρως) that the Therapeutae experience, that is, "a heaven-sent passion of love" (12 [cited above]; cf. 85 [cited above]). Although the sympotic discussion in Plato's *Symposium* was indeed centrally concerned with love, it was not at all confined to pederasty. In fact, Plato's point would seem to be rather that erotic love can be sublimated and refined in a way that draws the person to aspire to philosophical truth—a point that Philo would presumably find amenable to his portrayal of the Therapeutae as "philosophers."[26] As we shall see below, Philo's indebtedness to Plato's *Symposium* here is more than he acknowledges.

On the other hand, what Philo fails to mention is that the symposia in Xenophon and Plato prominently feature Dionysus. In Xenophon's *Symposium* (9.2–7), the symposium concludes with an erotic play in which an actor dressed as Dionysus approaches Ariadne dressed as a bride to the

---

erfunden wurde, muß man annehmen, daß es hier mit einer ptolemaischen Tradition zu tun haben. Der königliche Luxus ist in ihrem Zusammenhang eine Art Gottesdienst, da er nicht nur der Dionysos-Verehrung dient, sondern auch der Assimilation des Königs an diesen Gott." On Dionysiac luxuriousness, see also Diodorus Siculus 3.64.6: ". . . and since he grew to be of unusual beauty he at first spent his time at dances and with bands of women and in every kind of luxury (παντοδαπῇ τρυφῇ) and amusement. . . ."

[24] Vössing, *Mensa Regia*, 138. See further Hölbl, *Geschichte des Ptolemäerreiches*, 84: "Die materielle Grundlage einer erfolgreichen Regierung bildete der Reichtum des Königs, den er zur Schau stellte und in vieler Hinsicht zur Megalomanie steigerte, so bezüglich der Paläste, der Hofhaltung, der Festprozessionen, der Gastmäler etc. Ptolemaios III führte als erster offiziell den Beinamen 'Tryphon' (der 'Prunkende,' 'Glänzende') und propagierte damit die Tryphé (τρυφή), den Glanz und die Pracht, als Idealbild der Reichtum und Glück spendenden Ptolemäerherrschaft. Damit unterstrichen die Ptolemäer gleichzeitig ihre Nähe zu Dionysos als einem Stammvater der Dynastie und die dionysische Komponente des Herrscherkultes."

[25] Cf. Taylor, *Jewish Women Philosophers*, 317.

[26] In making this connection, we do not want to intimate that Philo would want the Therapeutae to be associated with any kind of erotic love. The difference between Plato and Philo is precisely that for Plato the actual act of love and drinking can be sublimated and given a new meaning and that Philo presents the Therapeutae as people without the actual act but only with the deeper meaning.

accompaniment of Bacchic music played on a flute, whereupon the two embrace passionately as lovers and then leave together for the bridal couch. In Plato's *Symposium*, Dionysus is even more integral to the development. To understand exactly how Plato's *Symposium* relates to Philo's treatment of the Therapeutae, it is necessary at this point to delve into some of the particulars of Plato's work, especially as interpreted recently by Steven R. Robinson.[27]

In his discussion of the *Symposium*, Robinson shows how wine and other Dionysiac symbols form a network that allows Plato to elaborate the nature of the contest of wisdom between Socrates and Agathon during the symposium under the auspices of Dionysus in the form of the drunken Alcibiades as an image of Dionysus who promptly appoints himself symposiarch. This contest of wisdom on the theory and practice of Eros exemplifies and highlights the fundamental difference between exoteric, public discourse (Agathon's wisdom = poetry, especially tragedy as the highest form of popular discourse for all citizens where Dionysus is the god of theater) and esoteric, private discourse (Socrates' wisdom = philosophy, particularly Dionysiac mystery-cult initiation as the highest form of esoteric discourse for the few), which is deemed superior. Thus, in the context of the symposium, where Dionysus is lord and is experienced by *ritual* drinking of wine,[28] Socrates and Agathon are made to exemplify a contrast within Dionysiac religious cult, i.e., the contrast between the civic cults of Dionysus (including that of the Lenaea, where Agathon's winning tragedy was performed) and the private, esoteric cults of Dionysus (to which philosophy is assimilated by Diotima's and Alcibiades' speeches). "Plato allows this *third form* of Dionysiac cult-event [i.e., the symposium]," writes Robinson, "to act as the common ground within which these two other Dionysiac forms can 'go to court.' And the person who does eventually render judgment is, of course, none other than the *drunken* Alcibiades, not only the very

---

[27] Steven R. Robinson, "The Contest of Wisdom between Socrates and Agathon in Plato's 'Symposium,'" *Ancient Philosophy* 24 (2004): 81–100.

[28] Cf. François Lissarrague, *The Aesthetics of the Greek Banquet: Images of Wine and Ritual* (Princeton, NJ: Princeton University Press, 1990), 25–28; Erwin R. Goodenough, *Jewish Symbols in the Greco-Roman Period* (Bollinger Series 37; 12 vols.; New York: Pantheon Books, 1953–68), 6.9–13. In Plutarch, *Quaest. conv.* 6.1 (*Mor.* 671 D), one of the symposiasts argues, in the context of identifying the God of the Jews with Dionysus, that what he is about to speak is "not forbidden in conversation with friends, especially over after-dinner wine, while we are enjoying the god's own bounty." In other words, it is intrinsically appropriate to speak circumspectly about the Dionysiac mysteries at a symposium, because everyone present is drinking wine, the gift of Dionysus. This is indeed the context in which Plato's famous *Symposium* also dealt with the subject of the Dionysiac mysteries as topic for the after-dinner conversation.

image of the wine god, but the only man in the house who is fully in his power (i.e., who is drunk)."[29] Nevertheless, it is Socrates himself who turns out to be the overwhelmingly Dionysiac presence: (1) he is immune to the effects of wine, no matter how much he drinks, ostensibly because he is always already possessed by Dionysus so that no amount of wine can make him more "drunk" than he already is; (2) Alcibiades describes Socrates as Silenus, Satyr, and even as Marsyas, the satyric "piper" who leads people to Bacchic rapture. Since the *Symposium* equates words and wine,[30] when Alcibiades compares Socrates to a satyr-figurine that opens up to reveal images of the gods (*Sym.* 215b), Socrates is seen to have gods inside of him and those gods are in his words, his philosophical talk. Socrates is therefore perpetually in a state of genuine possession by the wine god. "Socrates is possessed by Dionysus in a way that is for all intents and purposes equivalent to possession by wine, but without the wine. He is 'word-drunk': possessed by the divine words that fill up, and emanate from, his person. But since he is always already ἔνθεος ('drunk,' with words), wine has no effect upon him."[31]

---

[29] Robinson, "The Contest of Wisdom," 88. Cf. Helen H. Bacon, "Socrates Crowned," *The Virginia Quarterly Review* 35 (1959): 415–30, esp. 423–24:

> Socrates himself, the man who knows all about love, is drawn into the Dionysiac context, not only by his ability to drink everyone else under the table, and his mock love affair with the tragic poet (i.e., Agathon), but in several less obvious, and, I think more significant ways. The first interchange of raillery with Agathon develops into a contest in which each maintains with ironic courtesy that the other is wiser. Agathon has the last word. 'Socrates, you have no shame . . . as for our respective claims to wisdom, we'll argue them out in court a little later on, and Dionysus shall be the judge.' When Alcibiades comes in, his first act is to crown Agathon, the tragic poet of the hour, but when he turns and sees that Socrates is reclining on the other side of him, he takes some of the ribbons from Agathon's wreath and crowns Socrates too. 'Agathon,' he said, 'give me some of those fillets to crown this astonishing head here, . . . since in the contest of words he is victor over all men, not just day before yesterday, like you, but always.' In the judgment of this Dionysus at least, the crown of the tragic poet belongs to Socrates. The conclusion also seems to be making this point—in actions as much as in words. Certainly in the judgment of Dionysus, Socrates wins a victory over both poets. He drinks them both under the table. But perhaps in a more extended sense also; for Dionysus is the god of tragedy and comedy, and Socrates as he tucks in the tragic and the comic poet seems somehow to have beaten them at their own game. He seems to have known something about tragedy and comedy which they themselves did not know—that they are really the same art. Does the end of the 'Symposium' tell us that, in the judgment of Dionysus, it is not Agathon or Aristophanes but Socrates who carries off the prize for poetry?

[30] Cf. Robinson, "The Contest of Wisdom," 82–83.

[31] Robinson, "The Contest of Wisdom," 92.

Also important for our considerations is the fact that Plato's *Symposium* makes a connection between Socrates' "philosophical talk" and Dionysiac mystery-cult initiation.[32] In contrast to discourse that was readily accessible to the public, "the mysteries, with their *thiasoi*, their secret *hieroi logoi*, and their intellectualizing allegory, are the very definition of esotericism."[33] Specifically, Socrates' philosophical talk is portrayed as the pedagogical element of a Dionysiac mystery-cult.[34] "There are actually a remarkable number of similarities between Greek mystery cults and Plato's portrayal of philosophy (both in the *Symposium* and elsewhere). [...] As Burkert implies, Diotima's teachings as related by Socrates correspond to a so-called *paradosis*, or 'preparatory learning' phase of initiatory practice. Accordingly, it is the famous vision of The Beautiful (211) that would constitute the mysteries proper."[35] Robinson argues that this *paradosis* directly alludes to the Dionysiac mysteries rather than, as often assumed, to the Eleusinian cult.[36] For Dionysus was more closely associated with mysteries per se than any other god, and the mysteries to which Socrates refers are handed down personally in private succession, like the Dionysiac cults. Diotima is also a foreigner who performed mantic services for Athens in a time of crisis (*Sym.* 201d 3–5), and only the mysteries of Dionysus and Meter were transmitted by that sort of charismatic (with only the Bacchics using female mantics). Furthermore, the word-family surrounding τελετη (initiation), which is prominent in the *Symposium*, was "used with a certain preference with regard to Dionysos."[37]

From this exposition, it is easy to see how Plato's *Symposium* has fundamentally influenced Philo's portrayal of the Therapeutae. Here as elsewhere, Philo is an avowed admirer of Plato.[38] In both writings, esoteric, private discourse—the kind of "philosophy" that is exemplified by Dionysiac mystery-cult initiation—is deemed the highest form of wisdom. Philo's debt to Plato at this point can be seen by comparing *Phaedo* 69cd, which

---

[32] Cf. Riedweg, *Mysterienterminologie*, 1–69 (esp. 2–29, on the initiation rite described in Plato's *Symposium*). Note that Plutarch (*De profectibus in virtute* 10 [*Mor.* 81DE]) also compares initiation into the mysteries with introduction to philosophy. Cf. Reinhold Merkelbach, *Isis regina—Zeus Sarapis. Die griechisch-ägyptische Religion nach dem Quellen dargestellt* (Stuttgart/Leipzig: Teubner, 1995), 168.

[33] Robinson, "The Contest of Wisdom," 88.

[34] Ibid., 87.

[35] Ibid., 85 n. 7.

[36] Ibid., 84 n. 6.

[37] Burkert, *Antike Mysterien*, 16.

[38] Cf., e.g., John M. G. Barclay, *Jews in the Mediterranean Diaspora from Alexander to Trajan (323 B.C.E.–117 C.E.)* (Edinburgh: T&T Clark, 1996) 164–65; see also the special section on "Philo and Middle Platonism," in *Studia Philonica Annual* 5 (1993) 95–155.

interprets the lines uttered in the mysteries about the Dionysiac initiates being relatively few in number ("the thyrsus-bearers are many, but the Bacchants are few" [ναρθηκοφόροι μὲν πολλοί, βάκχοι δέ τε παῦροι]) to be an enigmatic reference to "the true philosophers" (οἱ πεφιλοσοφηκότες ὀρθῶς). As Seaford remarks, "How paradoxical that Plato should associate his ideal of the philosophical soul, abstracted from all bodily attractions, with the cult of the luxuriantly corporeal Dionysos!"[39] This is precisely Philo's point about the Therapeutae.

In both cases, what counts is not literal drunkenness, but rather being "word-drunk" with enthusiastic speech that takes possession of a person like wine (sober intoxication). In Plato's *Symposium*, there is an actual physical replacement of wine-drinking by speech-giving: "where heavy drinking is supposed to be, it has been excluded and replaced with speechifying; and when heavy wine-drinking resumes, the speechifying comes to an end."[40] Similarly in Philo's *De vita contemplativa*, the Therapeutae's singing of hymns after the communal meal functionally takes the place of the drinking-bouts of a symposium: they drink "as in the Bacchic rites of the strong wine of God's love" (85), and thus become "drunk with this drunkenness in which there is no shame" (89).

In both cases, it is the vision of the divine that is the object of the desire of those initiated into the Dionysiac mysteries. In Plato's *Symposium*, Socrates' discourse on Eros is based on the three stages of initiation into the mysteries, including the third and highest grade of initiation, Epopteia (seeing), which elsewhere is also called the "greater mysteries."[41] As Riedweg shows, Philo appropriates the language of the mysteries from Plato.[42] Hence, when Philo states that the Therapeutae are "initiated into the mysteries of the sanctified life" (τὰ τοῦ σεμνοῦ βίου μυστήρια τελοῦνται [25]), and that the Therapeutae's most essential characteristic is their mystical aspiration to reach the vision of the one God (11–12), we may assume that he has in mind the third stage of initiation into the mysteries. The framing of the treatise that we have observed (11–12 and 85, 89) shows that Philo is thinking particularly in terms of initiation into greater mysteries of the Dionysiac cult.[43] What techniques the Therapeutae employ in order to

---

[39] Seaford, *Dionysos*, 114.

[40] Robinson, "The Contest of Wisdom," 91.

[41] Cf. Riedweg, *Mysterienterminologie*, 2–29 (esp. 22–28 on Epopteia in Plato, *Symp.* 209e5–212a7).

[42] Cf. Riedweg, *Mysterienterminologie*, 70–115.

[43] On the quest to "see" God in Philo's writings, see further Taylor, *Jewish Women Philosophers*, 312, 318–20, 340, 343; Ellen Birnbaum, *The Place of Judaism in Philo's Thought:*

remain in their possessed state until they, like Bacchic ecstatics, see the object of their desire (12) is not explicitly stated in the text.[44] Based, however, on the end of the treatise (85, 89), which similarly refers to their Bacchic ecstasy and seeing the object of their desire, we may infer that their "drunkenness" is induced by their all-night vigil of choral singing (see above on word-drunkenness),[45] which is the collective parallel to their solitary composition and singing of hymns (29).[46]

Elsewhere, Philo's favorite expression for the things that he is talking about in *De vita contemplativa* is νηφάλιος μέθη ("sober intoxication"), by which he means initiation into the ultimate Dionysiac mysteries in order to attain to the mystical vision of the One God.[47] For example, in *Legum Allegoria* 3.82, Philo interprets

---

Israel, Jews, and Proselytes (BJS 290; Atlanta, GA: Scholars Press, 1996); Deutsch, "The Therapeutae," 293–95.

[44] Deutsch ("The Therapeutae," 299–303) argues that for Philo, contemplation of the sacred text via allegory is related to the vision of the Existent (*Contempl.* 11). On the role of sacred writings in the Dionysiac mysteries in Hellenistic Egypt, see Henrichs, "*Hieroi Logoi and Hierai Bibloi*," 224–31.

[45] Cf. Burkert, *Antike Mysterien*, 95–96. See also Tacitus, *Hist.* 5.5.5, who, noting that some have identified the Jewish God with Dionysus, discounts the evidence they cite, including, for example, that their priests chant to the music of flutes and cymbals. Pipes, cymbals, hand-drums, and ecstatic dancing were characteristic of Dionysiac ritual. Cf., e.g., Martin P. Nilsson, *The Dionysiac Mysteries of the Hellenistic and Roman Age* (Skrifter Utgivna av Svenska Institutet i Athen 8; Lund: Gleerup, 1957; reprint ed., New York: Arno, 1975), 59-60; *Anth. Gr.* 9.306 (Antipater of Sidon [mid-second century B.C.E.]: "These five votaries of Dionysus the Savior are entering upon the rapid dance. One lifts on high the body of a grim lion, another an antlered Arcadian stag, a third a bird with lovely plumage, a fourth a kettle-drum, and the fifth a heavy brazen clapper. All are frenzied and distraught by the Bacchic fury of the god."). The Corybantes (nature spirits), to whom Philo refers along with Bacchantes (*Contempl.* 12), guard the infant Dionysus in Orphic myth and dance to the sound of flutes in the orgiastic cult of Dionysus (Strabo 10.3.11; cf. Nonnus, *Dionysiaca* 9.162–68). On the connection between Dionysus and the Corybants, see further Burkert, "Bacchic *Teletai* in the Hellenistic Age," 270–71. Hence, when Philo mentions that the choral singing of the Therapeutae imitated the choir set up beside the Red Sea (Exod 15:1-20), with the men led by the prophet Moses and the women by the prophetess Miriam (*Contempl.* 85–87), then we should recall that Miriam danced and sang to the Lord on that occasion (Exod 15:20–21). See also Taylor, *Jewish Women Philosophers*, 336–37, on the question of whether the Therapeutae understood themselves to be "drunk" with the spiritual drink of Miriam's well.

[46] Hence, there seems to be a link between the community's two solitary textual practices—the allegorical interpretation of the scriptures and the composition and singing of hymns—and the communal choral singing that gives expression to ecstatic speech. Cf. *Contempl.* 89: "And after the prayers they depart each to his own sanctuary once more to ply the trade and till the field of their wonted philosophy."

[47] In the context of Bacchic revelry, according to Plutarch (*Aetia Romana et Graeca* [*Mor.* 291B]), ivy brings on a "wineless drunkenness" (ἄοινος μέθη) and joyousness in those who are precariously disposed towards spiritual exaltation. On the concept of "sober drunkenness," see further Hans Lewy, *Sobria Ebrietas. Untersuchung zur Geschichte der antiken*

allegorically the banquet of bread and wine that King Melchizedek of Salem provided for Abram (Gen 14:18) when the latter returned from defeating Chedor-laomer and the king with him: "But let Melchizedek instead of water offer wine, and give to souls strong drink, that they may be seized by a divine intoxication, more sober than sobriety itself (ἵνα κατάσχετοι γένωνται θείᾳ μέθῃ νηφαλεωτέρᾳ νήψεως αὐτῆς). For he is a priest, even Reason, having as his portion him that is, and all his thoughts of God are high and vast and sublime; for he is the priest of the Most High (Gen 14:18), not that there is any other not Most High—for God being One 'is in heaven above and on earth beneath, and there is none beside him' (Deut 4:39)—but to conceive of God not in low earthbound ways but in lofty terms, such as transcend all other greatness and all else that is free from matter, calls up in us a picture of the Most High."[48] The mystery-cult aspect of Philo's concept comes out clearly in *De opificio mundi* 71, which deals with the creation of man after the image of God and after his likeness in Gen 1:26: "And so, carrying its gaze beyond the confines of all substance discernible by sense, it comes to a point at which it reaches out after the intelligible world, and on descrying in that world sights of surpassing loveliness, even the patterns and the originals of the things of sense which it saw here, it is seized by a sober intoxication, like those filled with Corybantic frenzy (μέθῃ νηφαλίῳ κατασχεθεὶς ὥσπερ οἱ κορυβαντιῶντες ἐνθουσιᾷ), and inspired, possessed by a longing far other than theirs and a nobler desire. Wafted by this to the topmost arch of the things perceptible to mind, it seems to be on its way to the Great King himself; but, amid its longing to see him, pure and untempered rays of concentrated light stream forth like a torrent, so that by its gleams the eye of the understanding is dazzled."[49] Finally, if is it not already

---

Mystik (BZNW 9; Giessen: Töpelmann, 1929); Sebastian Brock, "*Sobria Ebrietas* according to Some Syriac Texts," *ARAM* 17 (2005): 185–91; David T. Runia, *Philo in Early Christian Litera-ture: A Survey* (CRINT 3.3; Assen: Van Gorcum; Minneapolis: Fortress, 1993), 179–80, 261, 308, 344; Taylor, *Jewish Women Philosophers*, 314. Lewy (*Sobria Ebrietas*, esp. 62–63, 89–90, 101–103) argues that Philo's concept of "sober drunkenness" was apparently derived from a pre-Gnostic dualism, analogous (but unrelated) to certain Dionysiac ideas. However, H. Chadwick, "Philo," in *The Cambridge History of Later Greek and Early Medieval Philosophy* (ed. A. H. Armstrong; Cambridge: Cambridge University Press, 1967), 137–57, esp. 150 n. 4, counters that Lewy may be mistaken in this regard: "Plutarch, *Qu. Rom.* 112, taken with *Anth. Pal.* IX 752 (Cleopatra's ring apparently inscribed with the formula) and Philostratus, *V. Apoll. Tyan.* II 37 (bacchants of sobriety), suggests the oxymoron may be a pre-Philonic coinage of Dionysiac origin with a metaphorical currency in Neopythagorean circles. A pre-Philonic origin is denied by H. Lewy, *Sobria Ebrietas* (1929). But I think the casual use of the phrase in *Fuga* 32 (cf. *V. Mos.* I 187) merely to enforce the lesson of temperance at the dinner-table tells against him."

[48] For another Philonic text that connects "sober intoxication" with spiritual banquet-ing, see *Mos.* 1.187.

[49] Cf. John J. Collins, "The Mysteries of God: Creation and Eschatology in 4QInstruc-tion and the *Wisdom of Solomon*," in *Jewish Cult and Hellenistic Culture: Essays on the Jewish Encounter with Hellenism and Roman Rule* (ed. John J. Collins; JSJSup 100; Leiden: Brill, 2005), 159–80, esp. 174: "He [sc. Philo] also distinguishes between the man made in the image of God in Gen 1:27 and the man fashioned from clay in Gen 2:7. The latter 'is an object of sense-perception, partaking already of such or such quality, consisting of body and soul, man or woman, by nature mortal; while he that was after the image was an idea

apparent that Philo's concept of "sober intoxication" is influenced by Platonic thought, then we have his direct statement about the matter in *Quod omnis probus liber sit* 13-14: "But since we have it on the sacred authority of Plato that envy has no place in the divine choir, and wisdom is most divine and most freehanded, she never closes her school of thought but always opens her doors to those who thirst for the sweet water of discourse, and pouring on them an unstinted stream of undiluted doctrine, persuades them to be drunken with the drunkenness which is soberness itself (μεθύειν τὴν νηφάλιον ἀναπείθει μέθην). (14) Then when like initiates in the mysteries (οἱ δὲ ὥσπερ ἐν ταῖς τελεταῖς ἱεροφαντηθέντες) they have taken their fill of the revelations, they reproach themselves greatly for their former neglect and feel that they have wasted their time and that their life while they lacked wisdom was not worth the living."[50]

This evidence suggests that the Therapeutae are viewed as a higher form of Dionysiacs. Very likely Philo's Platonism plays a role in this representation. For him, the Therapeutae as "citizens of heaven and the world" (90) live a heavenly existence on earth.[51] They embody the true Dionysiac mysteries, which is contrasted with the way that on earth Dionysus is often experienced in a distorted form characterized by bouts of drunken revelry (cf. 40–62).

Comparison of the God of the Jews with Dionysus?

We have seen that Philo uses the language of the mysteries, especially the Dionysiac mysteries, in order to describe, in an extremely positive way, the superior religious experience of the Therapeutae. The Therapeutae are

---

or type or seal, an object of thought, incorporeal, neither male nor female by nature incorruptible (ἄφθαρτος) [*De opificio mundi* 134].'"

[50] Plato (*Resp.* 363c–d) makes fun of both the ritual wine-drinking that presumably culminated the process of initiation and the eschatological belief that resulted from the ritual, when he described the "banquet of the pure" with its eternal drunkenness as a promise given by "Musaeus and his son" (i.e., by either Orpheus or the Eleusinian Eumolpus, although these banquets also mirrored those of Bacchic initiates). Cf. Graf and Johnston, *Ritual Texts*, 157.

[51] One wonders whether the Therapeutae's occasional dress in white garments (*Contempl.* 66) should be seen as part of an *imitatio vitae angelicae*. Cf. Eibert J. C. Tigchelaar, "The White Dress of the Essenes and the Pythagoreans," in *Jerusalem, Alexandria, Rome: Studies in Ancient Cultural Interaction in Honour of A. Hilhorst* (eds. Florentino García Martínez and Gerard P. Luttikhuizen; JSJSup 82; Leiden: Brill, 2003), 301–21, esp. 306–7, 312. In any case, the song and dance that are characteristic of the Therapeutae (*Contempl.* 84) are also common features of Elysium (e.g., Tibullus 1.3.59), especially cultic song and dance (e.g., Aristophanes, *Frogs* 316–459) and particularly Bacchic (e.g., *CIL* III 686.17–18). See, for example, the Dionysiac dancing, with cymbals, portrayed on a Roman sarcophagus from the second century C.E. (Museo Nazionale Romano no. 1303). Cf. Friedrich Matz, *Die dionysischen Sarkophage* (4 vols.; Berlin: Mann, 1968–75), 2.180–82.

portrayed as initiates into the highest divine mysteries who, possessed by the deity, engage in ecstatic speech and dance similar to that of the Dionysiacs. All these positive points of comparison between the acts of worship in the cult of Dionysus and in the Judaism practiced by the Therapeutae raise the question of whether Philo implies not only that the Therapeutae have the best of the worship of Dionysus in their worship of the one true creator God as he was revealed in Judaism, but also that there is a more direct comparison between Dionysus and the God of the Jews. After all, Plutarch[52] and Tacitus[53] independently provide evidence for a

[52] See the symposiasts' discussion of who the God of the Jews is in Plutarch, *Quaest. conv.* 4.6.1–2 (*Mor.* 671 C–672 B). Here, the identification of the God of the Jews with Dionysus proceeds in two main stages, according to the degree of probability of the evidence for the Dionysiac character of the Jewish cultus in each case. Each stage offers four pieces of evidence. On the one hand, the Athenian symposiast Moeragenes adduces rather circumstantial evidence that the God of the Jews should be identified with Dionysus, which falls short of direct proof. This "only probable" evidence relates to the supposed Dionysiac character and quality of four Jewish celebrations, the first three of which are closely connected: (a) the Fast (i.e., the Day of Atonement); (b) the Feast of Tabernacles (*Sukkot*); (c) the "Procession of Branches"; and (d) the Sabbath. On the other hand, the symposiast adduces supposedly even more convincing evidence for the identification of the God of the Jews with Dionysus. Whereas the first evidence provided only a probable argument, now, as the Athenian symposiast himself goes on to state, "the opposition is quite demolished" by the four proofs that he enumerates for the identification, again relating to the supposed Dionysiac character of the Jewish cultus: (a) the high priest's vestment; (b) the noise that was part of the Jews' nocturnal revelries; (c) the carved thyrsus in the relief of the pediment of the Temple; and (d) the Jews' nonuse of honey in their religious services. Hence, insofar as Philo likewise emphasizes the Dionysiac character of the cultic practice of the Therapeutae, he may similarly imply at least a comparison between Dionysus and the God of the Jews (direct identification being far less likely in this case). See further Louis H. Feldman, "The Jews as Viewed by Plutarch," in idem, *Studies in Hellenistic Judaism* (AGJU 30; Leiden: Brill, 1996), 529–52.

[53] Cf. Tacitus, *Hist.* 5.5.4–5: "The Egyptians worship many animals and monstrous images; the Jews conceive of one god only, and that with the mind only: they regard as impious those who make from perishable materials representations of gods in man's image; that supreme and eternal being is to them incapable of representation and without end. Therefore they set up no statues in their cities, still less in their temples; this flattery is not paid their kings, not this honor given to the Caesars. (5) But since their priests used to chant to the accompaniment of pipes and drums and wear garlands of ivy, and because a golden vine was found in their temple, some have thought that they were devotees of Father Liber [= Dionysus], the conqueror of the East, in spite of the incongruity of their customs. For Liber established festive rites of a joyous nature, while the ways of the Jews are preposterous and mean." Like Plutarch, Tacitus provides a checklist of similarities between Judaism and the Dionysiac cult that leads some to make the identification between the Jewish God and Dionysus. Indeed, there is a conspicuous overlap between the two descriptions. For example, both authors refer to the priests' Dionysiac headdress as evidence for the identification; both mention prominent Dionysiac emblems that are found in the architecture of the Jerusalem Temple; and both refer to chanting and musical

widespread identification of the God of the Jews with Dionysus in the Greco-Roman world, and this evidence is based on comparisons between the acts of worship in the two cults. Could it be, then, that Philo wished to exploit the Greco-Roman identification between the two gods for his own ends in Alexandria, Egypt, where Dionysus and his cult had long occupied a privileged position of power and prestige?[54] If so, then Philo's implied comparison can seen in light of other Jewish texts of the Second Temple period which make a comparison between the two deities in order to show that the God of the Jews is superior to Dionysus.[55]

---

accompaniment. This uncanny similarity of method and content cannot be explained as direct influence of one on the other, especially considering that the two authors come to a diametrically opposite conclusion based on the same evidence. Rather, we should see them both as examples of the kind of thinking about the Jews and Judaism that was probably quite prevalent in the Greco-Roman world by the end of the first century C.E. On the text, see further R. S. Block, *Antike Vorstellungen von Juden. Der Judenexkurs des Tacitus im Rahmen der griechisch-römischen Ethnographie* (Historia Einzelschriften 160; Stuttgart: Franz Steiner, 2002).

[54] Cf., e.g., P. M. Fraser, *Ptolemaic Alexandria* (2 vols.; Oxford: Clarendon Press, 1972), 1.193–94, 197, 201–7; J. Tondriau, "La Dynastie Ptolémaïque et la Religion Dionysiaque," *Chronique d'Égypt* 50 (1950): 283–316.

[55] Some Jewish texts view the imposition of the worship of Dionysus on the Jews, whether in Ptolemaic Egypt (3 Maccabees) or in Seleucid Jerusalem (2 Maccabees), as overwhelmingly negative—a great evil forced upon the people as the monarch's retaliation. In those situations, God is seen as triumphing over the persecutor of the Jews by "out-Dionysus-ing" Dionysus. In other words, Jews, whether in the Palestinian homeland or in the Diaspora, found themselves in situations in which they were confronted with a Hellenistic monarch who imposed the worship of Dionysus on them, but those who remained faithful to the God of the Jews were vindicated, and in the process the God of the Jews was shown to be more powerful than Dionysus, albeit like him in many ways. Moreover, Jews enjoy the benefits of the Dionysiac cult without its excesses and the debauchery. Thus, 3 Maccabees alludes to Euripides' *Bacchae* in order to spotlight Ptolemy IV Philopator as a Pentheus-like *theomachos*, and to emphasize that the God of the Jews has outdone the persecutor by turning against the king the very emblems and instruments of Dionysus by which he had sought to destroy the Jews. In 2 Maccabees (6:1–11), the persecutor again tries to impose the worship of Dionysus on the Jews, but ends up overplaying his hand and succumbing to defeat, whereupon the Jews, in turn, celebrate their triumph using Dionysiac emblems (10:7; cf. Judith 15:12–13). Philo's point about the Therapeutae seems to be similar: there is a brand of Egyptian Judaism that constitutes a higher form of Dionysiac-like mysteries. Both 3 Maccabees and Philo's treatment of the Therapeutae suggest that the Jewish laws themselves include activities similar to Dionysiac customs which, however, do not share the shortcomings of the Dionysiac cult. Philo also protests against the mystery cults and claims that it is the worship of the Jewish God that is the true mystery cult. See further Hacham, "3 Maccabees: An Anti-Dionysian Polemic," 167–83; N. Clayton Croy, *3 Maccabees* (Septuagint Commentary Series; Leiden: Brill, 2006); F. J. Dölger, "Die Gottesweihe durch Brandmarkung oder Tätowierung im ägyptischen Dionysoskult der Ptolemäerzeit," *Antike und Christentum* 2 (1930): 100–6, esp. 103; J. R. C. Cousland, "Dionysus *theomachos*? Echoes of the *Bacchae* in 3 Maccabees," *Biblica* 82 (2001): 539–48; idem,

Despite the apparent plausibility of such a comparison, there seems to be no evidence in Philo's other writings that he did indeed draw an analogy between Dionysus and the God of the Jews. In *Legatione ad Gaium*, for example, Philo criticizes Emperor Gaius' attempted self-identification with Dionysus, that is, "his most godless assumption of godship" (77), whereby he began by likening himself to the so-called demigods, Dionysus and Heracles and the Dioscuri (78).[56] Philo questions how Gaius could take the

---

"Reversal, Recidivism and Reward in 3 Maccabees: Structure and Purpose" *JSJ* 34 (2003): 39–51; Sarah R. Johnson, "Third Maccabees: Historical Fictions and the Shaping of Jewish Identity in the Hellenistic Period," in *Ancient Fiction: The Matrix of Early Christian and Jewish Narrative* (ed. Jo-Ann A. Brant et al., eds.; SBLSS 32; Atlanta, GA: Society of Biblical Literature, 2005), 185–97; Othmar Keel, "Die kultischen Maßnahmen Antiochus' IV. Religionsverfolgung und/oder Reformversuch?" in O. Keel and Urs Staub, *Hellenismus und Judentum. Vier Studien zu Daniel 7 und zur Religionsnot unter Antiochus IV* (Orbis Biblicus et Orientalis 178; Freiburg: Universitätsverlag, 2000), 87–121; Jonathan A. Goldstein, "What Really Happened: The Civic and Religious Policies of Antiochus IV," in idem, *1 Maccabees: A New Translation with Introduction and Commentary* (AB 41; Garden City, NY: Doubleday, 1976), 104–160; Joann Scurlock, "167 B.C.E.: Hellenism or Reform?" *JSJ* 31 (2000): 125–61.

[56] Cf. Athenaeus 4.148b–d, where Gaius, like Antony and many Hellenistic monarchs before him, was named "new Dionysus" (νέος Διόνυσος), and he actually put on the full Dionysiac outfit (τὴν Διονυσιακὴν πᾶσαν ἐνδύνων στολήν), and went out in public and sat in judgment dressed that way. Moreover, like Ptolemy IV, Emperor Gaius, in an apparent attempt to style himself as the "New Dionysus," had two luxury ships built that were outfitted with a great quantity of grapevines and fruit trees (cf. Suetonius, *Caligula* 37.2). On the two ships that Ptolemy IV had built with deluxe Dionysiac appointments, see Callixeinus of Rhodes, *ap.* Athenaeus 5.203e–204d; cf. Fritz Caspari, "Das Nilschiff Ptolemaios' IV," *Jahrbuch des Kaiserlich Deutschen Archäologischen Instituts* 31 (1916): 1–74. On Gaius' Dionysiac pretensions, see also Dio 59.26.5–9: "... and when some called him a demigod (ἥρωα) and others a god (θεόν), he fairly lost his head. Indeed, even before this he had been demanding that he be regarded as more than a human being, and was wont to claim that he had intercourse with the Moon, the Victory put a crown upon him, and to pretend that he was Jupiter, and he made this a pretext for seducing numerous women, particularly his sisters; again, he would pose as Neptune, (6) because he had bridged so great an expanse of sea; he also impersonated Heracles, Dionysus (Διόνυσον), Apollo, and all the other divinities, not merely males but also females, often taking the role of Juno, Diana, or Venus. Indeed, to match the change of name he would assume all the rest of the attributes that belonged to the various gods, so that he might seem really to resemble them. (7) Now he would be seen as effeminate, holding a wine-bowl and a thyrsus (τοτὲ μὲν γὰρ θηλυδριώδης ἑωρᾶτο καὶ κρατῆρα καὶ θύρσον εἶχε), and again he would appear as a man equipped with a club and lion's skin or perhaps a helmet and shield. He would be seen at one time with a smooth chin and later with a full beard. Sometimes he wielded a trident and again he brandished a thunderbolt. Now he would impersonate a maiden equipped for hunting or for war, and a little later would play the married woman. (8) Thus by varying the style of his dress, and by the use of accessories and wigs, he achieved accuracy inasmuch diverse parts; and he was eager to appear to be anything rather than a human being and an emperor. Once a Gaul, seeing him uttering oracles from a lofty platform in the guise of Jupiter, was moved to laughter, (9) whereupon Gaius summoned him and inquired, 'What do I seem to you to be?' And the other answered (I give his exact words):

insignia used to adorn the images of these deities (81), contrasting Dionysus
in especially positive terms (82–83): "Dionysus cultivated the wild vine and
drew pouring from it a drink most delicious and at the same time profitable
to souls and bodies. The soul he brings into a state of cheerfulness, creating
oblivion of evils and hopes of good, while he renders the body healthier
and stronger and more agile. In private life he improves each person and
converts large households and families from a squalid and toilsome existence to a free and gay mode of living, and for all cities Greek and barba-
rian he provides constant succession of banquets, merrymakings, galas,
festivals. For all these owe their existence to Dionysus." In other words,
Philo suggests that instead of identifying himself as a god, Gaius should
have emulated the virtues of Dionysus. There is no hint here of a comparison between Dionysus and the God of the Jews, let alone a direct identification of the two deities.

In other passages, Philo seems to contradict this positive portrayal of
Dionysus and literal drunkenness, as we might expect from someone who
holds "sober drunkenness" as the ideal (see further above), and the possibility of a comparison between the two gods becomes even less likely. In his
discussion of Noah's viticulture (*De plantatione* 140–77), based on Gen 9:20–
21 ("Noah planted a vineyard and drank of the wine, and became drunk"),
Philo makes it clear that literal drunkenness is to be eschewed: "It was for
this reason that the earliest inhabitants of the world called the inventor of
the culture of the vine Maenoles and the Bacchants whom its frenzy seized
Maenads, since wine is the cause of madness and loss of sound sense in
those who imbibe it over freely" (*Plant.* 148).[57] Interestingly enough, Lucius
Annaeus Cornutus, the Stoic literary and philosophical scholar of the Nero-
nian era,[58] makes the same etymological link that Philo does between
Dionysus as Μαινόλης and his female adherents as Μαινάδες (*Epidrome* 30.5
[ed. C. Lang 60.8]). Referring to the inexcusable outrage and insanity into

---

'A big raving maniac' (μέγα παραλήρημα)." On Plutarch's critique of Nero for identifying
himself with Dionysus, among other gods (*Quomodo adulator ad amico internoscatur* 56e), see
Kenneth Scott, "Plutarch and the Ruler Cult," *TAPA* 60 (1929): 117–35, esp. 121–22.

[57] The word μαινάς ("Maenad") is derived from μαίνομαι ("to be mad"; cf. μανία
["madness, frenzy"]); hence, μαινάδες are "mad women." The female worshipers of Dionysus are called Βάκχαι ("Bacchae"), whose name is derived from Βάκχος ("Bacchus"), the
Lydian name of the god.

[58] Cf. Robert S. Hays, "Lucius Annaeus Cornutus' *Epidrome* (*Introduction to the Traditions of Greek Theology*): *Introduction, Translation, and Notes*," (Ph.D. diss., University of
Texas at Austin, 1983) 30: "All the texts which refer Cornutus to a historical period agree
that he lived in Rome under Nero. His name suggests that he was a freedman either of
Seneca the Elder or Annaeus Mela, the brother of Seneca and the father of Lucan, or of
some other of Seneca's relatives."

which those involved in drunken bouts fall, Cornutus states: "That is why Dionysos was called 'frenzied' and why the women in his company were called 'mad women'" (ἀφ᾽ οὗ δὴ μαινόλης τε ὁ Διόνυσος ἐκλήθη καὶ Μαινάδες αἱ περὶ αὐτὸν γυναῖκες).[59] The *Epidrome*, Cornutus' only work that has survived intact (conjectural title Ἐπιδρομὴ τῶν κατὰ τὴν ἑλληνικὴν θεολογίαν παραδεδομένων, "Compendium of the Traditions of Greek Theology"), an educational treatise addressed to "Oh child" (ὦ παιδίον [1.1; ed. Lang 1.1]), uses etymology and also allegory to derive philosophical insights from divine names and myths.[60]

Despite the fact that Philo's other writings do not seem to encourage a comparison of the God of the Jews with Dionysus, one more line of evidence needs to be considered on the basis of *De vita contemplativa* itself, that is, the orientation of the Therapeutae on the sun during their nocturnal vigils: "… they stand with their faces and whole body turned to the east and when they see the sun (τὸν ἥλιον) rising they stretch their hands up to heaven and pray for bright days and knowledge of the truth and the power of keen sighted thinking" (*Contempl.* 89). Several later texts which point back to an earlier (Orphic) tradition from Egypt identify Dionysus with the Sun and possibly also with the God of the Jews.[61] For example, Cornelius Labeo, *De Oraculo Apollinis Clarii* (*ap.* Macrobius, *Saturnalia* 1.18.18–21) reads as follows:[62]

> That Liber [= Dionysus] is the Sun (*Solem*), Orpheus clearly proclaims in the line: 'The Sun that is called by the name of Dionysus' (Ἥλιος ὃν Διόνυσον ἐπίκλησιν καλέουσιν). And this verse certainly makes sense, but another line by the same poet is rather more elaborate: 'One Zeus, one Hades, one Sun, one Dionysus' (Εἷς Ζεύς, εἷς Ἀΐδης, εἷς Ἥλιος, εἷς Διόνυσος). (19) The authority of this last line is supported by an oracle of Apollo of Clarus, in which yet another name is attached to the sun, which is called in the same sacred verses, among other names, by the name of Iao. For when Apollo of Clarus was asked who among the gods should be identified with him that is called Iao he declared as follows: (20) 'Those who have learned the *Orgia* should keep them in secrecy, but if the understanding is little and the mind feeble, then ponder that Iao is the

---

[59] Cf. Hays, "Lucius Annaeus Cornutus' *Epidrome*," 107.

[60] Hays, "Lucius Annaeus Cornutus' *Epidrome*," 34: "Methodologically, the *Epidromē* relies primarily on etymology. Clearly dependent on studies of the Old Stoa, it is concerned with conceptions which the inventors of the myths were communicating by the names they chose for the gods. On Cornutus' dependence the Old Stoa, see also Hays, 37. Typically, two or more options will be listed without citation of the source…." See further G. W. Most, "Cornutus and Stoic Allegoresis: A Preliminary Report," *ANRW* II.36.3 (1989): 2014–65.

[61] On the Egyptian provenance of this tradition, see Reinhold Merkelbach, *Isisfeste in griechisch-römischer Zeit* (Beiträge zur klassischen Philologie 5; Meisenheim: Hain, 1963), 54–55.

[62] Cf. Stern, *GLAJJ*, 2.410–12.

supreme god among all, in winter he is Hades, at the beginning of the spring he is Zeus, in summer he is Helios, while in autumn he is the graceful Iao.' (21) The meaning of this oracle, and the explanation of the deity and the name by which Iao is denoted Liber pater and the sun, are expounded by Cornelius Labeo in a book entitled 'On the Oracle of Apollo of Claros.'"

Since Iao is often identified with the God of the Jews in the Greco-Roman world,[63] the identification of Dionysus, Helios, and Iao in this text (and others like it)[64] at least allows the possibility that Philo may have regarded the object of the Therapeutae's worship—the God of the Jews—as a Dionysus-like God, when he portrays them as greeting the rising sun after their nocturnal vigil.[65]

In sum, *De vita contemplativa* portrays the Therapeutae as an ideal group that practices a rarefied form of Judaism comparable to the highest form of the Dionysiac mysteries.[66] Whether Philo also entertains a comparison between the God of the Jews and Dionysus remains an open question. We have seen that Philo's portrayal of the Therapeutae is fundamentally influenced by the understanding of the Dionysiac mysteries in Plato's *Symposium*, which helps to explain how Philo can positively compare the cult of Dionysus even as he eschews its excesses.

Trinity Western University, Canada

---

[63] Cf. Stern, *GLAJJ*, 1.98, 171–72 (on Diod. Sic. 1.94.2: "among the Jews Moyses referred his laws to the god who is invoked as Iao"), 211–12 (on Varro, *ap.* Lydus, *De Mensibus* 4.53: "The Roman Varro defining him says that he is called Iao in the Chaldaean mysteries").

[64] See also Pseudo-Justin (*Ad Graecos de vera religione* 15.1 [Riedweg, 2.551] = *Orph. Fr.* 239 Kern), who ascribes to Orpheus the following witness to the one true God of the Jews: "And again, in some other place he [sc. Orpheus] says: 'There is one Zeus alone, one Hades, one Helios, one Dionysus; and in all things but one God. How do I speak of these as divided?" (καὶ αὖθις ἀλλαχοῦ που οὕτως λέγει· Εἷς Ζεύς, εἷς Ἀίδης, εἷς Ἥλιος, εἷς Διόνυσος, εἷς θεὸς ἐν πάντεσσι· τί σοι δίχα ταῦτ' ἀγορεύω;).

[65] On the identification of Dionysus with the sun, see further Diod. Sic. 1.11.3: "And of the ancient Greek writers of mythology some give Osiris the name Dionysus or, with a slight change in form, Sirius. One of them, Eumolpus, in his *Bacchic Hymn* speaks of 'Our Dionysus, shining like a star, with fiery eye in every ray,' while Orpheus says: 'And this is why men call him Shining One and Dionysus.'" Cf. Wolf Liebeschuetz, "The Significance of the Speech of Praetextatus," in *Pagan Monotheism in Late Antiquity* (ed. Polymnia Athanassiadi and Michael Frede; Oxford: Clarendon Press, 1999), 185–205, esp. 196 n. 61, 193, 198 n. 67, 204, 205; Burkert, *Antike Mysterien*, 69 with n. 95.

[66] Philo's own proclivities toward a Judaism similar to that of the Therapeutae are revealed in *Cher.* 48–49, where he claims to have been initiated into the mysteries by Moses, and in *Migr.* 34–35, where he describes his own mystical experience in terms very reminiscent of those used of the Therapeutae in *De vita contemplativa* (e.g. "as though under the inspiration of Corybantic frenzy"). See further Taylor, *Jewish Women Philosophers*, 126–53; Deutsch, "The Therapeutae," 299–300, 310–11.

The Studia Philonica Annual 20 (2008) 55–99

PHILOSOPHICAL ALLEGORESIS OF SCRIPTURE IN PHILO AND ITS LEGACY IN GREGORY OF NYSSA[1]

ILARIA L. E. RAMELLI

Philo and the First Patristic Philosophers:
Reading the Bible through Platonism and Allegory

Philo was the first comprehensive philosophical interpreter of the Bible who read it allegorically—he had forerunners such as Aristobulus, the Essenes, the Alexandrian Therapeutae and others[2]—in the light of Platonism

---

[1] This study is an expanded version of a lecture at the conference Philon von Alexandrien im Gespräch. Ratio Religionis. Religiöse Philosophie und philosophische Religion in der frühen Kaiserzeit, Göttingen, 21–23.VIII.2007. I am very grateful to the participants, especially Herwig Görgemanns, for discussion and useful comments, and to all colleagues and friends who read and commented on subsequent versions of this paper: Francesca Calabi, Rainer Hirsch-Luipold, Judith Kovacs, David Konstan, Roberto Radice, David Runia, and Gregory E. Sterling.

[2] See Carl R. Holladay, ed., *Aristobulus* (vol. 3: *Fragments from Hellenistic Jewish Authors*; Atlanta: Society of Biblical Literature, 1995); Roberto Radice, *La filosofia di Aristobulo* (Milan: Vita e Pensiero, 1995²). Biblical allegoresis among Essenes and Therapeutae is attested in *Prob.* 75ff. and *Contempl.* by Philo. In *Jos.* 151 he attests that the episode of Joseph in Egypt was allegorized by others before him (ἤκουσα καθ᾽ ἑτέραν ἰδέαν τροπικώτερον τὰ περὶ τὸν τόπον ἀκριβούντων): they took Egypt as the body, Pharaoh as the *nous*, and developed a coherent allegoresis of the story. For Philo on Essenes and Therapeutae see Laura Gusella, *Esperienze di comunità nel Giudaismo antico* (Florence: Nerbini, 2003); Smaranda Badilita, "La communauté des Thérapeutes," *Adamantius* 9 (2003): 67–77, who sees *Contempl.* as an emulation of Plato's *Republic*; Jörg Frey, "Zur historischen Auswertung der antiken Essenerberichte," in *Qumrankontrovers* (eds. J. Frey and H. Stegemann; Paderborn: Bonifatius, 2003), 23–56, who stresses the Essenes' interest in the eschatological exegesis of Scripture; Joan E. Taylor, *Jewish Women Philosophers of First-Century Alexandria* (Oxford: Oxford University Press, 2003), who considers the Therapeutae to have practiced a strong allegoresis. On them as allegorists also David M. Hay, "The Veiled Thoughts of the Therapeutae," in *Mediators of the Divine* (ed. R. M. Berchman; Atlanta: Scholars Press, 1998), 167–184, who thinks that Philo did not share their ideal of equality of genders and absence of slavery; Holger Szesnat agreed ("Mostly Aged Virgins," *Neot* 91 [1998]: 191–201; cf. Joan E. Taylor and Philip R. Davies, "The So-Called Therapeutae," *HThR* 91 [1998]: 3–24); Joan E. Taylor, "The Women 'Priests' of Philo's *De Vita Contemplativa*," in *On the Cutting Edge* (eds. J. Schaberg, A. Bach and E. Fuchs; London 2004), 102–122, thought that the senior Therapeutrides were equal to men. Philo's presentation of the Therapeutae

(in particular Middle-Platonism), Stoicism, and Pythagoreanism.[3] At the same time, he considered the Bible to be an inspired writing and sought an active synthesis between Hellenistic philosophy and revelation. His attention primarily focused on the Bible—as Nikiprowetzky, Runia, Radice, Borgen, and Winston have stressed—which he understood and explained through the theoretical lenses of Platonism. His primary intention was exegetical.[4]

A number of early Christian writers who knew Philo's works and depended on him shared these elements, i.e., a focus on the Bible as inspired writing and its philosophical interpretation through allegory, especially in the light of Platonism. I am referring in particular to Clement, Origen, and Gregory of Nyssa, three Fathers who were also influenced by Middle- or Neoplatonism and Stoicism, and were similary interested in the exegesis of Scripture through allegory.[5]

Among the aspects of Gregory's thought that still await a comprehensive and detailed assessment is the extent to which his interest in the allegorical exegesis of Scripture is indebted to Philo directly and indirectly through Origen. While Gregory's works are different than Philo's and Origen's since they are not primarily exegetical, he always looked for support in the Bible even in his highest theoretical constructions and strongest philosophical arguments.[6] As Macrina stated in *De anima*, Scripture remains the κανών throughout all philosophical reasoning. Surely this was the case

---

should not be considered fictional according to Per Bilde, "The Essenes in Philo and Josephus," in *Qumran between the Old and the New Testaments* (eds. F. H. Cryer and T. L. Thompson; Sheffield: Academic Press, 1998), 32–68; Otto Betz, "The Essenes," in *The Cambridge History of Judaism* (eds. W. Horbury, W. D. Davies and J. Sturdy; Cambridge: University Press, 1999), 3:444–470; and Manuel Alexandre, "The Eloquent Philosopher in Philo's *De Vita Contemplativa*," *Euphrosyne* 29 (2001): 319–330. Philo's description is a πλάσμα according to Troels Engberg-Pedersen, "Philo's *De vita contemplativa* as a Philosopher's Dream," *JSJ* 30 (1999): 40–64; *contra* Mary A. Beavis, "Philo's Therapeutae: Philosopher's Dream or Utopian Construction," *JSP* 14 (2004): 30–42. Philo's testimony on the Essenes in *Prob.* 75–91 and *ap.* Eus. *PE* 8.11.1–18 is critically analyzed by Joan E. Taylor, "Philo of Alexandria on the Essenes," *SPhA* 19 (2007): 1–28.

[3] I only cite, most recently, Francesca Alesse, ed., *Philo of Alexandria and Post-Aristotelian Philosophy* (Leiden: Brill, 2008), in particular the essays by A. A. Long, G. Reydams-Schils, R. Radice and M. Graver on Stoicism, and by J. Dillon and M. Bonazzi ("Towards Transcendence: Philo and the Renewal of Platonism in the Early Imperial Age," the most relevant to Middle-Platonism) on Platonism.

[4] See my "Allegory. II. Judaism," *Encyclopedia of the Bible and Its Reception*, 1:2.

[5] On Gregory of Nyssa as a philosopher and his relation to Neoplatonism see my *Gregorio di Nissa. Sull'anima e la resurrezione* (Milan: Bompiani, 2007). On Origen as a philosopher cf. eadem, "Origen, Patristic Philosophy, and Christian Platonism: Re-Thinking the Christianization of Hellenism," *VC* 63 (2009 forthcoming).

[6] See my "Christian Soteriology and Christian Platonism," *VC* 61 (2007): 313–356.

for Philo too who served as the *fons* of the tradition for his Christian successors. Origen had a predecessor in Clement who knew the works of Philo. The three of them belong to the Alexandrian tradition which found its heirs in the Cappadocians. Gregory the Wonderworker, a faithful pupil of Origen's who preached in Cappadocia and whose disciple was Macrina Senior, the grandmother of Macrina Junior, Basil, and Gregory of Nyssa, provided the link between Origen and the Cappadocians.[7]

Both Philo and these Patristic philosophers—Clement, Origen and Gregory—regarded Judaism and Christianity respectively as the true philosophy (Justin, deeply influenced by Platonism, inaugurated this line for Christianity by calling it φιλοσοφία θεία) and endeavored to interpret the Bible in the light of philosophy.[8] In order to do so, allegorical exegesis, already present in Philo and in Stoic (and then Neoplatonic) philosophy, but applied by Philo to the Bible, provided them with an invaluable instrument. In the line of Jewish-Hellenistic and early Christian apologetic,[9] these fathers, all allegorical exegetes of Scriptures, assumed that Moses lived before Plato and the Greek philosophers—an assumption shared by Philo himself—and that the convergences between the Bible and Greek philosophy were due to the common inspiration of the Logos, even if some articulations were not without distortions that Justin and Clement, for

---

[7] For the questions raised by recent scholarship concerning his identity and relation to Origen see Manlio Simonetti, "Una nuova ipotesi su Gregorio il Taumaturgo," *RSLR* 24 (1988): 17–41; Joseph W. Trigg, "God's Marvelous *Oikonomia*," *JECS* 9 (2001): 27–52; Gregorio il Taumaturgo (?), *Encomio di Origene* (ed. M. Rizzi; Milan: Paoline, 2002); *Il Giusto che fiorisce come palma* (eds. B. Clausi and V. Milazzo, Rome: Augustinianum, 2007). In his *Apology for Origen*, Pamphilus cited Gregory as a disciple of Origen's and placed his *Oratio Panegyrica* just after the *Apology* (Socr. *HE* 4.27). Eusebius' account is likely to be based on Pamphilus' reliable testimony. Basil and Nyssen were probably well informed thanks to the traditions known to their family and community.

[8] This, in a period in which the religious tradition began to become an important foundation of philosophy, e.g., in the Middle-Platonist Plutarch and, subsequently, in later Neoplatonists.

[9] See e.g., Aaron P. Johnson, *Ethnicity and Argument in Eusebius'* Praeparatio Evangelica (Oxford: Oxford University Press, 2006), 1–24 on Jewish apologetics of the second-third centuries; my "Le origini della filosofia: greche o barbare?" *RFN* 99 (2007): 185–214. For Philo's influence on Christian apologists, see Monique Alexandre, "Apologétique judéo-hellénistique et premières apologies chrétiennes," in *Les apologistes chrétiens et la culture grecque* (eds. B. Pouderon and J. Doré; Paris: Beauchesne, 1998), 1–40. Allegory in Philo is only partially used in support of 'apologetics' according to Ellen Birnbaum, "Allegorical Interpretation and Jewish Identity among Alexandrian Jewish Writers," in *Neotestamentica et Philonica* (eds. D. Aune, T. Seland and J. Ulrichsen; Leiden: Brill, 2003), 307–329.

example, explained as produced by φαῦλοι δαίμονες.[10] The Logos, which manifested itself fully in Christ-Logos according to these fathers, and in God's Logos according to Philo, had been present and active before the foundation of the world, and had inspired all rational creatures. Philo was so convinced of the common inspiration of the Bible and Platonism that he believed that the Bible taught the doctrine of the Ideas, especially in Exod 33:18 (*Spec.* 1.41.45–48) and Exod 25:40 (*QE* 2.82; *Mos.* 2.74–76, with an exegesis that was taken up by Origen),[11] even if he conceived of the Ideas in Middle-Platonic terms: he deemed them God's thoughts, situated in God's Logos and even tending to coincide with it. On the basis of this conception, he read the Bible as an allegorical exposition of fundamentally Platonic doctrines (although, as I mentioned, *ante litteram* from the historical point of view).[12] The Platonic Fathers who followed him did much the same thing.

There are previous analyses of Philo's influence on early Christian authors: David T. Runia has written an excellent survey of Philo's influence on the Christian fathers; there are also a number of specific contributions concerning the dependence of single Christian fathers on Philo.[13] I propose to provide a more comprehensive analysis for Gregory's indebtedness to Philo and for Origen's role in the process. The influence of Philo on Gregory is evident not only in his biblical allegoresis in general—which he

[10] See my "*Mystérion* negli *Stromateis* di Clemente Alessandrino: aspetti di continuità con la tradizione allegorica greca," in *Il volto del mistero* (ed. A.M. Mazzanti; Ravenna: Itaca, 2006), 83–120.

[11] Origen, *Hom. Ex.* 9.2. See Gregory E. Sterling, "Ontology *vs* Eschatology," *SPhA* 13 (2001): 190–211, esp. 200–210. Eusebius, who connected Exod 25:40 to Plato, *Rsp.* 500D-501C in *PE* 12.19 to prove that Plato taught the same things that Moses did well before him, may have drawn this connection from both Philo and Origen, even at the same time (I will argue in this article that this is often the case for Gregory). His argument is particularly close to that of the *Cohortatio* ascribed to Justin, 29.1–2, which argued for the derivation of Plato's Ideas from Moses on the basis of Exod 25:40. Eusebius inherited Philo's strategy of the "Mosaic philosophy": he legitimized the biblical doctrine through Plato by showing that the Mosaic philosophy is the perfection of Platonism (*DE* 3.6.129d; *pace* Johnson, *Ethnicity*, 126–152, who understands the passages in *PE* in which Eusebius expresses his admiration for Plato [173] as ironical).

[12] The total identification of philosophy and allegoresis in Alexandrian Judaism is highlighted by Roberto Radice, "Considerazioni sulle origini greche dell'allegoria filoniana," in *La rivelazione in Filone* (eds. A. M. Mazzanti and F. Calabi; Villa Verrucchio: Pazzini, 2004), 15–32.

[13] David Runia, *Philo in Early Christian Literature* (CRINT 3.2; Assen-Minneapolis: Van Gorcum, 1993); idem, *Filone di Alessandria nella prima letteratura cristiana* (tr. R. Radice; Milan: Vita e Pensiero, 1999); idem, *Philo and the Church Fathers: A Collection of Papers* (Leiden: Brill, 1995). Useful hints are also in David Dawson, *Allegorical Readers and Cultural Revision in Ancient Alexandria* (Berkeley: University of California Press, 1992). I shall refer to scholarship on the relationship between Philo and single Fathers subsequently.

inherited directly from Origen—but also in specific details of exegesis and thought. In each case it is important to consider whether the point was mediated through Origen (a similar proviso should be considered in other authors, e.g., Philo's influence on Didymus[14]). There have been a number of studies on the relationship between Philo and Gregory: Michel Aubineau has analysed the relationship between Philo's *Contempl.* and Gregory's *De Virginitate*; Jean Daniélou and Albert Geljon—to a greater extent—have compared Philo's and Gregory's *De Vita Moysis*; Daniélou has also studied Gregory's *Apologia in Hexaëmeron* and *De Hominis Opificio* against the background of Philo's *Opif.*, and has insisted on their common notion of a double creation; Runia, besides discussing previous scholarship, has offered a valuable study of the relationship between Philo's works and Gregory's *Contra Eunomium* and *De Vita Moysis*.[15] I will assess Philo's influence on Gregory's allegorical exegesis and philosophical thought with particular attention also to Origen's role in this connection.

Philo's and Gregory's De Vita Moysis *and* De Opificio

The choice of title and contents for one's writings is often telling and may already offer key hints in respect to the inspiration of a work. Gregory's *De Vita Moysis* (*VM*) has the same title as Philo's treatise,[16] and indeed is

[14] For this influence see Runia, *Philo in Literature*, 200–203; Richard A. Layton, *Didymus the Blind and His Circle in Late Antique Alexandria* (Urbana: University of Illinois Press, 2004), 144–151. For Didymus' dependence on Philo in his exegesis of Gen 12 see Albert C. Geljon, "Philonic Elements in Didymus the Blind's Exegesis of the Story of Cain and Abel," *VC* 61 (2007): 282–312, with detailed analysis.

[15] Jean Daniélou, *Grégoire de Nysse. La Vie de Moïse* (Paris: Cerf, 1955); idem, "Philon et Grégoire de Nysse," in *Colloques nationaux du CNRS* (Paris: CNRS, 1967), 333–345; Michel Aubineau, *Grégoire de Nysse. Traité de la virginité* (Paris: Cerf, 1966); Runia, *Philo in Literature*, 243–261, also with analysis of Philo's presence in Gregory's *De Virginitate, De Hominis Opificio*, and *Apologia in Hexaëmeron*; Albert C. Geljon, *Philonic Exegesis in Gregory of Nyssa's De Vita Moysis* (Providence: Brown, 2004); idem, "Philo of Alexandria and Gregory of Nyssa on Moses at the Burning Bush," in *The Revelation of the Name YHWH to Moses* (ed. G. H. van Kooten; Leiden: Brill, 2006), 225–236; briefly, with no mention of Geljon, Manuel Mira, "Filone di Alessandria," in *Gregorio di Nissa. Dizionario* (eds. L. F. Mateo-Seco and G. Maspero; Rome: Città Nuova, 2007), 287–289. A hint of Philo's influence on Gregory is also found in Beatrice Motta, *La mediazione estrema* (Padua: Il Poligrafo, 2004), 87–99; 104. The influence of Philo's Moses on early Christian conceptions of ideal rules is investigated by Sarah Pearce, "King Moses. Notes on Philo's Portrait of Moses as an Ideal Leader," in *The Greek Strand in Islamic Political Thought* (ed. G. Gannagé; Beirut: Bibliothèque Orientale, 2004), 37–74.

[16] Most mss. of Philo's *Mos.* bear the title Περὶ τοῦ βίου Μωϋσέως. The same is the case with Gregory's *VM*: in most mss. (5 out of 7) a precise reference to "The Life of Moses" is

inspired by it. Another title of Gregory echoes—in its meaning if not in its very wording—one of Philo's. His *De opificio hominis* (Περὶ κατασκευῆς ἀνθρώπου), a continuation of Basil's *Hexaëmeron*, echoes Philo's *De opificio mundi* (Περὶ τῆς κατὰ Μωϋσέα κοσμοποιίας), the first philosophical elaboration of the Biblical doctrine of creation. Philo, according to some scholars, might have anticipated the Patristic doctrine of *creatio ex nihilo*, unknown to Greek philosophy but embraced by Origen.[17] Gregory was concerned only with the creation of the human being, since the creation of the world was already addressed by his brother (who was less of an allegorist and a philosopher than he, Philo and Origen were). Philo's treatise also included a detailed discussion of the creation of the ἄνθρωπος, which was highly influential on Origen's and Gregory's protology and anthropology. Gregory's choice of these Philonic titles, topics, and the way of developing them is surely deliberate and seems to me very telling.

Some scholars situate Philo's *Mos.* among the writings devoted to the exposition of the Mosaic Law, in which the allegorical reading is sprinkled among general literal explanation; others locate it among the apologetic writings;[18] and still others consider it to be an introduction to the Pentateuch. Gregory, in his *VM*, presents Moses as a paradigm of the virtuous life, offering in Book 1 an account of Moses' life (ἱστορία) and in Book 2 an

---

found in the title, either Περὶ τοῦ βίου Μωϋσέως or Εἰς τὸν βίον Μωϋσέως (or, in the isolated case of Vat. 444, ʿΟ τοῦ Μωϋσέως βίος).

[17] Philo spoke of creation "from non-being to being," "from nothing," from non-existence. God is not only δημιουργός but also κτίστης (*Mos.* 2.267; *Leg.* 3.10; *Somn.* 1.76). In some works handed down in Armenian translation, the creation of matter is expressly stated, especially in *Prov.* In *Opif.*, where Philo follows Plato's *Timaeus*, he does not resume his argument concerning the pre-existence of matter. See Roberto Radice, "Modelli di creazione in Filone," in *Lingua e teologie nel Cristianesimo greco* (eds. C. Moreschini and G. Menestrina, Brescia. Claudiana, 1999), 35–38, who argues that divine creation is *ex nihilo* for the conceptual aspect and demiurgic for the material aspect. See also Giovanni Reale, "La dottrina dell'origine del mondo in Platone," *RFN* 88 (1996): 3–33: 28–33, according to whom, although Philo describes creation in Platonic terms, he goes beyond Plato in attributing the creation of matter to God; his Middle-Platonic doctrine of the Ideas as thoughts of God is an essential premise of the Christian doctrine of *creatio ex nihilo*. See Reale and Radice, *Filone di Alessandria. Filosofia mosaica* (Milan: Rusconi, 1987), LIVff.; Pierluigi Pavone, "Τὸ παθητόν: materia preesistente o intero creato?" in *La rivelazione in Filone*, 123–136, according to whom τὸ παθητόν may also be understood as a non-preexistent passive, which would be compatibile with the *creatio ex nihilo*. Differently David T. Runia, "Plato's *Timaeus*, First Principle(s) and Creation in Philo and Early Christian Thought," in *Plato's Timaeus as Cultural Icon* (ed. G. Reydams-Schils; Notre Dame: University of Notre Dame Press, 2003), 133–151.

[18] *Hypoth., Flacc., Contempl., Legat.* (which should be listed among Philo's exegetical writings according to Peder Borgen, "Application of and Commitment to the Laws of Moses," *SPhA* 13 [2001]: 37–58).

allegorical interpretation of it (θεωρία).[19] The work belongs to the last group of Gregory's writings, contemporary with his homilies on the Song of Songs. In both works Gregory deals with the soul's quest for and ascent to God within the framework of mystic thought and apophaticism. Whereas Philo's homonymous treatise does not include much allegorical exegesis, Gregory's hermeneutical approach to the Bible appropriates Philo's general allegorical technique; however, it also certainly drew from the example and inspiration of Origen, who was not only the greatest Christian allegorist of the Bible but also the first theorizer of biblical allegoresis.[20] (Philo was a great allegorist, but not a great theoretician).

Philo's *Mos.* was a major source of inspiration for Gregory's *VM*, although the precise relationship requires careful explanation. The structure of Gregory's *VM* in two books is borrowed from Philo, who in Book 1 of his *Mos.* narrated the life of Moses in chronological order and presented him as a philosopher and a king. Philo explicitly referred to Plato, *Rsp.* 473D on the necessity that kings be philosophers or philosophers kings and defined the king as νόμος ἔμψυχος, according to a formula that was spread by the Stoics but had Platonic roots and developments as well—as I have argued elsewhere.[21] In Book 2 Philo described Moses as legislator, high priest, and prophet.[22] In Philo's depiction of Moses' figure the influence of Stoicism is

---

[19] M. A. Bardolle, "La *Vie de Moïse* de Grégoire de Nysse," in *Le temps chrétien de la fin de l'Antiquité au Moyen Âge* (Paris: CNRS, 1984), 255–261; Adolf M. Ritter, "Die Gnadenlehre Gregors von Nyssa nach seiner Schrift *Über das Leben des Moses*," in idem, *Charisma und Caritas: Aufsätze zur Geschichte der Alten Kirche* (ed. A. Dörfler Dierken; Göttingen: Vandenhoeck & Ruprecht, 1993), 31–61; Hermann J. Sieben, "Die *Vita Mosis* (II) des Gregor von Nyssa," *Th&Ph* 70 (1995): 494–525; Andreas Sterk, "On Basil, Moses, and the Model Bishop," *ChHist* 67 (1998): 227–253.

[20] See, e.g. Manlio Simonetti, *Origene esegeta e la sua tradizione* (Brescia: Morcelliana, 2004).

[21] See my *Il Basileus come Nomos Empsychos: Spunti platonici del concetto* (Naples: Bibliopolis, 2006). Moses is also considered to be νόμος ἔμψυχος by Clement, *Strom.* 1.67.3 and Origen, *Hom. Ex.* 4.6; 2.4 (see Annewies Van den Hoek, *Clement of Alexandria and His Use of Philo in the* Stromateis [VCS 3; Leiden: Brill, 1988], 59). In *Abr.* 5, Philo described the Patriarchs, Abraham in particular, as ἔμψυχοι νόμοι. He regarded them as kings, as is clear in *Migr.* 8: βασιλεὺς ὢν ἄρχειν . . . πεπαίδευσο. This is reminiscent of the Stoic assumption that every wise man is king.

[22] Ian W. Scott, "Is Philo's Moses a Divine Man?" *SPhA* 14 (2002): 87–111, convincingly argued that Philo did not present Moses through the Hellenistic category of the θεῖος ἀνήρ. On Philo's Moses as a legislator and the relationship between the Mosaic Law and the law of nature in Philo's thought see Francesca Calabi, *The Language and the Law of God* (Atlanta: Scholars Press, 1998); Hindy Najman, "The Law of Nature and the Authority of Mosaic Law," *SPhA* 11 (1999): 55–73; eadem, "A Written Copy of the Law of Nature," *SPhA* 15 (2003): 54–63. See also Gregory E. Sterling, "Universalizing the Particular," *ibid.* 64–80; John W. Martens, *One God, One Law. Philo of Alexandria on the Mosaic and Greco-*

patent. The ideal of ἀπάθεια is represented by Moses and seen as clearly higher than that of μετριοπάθεια, which is incarnated by Aaron. Similarly Gregory—anticipated by Clement and Origen—presented ἀπάθεια as the highest ethical ideal, discussing it at length in *De anima*.[23] Clement had already linked Philo's Moses to the Stoic ideal of the wise in *Strom.* 2.19.4, where he ascribed to the Stoic sage the very same treats attributed to Moses by Philo: kingship, priesthood, prophecy, and legislation.[24] Gregory presented Moses as a model of virtuous life in its struggle against passions and in continual ascent in virtue, according to his ideal of ἐπέκτασις. He too saw Moses as the paradigm of the perfect human being who can be called "friend of God" (Exod 33:11), but left aside such Philonic characterizations of Moses as king or legislator. I think he may have conflated Philo's presentation of Abraham in *Abr.* and *Migr.*, as φιλαρέτου ψυχῆς τὸν ἀληθῆ ζητούσης θεόν (*Abr.* 68) with his presentation of Moses in *Mos.* Gregory dropped Philo's physical and cosmological interpretations in his allegory;[25] he tended to retain only the ethical ones which were more in line with his own perspective. Gregory also transposed some of Philo's interpretations to different objects,[26] and Christianized many of them in the very same way as Origen had. We will see that this is one of the cases in which Gregory regularly shows a close dependence on Origen rather than directly on Philo.

It is important to remember that Gregory's *VM* is based on Philo's larger corpus and not only on *Mos.*: the frequency and striking nature of Gregory's similarities to Philo's views are remarkable.[27] Most of them,

---

Roman Law (Leiden: Brill, 2003), for the theological and historical plane; and Roberto Radice, "La figura del legislatore in Filone e i suoi precedenti filosofici," *RStB* 15 (2003): 153–162, for the philosophical plane .

[23] See my philosophical essay in eadem, *Gregorio di Nissa*.

[24] As is correctly remarked by Geljon, *Philonic Exegesis*, 9.

[25] Philo refers to this as a φυσικός allegory, but this adjective has a more complex meaning in his exegetical vocabulary. See Steven Di Mattei, "Moses' *Physiologia* and the Meaning and Use of *Physikôs* in Philo," *SPhA* 18 (2006): 3–32, with analysis and ample documentation.

[26] As Geljon has shown very well, *Philonic Exegesis*, 173 and *passim*.

[27] Gregory had no problem in taking Philo as a recognized model in *VM*, even though elsewhere, for polemical purposes, as Geljon emphasized, he associated Philo with his opponent, the "Neo-Arian" Eunomius. In *C. Eun.*, he named Philo twice: in 3.5.24 ("There are also places where even Philo the Jew suffers the same fate, supplying him [Eunomius] with terms drawn from his own labors") and 3.7.8–9 (where he accuses Eunomius of relying on Philo) where the association is based on the Jews' and the "Arians'" denial of Christ's divinity. However, on the "Arian" category see now Lewis Ayres, *Nicaea and its Legacy* (Oxford: Oxford University Press, 2006). This book is discussed in an entire *HTR* issue (100 [2007]: 125–241, esp. Sarah Coakley's introduction, 125–138).

notably, are common to Origen, too. If we analyze Gregory's *Mos.* in light of the Philonic corpus more broadly, we see that he used Philo's *Opif.* and the allegorical commentary on Genesis, works that Origen also knew and used. Runia lists twelve passages in which Origen referred—anonymously—to Philonic exegeses of the Bible from the Allegorical Commentary.[28] It is not an accident that they both display an interest in those works of Philo in which the allegorical exegesis of the Bible is preeminent; neither of them was interested in Philo's non-allegorical writings of the Exposition of the Law. For both of them Philo was, first and foremost, a great allegorical exegete of the Bible.[29] The only exception to this scenario is Gregory's and Origen's use of Philo's *Opif.*, which is part of the Exposition of the Law;[30] however, it has a special status, because it is mostly philosophical and deals with the account of creation, which is also seen as the ontological foundation of all. For this reason it should have a place of its own in Philo's corpus, as Radice argued.[31] In sum, for both Origen and Gregory, Philo was an allegorical philosophical interpreter of the Bible, just as they were.[32]

The fact that Origen and Gregory both drew from the same section of the Philonic corpus poses the difficult but important question of the role that Origen played in transmitting Philonic influence to Gregory. When did

[28] Runia, *Philo in Literature*, 161–163 (for an assessment of Origen's debt to Philo, 157–183). This is also clear from the systematic analysis of Annewies Van den Hoek, "Philo and Origen: A Descriptive Catalogue of Their Relationship," *SPhA* 12 (2000): 44–121.

[29] That three papyri found in Egypt, possessed by Christians and containing works of Philo, all include treatises belonging to the Allegorical Commentary is a sign of the success of this work in Christian Alexandria. See David T. Runia, "One of Us or One of Them? Christian Reception of Philo the Jew in Egypt," in *Shem in the Tents of Japheth* (ed. J. L. Kugel; JSJSup 74; Leiden: Brill, 2002), 203–222. For the difficult question of the transmission of Philo's mss. in the first two centuries see Annewies Van den Hoek, "The Catechetical School of Early Christian Alexandria and Its Philonic Heritage," *HThR* 90 (1997): 59–87: 80–87. On the Philo papyrus discovered at Coptos in 1889, usually considered to come from Caesarea, see Theodore C. Skeat, "The Oldest Manuscript of the Four Gospels?," *NTS* 43 (1997): 1–34: 24–26, who thinks that it originated in Alexandria in the scriptorium of Pantaenus.

[30] So Abraham Terian, "Back to Creation: The Beginning of Philo's Third Grand Commentary," *SPhA* 9 (1997): 19–36; Cristina Termini, "La creazione come APXH della Legge in Filone (*Opif.* 1–3)," *RivB* 49 (2001): 283–318; David T. Runia, *Philo of Alexandria. On the Creation of the Cosmos According to Moses* (PACS 1; Leiden: Brill, 2001), against Cohn, who assigned it to the Allegorical Commentary.

[31] Introduction to *Filosofia mosaica*.

[32] He will still be such for the fifth-century compiler of the *Catena in Exodum*, who, besides the Fathers, quotes five passages from Philo's *Mos.* and twenty from his *QE* 2. See Françoise Petit, *La Chaîne sur l'Exode*, 2–4 (Leuven: Peeters, 2000–2001), with the review by David T. Runia, *SPhA* 15 (2003): 162–165. In the *Catena in Genesim* there are 73 citations of Philo, from *QG*: see idem, "*Philonica in the* Catena in Genesim," *SPhA* 11 (1999): 113–120.

Philo exercise direct influence? When was Philo's influence indirect, mediated by Origen,[33] and, in such cases, when did Gregory give preference to Origen's modifications of Philo's exegesis? I think that both direct and indirect influence of Philo on Gregory is evident; one does not exclude the other. For Gregory certainly read Philo directly, as verbal echoes show. At the same time, Gregory found many, often Christianized, modifications of Philo in Origen, whose writings he knew extremely well. He found a few such derivations in Clement, with whose works he was also familiar. While the general picture is clear enough, it is not always easy to establish in specific cases whether an exegetical tradition or philosophical conception, or even an expression, came directly from Philo or indirectly via Origen (or Clement).

The difficulty is heightened because Philo was well known both to Clement, Origen's master, and to authors who depended on Origen, such as Eusebius, Jerome, and the Cappadocians, especially Gregory himself and his brother Basil, who was influenced by Philo's *Opif.* in his *Homilies on the Hexaëmeron*—although his allusions to Philo's writings are sparse.[34] Clement, who was active in the same city as Philo more than a century after him, is the first Christian author who betrays a clear knowledge of him and of *Mos.* in particular:[35] he quoted ample sections from it in *Strom.* 1.151–157,

---

[33] In turn, it is not always an easy task to determine the extent to which Origen depends on Philo. See the methodological remarks of Antonio Cacciari, "Presenze filoniane nelle *Omelie sui Numeri* di Origene," in *La rivelazione in Filone*, 217–230.

[34] See Runia, *Philo in Literature*, 235–241.

[35] For Clement's knowledge of Philo see Paul Heinisch, *Der Einfluss Philos auf die älteste christliche Exegese* (Münster: Aschendorffsche Buchhandlung, 1908); Jacobus C. M. van Winden, "Quotations from Philo in Clement of Alexandria's *Protrepticus*," *VC* 32 (1978): 208–213; Van den Hoek, *Clement*; eadem, "How Alexandrian Was Clement of Alexandria?," *HeyJ* 31 (1990): 179–194; eadem, "Techniques of Quotation in Clement of Alexandria," *VC* 50 (1996): 223–242; 232–233; eadem, *The Catechetical School*; Eric F. Osborn, "Philo and Clement: Citation and Influence," in *Lebendige Überlieferung* (eds. N. El-Khoury, H. Crouzel, and R. Reinhardt; Beirut-Ostfildern: Rückert-Schwabe, 1992), 228–243, who noted that the 300 or so citations of Philo in the *Stromateis* do not indicate deep influence, since Clement extrapolated them from their contexts for his own, different, scope; idem, "Philo and Clement. Quiet Conversion and Noetic Exegesis," *SPhA* 10 (1998): 108–124; idem, *Clement of Alexandria* (Cambridge: Cambridge University Press, 2005), 1:4, who distinguished Philo as a "philosophical exegete" (93) and Clement as a "biblical theologian" (100) whose commitment to Plato was stronger than that of Philo (104); Runia, *Philo in Literature*, 132–156; idem, "Why Does Clement of Alexandria Call Philo 'The Pythagorean'?" *VC* 49 (1995): 1–22; Marcelo Merino Rodríguez, *Clemente de Alejandría: Stromata II–III* (Madrid: Ciudad Nueva, 1998); *IV–V (ibid.* 2003), who pointed out more than 100 Philonic derivations in Books 4–5, and almost 200 in Books 2–3; Andrew Dinan, "The Mystery of Play," *SPhA* 19 (2007): 59–80, who showed how Clement, *Paed.* 1.5.21–22, conflated two Philonic passages.

where he recounted Moses' birth and youth, and in 153.2 explicitly referred to Philo's *Life of Moses*. Clement retained the functions of legislator and prophet for Moses, but not that of high priest, which the Letter to the Hebrews had ascribed to Christ.[36] Manuscripts of Philo's works were certainly present in Alexandria, where Origen read and meditated on them.[37] He made extensive use of Philo's interpretation of the Bible, generally without mentioning his name, although occasionally he does so.[38] The assignment to Philo[39] of a papyrus fragment which proved to belong to Origen is a striking proof of the closeness between Philo and Origen.[40] Origen seems to be indebted to Philo's *Mos.* in at least five passages: *Hom. Ex.* 3.1; 4.3 and 6; 9.4; and *Hom. Num.* 20.1. In fact, in these homilies, preserved only in Rufinus' translation—a faithful version, as confirmed by the Greek fragments in the Catenae—Origen undertook an allegorical interpretation of the life of Moses that was extensively indebted to Philo and, in turn, highly influential on Gregory of Nyssa. The loss of so much of Origen's Greek writings, and especially of his monumental *Commentary on Genesis*, renders it difficult to assess the extent of Origen's role in the transmission of Philo's thought to Gregory (and of course to others, such as Calcidius).[41] The manuscripts Origen carried from Alexandria to Caesarea remained in that library, where they were at the disposal of a devoted admirer of the Alexandrian Christian, Eusebius, who used them when he prepared his list of Philo's writings (*HE* 2.18).[42] It is worth noting that in the preceding section (*HE*

---

[36] See my "The Universal and Eternal Validity of Jesus's High-Priestly Sacrifice," in *A Cloud of Witnesses: The Theology of* Hebrews *in Its Ancient Contexts* (eds. R. J. Bauckham, D. R. Driver, T. A. Hart and N. MacDonald; London: T&T Clark, 2008), ch. 14.

[37] Robert M. Berchman, *From Philo to Origen. Middle Platonism in transition* (Chico: Scholars Press, 1984); Christoph Blönnigen, *Die griechische Ursprung der jüdisch-hellenistischen Allegorese* (Frankfurt: Lang 1992), 205–265, esp. 228–262; Runia, *Philo in Literature*, 161–162; idem, "Filone e i primi teologi cristiani," *ASE* 14 (1997): 355–380; Van den Hoek, *Philo and Origen*; Hans G. Thümmel, "Philon und Origenes," in *Origeniana VIII* (ed. L. Perrone; Leuven: Peeters, 2003), 275–286. For a single aspect see Karen J. Torjesen, "The Alexandrian Tradition of the Inspired Interpreter," *ibid.* 287–299.

[38] E.g., in *Hom. Gen.* 1, 4, 6 and 7, in *Hom. Ex.* 9, *Hom. Lev.* 6 and 7; *Hom. Num.* 27.

[39] On the part of James Rendel Harris, *Fragments of Philo Judaeus* (Cambridge: Cambridge University Press, 1886), 6–8.

[40] See James R. Royse, *The Spurious Texts of Philo of Alexandria* (Leiden: Brill, 1991), 192.

[41] In *In Tim.* 278, Calcidius cited Philo and presented his wording closely, but we cannot exclude that he was borrowing from Origen's *Commentary on Genesis* (see Runia, *Philo in Literature*, 281–290), all the more in that he has just mentioned Origen and his only other reference to Philo (under the generic label *Hebraei*) and his creation exegesis in *In Tim.* 276 is admittedly drawn from Origen.

[42] This catalogue omits *Opif.* and *Mos.*, but they were probably present in the library of Caesarea, as Andrew J. Carriker argued (*The Library of Eusebius* [VCS 67; Leiden–Boston:

2.16–17), Eusebius claimed that the Therapeutae of Alexandria —described by Philo in Contempl. — were early Christians converted by St Mark.[43] Scholars have only occasionally investigated Eusebius' use of Philo: the most notable efforts have been by Runia, Ulrich, and Inowlocki.[44] One of the successors of Eusebius, Euzoius (376–379) a contemporary of Gregory, had Philo's mss. copied again. It was from these new exemplars in Caesarea that the whole manuscript tradition of Philo derives.[45]

Origen's Role in the Transmission (and Transformation) of Philo's Allegories to Gregory

We have already suggested that, while Gregory had a direct knowledge of Philo, he also read him indirectly through Origen. The evidence for this indirect influence consists of the numerous instances in which Philo's influence on Gregory is clearly paired with Origen's and sometimes superseded by it. When in VM 2.18 Gregory employed the image of the Logos who, as a shepherd, is a supervisor (ἐπιστατοῦντος) of the movements of the soul, he took up a notion attested in Philo, Sacr. 45 and 105, where the logos or logismos is ἐπιστάτης of the irrational powers of the soul, acting as their shepherd. In Hom. Ier. 5.6 Origen had already borrowed the image from Philo, but had Christianized it. For him the Logos, who shepherds the irrational movements of the soul, is Christ who in the Gospel of John was

---

Brill, 2003], 174–177; 303–304). For a reconstruction of the history of the transmission of Philo's corpus, see Runia, Philo in Literature, 16–31 (18 for a graphic representation).

[43] For the appropriation of the Therapeutae to early Christianity see Remo Cacitti, "I Terapeuti di Alessandria nella vita spirituale protocristiana." in Origene maestro di vita spirituale (eds. L. F. Pizzolato and M. Rizzi; Milano: Vita e Pensiero, 2001), 47–89. Although he does not include Philo's Mos. in his list, Eusebius is very likely to have known this treatise. He seems to reveal some influence in his presentation of Constantine as Moses, given that it was Philo who assimilated Moses to the perfect ruler, not without sacred traits.

[44] Runia, Philo in Literature, 212–234; idem, "Caesarea Maritima and the Survival of Hellenistic-Jewish Literature," in Caesarea Maritima (Leiden: Brill, 1996), 515–530; Jörg Ulrich, Euseb von Caesarea und die Juden (Berlin: De Gruyter, 1999), 88–110; Sabina Inowlocki, "The Reception of Philo's Legatio ad Gaium in Eusebius of Caesarea's Works," SPhA 16 (2004): 30–49, where she studied three passages that were paraphrased or quoted by Eusebius in DE and HE, and argued that they came from Philo's Legatio as we have it today. See also eadem, "Eusebius of Caesarea's interpretatio Christiana of Philo's De Vita Contemplativa," HThR 97 (2004): 305–328 and her Eusebius and the Jewish Authors: His Citation Technique in an Apologetic Context (Leiden–Boston: Brill 2006).

[45] Runia, Philo in Literature, 21–22; 241; James R. Royse, "The Text of Philo's Legum Allegoriae," SPhA 12 (2000): 1–28: 1–2; Runia, Caesarea, 479–482.

described as ὁ ποιμὴν ὁ καλός. He was—Origen explained— ἐν ταῖς ψυχαῖς ἡμῶν. Origen clearly had Philo in mind for this own image; he referred to Philo (*Opif.* 24; *QG* 1.4) as a predecessor who spoke of the Logos's ruling function.[46] Gregory, I think, shows traces of reading both Philo and Origen: he demostrated his reading of Philo when he used the keyword ἐπιστα-τέω—like Philo and differently from Origen who used only ποιμήν and ποιμαίνω—and of Origen when he used the expression κινήματα for the soul's movements—like Origen who described the Logos as ποιμαίνων τὰ ἐν ἐμοὶ ἄλογα κινήματα but differently from Philo who used ἄλογοι δυνάμεις. He appears to have read and conflated both texts.

At the beginning of *VM*, Gregory contrasted the "sea of life" and its waves of passions with the calm "harbour of virtue." These are typical Philonic expressions—as Geljon has rightly pointed out; however, the first also occurs in Clement and frequently in Origen,[47] both readers of Philo, as well as in Eusebius who knew both Philo and Origen, and sometimes read Philo *through* Origen.[48] So, the expression τὴν τοῦ βίου θάλασσαν (*VM* 1.11) and πέλαγος τοῦ βίου (*Hom. Cant.* 81.13) could easily derive either from Philo (*Spec.* 1.224: τοῦ βίου πέλαγος) or from Origen. The second phrase is present in Philo, *Sacr.* 90 (λιμένα τὴν ἀρετήν) and *Somn.* 2.225 (τῆς ἀρετῆς . . .

---

[46] *Regere, moderare* (*Hom. Gen.* 14.3). It is a citation rated A, i.e., the highest level of closeness, in Van den Hoek's *Philo and Origen*, 72.

[47] In Origen it occurs many times: *Hom. Lev.* 7.7; *Hom. Ios.* 19.4; *Hom. Jer.* 18.5; *fr. Ps.* PG 17.141A. These are just the occurrences in the Greek extant writings.

[48] A good example is given by a quotation of Philo, *Legat.* 299ff. in Eusebius *DE* 8.2.403Aff., who located the profanation ἐν τῷ ἱερῷ, whereas Philo put it in Herod's palace. Eusebius' passage cannot be influenced by Josephus, *Ant.* 18.55 and *Bell.* 6.299, who loca-ted it in Jerusalem; however, it is surely reminiscent of Origen's account in *Co. Mat.* 17.25, where the same deviation from Philo is already patent. Origen stated that the profanation took place ἐν τῷ ναῷ, for he assimilated the episode of Caligula's statue with that of Pilate's shields (τοῦ μὲν Πιλάτου βιαζομένου ἀνδριάντα Καίσαρος ἀναθεῖναι ἐν τῷ ναῷ, τῶν δὲ καὶ παρὰ δύναμιν κωλυόντων· τὸ δ᾽ ὅμοιον ἀναγέγραπται γεγονέναι καὶ κατὰ τοὺς χρόνους Γαίου Καίσαρος). Origen said that his sources were "historical writings of the time of Tiberius" (εὕρομεν δὲ ἐκ τῶν κατὰ τὸν χρόνον Τιβερίου Καίσαρος ἱστοριῶν γραφὰς ὡς. . .). Origen's account was followed by Eusebius, who stated that the profanation took place in the Temple in *Chron.* 175 Helm, and by Jerome, *In Mat.* 24.15, PL 26.184. The same apologetic purpose that Inowlocki, *Reception*, 42, correctly saw in Eusebius when he changed Philo's and Josephus' places into the Temple is, to my mind, already present in Origen, who commented: αὐτὸς πρῶτος ἐτόλμησε μιᾶναι τὸν ναὸν τοῦ θεοῦ ὁ Πιλᾶτος, ᾧ παρέδωκαν τὸν Ἰησοῦν. For Origen as well as Eusebius the placement of the profanation in the Temple of God was crucial. Indeed, I think that Eusebius was inspired by Origen in this. He was a disciple of Pamphilus, who wrote the Apology for Origen while he was in prison waiting for his martyrdom. Eusebius helped Pamphilus write the Apology and completed it after his martyrdom. He devoted almost a full book of his *HE* to Origen, where he depicts him as a hero, *defensor fidei* and *magister ecclesiae*, unjustly accused.

λιμέσι), but is absent in Clement and in the extant Greek works of Origen, as well as in other authors dependent on Origen such as Eusebius, Basil, and Gregory Nazianzen. In Gregory, however, it is present, in *VM* 1.13, τῆς ἀρετῆς λιμένι, where it probably depends directly on Philo, although—as always—we cannot exclude its presence in the numerous works of Origen that have been lost or survive only in translation. Moreover, this expression occurs in Gregory together with λιμένα τοῦ θείου θελήματος (*VM* 1.11), which recalls Origen's reflection on virtue as a harbor in *Fr. Ps.* 106.30: ὁδήγησεν αὐτοὺς ἐπὶ λιμένα θελήματος αὐτῶν· λιμὴν μὲν ψυχῆς ἡ ἀπάθεια.[49]

Many parts of Gregory's *VM*, in fact, just as much of his thought, betray a profound influence of Origen. For example, the discussion of the hardening of Pharaoh's heart in 2.73–77, 80, 86, is reminiscent of Origen's ample and important treatment of the same subject in *Princ.* 3,[50] where it is closely related to the question of free will, as it is in Gregory's treatise. Another example is the soul giving birth to virtue through its spiritual marriage with God. This theme is found both in Philo (*Leg.* 3.180; *Congr.* 5–8; cf. *Cher.* 41–50) and in Gregory (*VM* 2.4), although with a slight variation. In Gregory, it is the rational faculties of the human being, constituting the soul, that generate virtue with the help of free will. Gregory found the idea of the soul's spiritual marriage with God not only in Philo but also in Origen. The latter, in my view, provided the link between Philo and Gregory. In *Hom. Num.* 20.2, Origen depicted the soul's intercourse with the Logos, the intermediary between God (since it is God's Logos and thus associated with God) and the soul (since it is the rational faculty of the soul). It appears that Gregory found in Origen the inspiration to transform Philo's intercourse of the soul with God for the begetting of virtue into begetting virtue by human faculties. Moreover, the theme of the begetting of virtues on the part of the converted soul is also found in Didymus (*Co. Gen.* 119.1–10), the faithful follower of Origen and supporter of his doctrine of apokatastasis, who surely knew Origen's interpretation as well. The same is the case with the allegorical interpretation of male and female as virtue *vs* passions in *VM* 2.2–3 and 2.49 (ἀρετή *vs* ἐμπαθεστέρα διάθεσις and κακία, τὸ μαλακώτερόν τε καὶ ἀσθενέστερον in the exegesis of Pharaoh's order to kill all baby boys), although Gregory clearly states that men and women, both constituting the same human nature, are equally capable of

---

[49] This is the following: λιμὴν δὲ νοῦ γνῶσις σωμάτων καὶ ἀσωμάτων. Cf. *ibid.* 106.23, τῶν ψυχῶν τὴν γαλήνην καὶ τῆς ἀναστάσεως τὸν λιμένα.

[50] See my "La coerenza della soteriologia origeniana," in *Pagani e cristiani alla ricerca della salvezza* (SEA 96; Rome: Augustinianum, 2006), 661–688.

virtue.[51] Philo had already allegorized male and female as rationality *vs* senses or incorporeality *vs* matter (*Leg.* 3.3 and 243 and *QE* 1.8).[52] But Gregory could also have drawn the contrast from Origen, whose exposition seems to be closer to his than Philo's. In *Hom. Ex.* 2.2–3, Origen allegorized man as rationality and intellect, which is lifted up to heavenly realities, and precisely as virtue, and woman as flesh and bodily matter, and explicitly as vice and pleasure.[53] The same ideas occur in *Hom. Gen.* 4.4; 5.2. Almost all of these allegorizations, in Philo, Origen, and Gregory, appear in connection with the allegorical exegesis of the Hebrews' Egyptian captivity. But Origen's interpretation, in which virtue and vices, rather than incorporeality and matter, are expressly presented as the allegorical counterpart of male and female, is closer to Gregory's.

The exegesis of the skin tunics of Gen 3:21 in *VM* 2.22 as the dead and earthly covering placed around human nature after the fall that represent the irrational and passion-filled disposition that was added to our nature together with reproduction, growth, nutrition, disease, and death (*An.* 148C–149A), and the loss of immortality and ἀπάθεια, derives more from a meditation of Origen's and Methodius' interpretations of the skin tunics[54] than from Philo's, from whom (*Leg.* 2.56) Gregory simply drew the exegetical detail of the tunic of skin as a symbol of the wrong opinion that one ought to take off. In *QG* 1.53 Philo interpreted the skin tunics as the body

---

[51] *VM* 1.12: πρὸς τὸ θῆλύ τε καὶ ἄρρεν ἡ ἀνθρωπίνη μεμέρισται φύσις καὶ ἀμφοτέροις ἐπίσης κατ᾽ ἐξουσίαν ἡ πρὸς ἀρετὴν καὶ κακίαν αἵρεσις πρόκειται. On Philo's misogynist theory of gender, which is less emphasized in Origen and not at all in Gregory (one of the most illuminated Fathers in this respect), see Dorothy Sly, *Philo's Perception of Women* (Atlanta: Scholars Press, 1990), esp. 91–110 on woman as sense perception; Gérard H. Baudry, "La responsabilité d'Ève dans la chute," *MSR* 53 (1996): 293–320: 303–305; Petra von Gemünden, "La femme passionnelle et l'homme rationnel?," *Biblica* 4 (1997): 457–480; Judith M. Gundry-Wolf, "Paul on Women and Gender," in *The Impact of Paul's Conversion on His Life, Thought, and Ministry* (ed. R. Longenecker; Grand Rapids: Eerdmans, 1997), 184–212: 195–201; Joan E. Taylor, "Virgin Mothers: Philo on the Women Therapeutae," *JSP* 12 (2001): 37–63; Elad Filler, "Notes on the Concept of Woman and Marriage in Philo," *Iyyun* 53 (2004): 395–408, who argued for a positive view of marriage in Philo and a not only negative evaluation of women; William Loader, *The Septuagint, Sexuality, and the New Testament* (Grand Rapids: Eerdmans, 2004), esp. 69, where the author reached the conclusion that Philo tended to see women as flawed by nature.

[52] See e.g., Annewies Van den Hoek, "Endowed with Reasons or Glued to the Senses," in *The Creation of Man and Woman* (ed. G. P. Luttikhuizen; Leiden: Brill, 2000), 63–75.

[53] On Philo's conception of ἡδονή see Alain Le Boulluec, "La place des concepts philosophiques dans la réflexion de Philon sur les plaisirs," in *Philon d'Alexandrie et le langage de la philosophie* (éd. C. Lévy; Turnhout: Brepols, 1998), 129–152.

[54] See my philosophical essay in *Gregorio di Nissa* also for an assessment of Origen's true view of the skin tunics, which are not simply the body in his thought.

tout court, an interpretation that neither Origen nor Gregory share. Gregory, who reflects on the meaning of the skin tunics in many passages (including *Beat.* 151; *Mort.* 55; *Or. Cat.* 30), seems to stick more closely to Origen, who identified the skin tunics with mortality and heavy corporeality insofar as the body is liable to passions and corruption, than to Philo.

There is another interpretation, similar to this, in which Gregory adhered to Origen more than to Philo, in that he tries to avoid an exegesis in which the body *per se* is seen in a negative way and transfered all negativity to vices and passions rather than to pure corporeality, the exegesis of Egypt and liberation from Egypt. In *VM* 2.26–27 Gregory interpreted Pharaoh's tyranny over the Hebrews in Egypt as a symbol of the tyranny of passions and sin over the human being, who is an image of God and thus enjoys freedom as an essential feature. This image was blurred by the fall and human freedom was partially lost, but both can be recovered through ἀπάθεια. So, the exodus from Egypt is read as the liberation of the soul from the tyranny of the passions. Accordingly, in 2.54–62 Gregory interpreted the making of bricks in the land of Egypt as material enjoyment and the pursuit of pleasures, and Pharaoh as a lover of the material life (2.35). Philo in *Her.* 268–272 interpreted the passions of the body as alien to the intellect. Philo equated Israel's captivity in Egypt to a life according to bodily passions and Pharaoh to a lover of the body, of matter, and of pleasures (*Leg.* 3.13; 38; 212; 243; *Ebr.* 209; *Abr.* 103), an ἄθεος and ἀντίθεος (*Leg.* 3.12; 212; *Ebr.* 19; *Conf.* 88; *Congr.* 118; *Somn.* 2.183), a symbol of those who do not know God and thus forget their humanity due to the enjoyment of bodily things (*Post.* 115).[55] He is a lover of passions who dwells in the darkness (*Ebr.* 209). The making of bricks in Egypt in *Conf.* 83–100 is related to the tower of Babel and interpreted as an engagement in material and earthly activities characterized by passions and vices. Philo's interpretation of Egypt as the body and its passions and sense-perception[56]—perfectly in line with his statement that the principle of παντελὴς σωτηρία consists in abandoning σῶμα and αἴσθησις, τὸ παμμίαρον ἐκφυγὼν δεσμωτήριον, τὸ σῶμα, καὶ τὰς ὥσπερ εἰρκτοφύλακας ἡδονὰς καὶ ἐπιθυμίας αὐτοῦ, just as Abraham abandoned his land and family (*Migr.* 2; 9)—was transformed by Origen into an interpretation of sin and the passions of this world, with a stress on

---

[55] For the delineation of Pharaoh in Philo see Frédéric Deutsch, "La philautie chez Philon d'Alexandrie," in *Philon d'Alexandrie*, 87–98.

[56] On Egypt as the body, sense-perception and passions according to Philo see Sarah Pearce, "Belonging and not Belonging: Local Perspectives in Philo," in *Jewish Local Patriotism and Self-Identification in the Greco-Roman Period* (eds. eadem and S. Jones; Sheffield: Academic Press, 1998), 79–105 and eadem, *The Land of the Body. Studies in Philo's Representation of Egypt* (WUNT 208; Tübingen: Mohr Siebeck 2007).

sin rather than on the body, which will be retained by Gregory. In both fathers the emphasis lies not on the body which disappears, but on passions and sins. In fact, in *Hom. Ex.* 3.3, Origen interpreted Egypt as a symbol of this world and its passions and darkness; in 7.2 he considered it as a figure of the passions, namely luxury, voluptuousness, sensuality. He understood Pharaoh as a symbol of the devil—Philo's ἀντίθεος, who opposed God—the ruler of this world's darkness (*Hom. Ex.* 1.5; 2.1; 3.3; 6.1; *Hom. Ps. 36*, 3.1), an interpretation taken up by the Origenist Methodius, *Symp.* 4.2.[57] Indeed, the devil, in Origen's view, is a creature that—like all humans and angels—sinned in making a bad choice but will be restored in the end *qua* creature of God. Origen allegorized the making of bricks in Egypt as earthly works (*Hom. Ex.* 1.5). Gregory seems to follow Origen by dropping the negative characterization of the body in Philo's exegesis when he omitted Egypt as body and Pharaoh as lover of the body, but retained the reference to passions and sin deriving from bad will as well as the decayed status of humanity after the fall.

There is another example of Gregory's familiarity with Philo, but a familiarity mediated by Origen, the exegesis of Moses' foreign wife as a symbol of pagan culture and philosophy. This is interpreted by Gregory in the same way as he interpreted Pharaoh's daughter. In Philo it was Hagar, Sarah's slave, who was considered to be the symbol of education (*Leg.* 3.244–245; *Congr.* 15–18); however, this education was seen positively by Philo as leading to virtue: θεραπαινὶς δὲ σοφίας ἡ διὰ τῶν προπαιδευμάτων ἐγκύκλιος μουσική . . . γραμματικῇ, γεωμετρίᾳ, ἀστρονομίᾳ, ῥητορικῇ, μουσικῇ, τῇ ἄλλῃ λογικῇ θεωρίᾳ . . . ἀρετῆς πρόκεινται τὰ ἐγκύκλια· ταῦτα γὰρ ὁδός ἐστιν ἐπ᾽ ἐκείνην φέρουσα (*Congr.* 10–11). Gregory's views are closer to Origen's who interpreted Hagar as pagan education—not as slave, but as a foreign wife (*Hom. Gen.* 11.2)—and who underlined the negative aspects of this education.[58] Gregory, who warned that philosophy can lead to virtue only if its fruits do not bear alien defilement (*VM* 2.37), emphasized the necessity of removing all pagan elements in philosophy. He saw circumcision precisely as an allegory of this removal, whereas Philo allegorized it as the cutting off of pleasure, passions, and impious opinions in *Migr.* 92. A similar allegorization concerns the spoiling of the Egyptians, where

---

[57] On Methodius' Origenism see my "L'Inno a Cristo-Logos nel *Simposio* di Metodio," in *La poesia cristiana* (SEA 108; Rome: Augustinianum, 2008), 257–280.

[58] John L. Thompson, *Writing the Wrongs. Women of the OT among Biblical Commentators* (Oxford: Oxford University Press, 2001), 24–27, went through the *Wirkungsgeschichte* of Philo's interpretation of Hagar, taken over by Clement and joined by Origen and Didymus to the interpretation of Gal 4. Gregory, due to Origen's influence, is closer to Paul's exegesis than to Philo's.

Gregory's exegesis (*VM* 2.112–116) followed Origen's rather than Philo's. Gregory openly refused to understand that the Jews, by spoiling the Egyptians, took what they had earned by their work (μισθώματα). As Runia pointed out,[59] this is precisely Philo's interpretation in *Mos.* 1.141 (μισθὸν κομιζόμενοι), an interpretation also found in Clement, *Strom.* 1.157; Irenaeus, *AH* 4.30.2; Eusebius, *Co. Ps.* 1309B; Nazianzen, *Or.* 45.20 and *Poem. Mor.* 10.499. Origen knew this interpretation—probably from both Philo and Clement—but turned it into spiritual exegesis. It was his allegorization of the spoils from Egypt[60] that was taken over by Gregory. In fact, in his letter to his pupil Gregory the Wonderworker, 2–3, Origen, after stating that he considers Greek philosophy to be propaedeutic to Christianity, just as the Greeks considered the ἐγκύκλια μαθήματα to be προπαιδεύματα to philosophy, claimed that from such richness the Hebrews made things for their sanctuary, whereas the Egyptians were unable to use those riches properly. Now, those spoils are τὰ τοῦ κόσμου μαθήματα, which must be used to honor God (εἰς θεοσέβειαν). Origen, while transforming Philo's wages into the acquisition of knowledge, observed that the Hebrews profited (κεκερδήκασι) from the fact that they had at their disposal (εὐπορῆσαι) such treasures of knowledge to employ for the honor of God (τιμίας εἰς τὰ χρήσιμα τῇ λατρείᾳ τοῦ θεοῦ). Gregory entirely relied on Origen when in *VM* 2.115–116 he affirmed that the spoils represented pagan education whose richness ought to be used to adorn the divine sanctuary, just as the Hebrews used the precious spoils from Egypt to furnish the divine tabernacle.

Likewise, in the interpretation of Moses' rod in the episode of the contest between Moses and the Egyptian sorcerers (*VM* 2.63–64), the verbal echoes of Philo, *Migr.* 83–85, and resemblances in phrasing—pointed out by Geljon[61]—guarantee that Gregory read and employed Philo's text; however, he was even more influenced by Origen's exegesis of this passage. His Christological interpretation of Moses' staff in 2.31–34 clearly derives from Origen, *Hom. Ex.* 4.6, whereas Philo, in *Leg.* 2.88–93, understood the rod as an allegory of education. Origen saw in Moses' rod the cross of Christ which defeats the world and its prince together with its powers. The swallowing of the Egyptians' staffs by Moses' staff that was changed into a serpent is consequently interpreted by Origen as a symbol of the defeat of

---

[59] Runia, *Philo in Literature*, 258–259.

[60] For a specific and comprehensive examination of this theme in Patristic authors see Joel S. Allen, *The Despoliation of Egypt in Pre-Rabbinic, Rabbinic and Patristic Traditions* (Leiden: Brill, 2008). See also Pier Franco Beatrice, "The Treasures of the Egyptians," in *StPatr* 39 (2006): 159–183.

[61] Geljon, *Philonic Elements*, 108.

this world's wisdom by Christ crucified. Moreover, Philo's designation of the Egyptian sorcerers as magicians, repeated by Gregory, was present in Origen as well (*Hom. Ex.* 4, 4; 13, 4; *Hom. Ier.* 19.2; *Fr. Ex.* 281C).[62]

Similarly, closer resemblances between Gregory and Origen than between Gregory and Philo appear in the allegorization of the ten plagues of Egypt, treated in Gregory's *VM* 2.65ff. and in Origen's *Hom. Ex.* 4. This is, moreover, the context in which Gregory inserted the digression on free will occasioned by the reflection on the hardening of Pharaoh's heart that— as I mentioned—is heavily indebted to Origen's treatment in *Princ.* 3. It is also worth noting that in this context, while speaking of the plague of darkness, Gregory inserted a clear hint to the doctrine of apokatastasis, a view that he shared with Origen (2.80–84).[63] In this connection, it comes as no surprise that Gregory drew inspiration from Origen in the interpretation of the plagues. The tenth plague, the Egyptian firstborns' death, was allegorized by Gregory as a sign that it is necessary to destroy the first beginnings of evil in order to avoid the Egyptian life, a life according to passions (2.90). The lamb, whose blood protects the Jews against death, is a symbol of Christ whose sacrifice has saved humanity from death (2.95). The same interpretation of the lamb can be found throughout Origen's *De Pascha*, in *Hom. Gen.* 10.3, and *Co. Io.* 10.92–93. The same exegesis of the tenth plague is present in Origen's *Hom. Ex.* 4.8, where he explained that it is necessary to kill the first movements of the soul made according to passions in order to avoid a vicious life. Origen's exegesis is much closer to Gregory's than to Philo's, who—of course—had no Christological interpretation of the Lamb and who allegorized the Egyptian firstborn not as the beginnings of evil choices and of bad movements of the soul, but as the most dominant passions. Philo believed that the elimination of these passions provides the sanctification of the offspring of the one who sees God (*Sacr.* 134).

Gregory's exegesis of the doorposts on which the blood of the lamb must be spread exactly coincides with that of Origen, *Fr. Ex.* PG 12.285A, who assimilated the lintel to the λογικόν and the two side-posts to the

---

[62] Van den Hoek, "Philo and Origen," 77, did not think that Origen depended on Philo for the interpretation of the magicians in terms of false and true miracles and the link with sophists, since both were already present in the Septuagint.

[63] Gregory assimilated the Egyptian darkness to that of hell, the evangelical "outer darkness," and considered Moses, who dispelled it by stretching out his hands, to be a τύπος of Christ, who, by stretching out his arms on the cross, dispelled the darkness of hell. I find it most interesting that precisely in his interpretation of the "outer darkness," which he regards as the darkness outside the *kosmos* where sinners will be thrown, Origen (*Co. Mat. S.* 69) depended on Philo (*Opif.* 32), whom he cites as a predecessor. See below.

θυμικόν and the ἐπιθυμητικόν. Here Origen followed Plato's tripartition of the soul, which of course is also present in Philo but in different contexts (*Migr.* 66; *Leg.* 1.70; *Spec.* 4.92) as well as in Didymus (*Co. Gen.* 119.24–26); however, as Runia and Geljon have pointed out,[64] it differs from that of Philo (*QE* 1.12) who equated reason to the two side posts, the heart to the lintel, and desire to the house.[65] Gregory's interpretation of Passover regulations betrays the same close similarity to Origen's exegesis (*VM* 2.102–111). Again, there are resemblances to Philo (*QE* 1.19), but Gregory is closer to Origen's detailed exegesis in his *De Pascha* discovered in a Toura papyrus, 35–39.[66] According to Gregory, the girdle around the loins represents self-restraint, the shoes symbolize readiness to depart from this life as well as an austere conduct which protects from the thorns of this life, and the staff is the word of hope. In Philo, the girdle indicates drawing passions together, the shoes are protection on the path leading to virtue, and the rod is a symbol of kingship. In Origen, according to an interpretation which also influenced Eusebius, *Pas.* 4.697C, and Nazianzen, *Or.* 45.18, the girdle is a symbol of self-restraint generally, and, specifically, of abstention from intercourse; the shoes represent promptness to depart from this life for resurrection and, spiritually, to depart from vices for virtue; and the rod symbolizes παιδεία understood as correction. From the interpretation of the shoes it is evident that Gregory took over both Philo's and Origen's exegeses, while Gregory's allegorizations of the girdle and rod are closer to those of Origen.

Origen's influence on a Philonic exegetical tradition is also found in *VM* 2.131–132, where Gregory allegorized the bitter water at Marah that sweetened when Moses threw a piece of wood into it as a symbol of the virtuous life. For such a life is difficult and bitter, but becomes sweeter thanks to the wood, an allegory of the resurrection, in that the latter had its beginning in the wood of the cross. Philo had interpreted the water at

---

[64] Runia, *Philo in Literature*, 258; Geljon, *Philonic Exegesis*, 112.

[65] Origen said that his own exegesis, taken over by Gregory and partially by Eusebius, *Pas.* 11.705B, and Nazianzen, *Or.* 45,15, was already offered by τις τῶν πρὸ ἡμῶν. It was on this source, or more likely on Origen again, who was the inspirer of a large part of the subsequent allegoresis of the Bible, that an anonymous fourth-century Easter homily depends (Ps. Chrys. *Hom. Pasch.* 2.8: *Homélies pascales, II. Trois homélies dans la tradition d'Origène* [éd. P. Nautin; Paris: Cerf, 1953], 83). It likened λογισμός to the lintel and πάθος to the side posts, which are below because they should submit to reason, ἡγεμονικὸς καὶ ἀνώτερος τῇ φύσει. The two forms of passion, μαλακτικὸν τῆς ψυχῆς εἰς ἀπαλότητα, σκληροποιὸν εἰς τραχύτητα, recall Origen's (i.e. Plato's) ἐπιθυμητικόν and θυμικόν, all the more for the respective characterizations, εἰς ἡδονὰς ἐκλυόμενοι and εἰς θυμοὺς ἐκτραχυνόμενοι.

[66] In addition to the text, see Octave Guéraud and Pierre Nautin, "L'exégèse d'Origène sur la Loi de la Pâque," in Origène, *Sur la Pâque* (Paris: Beauchesne, 1979), 112–150.

Marrah as a symbol of the bitter toil of the virtuous life in *Post.* 154–157. Gregory likely knew Philo's exegesis—as Geljon correctly assumed[67]—but the Christological interpretation of the wood derives from Origen, *Hom. Ex.* 7.1, and *Hom. Ier.* 10.2. This exegesis was "prepared" by Philo, who interpreted the wood as a promise of immortality, because the tree of life was in the middle of paradise (*Migr.* 36–37), an interpretation accepted by Origen, *Hom. Ex.* 7.1[68] and later influential not only upon Gregory of Nyssa but also upon Nazianzen, *Or.* 36.4. Of course, Origen linked the promise of immortality to the wood of the cross, the beginning of resurrection. A further proof of the influence of Origen's interpretation of the bitter water at Marrah upon Gregory is the fact that Origen's allegorization of this water as the literal sense of the Law in *Hom. Ex.* 7.1 was well known to Gregory and transferred by him to the position of Moses' hands in the battle against the Amalekites. According to Gregory, the lowering of Moses' arms symbolized the literal exegesis of the Law, whereas the lifting up of Moses' hands indicated spiritual interpretation. Another example of Gregory's double dependence on Philo and Origen together for his allegory is his interpretation of the high priest's ritual garments in *VM* 2.189–201, where the cosmological allegoresis—in line with the Stoic tradition—came from Philo, whereas the ethical allegoresis was drawn from Origen.[69] All this, again, suggests that Gregory's allegoresis was inspired by both Philo and Origen, through direct reading of both.

There are only a few examples—but there are a few—in which we can exclude Origen's influence on Gregory's understanding of the allegorical interpretations in Philo. For instance, the interpretation of Moses' cry in

---

[67] Geljon, *Philonic Exegesis*, 121.

[68] Philo's influence on *Hom. Ier.* 10.2, instead, is denied, on good bases, by Van den Hoek, "Philo and Origen," 75: the Christological interpretation of Exod 15:25 in reference to the cross was already in Justin, *Dial.* 86.1. On Justin see my "S. Giustino Martire: il multiforme uso di *mystérion* e il lessico dell'esegesi tipologica delle Scritture," in *Il volto*, 35–66.

[69] Gregory kept some distance from the cosmological allegoresis: while he did not know whether it was valid or not, he did not reject it (2.191): φασὶ δέ τινες τῶν πρὸ ἡμῶν τεθεωρηκότων τὸν λόγον τὸν ἀέρα σημαίνεσθαι τῇ βαφῇ. Ἐγὼ δὲ εἰ μέν τι τὸ τοιοῦτον τοῦ χρώματος ἄνθος πρὸς τὸ ἀέριον χρῶμα συγγενῶς ἔχει, ἀκριβῶς οὐκ ἔχω διϊσχυρίζεσθαι, τὸν μέντοι λόγον οὐκ ἀποβάλλω. He preferred to develop his exegesis in reference to virtue (συντείνει γὰρ πρὸς τὴν κατ᾽ ἀρετὴν θεωρίαν τὸ νόημα) and interpreted the parts of the vestment in reference to virtuous life, e.g., the colors of the ephod symbolized different virtues. The cosmological interpretation of the priestly vestment was offered by Philo, *Mos.* 2.109–135, to whom it is almost certain that Gregory referred (Runia, *Philo in Literature*, 259–260). But the allegorization in terms of virtue was provided by Origen, who is Gregory's source of inspiration. In *Hom. Ex.* 9.3, he interpreted the colors of the priestly apparatus as the virtues: purple is love, green is hope, etc.

Mos. 1.29 that contains the distinction between his uttered words, with which he encourages his people to hope, and his mental prayer to God for those who fear, is missing in the extant works of Origen and was apparently not in the lost works—at least this is suggested by its absence in the authors who depended on Origen: Eusebius, Jerome, Didymus, and the other two Cappadocians. Gregory seems here to rely only on Philo, *Mos.* 1.173, who drew a distinction between word and intention, λόγος and νοῦς. According to Philo, with the former Moses uttered words of encouragement, with the latter he prayed to God to deliver them from a difficult situation.

On the other hand, there are also cases in which Gregory betrays a direct influence of Origen and none of Philo, even though they interpreted the same biblical passage. For example, Gregory allegorized the twelve springs and seventy palms at Elim as the twelve apostles, who made Christ's word to spring, and the seventy disciples (*VM* 2.133–134). This exegesis was—of course—not in Philo; rather it came from Origen's *Hom. Ex.* 7.3 and *Hom. Num.* 27.11. Further derivations from Origen rather than Philo are the Christological allegorizations of both the rock in the desert (*VM* 2.135–136) and the manna (2.137–146). Origen had already made these identifications in many passages: the rock in *Hom. Gen.* 10.3; *Hom. Ex.* 11.2, and *Co. Rom.* 10.6; the manna in *Hom. Ex.* 7.8 and *Hom. Num.* 3.1, where he interprets it as the Logos of Christ, exactly as Gregory does. Of course, the Christological exegesis of the rock was already in 1Cor 10:4, and was certainly prepared by Philo, who interpreted the rock as Wisdom and Logos (*Det.* 115; 118), precisely the two principal ἐπίνοιαι of Christ according to Origen. We should also note that Philo interpreted the manna as God's Logos (*Leg.* 3.175). Origen found in Philo a sort of preparation for the Christological interpretations that he made and that Gregory drew from him [70]

---

[70] In other cases, Christological allegorizations, naturally absent in Philo, were already present not only in Origen but also in other Christian authors. For example the presentation of Joshua as a τύπος of Christ in *VM* 2.148 and the stretching of Moses' hands for the victory in 2.151 as a symbol of Christ's cross were already present in a number of authors: the former in Justin, Irenaeus and Clement before Origen (*Hom. Ex.* 11.3; *Hom. Jos.* 1.1–4; 2.1; *Co. Io.* 6.229) and Eusebius (*HE* 1.3.3–5); and the latter in Justin before Origen (*Hom. Jos.* 1.3; *Hom. Reg.* 1.9) and Nazianzen (*Or.* 2.88; 12.2). Another example is the Christological allegorization of the brazen serpent in the desert (*Mos.* 2.271–277), which was already present in John 3:14 and, accordingly, in Justin and Irenaeus, in addition to Origen, *Pasch.* 14 and Basil. See my "Serpente nei Padri," in *Nuovo Dizionario Patristico e di Antichità Cristiane* (ed. A. Di Berardino; Genoa: Marietti, 2008), 3:4881–4889. For Philo's and the rabbis' interpretation see Amy Birkan-Shear, "Does a Serpent Give Life?" in *The Changing Face of Judaism* (eds. I. H. Henderson and G. S. Oegema; Gütersloh: Gütersloher Verlagshaus, 2006), 2:416–426. A direct reading of Philo on the part of Gregory is

One last example: both Philo and Gregory offered spiritual interpretations of the Jewish feasts, and in particular of that of the Tabernacles, treated by Philo in *Spec.* 2.204ff. and presented by Gregory at the end of his *De Anima* as a prefiguration of the apokatastasis. Now the eschatological and Christological exegesis of the Jewish feasts did not derive from Philo but from Origen (esp. *Hom. Num.* 23), like the doctrine of apokatastasis itself.[71] Both for Origen and for Gregory the feasts will be truly and wholly celebrated in the glorious τέλος.

Etymology and Allegory between Philo and Gregory:
Origen's Role and the Relation to Pagan Allegory

An important feature in allegoresis that Gregory failed to inherit either from Philo or from Origen, but for which Origen probably played a key role in the transmission of Philonic materials, is etymology. It was associated with allegorical hermeneutics in the Stoics[72] and remained an important feature through the centuries, as in Philo's own days Cornutus' Ἐπιδρομή shows.[73] But it was also used in the Jewish tradition, in all likelihood before Philo, in the interpretation of the Bible, e.g., an etymology of *shabbath* as "rest"—the same etymology subsequently given by Philo—as attested in Aristobulus, fr. 5.13. Philo, probably on the basis of earlier etymological lists,[74] made extensive use of etymologies in his allegoresis, usually in

---

guaranteed by his allegorization of the other serpents as desires, which, absent in the aforementioned Fathers, is present in Philo, *Leg.* 2.76–81. For Philo's double allegorization of the snake see Francesca Calabi, "Il serpente e il 'cavaliere'," *AnnScRel* 8 (2003): 199–215. Philo's four interpretations of the snake in *Leg.* 2.71–105 is analyzed by Marta Alesso, "La alegoría de la serpiente en Filón de Alejandría," *Nova Tellus* 22 (2004): 97–119. An allegorization common to Philo (*Mos.* 2.88), Clement (*Strom.* 5.32.3), Origen (*Hom. Ex.* 13.3), and Gregory, so that Gregory may depend on all others, is that of the four colors of the curtains of the tabernacle as the elements. Origen attributed this allegorization to "some before us," referring maybe to Philo and Clement together, and even to Josephus, who offered the same allegoresis in *Ant.* 3.183; *Bell.* 6.212–213. For the interpretation of the inner veil as Christ's flesh and of the tabernacle as Christ, Gregory did not depend on Philo, of course, but on Paul, on whose authority already Origen relied for his own interpretation of the veil as the flesh of Christ in *Hom. Ex.* 9.1, and on John 1:14, to which Gregory expressly appealed.

71 See my *Apocatastasi* (Milan: Vita e Pensiero, 2009) and my Integrative Essay I in *Gregorio di Nissa*.
72 See my *Allegoria*, I, *L'età classica* (Milan: Vita e Pensiero, 2004), chs. 2 and 9, and my *Allegoristi dell'età classica* (Milan: Bompiani, 2007).
73 See my *Anneo Cornuto. Compendio di teologia greca* (Milan: Bompiani, 2003).
74 They are presupposed also by Gerhard Sellin, "Die Allegorese und die Anfänge der Schriftauslegung," in *Theologische Probleme der Septuaginta* (ed. H. Reventlow; Gütersloh:

etymologizing the names of biblical characters. He provided almost all of the biblical names he mentioned with a Hebrew etymology: there are 166 such etymologies in the Philonic corpus, some of which occur in more than one passage. In a pioneering study of Philo's etymologies,[75] Lester Grabbe argued that the cases in which an etymology is the sole source of an allegorization are few. Subsequently, in a substantial article on Philo's conception of language and the relevance of the etymological technique to his allegoresis,[76] Runia showed that the distribution of the etymologies within the Philonic corpus attests to their strong link with allegoresis: they are much more numerous in the Allegorical Commentary than in the Exposition of the Law, where allegory is absent and etymologies are very few. An intermediate concentration is found in *QG* and *QE*, where allegorical exegesis flanks literal interpretation. Also, when more than one etymology is offered by Philo, its bearer is often allegorized in more than one way.[77] The massive presence of etymologies of biblical names and the appearance of the relevant etymology generally at the beginning of the allegorization of a given character, led Runia to conclude that in Philo "the etymologies of Biblical names contribute to the exegesis and help to give it a solid foundation" (111). This is especially the case in genealogies and in name changes (e.g. *Abr.* 81–82), on the importance of which, I would like to point out, Origen will agree with Philo.[78] But the allegorical pictures that Philo traced in his ethical and spiritual interpretations are too broad and complex to be simply based on etymology, although they are supported by it. By

---

Gütersloher Verlagshaus, 1997), 91–132, esp. 108–126. Grabbe, *Etymology*, 108, provided a good clue for Philo's employment of onomastical lists, the use of lexical forms different from those usually employed by him, exclusively in connection with a given etymology, e.g., the use of περισσός in connection with the etymology of "Jethro," as opposed to the Attic form πορυττός, which represents Philo's normal usage (based on a Hebrew article by Yehoshua Amir, "The Interpretation of Hebrew Names According to Philo," *Tarbiz* 31 [1961]: 297, translated by Grabbe in an appendix to his book and praised by Runia, *Etymology*, 114). See also the use of ὠμίασις always in relation to the etymology of "Shechem," as opposed to Philo's usage ὠμός.

[75] Lester Grabbe, *Etymology in Early Jewish Interpretation* (BJS 115; Atlanta: Scholars Press, 1988).

[76] David T. Runia, "Etymology as an Allegorical Technique in Philo of Alexandria," *SPhA* 16 (2004): 101–121.

[77] Philo occasionally offered Greek etymologies of Hebrew names, besides Hebrew etymologies, but he did not introduce them through his standard formula, and he is likely to be, in a way, "playful."

[78] Philo, *Mut.* 65 (cf. *QG* 3.43) was probably taken up by Origen, *Hom. Num.* 25.3; *Cat. Gen.* B 12.115. Van den Hoek, "Philo and Origen," 105, is right that dependence in this passage is uncertain; however, it is clear that for the general conception Origen was inspired by Philo.

relying especially on *Abr.* 99, which shows that Philo derived his etymological material from his exegetical predecessors, Runia shares the hypothesis that Philo depended on a rich onomastical list specifically prepared for the purpose of allegoresis, although he disagrees with Goulet that Philo adapted a full-blown and coherent pre-existent allegorical commentary on the Pentateuch. For his own allegoresis Philo was probably inspired by Hellenic models comparable to the Middle-Platonist Plutarch, the Stoic Cornutus, and allegorical works that were variously influenced by the Stoic tradition such as Heraclitus' *Homeric Allegories* and the *Cebetis Tabula*; however, the extensiveness, coherence, and systematic approach of Philo's allegoresis go well beyond the achievements of the Stoics. They are more comparable to Plutarch and, on the Christian side, Origen, both belonging to the Platonic tradition. We should also remember that they were applied to a completely different text.

It is remarkable that Philo's etymologies of biblical names reappear in Clement, and above all in Origen, and then in authors that were powerfully influenced by Origen, especially Eusebius, Jerome, and Ambrose—most of Philo's etymologies, indeed, appear again in Jerome. For this reason I suspect that Origen may have functioned as a mediator in many cases. In the extant works of Origen, at least thirty-nine etymologies coincide precisely with those offered by Philo, and many others show some correspondence. Origen surely drew many etymologies from Philo, in addition to having some other sources.[79] Almost half of the examples of Origen's dependence on Philo that van den Hoek collected ("Philo and Origen") are etymologies. What is most interesting, moreover, is that in both Origen and the authors depending on him—including the few examples that Gregory offers—these etymologies are not simply listed or introduced merely for erudite purposes, but are instrumental to the allegorical interpretation of the Bible, precisely as they are in Philo. Origen and his followers did not pick up single etymological derivations, but the whole method. In his *De Anima*, in the exegesis of the parable of Dives and Lazarus, Gregory offered the etymology of Hades as "invisible" in support to his interpretation of it not as a physical place, but as a condition of the soul after physical death and separation from the body. Remarkably this was a Greek not a Hebrew etymology and was widespread in the Greek allegorical tradition, e.g., in

---

[79] See Richard P. C. Hanson, "Interpretation of Hebrew Names in Origen," *VChr* 10 (1956): 103–123; Annewies Van den Hoek, "Etymologizing in a Christian Context: The Techniques of Clement and Origen," *SPhA* 16 (2004): 122–168.

Cornutus, 5.[80] Greek etymologies, mostly stemming from the Stoic tradition and often from Chrysippus, were already present and frequent in Clement, who linked them to allegoresis. Van den Hoek suggests that Clement approximated Cornutus in his treatment of names and myths.[81] Clement shared with Origen an interest in Philo's etymologies of biblical names. In *Strom.* 1.13.1–5 he openly mentioned Philo as a source for his own etymologies for the names of the Patriarchs and their wives. At other times, however, he shows a total independence from Philo. Origen was much more interested than Clement in the Hebrew language and Hebrew etymologies of biblical names; correspondingly, he is far less interested than Clement in Greek mythology and etymology. Gregory reported the Hebrew etymology of Adam as terrestrial in *Opif.* 204.42, because this is fundamental for his anthropology in drawing the (Philonic and Origenian!) distinction between the ἄνθρωπος κατ᾽ εἰκόνα θεοῦ and the γήϊνον πλάσμα that is called Adam κατά τινα ἐτυμολογικὴν ὀνομασίαν. After he related this etymology to οἱ τῆς Ἐβραίων φωνῆς ἐπιΐστορες, he attributed it to St Paul as expert in the Hebrew language since he understood χοϊκός as the ἄνθρωπος ἐκ γῆς, the translation of "Adam" into Greek (Gregory similarly cited Paul as a warrant for biblical allegoresis, just as Origen had done).[82] Gregory was not fond of picking up etymologies from Philo or Origen or Clement. In *In Illud* 26, he even described etymologies as ψυχραί and in *Abl.* GNO 3/1.43.6, he said that there was no need for etymologies for the names of all that exist because names have been assigned to things κατὰ τὸ συμβάν. He reasoned that we need names to designate things in order to avoid confusion in knowledge. These names are different than the names of God that are never devoid of διάνοια and νόημα, although they do not grasp God's essence. Likewise, Gregory was scarcely interested in the Hebrew *Vorlage* of the Septuagint, although he indirectly referred to the Hebrew original of the Old Testament on occasion and—like Origen—compared the different Greek versions.[83] However, he was much less of a philologist than Origen.

---

[80] Of course both Philo and Origen made use also of Greek etymologies, e.g., θεός from τίθημι in *Abr.* 121.

[81] Van den Hoek, "Etymologizing," 139.

[82] In *CE* 2.85 GNO 1.251 Gregory observed that Paul taught ἀλληγορικῶς τὸν νοῦν τῆς ἱστορίας κατανοῆσαι, μενούσης δηλαδὴ καὶ τῆς ἱστορικῆς ἀληθείας. In *Hom. Cant.* prol. GNO 6.5–6, he cited Paul again, who spoke of ἀλληγορία and τύπος in Gal 4:24 and 1Cor 10:11. Paul's allegoresis of Hagar and Sarah in Gal 4:22 is cited by Gregory in *In diem lum.* GNO 9.230, where he also allegorized Laban and Jacob. The Bible, at any rate, maintained its literal meaning, independently of the τροπικὴ ἀλληγορία (*In Hex.* PG 44.121D).

[83] W. Völker, *Gregor von Nyssa als Mystiker* (Wiesbaden: Steiner, 1955), 167ff.

Once more, in the parallels that can be traced between the aforementioned Christian authors and Philo, the question arises—that probably
has not been sufficiently asked by scholars: how much of this material was
handed over by Origen? Ambrose and Jerome depended heavily on Origen
for their allegorical interpretation of the Bible, to the point that Jerome
reproduced, with only slight paraphrases and summarizing, Origen's allegorical treatises. Rufinus denounced this in his polemic against Jerome and
defense of Origen, when Jerome, once a fervent admirer of Origen, sudden-
ly became a detractor. It is noteworthy that Ambrose's etymologies agree
with Philo's in at least thirty-six cases, and in twenty-four cases out of the
twenty-five etymologies that Jerome has in common with Philo.[84] For both
these authors, especially Ambrose, it is likely that they read some of Philo's
works directly,[85] but it is also probable that they knew intermediate
sources, among which I suspect that Origen was especially important. For
not only did both of them know Origen well, but in most cases in which
Ambrose's and Jerome's etymologies agree with Philo's, the etymology
under consideration appears already in Origen and the context is always
that of biblical allegoresis. Origen's role as a major source for Philonic
etymologies for Ambrose and Jerome is also demonstrated by several Onomastica Sacra. These are rightly labeled the "Origenian group" in Wutz's
classification,[86] but have many agreements with Philo. In Ambrose and
Jerome, thus, we find the same combination of knowledge of Philo and
dependence on Origen that we find in Gregory, albeit with a different
interest: the three of them were deeply interested in Origen's allegorical
exegesis of the Bible, whereas only Jerome and Ambrose were also interested in biblical etymologies. Gregory was more attracted by Origen's (and
Philo's) philosophy and theology and his (their) profound allegorization of
the Bible.

Philosophical allegoresis of Scripture was undertaken by Philo and then
Origen and Gregory, who defended the legitimacy of this approach against
both internal and external attacks. For inside Judaism and Christianity
there were exegetes who opposed the allegorical interpretation of the Bible,

---

[84] Grabbe, *Etymology*, 110. An example of Ambrose's heavy dependence on Philo is in
his *Ep.* 55 (from Philo, *Fug.* 132–136). On this see Adam Kamesar, "Ambrose, Philo, and the
Presence of Art in the Bible," *JECS* 9 (2001): 73–103.

[85] On Philo's presence in Ambrose and Jerome see Runia, *Philo in Literature*, 291–311
and 312–319 respectively, esp. 292–297 for remarkable and extensive correspondences
between Ambrose's and Philo's works.

[86] Franz Wutz, *Onomastica Sacra* (TU 41; Leipzig: Hinrichs, 1914). The Onomastica of
this group, e.g. Coislinianum and Colbertinum, show close affinities with Origen's
writings and were assumed by later authors to be due to Origen.

e.g., in the so-called School of Antioch. Similarly, the pagan allegorists, especially the Neoplatonists, denied that any allegoresis could be applied to such a text as the Bible, where no deep meaning could be expected to be concealed.[87] One remarkable exception is the Middle-Platonist and Neo-Pythagorean Numenius of Apamea (Syria), who lived in Alexandria and appears to have allegorized the Bible himself (frs 1c and 10a Des Places = Origen *CC* 4.51). He was known to Origen, as is attested also by Porphyry *ap.* Eus. *HE* 6.19. Moreover, whereas pagan allegorists did not believe in the literal sense of the objects of their interpretation, i.e., myths—so that Salustius in *De diis et mundo* declared that the facts recounted in myths had never happened, but they were mere allegories of eternal truths—Philo, Origen, and Gregory maintained the validity and truth of the literal, historical level of the Bible—an expression of a revelation unknown to pagan Hellenism—together with its deeper meanings.

The conception of the literal and spiritual meaning of the Bible as the body and soul of Scripture, a conception that Origen developed into a threefold division of σῶμα, ψυχή, πνεῦμα in his theorization of biblical allegoresis in *Princ.* 4 (cf. *Hom. Lev.* 5.1), and which was adopted by Gregory, was already present in Philo who attributed it to the Therapeutae (*Contempl.* 78), and then in Clement, as van den Hoek has rightly pointed out.[88] It is thus possible to trace a line of continuity in Alexandria from Hellenistic Jewish allegorists to early Christian philosophers, all related to Platonism, and precisely in respect to a notion that was crucial to biblical allegoresis.

Philo's Philosophical Concepts in Gregory, Origen's Mediation,
and their Relation to the Allegoresis of Scripture

Philo's scriptural exegesis often influenced Origen and Gregory in the smallest details. For instance, the idea that the creation of the human being came after that of all other creatures because God invited his guests after all was ready, in *Opif. Hom.* 132D–133B derived from Philo, *Opif.* 77–78. More importantly, there are a number of important philosophical and theological conceptions attached to this detail, conceptions that passed from Philo to

---

[87] See my "Origen and the Stoic Allegorical Tradition: Continuity and Innovation," *InvLuc* 28 (2006): 195–226; eadem, "Giovanni Crisostomo e l'esegesi scritturale: le scuole di Alessandria e di Antiochia e le polemiche con gli allegoristi pagani," in *Giovanni Crisostomo* (SEA 93.1; Rome: Augustinianum, 2005), 121–162.

[88] "The concept of σῶμα τῶν γραφῶν in Alexandrian theology," in *StPatr* 19 (1989): 250–254.

these Fathers. The result is that the philosophical materials are often insepa-rable from the allegorical exegesis both in Philo and in Origen and Nyssen.

One of the notions that these Fathers inherited from Philo was the infinitude of God, which was the metaphysical ground for Gregory's core theory of ἐπέκτασις, a theory that he drew significantly from Origen.[89] This notion is related to the allegorical exegesis of Abraham's migration from his native land, for which Gregory heavily relied on both Philo and Origen. In *C. Eun.* 2.85–105, Gregory interpreted Abraham's migration as the quest for the knowledge of God, which is an infinite striving and ascent (85–89) directed to the incomprehensible nature of God, an ascent that requires the mediation of faith (90–91). Much of this is rooted in Philo's *Migr.* The reflection on Abraham's faith that counted to him for righteousness echoes Origen's meditations on the same subject in his *Commentary on Romans*, where Origen interpreted God's promise to Abraham as the promise of the apokatastasis, a perspective shared by Gregory.[90] The stress on the charac-terization of Abraham as a friend of God is common to both Origen[91] and Philo, who also applied it to Moses (we have already noticed that Gregory —just like Origen—tended to conflate Philo's characterizations of Abraham and Moses). The subsequent distinction between knowledge of God's existence and knowledge of God's nature and essence is rooted in both Philo (*Fug.* 161–165; *Post.* 167–169) and Origen.[92] The incomprehensibility of God's nature, Gregory argues, is due to the divine infinitude (*C. Eun.* 3.1.103–110; *VM* 2.238), which was already stated, not without some

---

[89] For this idea in Origen and Gregory and its roots in Philo see my philosophical essay in *Gregorio di Nissa*. For Philo in comparison with Gregory, see Albert C. Geljon, "Divine Infinity in Gregory of Nyssa and Philo," *VC* 59 (2005): 152–178.

[90] Origen, *Co. Rom.* 4.2–3, stated that the full meaning of God's promise to Abraham will be revealed at the end, at the salvation of all humanity (all gentiles and all Israel): Quod signaculum illo utique in tempore dissignabitur cum in novissimis diebus, post-quam *plenitudo gentium introierit, omnis Israhel salvus fiet* [Rom 11:25–26]. Per istud ergo signaculum … iustitia fidei quam in praeputio positus Abraham accipere meruit indicatur et pater esse multarum gentium, quod tunc credimus resignandum cum *plenitudo gentium introierit et omnis Israhel salvabitur* … Benedicentur in te *omnes tribus terrae*, hoc est heredem factum esse *totius mundi* … per iustitiam fidei. That God made Abraham heir of all human-ity through faith will be evident in the end, when all will come to believe and will be justified and saved.

[91] Origen, *Co. Rom.* III 3: Deo credidit Abraham et iustificari meruit atque amicus Dei appellari.

[92] Particularly interesting is Philo's late fragment *De Deo*, preserved only in an Arme-nian translation. On this fragment see F. Siegert, "The Filonian Fragment *De Deo*," *SPhA* 10 (1998): 1–33.

controversial interpretations, by both Philo and Origen.[93] In *VM* 1.6.7, Gregory tried to explain why God is infinite: since God is the Good and goodness, i.e., virtue, is limitless and boundless—as Plato maintained— then God is unlimited. Moreover, there is nothing opposite to the divine and so nothing is capable of limiting it. Accordingly, human perfection does not consist in reaching the Good, which is unattainable because of its infinity, but in wishing to grow in the Good endlessly (*VM.* 1.10; see also *Perf.* 214).

A theme related to this and belonging to the spiritual theology of both Philo and Gregory is that of the "sober drunkenness" representing mystical experience.[94] It passed to Gregory in a Christianized form, very likely through Origen (*Co. Io.* 1.30.206 *et al.*). This is suggested by its presence in Ambrose (*Fid.* 1.20.135 *et al.*), who depended heavily on Origen. Gregory developed it in *Hom. Cant.* 5.10, and 13, and *Ascens.* GNO 9.324, and aligned it to his other oxymoronic expressions denoting the paradoxical nature of our relation to the infinite, unknowable, and unattainable divine: impassible passion, bright darkness,[95] and awake sleep.

Another theme, not included in van den Hoek's most helpful catalogue of Origen's derivations from Philo, that indicates a deep influence of Philo on Origen and, then, Gregory is related to human spiritual progress: doing good through fear, which is typical of spiritually immature people, or out of love.[96] Philo, *Immut.* 69, like Origen later, noticed that the Bible leads us to do good either through fear, for those who think that God punishes us out of anger and passions, or through love, for those who know that God is not liable to human passions.[97] Clement embraced the theme of biblical pedagogy as did his successor, but Origen's resemblance to Philo is so close that it suggests a direct dependence. Similarly, the so-called "theology of

---

[93] On the infinity of God in Gregory, Origen, and Philo see my philosophical essay in *Gregorio di Nissa*. A good synthesis on Gregory is Lenka Karfíková, "Infinito," in *Gregorio. Dizionario*, 349–351, with further bibliography.

[94] On this theme in Gregory, Origen, and Philo see my philosophical essay in *Gregorio di Nissa*. For Gregory, with no references to Origen but with rich documentation, see Lucas F. Mateo-Seco, "Sobria ebbrezza," in *Gregorio. Dizionario*, 498–500. For Philo, see Clara Kraus Reggiani, "L'inebriamento spirituale in Filone," in *Una manna buona per Mantova* (ed. M. Perani; Florence: Olschki, 2004), 41–47.

[95] See Brian E. Daley, "'Bright Darkness' and Christian Transformation," *SPhA* 8 (1996): 83–98.

[96] For this motif in Origen and Gregory see my philosophical essay in *Gregorio di Nissa*; eadem, "Origen's Exegesis."

[97] Τὰς διὰ τὸν νόμον εἰς εὐσέβειαν ὁρῶ παρακελεύσεις ἁπάσας ἀναφερομένας ἢ πρὸς τὸ ἀγαπᾶν ἢ πρὸς τὸ φοβεῖσθαι τὸν ὄντα. Τοῖς μὲν οὖν μήτε μέρος μήτε πάθος ἀνθρώπου περὶ τὸ ὂν νομίζουσι, ἀλλὰ θεοπρεπῶς αὐτὸ δι᾽ αὑτὸ μόνον τιμῶσι τὸ ἀγαπᾶν οἰκειώτατον, φοβεῖσθαι δὲ τοῖς ἑτέροις.

the image," which plays a central role in Origen's and Gregory's anthropology, protology, and eschatology, is firmly rooted in Philo's thought, and, once again, is grounded in the Bible and constitutes a chief point in Philo's exegesis. If both Origen and Gregory, appealing to Gen 1:26–27, insisted that the ἄνθρωπος was created as an εἰκών of God and more specifically of Christ-Logos (see e.g. *Hom. Gen.* 1.13; *Princ.* 1.2.6)[98] who moreover has taken up our human nature, Philo thought that the Logos was the image of God (*Conf.* 97) and that the ἄνθρωπος was created as an image (εἰκών) of the Logos (*Opif.* 134 and 139); he even defined the Logos as the ἄνθρωπος κατ' εἰκόνα (*Conf.* 146). This is why the ἄνθρωπος can be an image of God.[99] Moreover, exactly as Gregory and Origen argued, Philo also assumed that the image of God in the human being was properly carried only by the νοῦς.[100]

Another clear indicator of Philo's theological and metaphysical influence on Origen, and afterwards on Gregory, is found in the absolute preeminence assigned by Philo to Logos and Wisdom among the realities that mediate between God and the creation, like the δυνάμεις.[101] They both are

---

[98] See my philosophical essay in *Gregorio* for Origen and Gregory. Origen drew a sharper distinction than Gregory and Philo did between εἰκών, acquired at the beginning, and ὁμοίωσις, accomplished in the end, e.g., in *Co. Rom.* 4.5: In initiis homo, cum propositum fuisset ut ad imaginem et similitudinem Dei fieret, ad imaginem quidem factus est, *similitudo autem dilata est* ob hoc, ut prius confideret in Deum, et ita similis fieret ei.

[99] Another reflection of Philo on the Logos influenced the understanding of Christ in Origen's interpretation of the Letter to the Hebrews. In *Gig.* 52, Philo identified the Logos with the Hebrew high priest who could enter the Holy of Holies once a year. In Hebrews, Christ was assimilated to the high priest—and we should remember that in the Johannine Prologue Christ was assimilated to the Logos. Now in Origen's reflection on the Letter, the assimilation of Christ/Logos to the Hebrew high priest and his differentiation from that τύπος, are fundamental for Origen's demonstration of the universal and eternal validity of Jesus' sacrifice (see my "Validity"). Origen found in Philo the assimilation of the high priest as performer of an annual sacrifice with the Logos, and identified Philo's Logos with Christ. For remarkable affinities and differences between the Philonic and the early Christian Logos see Harold W. Attridge, "Philo and John: Two Riffs on One Logos," *SPhA* 17 (2005): 103–117. For the intriguing relationship between Philo and the Letter to the Hebrews, see Bernhard Heininger, "Sündenreinigung (Hebr 1,3)," *BibZ* 41 (1997): 54–68; Sterling, *Ontology*; Kenneth L. Schenck, "Philo and the Epistle to the Hebrews," *SPhA* 14 (2002): 112–135; Luís H. Rivas, "La Cristología de la Carta a los Hebreos," *RevistB* 65 (2003): 81–114. Both Philo and the Letter place the Logos above the angels and provide a similar presentation of Melchisedek.

[100] For Philo see Francesca Alesse, "Il luogo del *nous*," in *La rivelazione in Filone*, 105–122; for Gregory and Origen see my philosophical essay in *Gregorio di Nissa*, with documentation.

[101] There are 187 occurrences in Philo's corpus: 108 in the plural and seventy-nine in the singular. See Cristina Termini, *Le potenze di Dio. Studio su* δύναμις *in Filone* (Rome: Augustinianum, 2000), who strongly argued for their theophanic nature *vs* an independent

"principle, image, and vision of God" (*Conf.* 146; *Leg.* 1.43). They are before and beyond all existing creatures (*Leg.* 2.86). They are the sources of all virtues and are depicted with the same symbolism. It is surely also due to the influence of Philo that Origen presented Logos and Wisdom as the two chief ἐπίνοιαι of Christ, a conception that, in turn, influenced Gregory.[102] Of course, Origen's and Gregory's idea of the Logos as Christ, and thus God, is necessarily different from that of Philo, but much of Philo's characterization of the Logos is in their thought.[103] In relation to Origen's and Gregory's interpretation of Philo's Logos as Christ, which is also present in Eusebius as a result of Origen's influence,[104] it is remarkable that Philo called the Logos "the first-born" (*Agric.* 51; *Conf.* 146), "antecedent to all beings that have come into existence" (πρεσβύτερος τῶν γένεσιν εἰληφότων, *Migr.* 6), "man of God" and "Son of God" (*Conf.* 41; 145).[105]

---

ontological reality—rightly denied by her; Francesca Calabi, "Tra Platone e la Bibbia: ontologia e teologia in Filone," *Oltrecorrente* 9 (Oct. 2004): 47–59, who saw in Philo the conception of the δυνάμεις and the Logos both as modes of God's activity or sometimes as autonomous entities and as forms of human knowledge; Martin Neher, *Wesen und Wirken der Weisheit in der* Sapientia Salomonis (Berlin: De Gruyter, 2004), 155–163. See also Baudouin Decharneux, "De l'évidence de l'existence de Dieu et de l'efficacité de ses puissances dans la théologie philonienne," in *Dire l'évidence* (eds. C. Lévy and L. Pernot; Paris-Montreal: L'Harmattan, 1997), 321–334; Shlomo Naeh, "Ποτήριον ἐν χειρὶ Κυρίου. Philo and the Rabbis on the Powers of God," *SCI* 16 (1997): 91–101. On the Logos as the principal mediating figure in Philo see Clara Kraus Reggiani, "Il monoteismo ebraico e il concetto di mediazione," *SMSR* 25 (2001): 5–35, esp. 12–21; Marian Hillar, "The Logos and its Function in the Writings of Philo," *Journal from the Radical Reformation* 7 (1998): 22–37. On the Aristotelian basis of the δυνάμεις in Philo see Abraham P. Bos, "Philo of Alexandria: A Platonist in the Image and Likeness of Aristotle," *SPhA* 10 (1998): 66–86. Other Aristotelian features in Philo's thought are pointed out by José P. Martín, "La configuración semántica ἀρχή-νοῦς-θεός en Filón," in *Philon d'Alexandrie et le langage*, 165–182. David T. Runia, "Clement of Alexandria and the Philonic Doctrine of the Divine Powers," *VC* 58 (2004): 256–276, studied the transfer of Philo's δυνάμεις to the Logos. A somewhat more independent relevance of the δυνάμεις in Clement is supposed by Bogdan G. Bucur, "Revisiting Christian Oeyen," *VC* 61 (2007): 381–413.

[102] Both Philo and Origen explicitly identify Σοφία with God's Logos (*Leg.* 1.65; *Princ.* 1.4.4; 1.2.2).

[103] Geljon, *Philonic Exegesis*, 56–58, noted the basic difference in the conception of the Logos between Gregory and Philo; of course it is the same that also obtains between Philo and Origen.

[104] In his *PE*, Eusebius cited Philo a great deal and identified Philo's Logos with Christ. See Inowlocki, *Eusebius and the Authors*. On Philo's Logos as apt for Christian reception see Gerhard Sellin, "Eine vorchristliche Christologie," *ZNT* 4 (1999): 12–21; Daniel Boyarin, "The Gospel of the Memra: Jewish Binitarians and the Prologue to John," *HThR* 94 (2001): 243–284; 249–252.

[105] The question of Philo's knowledge of Christians is open. Birger A. Pearson, "Cracking a Conundrum," *ST* 57 (2003): 61–75, hypothesized that the first Christians in Egypt stemmed from local Jewish communities and some of them might have been Philo's

Philo's notion of the divinity as unknowable in its essence, and thus properly ineffable, but knowable through its activity and manifestation (e.g. *Abr.* 122),[106] is a conception that will be crucial to Origen's and

disciples. I regard it as notable that Philo, while criticizing Caligula's pretence to be called *dominus et deus*, in *Legat.* 118 states: θᾶττον γὰρ ἂν εἰς ἄνθρωπον θεὸν ἢ εἰς θεὸν ἄνθρωπον μεταβαλεῖν. At the time of the *Legatio* (read in the Senate under Claudius according to Eus. *HE* 2.18.9), the Christian message was already being preached in Rome and Alexandria, even though we do not know whether Jesus Christ's divinity was already proclaimed. Paul's letters, which are close to that time, have clear statements, e.g., Phil 2:5–6 (for their dating see, e.g., John Fitzgerald and Wayne A. Meeks, *The Writings of St Paul* [New York-London: Norton, 2007], 1–97, who offer the following dates: 1Thess in AD 50–51, Gal ca. 54, 1 Cor in 53–55, 2 Cor in 54–56, and Rom in 57). Gregory Sterling, "The Place of Philo of Alexandria in the Study of Christian Origins," in *Philon und das Neue Testament* (Tübingen: Mohr Siebeck, 2004), 21–52, denied any direct influence between Philo and the NT, but did think that they both shared common traditions, e.g., the creative role of the Logos. Folker Siegert, "Der Logos, 'älterer Sohn' des Schöpfers und 'zweiter Gott'," in *Kontexte der Johannesevangelium* (eds. J. Frey and U. Schelle; Tübingen: Mohr Siebeck, 2004), 277–294, underlined the closeness between Philo's Logos and the Logos in John.

Another Philonic assertion that was to strike Christian readers is *Congr.* 7 that allegorized Sarah as virtue bearing virtues (*Congr.* 2: φρόνησις, σωφροσύνη, δικαιοσύνη, καὶ ἑκάστη τῶν ἄλλων ἀρετῶν). Philo said that Sarah/virtue εἴωθε θεῷ μόνῳ τίκτειν, τὰς ἀπαρχὰς ὧν ἔτυχεν ἀγαθῶν εὐχαρίστως ἀποδιδοῦσα τῷ τὴν ἀειπάρθενον μήτραν . . . ἀνοίξαντι, alluding to Gen 29:31, which, however, simply says that God ἤνοιξεν Leah's μήτραν, with no mention of παρθενία (of course, in Philo's days Christianity was still far from Marian dogmas, but an early gospel such as the *Infancy Gospel of James* attests to the widespread belief concerning Mary's ἀειπαρθενία, and, still earlier, at the beginning of Luke's Gospel that of Jesus is already presented as a virginal birth). Origen picked up this interpretation referring both to Mary and to each soul in *Cat. Gen.* B 124C: God ψυχῆς ἀνοίγει μήτραν ἵνα γεννήσῃ Θεοῦ Λόγον ἡ ἐσομένη αὐτοῦ μήτηρ, based on the understanding of the birth of Christ in the νοῦς of each believer (for which see my philosophical essay in *Gregorio di Nissa*). The mystery of Mary's ἀειπαρθενία became an important topic of reflection in Gregory of Nyssa, who included the spiritual sense of total purity in his reflections on it, since only the fully pure can receive God's descent into the world (*Virg.* 2; cf. Lucas F. Mateo-Seco, "Mariologia," in *Gregorio. Dizionario*, 374–378).

[106] Μὴ δύνηται τὸ ὂν ἄνευ ἑτέρου τινὸς ἐξ αὐτοῦ μόνου καταλαβεῖν, ἀλλὰ διὰ τῶν δρωμένων ἢ κτίζον ἢ ἄρχον (in the context of the three persons hosted by Abraham as God, ὁ ὤν, accompanied by his two main δυνάμεις, ἡ μὲν ποιητική, ἡ δ᾽ αὖ βασιλική). See e.g., David Bradshaw, "The Vision of God in Philo of Alexandria," *AmerCathPhilos Quart* 72 (1998): 483–500; Roberto Radice, *Allegoria e paradigmi etici in Filone di Alessandria* (Milan: Vita e Pensiero, 2000), 1–35; idem, "The 'Nameless Principle' from Philo to Plotinus: An Outline of Research," in *Italian Studies on Philo of Alexandria* (ed. F. Calabi; Leiden: Brill, 2003), 167–182. God's namelessness in Philo's thought is emphasized by Sean McDonough, *YHWH at Patmos: Rev. 1:4 in its Hellenistic and Early Jewish Setting* (Tübingen: Mohr Siebeck, 1999), 79–84. For the Middle-Platonic background of the idea of God's ineffability in Philo see R. M. García, "La concepción de Albino y Apuleio de los atributos del Dios transcendente, con especial referencia al término *árrhêtos*," in *Arrhetos Theos* (ed. F. Calabi; Pisa: ETS, 2002), with my review *Stylos* 14 (2005): 177–182; and Anna Passoni Dell'Acqua, "Innovazioni lessicali e attributi divini: una caratteristica del Giudaismo alessandrino?" in *La Parola di Dio cresceva* (ed. R. Fabris; Bologna: Dehoniane, 1998), 87–108.

Gregory's moderate apophaticism and "negative theology." This was already present in Clement of Alexandria, Origen's master, who shared with Philo, Origen and Gregory the conceptual distinction between God's essence and powers.[107] The distinction also appears in other Fathers who knew Origen's thought well, such as the other two Cappadocians and John Chrysostom, who also wrote twelve homilies *On the Incomprehensible Nature of God*. The biblical passage by which both Philo (*Post.* 14; *Mut.* 7) and Clement (*Strom.* 2.6.1; 5.78.3) and, then, Origen and Gregory[108] buttressed their theory of the unknowability of God is Exod 20:21. They understood the darkness that Moses entered and where God dwelled to be a reference to divine unknowability. The idea became widespread, up to Dionysius the Ps. Areopagite's—remarkably, an Origenist, according to István Perczel[109] —the *Cloud of Unknowing* and the entire mystical tradition. Referring to this biblical text in *VM* 1.47 and 2.110, Gregory drew a distinction between God's essence, which is unknowable, and God's existence, which is knowable. In 2.163–164, he referred to Psalm 17:12, "God made darkness his secret place." The connection of Exod 20:21 and Psalm 17:12 in reference to the allegorical interpretation of the unknowability of God's nature is already found in Origen, *CC* 6.17; *Co. Io.* 2.172; and *Fr. Luc.* 162. Gregory apparently took the connection from Origen. God's unknowability is also treated by Nazianzen, *Or.* 28. However, Nazianzen, in contrast to Origen and Gregory, did not allegorize darkness in reference to the unknowability of God's essence. In his imagery of light in relation to God and the Logos, Gregory[110] drew inspiration from Origen, whose imagery of light in *Princ.* has been traced back to Philo by Francesca Calabi.[111] Origen, drawing from Plato, equated the Good and the source of light that makes things

---

[107] This aspect in Clement was emphasized by Henny F. Hägg, *Clement of Alexandria and the Beginning of Christian Apophaticism* (Oxford: Oxford University Press, 2006), 236, 251, 268 and *passim*, who, however, did not highlight Philo's influence.

[108] *Bas.* 129.5–9; *Cant.* 181; 322–323; *Inscr. Ps.* 44; *Thaum.* 10.10–14; *VM* 2.163.

[109] István Perczel, "Le Pseudo-Denys, lecteur d'Origène," in *Origeniana VII* (eds. W. A. Bienert and U. Kühneweg; Leuven: Peeters, 1999), 673–710; idem, "Une théologie de lumière," *REA* 45 (1999): 79–120; idem, "Pseudo-Dionysius and the Platonic Theology," in *Proclus et la théologie platonicienne* (eds. A. P. Segonds and C. Steel; Leuven-Paris: Leuven Univ. Press, 2000), 491–532: 516–519; idem, "Pseudo Dionysius and Palestinian Origenism," in *The Sabaite Heritage in the Orthodox Church* (ed. J. Patrich; OLA 98; Leuven: Peeters, 2001), 261–282; idem, "Théologiens et magiciens dans le Corpus dionysien," *Adamantius* 7 (2001): 54–75; idem, "God as Monad and Henad: Dionysius the Areopagite and the *Peri Archon*," in *Origeniana VIII* (ed. L. Perrone; Leuven: Peeters, 2003), 1193–1209.

[110] For a survey of the theme of light in Gregory—in whose writings the word φῶς occurs 582 times—see A. M. Ritter, "Luce," in *Gregorio. Dizionario*, 360–363.

[111] Francesca Calabi, "La luce che abbaglia: una metafora della inconoscibilità di Dio in Filone," in *Origeniana VIII*, 223–232.

knowable, but held that it is impossible for anyone to contemplate it. Philo used the same metaphor to express the unknowability of τὸ ὄν as ἀόρατον and, at the same time, the source of all intellectual sight, i.e., of knowledge. The similarity between Origen and Philo extends to the beams of this light, which in Philo are the δυνάμεις and in Origen the Son-Logos; in both cases they are the main mediators between God and humanity.

Philo (*Spec.* 1.32.50) and Gregory (*VM* 2.219–255) share a common allegorical interpretation of another biblical passage on the unknowability of God, namely Exod 33:12–32, where God says to Moses that he cannot see his face, only his back. Philo commented that God's existence is easy to know, whereas God's essence is unknowable. Nevertheless, he held that the quest for God is the best human activity, even though humans cannot attain the knowledge of divine nature. Also in *Fug.* 165, Philo allegorized Exod 33:23 to suggest that only what is behind God is knowable to humans, not God's essence. Gregory knew this exegetical tradition, but his interpretation is closer to Origen's. Gregory, in stating that this episode has no literal meaning and hence must be interpreted allegorically, directly followed Origen's theorization of biblical allegoresis in *Princ.* 4, according to which the ἄλογα and ἀδύνατα in the biblical *littera* reveal that the passages containing them have no literal meaning but ought to be interpreted allegorically.[112] Gregory linked the absence of a literal meaning in this passage with the mention of God's "back," an anthropomorphism that implied an absurd notion of corporeality in reference to God. This is exactly the kind of absurdity adduced by Origen as a reason for rejecting the literal meaning of a biblical passage and interpreting it allegorically. Also, Gregory connected Exod 33:23, interpreted as a prescription to follow God, with Deut 13:5 on going behind God, and with Ps 62:9 on clinging to God's back, an association already made by Origen, *Fr. Ps.* PG 12.1489B. He did not apply to the expression τὰ ὀπίσω μου (Ex 33:23) the eschatological interpretation that is offered by Philo, *Fug.* 165 and was known to Origen, *Hom. Ps.* 36.4 (*poste-*

---

[112] See my "Origen and the Stoic Allegorical Tradition." Both Philo and Origen, similarly, used allegory to explain away passages in Scripture where God is said to order or perform the destruction of kingdoms and peoples. Philo either omitted such passages or allegorized them, e.g., he interpreted the destruction of the Amalekites as the annihilation of passions (see Louis H. Feldman, "The Command, According to Philo, Pseudo-Philo, and Josephus, to Annihilate the Seven Nations of Canaan," *AUSS* 41 [2003]: 13–29). Much in the same way, Origen in his *Homilies on Jeremiah* stated that, when speaking of the destruction of peoples and kingdoms, the Bible means the annihilation of vices and the total eviction of the kingdom of evil. See my "Origen's Exegesis of Jeremiah: Resurrection Announced throughout the Bible and Its Twofold Conception," *Augustinianum* 48 (2008 forthcoming).

riora mea = quae in novissimis temporibus implebuntur); Co. Cant. 3.4; *Hom. Ier.* 16.2–4; *Princ.* 2.4.3.

But it is above all Philo's protology and anthropology that turn out to be most influential on Origen's and Gregory's conception, especially in his theory of double creation and threefold composition of the human being in σῶμα, ψυχή, and πνεῦμα-νοῦς. According to Philo, the creation of the ἄνθρωπος was double, not in time but in principle (*Opif.* 69–71; *Leg.* 1.31; 53; 88–90): intelligible (Gen 1:26–27) and corporeal (Gen 2:7). The ἄνθρωπος who is said to be in the image and likeness of God is the noetic ἄνθρωπος, since the human being is an image of God not in the body but in the intellect (*Opif.* 69: τὴν δ᾽ ἐμφέρειαν μηδεὶς εἰκαζέτω σώματος χαρακτῆρι . . . ἡ δὲ εἰκὼν λέλεκται κατὰ τὸν τῆς ψυχῆς ἡγεμόνα νοῦν). The ἄνθρωπος-image of God is an Idea, a *typos*, intelligible, incorporeal, neither male nor female, immortal; the human being described in Gen 2:7, derived from a mold, is corporeal, mortal, and divided into genders.[113] The body derives from the earth, the soul from God, ἐκ τοῦ πατρὸς καὶ ἡγεμόνος τῶν πάντων (*Opif.* 135; *Migr.* 3).[114] Such a "double creation" is clearly present in Origen (*Hom. Gen.* 1.13; *Princ.* 1.2.6; *Her.* 15.28; *Hom. Ier.* 1.10; *Co. Mat.* 14.16)[115] and Gregory (*Opif.* 181AD), too, and so is Philo's threefold division of the human being.[116]

Similarly, Philo's Platonizing account of the double creation of the world in *Opif.* 15–35, the intelligible on "day one"[117] and the sense-

───────

[113] *Opif.* 134: διαφορὰ παμμεγέθης ἐστὶ τοῦ τε νῦν πλασθέντος ἀνθρώπου καὶ τοῦ κατὰ τὴν εἰκόνα θεοῦ γεγονότος πρότερον· ὁ μὲν γὰρ διαπλασθεὶς αἰσθητός, ἐκ σώματος καὶ ψυχῆς συνεστώς, ἀνὴρ ἢ γυνή, φύσει θνητός· ὁ δὲ κατὰ τὴν εἰκόνα ἰδέα τις ἢ γένος ἢ σφραγίς, νοητός, ἀσώματος, οὔτ᾽ ἄρρεν οὔτε θῆλυ, ἄφθαρτος φύσει. *Leg.* 1.31: διττὰ ἀνθρώπων γένη· ὁ μὲν γάρ ἐστιν οὐράνιος ἄνθρωπος, ὁ δὲ γήϊνος.Ὁ μὲν οὖν οὐράνιος ἅτε κατ᾽ εἰκόνα θεοῦ γεγονὼς φθαρτῆς καὶ συνόλως γεώδους οὐσίας ἀμέτοχος, ὁ δὲ γήϊνος ἐκ σποράδος ὕλης, ἣν χοῦν κέκληκεν, ἐπάγη· διὸ τὸν μὲν οὐράνιόν . . . κατ᾽ εἰκόνα τετυπῶσθαι θεοῦ, τὸν δὲ γήϊνον πλάσμα, ἀλλ᾽ οὐ γέννημα.

[114] *Leg.* 1.53: δύο ἀνθρώπους εἰς τὸν παράδεισον εἰσάγεσθαι, τὸν μὲν πεπλασμένον, τὸν δὲ κατ᾽ εἰκόνα . . . τοῦτον μὲν λαμβάνει, ἐκεῖνον δὲ ἐκβάλλει; 1.88-90: ὁ μὲν γὰρ πλασθεὶς νοῦς ἐστι γεωδέστερος, ὁ δὲ ποιηθεὶς ἀϋλότερος, φθαρτῆς ὕλης ἀμέτοχος, καθαρωτέρας καὶ εἰκλινεστέρας τετυχηκὼς συστάσεως . . .᾽Αδὰμ γήϊνον καὶ φθαρτὸν νοῦν εἶναι νόμιζε.Ὁ γὰρ κατ᾽ εἰκόνα οὐ γήϊνον ἀλλ᾽ οὐράνιον; 2.4: δύο γὰρ ἀνθρώπων γένη, τό τε κατὰ τὴν εἰκόνα γεγονὸς καὶ τὸ πεπλασμένον ἐκ γῆς.

[115] See now Anders L. Jacobsen, "Genesis 1–3 as Source for the Anthropology of Origen," *VC* 62 (2008): 213–232.

[116] See my philosophical essay in *Gregorio di Nissa*, with documentation; and eadem, "Tricotomia," in *Enciclopedia Filosofica*, 11772–11776.

[117] Οὐδὲ πρώτην, ἵνα μὴ ταῖς ἄλλαις συγκαταριθμῆται, καλεῖ, μίαν δ᾽ ὀνομάσας ὀνόματι εὐθυβόλῳ προσαγορεύει τὴν μονάδος φύσιν καὶ πρόσρησιν ἐνιδών . . . χρώμενος ἀσωμάτῳ καὶ θεοειδεστάτῳ παραδείγματι, τὸν σωματικὸν ἀπεργάσηται· . . . τὸν ἐκ τῶν ἰδεῶν συνεστῶτα κόσμον . . . κόσμον νοητὸν συστησάμενος, ἀπετέλει καὶ τὸν αἰσθητόν.

perceptible world on the second to sixth days, passed to Clement (*Strom.* 5.93–94), to Origen (*Hom. Gen.* 1.2, in addition to his lost Commentary on *Genesis*) and, thanks to Origen's influence and probably also to a direct reading of Philo's writings, to Eusebius, *PE* 11.6.19, and on to Gregory, who distinguished the intelligible creation on the first day as God's comprehensive plan, and the sense-perceptible creation as the development of the intelligible one into six days (*Hex.* PG 44. 72).[118]

Another important conception in Philo, directly derived from his reading of the Bible in the literal and spiritual senses but also owing much to his Platonic frame of mind, is found also in Origen and Nyssen: the twofold notion of death as physical and spiritual.[119] Philo often used θάνατος and the like to indicate spiritual death. For example, in *Congr.* 57, he affirmed that "the true Hades is the life of the wicked man"; in *Leg.* 2.77–78, he drew a clear distinction between the death of the body and that of the soul;[120] and in *Fug.* 58, he described life as ἀγαθόν and ἀρετή and death as

---

[118] For Philo's account see David T. Runia, "The King, the Architect, and the Craftsman," in *Ancient Approaches to Plato's* Timaeus (eds. R. W. Sharples and A. Sheppard; London: Institute of Classical Studies, 2003), 89–106; Gregory E. Sterling, "Day One," *SPhA* 17 (2005): 118–140; Jutta Leonhardt-Balzer, "Creation, the Logos and the Foundation of a City," in *Philon und das Neue Testament* (eds. R. Deines and K. W. Niebuhr; WUNT, 172; Tübingen: Mohr Siebeck, 2004), 323–344. For Clement's account see Van den Hoek, *Clement*, 196. For Origen's account see eadem, "Philo and Origen," 65; Runia, *Philo in Literature*, 173. Runia, *ibid.* 326, noted the presence of this theory in Augustine and hypothesized that he read the beginning of Philo's QG 1 in the Old Latin translation and perhaps something of Philo's *Opif.*, either in a Latin translation or in Greek, although he knew very little of it. I add the possibility that Augustine may have known Origen's account of the creation in a Latin version. Recent scholarship has pointed out Augustine's knowledge of Origen, e.g., György Heidl, *Origen's Influence on the Young Augustine* (Louaize, Lebanon: Notre Dame University/Piscataway, NJ: Gorgias, 2003), with my review in *Stylos* 14 (2005): 194–198. The derivation of Augustine's conception of time from Origen is maintained by Panayiotis Tzamalikos, *Origen: Cosmology and Ontology of Time* (Leiden-Boston: Brill, 2006), with my review in *RFN* 99 (2007): 177–181.

[119] On the bivalence of death, physical and spiritual, in Philo see Dieter Zeller, "The Life and Death of the Soul in Philo of Alexandria," *SPhA* 7 (1995): 19–55; Karina Martin-Hogan, "The Exegetical Background of the 'Ambiguity of Death' in the Wisdom of Solomon," *JSJ* 30 (1999): 1–24; Menahem Kister, "Leave the Dead to Bury their own Dead," in *Studies in Ancient Midrash* (ed. J. L. Kugel; Cambridge, MA: Harvard University Press, 2001), 43–56; Emma Wassermann, "The Death of the Soul in Romans 7," *JBL* 126 (2007): 793–816, esp. 807–809. More below in n. 136.

[120] The context is the above-mentioned allegorical reading of the serpents in the desert: "The part that, in us, is like a random mass, when it tends to the sojourn in Egypt, that is, in the corporeal mass, falls in the pleasures that bring about death, not that consisting in the separation of the soul from the body, but that consisting in the corruption of the soul operated by evil . . . [quotation of Num 21:6] In fact, nothing more than immoderate pleasures brings death to the soul. The part that is liable to death in us is not the

κακόν and κακία. Origen and Gregory also spoke of death—and, accordingly, of life and resurrection—in both the physical and the spiritual senses.[121] When they mentioned death, they often meant being far from God and the Good, in sin and darkness; and, correspondingly, when they spoke of resurrection they often meant salvation. (Gregory's definition of resurrection in *De Anima* and elsewhere is meaningful: ἡ ἀνάστασίς ἐστιν ἡ εἰς τὸ ἀρχαῖον τῆς φύσεως ἡμῶν ἀποκατάστασις, i.e., restoration to the original state before sin, thence liberation from evil and ultimate salvation; and since resurrection is universal, salvation too must be universal in the end). It is important to note that it was in connection with the spiritual interpretation of death as sin that we find in one of the few references to Philo as *quidam ex his qui ante nos interpretati sunt locum hunc* (in *Her.* 201 Philo interpreted the "dead" as the impious and foolish) in Origen, *Hom. Num.* 9.5.

In fact, I found other examples that lead to an important remark: Origen tends to refer expressly to Philo as a predecessor precisely in points that are crucial to his scriptural allegorical method. A significant example is in *Co. Mat.* 17.17, where the inspiration from Philo, *Deus* 52–53, is close and declared (τῶν μὲν πρὸ ἡμῶν ποιήσας τις βιβλία νόμων ἱερῶν ἀλληγορίας).[122] In these passages, Philo and Origen deal with one of the pivotal motifs of their allegorical exegesis, namely the therapeutic and didactic aim of the biblical anthropomorphical language applied to God, i.e., when not only bodily features, but also anger, punishment and threats are applied to the divinity. This conception is fundamental to Gregory as well. In both Origen and Gregory, the didactic and therapeutic function of divine threats and punishment is one of the main premises for their theory of apokatastasis. It is no accident that another close parallel between Origen (*Hom. Ier.* 20.3) and Philo (*Deus* 65)[123] regards the therapeutic and didactic function of anthropomorphic language about God in the Bible. A further example of Origen's

---

hegêmonikon, but the mass of the faculties that are under it will remain in death until conversion."

[121] See my "Origen's Exegesis of Jeremiah." Let me add two examples. *Co. Rom.* 4.5, when Scripture says that God gives life to the dead it chiefly means the spiritually dead (Qui vivificat mortuos . . .: *mortuos hic secundum animae peccatum* intellegimus, quoniam anima—inquit—quae peccat ipsa morietur). Thus, their return to life means their salvation. *Fr. Ps.* PG 12.1549CD, spiritual death is κακία and ἀγνωσία while spiritual life is ἀρετή and γνῶσις.

[122] Accordingly, in Van den Hoek's list ("Philo and Origen," 94–95), the relation between the two passages is rated A.

[123] It is one of the closest, rated B in Van den Hoek's catalogue ("Philo and Origen," 77–78), although similar ideas were already in Clement (see David Satran, "Pedagogy and Deceit in the Alexandrian Theological Tradition," in *Origeniana V* [Leuven: Peeters, 1992], 119–124). Origen clearly drew his inspiration directly from Philo.

expressly referring to Philo in connection with essential exegeses is in *Co. Mat.* 10.22, where he has Philo, *Ebr.* 208–209 in mind. The text deals with Pharaoh who was a key-figure in Origen's exegesis and reflections on free will and providence in *Princ.* 3.[124] Moreover, both Origen and Philo ground their criticisms of the celebration of Pharaoh's birthday in the conviction that the life that should be celebrated is the true imperishable life, not the earthly life.[125]

The last instance is probably the most important in this connection. In *CC* 7.20, Origen referred to Philo as a predecessor, τῶν πρὸ ἡμῶν τινες ἐδίδαξαν, precisely in relation to the basic methodological feature of his exegesis, i.e., the distinction between a literal and a spiritual meaning in the Law (ὁ νόμος διττός ἐστι, πρὸς ῥητόν and πρὸς διάνοιαν). I think that we can safely suppose, on the basis of the present analysis, that Origen tended to refer to Philo openly in those cases—among the many instances of Origen's dependence on him—in which a particularly important aspect of his allegoresis or his thought is at stake. For the most part, these are aspects taken over by Gregory.

Gregory of Nyssa transposed many other notions to the intelligible and spiritual plane according to the same procedure as that used in Biblical allegoresis, a procedure that can be traced back to Philo. For example, he incorporated the idea of mystical wedding (Gregory, *Virg.* 305. 308; Philo, *Contempl.* 68; *Cher.* 40–52). Perhaps more noteworthy is his acceptance of the crossing of the Red Sea by Israel as the passage from the sense-perceptible world and its passions to the intelligible world (Gregory, *Virg.* 274; 320–322; Philo, *Contempl.* 83–88).[126] What makes this interpretation remarkable is that Gregory differed from the majority of Christian authors who interpreted it in a sacramental sense as a figure of baptism. Yet even here, Gregory does not differ from Origen. The idea itself of "passage" is

---

[124] See my *La coerenza*. Another example, in which Origen (*Co. Mat.* 15.3) even mentioned Philo by name and praised him as εὐδοκιμῶν καὶ παρὰ συνετοῖς ἀνδράσι, deals with the good of being a eunuch (*Det.* 176), which indeed played a fundamental role in Origen's exegesis and life.

[125] See my "Osservazioni sul concetto di 'giorno natalizio' nel mondo greco e romano e sull'espressione di Seneca *dies aeterni natalis*," *'Ilu* 6 (2001): 169–181. Likewise, Origen explicitly referred to Philo when he disagreed with him on important allegorical interpretations, e.g., in *Co. Io.* 6.217, where under the epithet of τινες he referred to Philo in order to reject his exegesis of Gen 6:2 that equated the women with bodies and the angels with souls in their fall into the bodies, a critical notion in Origen's thought.

[126] On Philo's interpretation of the crossing of the Red Sea in *Contempl.*; in *Ebr.* 111; and in *Mos.* 1.163–180; 2.246–257, see Peder Borgen, "The Crossing of the Red Sea as Interpreted by Philo," in *Common Life in the Early Church* (ed. J. V. Hills *et al.*; Harrisburg: Trinity Press, 1998), 77–90.

perfectly in line with the interpretation of πάσχα as "passage" that is offered by Origen, *Pasch.* 1, according to the etymology of the Hebrew פסח already known to Clement (*Strom.* 2.11.51.1–2 from Philo *Congr.* 100–106),[127] in contrast with other Christian interpretations such as "suffering" from πάσχω (Ps. Melito, *Pasch.* 46; Apollinarius, *Apol.* PG 92.80C–81A; Hippolytus, *Pasch.* PG 92.80BC).

Again, in these and in all other cases, we should always ask the question concerning the possible mediation of Origen (surely not in order to exclude Gregory's own reading of Philo, which is certain, but to recognize the enormous influence of Origen on Gregory). For example, the idea of the logical sequence in which creation occurs, expressed by the terms εἱρμός and ἀκολουθία, is present in Gregory's *Hex.* 72C, 76B, 145B etc. This corresponds not only to Philo's use in *Opif.* 28, 65 and 131,[128] but also to Origen's use in *Cat. Gen.* B 97BC, where he includes Philo among the τινες (cf. *Hom. Gen.* 1.1; *Cat. Gen.* 27). Origen must have treated the issue to a greater extent in his commentary on Genesis. At the same time, this is a common idea in Gregory:[129] he insists on εἱρμός and ἀκολουθία in argument (e.g., in *De anima*) and in Scripture. These are also core concepts in Origen who claimed that a perfect εἱρμός and ἀκολουθία were present in Scripture and must also be present in its interpretation (a point also made by Philo, *Abr.* 3: τοὺς νόμους κατὰ τὸ ἑξῆς ἀκόλουθον ἀναγκαῖον διερευνᾶσθαι).[130] The understanding that allegoresis permitted the discovery of the "soul" of Scripture, i.e., its spiritual meaning, under its "body" (*Contempl.* 78) is present in Origen's

---

[127] Origen, by transliterating the term as φασ´, attests to the ancient pronunciation *phash* (different from the later Masoretic p⁽ᵉ⁾sah) confirmed by the transliterations of the Septuagint, Aquila, Symmachus, and Philo himself (*Leg.* 3.94): φασεχ or φασεκ. Philo, according to the correct Hebrew etymology he offers, calls Pesach διάβασις or διαβατήρια. See Karl Gerlach, *The Antenicene Pascha: A Rhetorical History* (Leuven: Peeters, 1998), 86–90.

[128] See Aristobulus, fr. 5.12, according to whom the creation in six days foretold the τάξις of reality, although Aristobulus seemed to think that the creation took place in time (Radice, *Aristobulo*, 110–115), whereas Philo, *Opif.* 24 (cf. 26), denied it: τὴν ἀρχὴν παραλαμβάνων οὐχ, ὡς οἴονταί τινες, τὴν κατὰ χρόνον· χρόνος γὰρ οὐκ ἦν πρὸ κόσμου. Holladay, *Aristobulus*, 229, is uncertain regarding Aristobulus' conception of creation in time: "perhaps this is an ambiguous, undeveloped statement of the position more fully elaborated in Philo that 'time' did not precede creation" (*Leg.* 1.8.20; *Opif.* 7.26; *Sacr.* 18.68).

[129] See my philosophical essay in *Gregorio di Nissa*; Jean Daniélou, "*Akolouthia* chez Grégoire de Nysse," *RSR* 27 (1953): 219–249; and Juan A. Gil-Tamayo, "Akolouthia," in *Dizionario*, 49–55 (an excellent synthesis, even though it completely overlooked Origen's influence on Gregory in this respect).

[130] See my "Origen and the Stoic Allegorical Tradition," and for Gregory eadem, "Allegoria ed escatologia: l'uso della retorica nel *De anima et resurrectione* di Gregorio di Nissa e il suo rapporto con la tradizione filosofica classica e la dottrina cristiana," in *Approches de la Troisième Sophistique. Hommages à Jacques Schamp* (ed. E. Amato; Coll. Latomus 296; Brussels: Latomus, 2006), 193–220.

theorization of Biblical allegoresis corresponding to the levels of body, soul, and spirit.[131]

Another fundamental conception shared by both Philo and Gregory is that of the human being as intermediate: θνητῆς καὶ ἀθανάτου φύσεως μεθόριον (Gregory, *Opif.* 135).[132] According to Gregory, the human being makes the invisible world present in the visible (*Inf.* GNO 3/2.77–79) and enables the sense-perceptible world to participate in the intelligible (*Or. Cat.* GNO III/4.22; *Or. Dom.* GNO 7/2.48–49). The human soul is intermediate between the intelligible and the material worlds (*Hom. Cant.* GNO 6.333–334), between spirit and passions (*An.* PG 46.57C), and between good and evil (*Beat.* GNO 7/2.164). According to Philo, the ἄνθρωπος is linked to the Logos through its soul and to the world through its body (*Det.* 82–86), a double condition often stressed in *Opif.* Now, in this notion, Gregory was heavily influenced by Origen who shared with him and Philo a two-level conception of reality that regarded humans as intermediate between these levels. Origen also employed μεθόριον and μετέχω terminology (more than a hundred occurrences of μετέχω in the surviving Greek writings). He inspired Gregory by stating that humans participate in the material and the intelligible world, in good and evil (*Princ.* 4.3.1; *Philoc.* 1.17), that is, in spiritual life and death (*Co. Io.* 2.6.53), and even in the divine nature. This notion is absent in Philo, but is taken over by Gregory in his doctrine of θέωσις,[133] which is made possible by the incarnation. Origen assumed that it was necessary for God to become a human in order for humans to participate in God's spirit, in God (*CC* 4.5; 6.64; 6.70; 7.65; *Fr. Ier.* 28.13; *Philoc.* 13.4; *Ep. Greg.* 4; *Fr. Eph.* 8; *Sel. Ps.* 12.1164.44; 12.1236.18), and in God's divinity (*Sel. Ps.* 12.1165.50). Humans can participate in God, and thus can truly exist, or they can participate in sin and evil or non-being, and thus not exist (*Co. Io.* 2.13.98; *Or.* 22.3; 27.8; *Fr. Eph.* 2; *Co. Rom. Cat.* 25; *Co. Ro.* 3–5 p. 210.7–8). They can participate in the light or in the darkness (*Co. Io.* 2.23.153; *Fr. Luc.* 121e.3; *Sch. Luc.* 17.336.26), in sanctity and the

---

[131] See my "Origen and the Stoic Allegorical Tradition"; David Dawson, "Plato's Soul and the Body of the Text in Philo and Origen," in *Interpretation and Allegory* (ed. J. Whitman; Leiden: Brill, 2000), 89–107; and idem, *Christian Figural Reading and the Fashioning of Identity* (Berkeley: University of California Press, 2002), with my review in *InvLuc* 26 (2004): 361–363.

[132] Cf. Jean Daniélou, *L'être et le temps chez Grégoire de Nysse* (Leiden: Brill, 1970) and Angela M. Mazzanti, *L'Uomo nella cultura religiosa del tardo-antico tra etica e ontologia* (Bologna: Pàtron, 1990).

[133] Norman Russell, *The Doctrine of Deification in the Greek Patristic Tradition* (Oxford: Oxford University Press, 2004); Michael J. Christensen and Jeffrey A. Wittung, *Partakers of the Divine Nature. The History and Development of Deification in the Christian Tradition* (Grand Rapids: Eerdmans, 2008).

knowledge of truth or in their opposites (*Fr. Io.* 10.32; *Sel. Ps.* 12.1552.12). Philo's conception of the participation of humans in the Logos becomes the notion of their participation—which will be full in the perfection of the τέλος—in Christ (under all his ἐπίνοιαι, Logos, σοφία, δύναμις, ἀνάστασις, ζωή, αὐτοζωή, δικαιοσύνη . . .) in Origen.[134] This, in turn, became one of the most important conceptions in Gregory's anthropology and eschatology and one of the pillars of his doctrine of apokatastasis, which—as it is in Origen—is grounded in Christ and his assumption of humanity.[135]

Philo's eschatology is different from that of Origen and Gregory who both were strong supporters of the theory of ἀποκατάστασις, that is, not only of universal resurrection (of all human beings) but also of universal salvation (of all rational creatures: angels, humans, and demons). Philo, instead, appears to have maintained that eternal life was a privilege granted by God's grace only to virtuous souls, whereas others would seem to be destined to perish altogether since only the rational soul is immortal and incorruptible and destined to return home. Only those who have exercised it will survive: "The soul quits its residence in its mortal body and returns to its homeland, which it had abandoned to come to this place . . . another life without a body, which only the soul of the wise will live" (*QG* 3.11).[136] For only a purified soul is really incorruptible: "The kind of soul that is

---

[134] *Co. Io.* 1.33.242; 1.34.246; 1.37.268–269,273; 2.3.22–30; 2.7.57; 2.8.60; 2.11.80; 2.16.114; 2.37.227; 13.10.60; 20.28.245–246; *Hom. Ier.* 14.10; *Co. Mat.* 12.9; 14.6; *Fr. Eph.* 15; *Sel. Ps.* 12.1136.46; 12.1473.12; 12.1481.8; 12.1564.36; *Exp. Prov.* 17.196. On "participation" in Origen and its Platonic roots, see David L. Balas, "The Idea of Participation in the Structure of Origen's Thought," in *Origeniana* (ed. H. Crouzel; Bari: Edipuglia, 1975), 257–275.

[135] See my Integrative Essay 1 in *Gregorio di Nissa*; eadem, "*In Illud: Tunc et Ipse Filius*: Gregory of Nyssa's Exegesis, Some Derivations from Origen, and Early Patristic Interpretations Related to Origen's," forthcoming in *StPatr*.

[136] Cf. *Spec.* 3.206–207; *Chor.* 114; *Sacr.* 6; *Prob.* 117–118. On Philo's eschatology see Francesca Calabi, "Tra Atene e Gerusalemme: Anima e parola in Filone," in *Gli irraggiungibili confini* (ed. R. Bruschi; Pisa: ETS, 2007), 217–236: 235–236; Dieter Zeller, "Philons spiritualisierende Eschatologie und ihre Nachwikung bei den Kirchenvätern," in *Vom Jenseits. Jüdisches Denken in der europäischen Geistesgeschichte* (ed. E. Goodman-Thau; Berlin: Akademie Verlag, 1997), 19–35; Lester Grabbe, "Eschatology in Philo and Josephus," in *Judaism in Late Antiquity* (eds. A. J. Avery-Peck and J. Neusner; Leiden: Brill, 2000), 4:163–185; Wilfried Eisele, *Ein unterschütterliches Reich: Die Mittelplatonische Umformung des Parusiegedankens im Hebräerbrief* (Berlin: De Gruyter, 2003), 160–240, according to whom Philo can be said to have an eschatology only to a limited extent, it is better to speak of human destiny in terms of aretalogy; and also Christian Noack, *Gottesbewußtsein. Exegetische Studie zur Soteriologie und Mystik bei Philon* (Tübingen: Mohr Siebeck, 2000). Philo's lack of interest in eschatology is also pointed out by Gian Maria Vian, "L'escatologia nel Giudaismo ellenistico," *ASE* 16 (1999): 21–34. According to Reale-Radice, *Filosofia mosaica*, CXXIX–CXXX, the problem is intensified by the above-mentioned double sense of "death," physical or spiritual, in Philo's works.

perfectly purified is inextinguishable and immortal and destined to travel from here up to heaven, and not to the dissolution and corruption that death brings about" (*Her.* 276). Origen was also convinced that the vicious soul perishes—for the soul is not immortal in respect to the true death, i.e., spiritual death, as he explains in his *Dialogue with Heraclides*—but he did not regard this ἀπώλεια or perdition or state of "being lost" as eternal since Christ has come to rescue the lost sheep and the Bible announces resurrection after death (οὐ βλέπεις ἐν ταῖς Γραφαῖς ἐπαγγελίαν ἀναστάσεως νεκρῶν;), as Origen insists in his *Homilies on Jeremiah*, on the basis of his twofold conception of resurrection, i.e., it is physical and spiritual.[137]

Why such a difference in eschatology, if Philo's protology and anthropology, even his theology, and his biblical allegoresis—and even the extremely close relation between philosophy and allegorical exegesis, as I have argued in the last part of this study—are so similar to those of these two Christian philosophers?

I think that the explanation must be sought in the difference between their sacred texts. Philo did not have Paul at his disposal or the rest of the New Testament or some so-called apocrypha (which Clement and Origen considered to be inspired writings) such as the *Apocalypse of Peter*, all texts in which both Origen and Gregory found fundamental support for the doctrine of apokatastasis, most of all in Paul.[138] Granted, not all of the Christian Fathers maintained the apokatastasis, even if they all had Paul and the rest at their disposal. But Basil attests that in his days the doctrine of universal restoration was still maintained by many Christians. Certainly both Origen and Gregory saw in Paul (1Cor 15:22–28; 3:14–15; Rom 5:18–19; 11:11–32; Phil. 2:10–11; 1Tim 2:4–6, and many other passages, in addition to Acts 3:20–21, John 17, 1Pet 3:19–21) the main biblical pillars for the idea of apokatastasis and universal salvation.[139]

Conclusions

On the basis of this analysis, Philo's influence upon Gregory's allegorical exegesis and philosophical thought has proved remarkable. More noteworthy is that it seems to have passed through Origen on a regular basis. Origen's role in this transmission cannot be dismissed, as I have endeavored to

---

[137] See my "Origen's Exegesis of Jeremiah."

[138] As is pointed out in my *Apocatastasi*.

[139] Cf. my "Christian Soteriology" and my introductory essay to Gregory's *In Illud* in my *Gregorio di Nissa*.

demonstrate. There are cases in which a direct knowledge and usage of Philo on the part of Nyssen without Origen's mediation is virtually sure. In most cases, however, Gregory follows Origen's modified version of Philo's interpretation or conception, e.g., when Origen transposes some of Philo's interpretations to different objects or Christianizes them. Philo's influence upon Origen and Gregory is profound and involves the main lines of their thought and exegesis, as well as the tiniest interpretive details. In the case of etymology, too, which is closely related to allegory, Origen seems to have played a crucial role in the transmission and transformation of Philo's material, although in this case the recipients were Eusebius, Ambrose, Jerome, and other authors depending on Origen and Philo, rather than Nyssen, who was not so fond of etymologies and was much less of a philologist than Origen.

An important point that has emerged is that philosophy (especially Middle- and Neoplatonism) and allegorical exegesis of Scripture are deeply interwoven in all three authors: Philo, Origen, and Gregory. Indeed, many theological and philosophical conceptions passed from Philo to Origen and Nyssen through allegory. In fact, Philo was the first comprehensive philosophical interpreter of the Bible who read it allegorically. Origen was the first, and undoubtedly the greatest, who did so in Christianity. He was closely and brilliantly followed, in this as in many other aspects of his thought, by Gregory of Nyssa. These Fathers shared with Philo a primary interest in Scripture as an inspired writing, as well as its philosophical interpretation chiefly along the lines of Platonism. Both of them were interested in those works of Philo in which the allegorical exegesis of the Bible is predominant, and indeed they both seem to have employed the same selected group of Philo's writings. What is more, I have shown that Origen tends to expressly refer to Philo as a predecessor precisely in points that are crucial to his Scriptural allegorical method, which cannot be accidental. Mostly, these are points that Gregory will take over.

In my investigation, as the nature of the task demanded, I have dealt with the similarities between Philo, on the one side, and Origen and Gregory on the other, more than with the dissimilarities, which also exist and are notable. The discrepancy to which I have called attention is eschatology (whereas Philo's protology and anthropology, as well as theology and biblical allegoresis, display striking correspondences with Origen's and Nyssen's). I have suggested that what made a substantial difference and served as the basis for Origen's and Gregory's doctrine of universal salvation is the New Testament and its announcement of Christ's work (indeed, according to both Origen and Nyssen the apokatastasis primarily rests upon Christ's assumption of humanity, sacrifice, and resurrection[140]). Again, the first key that discloses Philo's and these Fathers' thought, in either their convergence or their divergence, is Scripture.

Milan, Italy

[140] See my *Gregorio di Nissa*, first Integrative Essay.

The Studia Philonica Annual 20 (2008) 101–127

HEGEL'S RETRIEVAL OF PHILO: CONSTITUTION OF A CHRISTIAN HERETIC

CYRIL O'REGAN

The fact that G. F. W. Hegel is, when all is said and done, a thoroughly modern philosopher—post-Cartesian, indeed post-Kantian—whose horizon of thought, even in its most religious dimension, is determined in significant part by the huge discursive shift away from the ancients encouraged by the Enlightenment, does not prevent him turning to ancient Greece as a resource in rethinking the nature and limits of discourse, reconsidering the normative in art, and imagining forms of life and institutions that would, at a minimum, temper the fragmentation and alienation characteristic of modernity and, at a maximum, overcome and heal it. Nor does this fact on the level of philosophical articulation prohibit a profound engagement with classical Greek philosophy in general, and Aristotle in particular,[1] that goes well beyond his explicit statements with regard to their general positions and their texts. But it does not encourage the presumption that relatively belated thinkers in the Greek tradition, especially religio-philosophical thinkers, such as Philo of Alexandria could play a significant role in his own self-consciously modern, religious and speculative thought. To recall a figure like Philo would seem to exhibit a regression to mere erudition, and import the baggage that most impeded the development of philosophy. It comes as something of a surprise then that in Hegel's various lectures series on religion and on history that there is explicit discussion of the contribution of Philo to philosophical thought,

---

[1] It is not only that Hegel expostulates at some length concerning Plato and Aristotle in his treatment of the history of philosophy, but that these thinkers, and especially the latter, influence Hegel's fully elaborated position. Aristotle is a presence in Hegel's constructive work of an order comparable to any modern philosopher with the exception of Kant and Spinoza. The secondary material on the relation between Hegel and Aristotle is already quite considerable. In English, arguably, the work of Alfredo Ferrarin has surpassed that of G. R. G. Mure, who set the old standard. See A. Ferrarin, *Hegel and Aristotle* (Cambridge: Cambridge University Press, 2001); G. R. G. Mure, *An Introduction to Hegel* (Oxford: Oxford University Press, 1959); as well as idem, *A Study of Hegel's Logic* (Oxford: Clarendon Press, 1948).

consistent citation when the issue concerns both the adumbration of the
Trinity in the thought of non-Christian religious traditions (e.g., Hinduism,
Judaism) and its more adequate formulation in Christianity, and that there
is non-trivial evocation of Philo when discussing the understanding of
Judaism and its relation-difference to Christianity.[2]

Perhaps this surprise is sufficient justification for elucidating Hegel's
take on and relation to Philo. The benefits to scholars of Philo or Hegel are
obvious. For the Hegel afficionados, Hegel's recall of Philo supports the
view of a multi-dimensional Hegel with masterly knowledge of the
philosophical and religious traditions. For the admirers of Philo, it offers
the solace that, whatever the vicissitudes of Philo in Western thought, a
modern philosophical and theological giant thought Philo worthy of his
attention, all the more noteworthy in light of the fact that Hegel did not
extend this compliment to Augustine or Aquinas or any of Philo's Christian
appropriators in the earliest centuries, whether Justin Martyr, Clement of
Alexandria, Origen, Gregory of Nyssa, Jerome, or Eusebius. Focusing here
solely on the benefit to Philo, one wonders whether this kind of approval is
sufficient to construct Philo as anything other than a thoroughly antique
figure. I would like to pursue a more specific line of questioning. In
particular I would like to ask whether Hegel's commentary on, citation of,
and evocation of Philo might be viewed in three different ways or under
three different aspects: (i) as actually affecting or confirming basic Hegelian
commitments to the divine and the divine's relation to the world and

---

[2] The following texts of Hegel are especially relevant: *Lectures on the Philosophy of
Religion* (3 vols,; ed. Peter Hodgson; trans. R. F. Brown, P. C. Hodgson, J. Steward, with
assistance from H. S. Harris; Berkeley: University of California Press, 1985–87), which
represents the English translation of a simultaneous German edition under the editorship
of Walter Jaeschke published by Meiner Verlag in Hamburg. A second major text is
Lectures on the History of Philosophy (trans. E. S. Haldane and Frances H. Simson; vol. 2;
Lincoln and London: University of Nebraska Press, 1995. This is a reprint of the 1894
translation published by Kegan Paul, Trench, Trübner & Co., in London) which is, in turn,
the translation of the *Geschichte der Philosophie* (1840). The German edition of this work
consulted is *Vorlesungen über die Geschichte der Philosophie* (Frankfurt: Suhrkamp, 1971).
This is volume 19 of *Werke*, ed. R. E. Moldenhauer and K. M. Michel. I will adopt the
abbreviation of *LPR* for *Lectures on the Philosophy of Religion*, *LHP* for *Lectures on the History
of Philosophy*. In the case of the former, I will cite the English first and mark it by putting E
before the page number, and the German second and mark it the letter G before the page
number. The recent German edition of *Vorlesungen über die Geschichte der Philosophie. 3.
Griechische Philosophie II. Plato bis Proclus* (ed. Pierre Garniron and Walter Jaeschke; Hamburg: Felix Meiner, 1996), is a veritable gold-mine for tracking Hegel's sources on Philo,
who is discussed over three pages (169–72). See especially pages 421–33 in which Hegel's
main historiographical sources are pointed out, his references tracked with respect to these
sources, and the Greek texts of Philo presented in full.

human being—thus Philo is a Hegelian *avant la lettre*; (ii) as showing that Hegel's retrieval is at once patterned after Platonic Christian or Christian Platonic assimilations of Philo, while ultimately deviating radically from them; (iii) as showing how Hegel's appropriation of Philo effects an important shift in how Hegel understands Judaism. While ideally I would like to address all these questions fully and answer in detail, page constraints compel me to sketch and to prioritize. My central and integrating question is the second one: In what way or ways does Hegel repeat early Christian appropriations of Philo with respect to the view of God, God's relation to the world and human beings? And more specifically in what way does Hegel actually reverse the pattern of appropriation, availing of Philo not so much as a means to validate orthodox Christianity, but to deconstruct and reconstruct it, especially as it is represented by the Trinity. The other two questions will be attended to superficially, because instrumentally. They will be viewed in significant part at least for the light they shed on Hegel's dismantling of Christian orthodoxy with the assistance of a Jewish thinker. Still, I will say something—if only in passing—to the way in which affirmation of Philo, as well as other species of ancient religious thought, functions to support a religious philosophical position in which the symbol of the Trinity is regulative and functions critically regarding alternative philosophical understandings of the divine in the modern period. Given H. A. Wolfson's well-known contrast between Philo and Spinoza,[3] I will note that not only is Hegel much more appreciative of Philo than Spinoza, but uses something like a Philonic lens to expose Spinoza's deficiencies, which in the end Hegel thinks are specifically Jewish. And I will also say something about the way Hegel deals with and fails to deal with Philo's Jewishness; more specifically how, on the one hand, Philo is scoured of his Jewishness in its very acknowledgment and, on the other, how a recognition of this Jewishness effects a curing of Judaism whereby Judaism is no longer defined, as is typical in the texts of Hegel, by a God that cannot be thought and a created world that is as unliveable as it is unintelligible.

---

[3] Writing two volumes on both these Jewish thinkers, H. A. Wolfson saw them as structurally opposed when it came to the understanding of exegesis, the proper relation between philosophy and the Bible, and on such central issues as the God-world relation. Although this kind of interest means that Wolfson does not feature in the contemporary secondary literature on Philo, his two-volume work is still consulted for the breadth of its knowledge of Hellenistic Judaism, its comprehensive grasp of ancient philosophy, and his drawing out of broad trajectories of Philo's influence in Western thought. See H. A. Wolfson, *Philo: Foundations of Religious Philosophy in Judaism, Christianity and Islam* (2 vols.; Cambridge, MA: Harvard University Press, 1947).

Obviously, one is in no position to render verdicts on these questions without consideration not only of the contexts of Hegel's discussion, citation, and evocation of Philo, but also his sources. This is especially important if it turns out that Hegel depends heavily—if not exclusively—on secondary rather than primary sources that construct Philo in such a way that his Jewishness will not represent intolerable baggage for Christians fated to integrate Christian beliefs and ethos with the Enlightenment (an issue for eighteenth century and nineteenth century historiography). I begin therefore, with a discussion of Hegel's texts in which Philo is discussed, cited, or evoked, and then turn to the issue of Hegel's sources.

Philo in Hegel's Texts: Discussion, Citation, Evocation of Hegel's Sources

There exist three distinct modes of recall of Philo in Hegel's texts. These are explicit discussion, citation, and evocation. For purposes of making the connection between Hegel and Philo, obviously explicit discussion is primary (although not necessarily on any other account). Hegel's most extensive discussion of Philo occurs in *Lectures on the History of Philosophy*, vol. 2 (89–96) and occupies about six pages of the German text (*Werke* 19:418–25). Leaving in parenthesis for the moment the extraordinarily interesting way in which the discussion of Philo is framed, Hegel in these pages shows none of the obscurity for which he is justifiably famous. Indeed, Hegel is pedagogically appropriate to a surprising degree. Opening with a reference to the publication in 1691 of a folio edition of Philo by Pfeiffer at Erlangen, Hegel uncontroversially goes on to propose that Philo represents a synthesis of Hebrew scriptures and Platonic philosophy. If there is any tweaking of this scholarly cliche, it is the emphasis Hegel puts on Platonic philosophy functioning as the interpreting discourse. Possible negative implications with respect both to the transparency and authority of the biblical text are not attended to as Hegel lets pass without comment Philonic allegory. Later on in *Lectures on the History of Philosophy* (*LHP* 3:12–13; *Werke* 19:503),[4] and also in other texts from the same period, for example, *Lectures on the Philosophy of Religion*, Hegel indicates quite clearly that he has no truck with literal modes of interpreting the biblical text. In *Lectures on the Philosophy of Religion*, continuing a long-standing practice, Hegel appeals to the authority of Paul's contrast between the letter and the

[4] See *Lectures on the History of Philosophy* (trans. E. S. Haldane and F. R. Simsom; vol. 3; Lincoln: University of Nebraska Press, 1995). This is a reprint from an original translation published by Kegan Paul, Trench, and Trübner (see n. 2).

spirit (*LPR* 1, E 167, G 77). But he also adduces the general hermeneutic warrant about the multivalency of interpretation: the biblical text is a veritable "wax nose" capable of an unlimited number of impressions (*LPR* 1, E 123, G 40). Hegel goes one step further when he suggests that the biblical text admits, even requires, specifically philosophical translation. If Kant provides the precedent for this move,[5] as the work of Spinoza and its Reimarus offshoots in the second half of the eighteenth century indicates clearly,[6] both the demand and performance of philosophical interpretation had become something of a commonplace.[7] While, arguably, there are a number of relatively adequate philosophical translations,[8] Hegel is being consistent rather than immodest when he insists in *Lectures on the History of Philosophy* that the most adequate philosophical translation is provided by his own speculative philosophy, which is nothing less than the telos of all development in philosophy.

Introductory courtesies over, Hegel proceeds to offer a synoptic account of Philo's thought, the structural elements of which are Philo's understanding of the divine, the divine's relation to the world, the status of the physical world, and the status of human beings essentially as knowers. This is a distillation that leaves no room for such important Philonic themes as Law (divine and natural), the practice of virtue, asceticism and its relation to contemplation. Although Hegel is extraordinarily positive here as

---

[5] Although Kant made a number of forays on the this topic, by far his most important contribution was *Die Religion innerhalb der Grenzen der blossen Vernunft* (1793). The new English translation goes under the title of 'Religion within the Boundaries of Mere Reason' and can be found in *Immanuel Kant: Religion and Rational Theology* (trans and. ed. Allen Wood and George di Giovanni; Cambridge: Cambridge University Press, 1996), 39–215.

[6] In the *Tractatus Theologico-Politicus* (1670) Spinoza argued that reason and faith are two completely different discourses with two different functions. Properly understood only the former pursues truth; the latter is in the business of edification and consolation. The famous fragments of Reimarus, which developed further Spinoza's historical-critical apparatus with respect to the biblical text, were published by Lessing between 1774–78.

[7] Here I am limiting myself to those kinds of biblical interpretation which were most pertinent in German intellectual culture at the end of the eighteenth century. Of course, the bible was also submitted to philosophical critique in English deist circles and in France by Voltaire and by Diderot and his circle.

[8] For Hegel, by contrast with the Spinozist brand of biblical interpretation, Kant's *Religion* provides a relatively adequate rendition. It does so for two main reasons. First, *Religion* is characterized not by outright critique of the biblical text, but by a serious attempt to retrieve the true, that is, 'philosophical' meaning of such central biblical symbols as creation, fall, redeemer figure, redemption, conversion, forgiveness, church, and end of history. Second, *Religion* thinks of these symbols as articulating a salvation-history narrative. For Hegel, the 'salvation-history' narrative represents the summary of Christianity, and thus the starting point for any interpretation of Christianity in which philosophy plays a guiding role.

elsewhere in his assessment of Philo, he expresses disappointment with a key feature of Philonic discourse about God. Philo's emphasis on beholding or *horasis* gives the impression that we have unrestricted access to the divine as such. As it turns out, however, we behold not *what* God is—God's essence (*Wesen*)—but simply *that* God is (*LHP* 2:389–91; *Werke* 19:421–12). From the opening bell, then, Hegel resists a fairly constitutive feature of Philo's thought that proved so attractive to Christian Platonic thinkers anxious to protect at all costs divine transcendence. In light of Hegel's complimentary assessment of Philo's articulation of Logos that immediately follows his expression of disappointment (*LHP* 2:391–93; *Werke* 19:423–24), it is clear that what is wrong is a kind of negative theology double faulting. Philo gets it wrong ontologically because the supereminent divine in principle—if not necessary in fact—transcends relation to the world and to human being. Philo gets it wrong epistemologically when he shortchanges human being's noetic capacity, which cannot be stopped short by the divine itself, which is defined by knowledge.[9] Hegel will make a similar criticism of other forms of thought of the Hellenistic period he deems to make the same error, for example, Gnosticism, the classical Neoplatonism of Plotinus and Proclus, and most surprising of all the Kabbalah.[10] This is an error, however, that is far from unique to the Hellenistic period. This mistake is a modern mistake also, since Kant and various species of post-Kantian thought, which include the fideism of Jacobi and the experientialism of Schleiermacher, resolutely insist that the divine is not an object of conceptual thought. In a very interesting deployment of Acts 17:24 in the *Encyclopedia*—one that indicates a direction of interpretation for Philo—Hegel rails against what he takes to be the the worship of the Unknown God, which must be regarded as the anachronism of anachronisms given his view of the status of Christianity as revealed (*geofffenbarte*) or revelatory (*offenbare*) religion.[11]

[9] Evidence of this is to be found in Hegel's references to Philo in *LPR* 3 E 84, G 22; E 196, G 129–30; E 287, G 212.

[10] Importantly, Hegel treats all these species of thought together in *LHP* 2. In *LPR* 3, in criticizing Philo, he makes essentially the same criticism of these forms of thought.

[11] See especially, *Encyclopaedia of the Philosophical Sciences. vol. 1: Logic* (trans. William Wallace; Oxford: Oxford University Press, 1971; repr. of original text of 1873 that translates the 1830 German edition), #73 (p.107): "If it were really needful to win back and secure the bare belief that there is a God, or even to create it, we might well wonder at the poverty of the which can see a gain in the merest pittance of religious consciousness, in which in its church has sunk so low as to worship at the altar that stood in Athens long ago, dedicated to the 'Unknown God.'" For a fuller discussion of these and other similar statements from Hegel, as well as his critique of Kant, Jacobi, and Schleiermacher on grounds of their

Criticism ceases, however, when Hegel discusses Philo's account of the Logos. Hegel accounts for the Logos in the double register of metaphysics and theology. The Logos is identified with being as such (*to on*). Presumptively, this is the reality which can be beheld, the reality to which the mind at least in its uppermost reach is commensurate. At the same time, the Logos is the first-born (*Protogenes*) of the Father. The second form of identification is important in light of Hegel's appeal in *Lectures on the Philosophy of Religion* to Philo as a trinitarian thinker. Proceeding more on the metaphysical than the theological front, Hegel remarks that the Logos is articulated by a totality of *logoi*, which constitutes the basic semantics for every expression of the divine outside itself. In its aspect of being as such and as first born, the Logos is the eternal Logos, or in Stoic terminology, the *logos endiathetos*. Hegel does not explicitly recall the Greek locution, but it is implied as the second element of a binary pair when Hegel speaks explicitly of the *logos prophorikos* (*LHP* 2:392; *Werke* 19:423), the external Logos, which played an important role in Christian thinkers such as Justin Martyr, Clement, and Origen.

I will return to the *logos prophorikos* momentarily, but I want to note another lexical association Hegel makes, that is, the association between Logos and Wisdom (Sophia) (*LHP* 2:392, *Werke* 19:423). In one sense the recall is trivial, since the connection is to be expected of a Jewish thinker of the Hellenistic period. But once again, even the trivial—or especially the trivial—is motivated in Hegel, and serves some broader agenda. The framing context of Hegel's discussion of Philo in *Lectures on the History of Philosophy 2* should be noted. Discussion of Philo, Gnosticism, the Kabbalah as well as Neoplatonism proper is carried out under the canopy of "Neoplatonism." Importantly, in this context Philo and Gnosticism are not only contiguous, but Hegel has indicated from the beginning that they are different species of an original type of "religious philosophy" (*Religionsphilosophie*).[12] Thus, Hegel's emphasis on the connection between Logos and Wisdom is at least overdetermined. It is not simply a matter of pointing to a

---

privileging a divine that is not available to thought, see my *The Heterodox Hegel* (Albany: SUNY Press, 1994), 31–44.

[12] Hegel's organization is influenced in this respect by August Neander's very important text, *Genetische Entwicklung der vornehmten gnostischen Systeme* (Berlin: Dümmler, 1818). Indeed, his knowledge of historical Gnosticism and Neoplatonism comes from this source. It should be pointed out, however, that Hegel does seem to have detailed knowledge of both the work of Plotinus and Proclus. While Hegel does refer to standard secondary sources in the case of Proclus *LHP* 2:432–50), it is evident that he has available to him the edition of Proclus's work edited by Friedrich Creuzer (1771–1858) which was published in Frankfurt in 1820.

prominent feature of Philo's thought, which indicates his own synthesis of Hellenistic philosophy and the biblical Wisdom tradition, or even of Hellenistic philosophy and Hebrew scripture, which as a whole is interpreted as a Wisdom tradition. The connection provides him with a way of justifying or underwriting the connection between the discourse of Philo and that of Gnosticism. This Hegelian reading is continued by, indeed, amplified by, Ferdinand Christian Baur, whose magisterial *Die christliche Gnosis* (1835) proceeds largely on the authority of Hegel.[13] Just as interesting is Hegel's recall of the association of the Logos with Primordial Man (*LHP* 2:392; *Werke* 19:423). While once again this is justified by Philo's texts—the identification is conspicuous in such texts as *De somniis* and *De vita Mosis* among others—again the recall seems motivated, since discussion of Philo's discourse is also associated with the Kabbalah by both discourses being included under the same generic rubric of 'Neoplatonism' (*LHP* 2:394–96; *Werke* 19:426–28). I will return to these associations later, not only because they suggest that Philo is better identified as a species of a generic religious philosophy, but also, and especially, because these associations are grist for the mill in making the case that in Hegel's hands Philo is used not so much as an aid to the construction of adequate Christian thought—for example, the notion of the Trinity and the God-world relation—but to assist in their radical reconstruction or revision.

Hegel also thinks that Philo's view of the operation of *logos prophorikos* in the physical world is worthy of brief elaboration. As he understands it, it is Philo's view that the external Logos informs matter, which is characterized as "nothing." Interestingly, in retrieving the Greek term of *ouk on* (*LHP* 2:393; *Werke* 19:424),[14] Hegel does differentiate between the more Parmenidean sense of absolute nothing and the more specifically Platonic sense of relative nothing, which Plato called *me on*. In addition, somewhat strangely, given Plato's classical discussion of matter and Plotinus's authoritative interpretation,[15] Hegel insists on the *positive* character of nothing. At

---

[13] The full title of Baur's work is *Die christliche Gnosis; oder die christlichen Religionsphilosophie in ihrer geschichtlichen Entwicklung* (Tübingen: Ossiander, 1835). In addition, although the overall structure of Baur's argument is supplied by Hegel, Baur is dependent for much of his content on Neander, who also is Hegel's source for this knowledge of Gnosticism.

[14] Hegel refers to *ouk on*, which connects with matter and evil, later on in the *Lectures on the History of Philosophy* when he briefly discusses Manichaeism (*LHP* 3:17–8).

[15] Hegel shows clearly that he has grasped Plotinus on this point. In his free–ranging discussion of Plotinus on matter in *LHP* 2:422–26, Hegel goes well beyond the precis of Plotinus he could have found in the secondary sources to which he refers. He quotes liberally from the *Enneads*, and grasps the identification that Plotinus makes between matter,

one end, the point is simply that the nothingness of matter is not nothing *absoluter*, a point made already by Plato in the *Sophist*. At another end, it is evident that Hegel is anxious to deny that nothing is privative, which is definitely the view of Plotinus and plausibly the view of Plato.[16] Reading Hegel's presentation of Plotinus's discussion of nothing in the *Enneads* in *Lectures on the History of Philosophy 2* (434–36), in light of his own work, which disavows a privative understanding of nothing,[17] there is a principled distinction between privative and positive nothing. Interpreted positively, nothing is the aggressive other to Spirit, what resists and is recalcitrant with respect to it, and thus synonymous with evil. Reading Philo's discourse on matter in this aggressive light facilitates making the connection between it and Gnostic *hylé*,[18] and helps forge a united stance regarding constructive options to the inadequate views of the Christian confessional traditions and the bland theistic and deistic alternatives.

In due course I will return to what accounts for the phenomenon of blurring between Philo and Valentinianism and what it licences regarding Hegel's reconstruction of Christianity. But, perhaps, it is appropriate to end my analysis of Hegel's longest explicit discussion of Philo by observing that in his discussion of matter as evil Hegel has not forgotten the *logos prophorikos*. Matter after all, evil or not, is what resists the semantic force of the *logos prophorikos*, which alone makes the world intelligible and gives direction and meaning to history.[19] For without the *logos prophorikos* history

---

evil, and nothingness, and understands that the use of nothing (*ouk on*) is quite different from its use in dualistic systems of thought.

[16] Plotinus's view is classically articulated in *Enneads* 1.6, and 2.9 in which he refutes Gnostic interpretations of Plato's texts. This sets the table for Augustine's refutation of Manichaeism, which is conducted over a period of twenty years and which finds its most succinct expression in the *Confessions*.

[17] A classic expression of the positive (and agressive) view of evil is to be found in the *Science of Logic*. See *Science of Logic* (trans. A. V. Miller; New York: Humanities Press, 1969), 437. This is not to say, however, that Hegel sides with ontological dualism over monism, but rather that his view is dialectically monistic: the self-development of Spirit demands aggressive opposition, and it is in and through its overcoming of this opposition that the divine comes to be.

[18] See *LPR* 3 E 88–89, G 26–7. We are not to think that Hegel has the kind of warrant a modern scholar would have in seeing the connection between Philo and the spectrum of Middle Platonists, which would have Alcinous and perhaps Iamblichus at one end and Numenius and Plutarch at another. In his revealing note to the above passage, Peter Hodgson, the editor of the English translation of the *Lectures on the Philosophy of Religion*, points to Neander as Hegel's source for his understanding of the polarizing feature of matter and nothing.

[19] Here Hegel resembles early Greek Christian thinkers such as Ignatius of Antioch and Justin Martyr.

is chance, erring, Abrahamic wandering without conclusion.[20] In any event, Hegel gives a dramatic twist to Philo's view of the relation: Logos is involved in a life and death struggle either to impose or extract meaning from matter. The fact that victory is guaranteed does not for Hegel alter the fact that the relation has to be construed as agonistic. Philo is being read not in the light of mainline early Christian writers, but rather by the Gnostic system of Ptolemy, made famous in Irenaeus's *Against Heresies* (Bk. 1), as this is relayed in the post-Reformation historiography by a figure such as Gottfried Arnold.[21]

Lectures on the History of Philosophy 2 is not the only place in Hegel's oeuvre where Philo comes in for discussion. While for the most part in *Lectures on the Philosophy of Religion* recall of Philo does not go beyond citation, on occasions it extends to a paragraph or two. In every case, Philo is recalled as a genuinely trinitarian thinker: Philo can assist in the trinitarian remapping of Christian discourse, whose trinitarian substance has been stifled within the magisterial tradition of Catholicism, and effectively evacuated by evangelicals and rationalists alike. Catholicism is right in drawing attention to the importance of the symbol of the Trinity, but completely inadequate in its articulation of it as a reality. As with its articulation of the eucharist, the Catholic view of one essence and three persons displays a penchant for entifying when it considers each of the three persons as an individual self-consciousness. Hegel considers Protestantism to have largely dispensed with the doctrine of the Trinity. For an Enlightenment figure such as Kant the Trinity is an *adiaphora*,[22] a doctrinal extra that Christian faith can well do without. Schleiermacher's view in *The Christian Faith* (#170–172) essentially reprises Kant's reason for marginalizing of the doctrine, namely that the doctrine of the Trinity cannot be experientially reduced in Schleiermacher's case to the sense of absolute dependence on a divine whence. For these purposes Hegel does not assume

---

[20] Before his 1824 and even more his 1827 account of Judaism in *Lectures of the Philosophy of Religion*, which seem to evince something like a Philonic understanding, Hegel's view is that Judaism is structurally non-providentialist. See *LPR* 2 E124, G 30–1. Hegel worries, of course, not only whether Judaism rises to the Christian view of meaning in history, but also whether Judaism continues to affect systems of thought that discount a teleology in the generation of meaning and truth. Thus, his persistent attack on Fichte's "unrealized eschatology" and his sometime attack on Spinoza.

[21] Arnold, a Pietist, was, arguably, the single most important transmitter of marginalized religious discourses in Protestant thought until the latter half of the eighteenth century. See his *Unparteiische Kirchen-und Ketzerhistorie* (Hildesheim: Olms, 1967). This text was originally published in 1697.

[22] This is the position that Kant adopts in *Religion within the Boundaries of Religion Alone*. See *Religion and Rational Theology*, 167–69.

with Eusebius that Philo is in the strict sense a Christian thinker—one of the recalls of Philo occurs in the context of a discussion of trinitarian tendencies in Hindu and Jewish thought (*LPR* 2 E 339, G 243).[23] Nor is Philo claimed as an orthodox trinitarian thinker, as with Jerome. Genuine and orthodox are not coextensive in Hegel's reflections on the Trinity. (i) In all of Hegel's reflections on the Trinity there is not a single reference to Athanasius, Gregory of Nazianzen, Augustine, or Aquinas. (ii) When Hegel refers to important trinitarian thinkers, in addition to Philo, he finds no inconsistency in also appealing to Valentinus (*LPR* 3 E 84–85; G 22–23), whose thought is so non-trinitarian that it provokes Irenaeus to stake the survival of Christianity on its refutation. Similarly, Proclus (*LHP* 2:440), who while he articulates his thought in triads such as Being-Life-Intellect and progress-remaining-reversion (*LPH* 2:448), has nothing to do with a tripersonal God of Christian worship, is also regarded as a positive resource for Christian thought badly in need of revision. Arguably, the heterodox Lutheran mystic, Jacob Boehme (1575–1624), is the most immediate resource for Hegel's creative revisioning of the Trinity. His thought comes in for singular praise in *Lectures on the History of Philosophy* 3.[24] (iii) In texts such as the *Phenomenology*, the *Encyclopedia of the Philosophical Sciences*, and *Lectures on the Philosophy of Religion* Hegel criticizes the classical view of Trinity as being inherently tri-theistic since it freezes what in his view is best regarded as a complex unitive process of divine self-manifestation into three distinct entities,[25] and shows itself further incapable of thought by thinking of these entities as persons. It is of no concern to Hegel that the erasure of persons amounts structurally to a regression to Sabellianism, the rejection of which in and by the early church was regarded as a requirement for a viable view of the triune God.

Hegel's most extensive discussion of Philo in *Lectures on the Philosophy of Religion* 3 occurs in the 1821 ms and the 1824 Lectures. No obvious differences between Hegel's treatment here and that of *Lectures on the History of Philosophy*, which are relatively contemporaneous productions, suggest

---

[23] Peter Hodgson, the English editor of the *Lectures on the Philosophy of Religion*, makes a note on p. 340 that the "Jewish" view is a generalization for Philo's view, as this view is relayed by Neander. Hodgson provides cross-references with other texts such as *LPR* 3:277 and *LHP* 2:398–99.

[24] See *LHP* 3:188–216. For Boehme on the Trinity, and its connection to earlier "Neoplatonic" construals, see also *LPR* 3 E 288–89, G 213–14.

[25] See for example *LPR* 3 E 82–3, G 20; *Phenomenology of Spirit* (trans. A. V. Millee; Oxford University Press, 1977), #771 on p. 465. See also the *Encyclopaedia of the Philosophical Sciences* (trans. A. V. Wallace; vol. 3); *Zusätze* (trans. A. V. Miller; Oxford: Clarendon Press, 1971), #564–573 on pp. 297–313.

themselves. Hegel is enthusiastic about the eternal Logos which he understands to be differentiated by logoi, and reserved with respect to Philo's
tendency to relativize the Logos as the divine essence exposed to and
commensurate with—merely commensurate with—the human gaze. Correspondingly, he is reserved about Philo's tendency to think of an ultimate
divine ground that is intrinsically unknowable (*LPR* 3 E 84–5, G 22–3; E196–
97, G 129–30). For Hegel this is degenerative both from a philosophical and
theological point of view. It is unworthy of the vocation of the philosopher
whose ambition is to know without reserve; it is unfaithful to Christianity
as the religion of revelation, that is, the religion in which God is revealed
without remainder, and which in consequence is kataphatic all the way
through. In light of associations made in *Lectures on the History of Philosophy*,
it is interesting that in *Lectures on the Philosophy of Religion* Hegel continues
to link Philo not only to Platonism and Neoplatonism but also to Gnosticism. The latter linkage is made in the 1821 manuscript and in 1827
Lectures (*LPR* 3 E 84–85, G 22–23; E 287–88, G 212–13). The *raison d'être* is
the identity of Logos and Sophia. In the same passages in which Hegel links
Philo with Gnosticism, he links Philo with the Kabbalah: in the former case
in and through the identity of the Logos with *Chokhma*,[26] one of the ten
sephirot or names of God in the *Zohar*; and in the latter case by associating
the Logos with Primordial Man or Adam Kadmon, the figure formed by the
ten names that express the inexpressible God or the *En Sof*.[27]

It is in *Lectures on the Philosophy of Religion* also that one finds an
important evocation of Philo that reflects not so much Hegel's concern to
enlist Philo in a trinitarian rehabilitation of modern theology (which involves a correction of classical trinitarianism), but his interest in modifying
his erstwhile highly negative construal of Judaism. This is especially to the
fore in the 1827 Lectures, which mark something of a high-point of Hegel's
evaluation of Judaism (*LPR* 2 E 669–87; G 561–79). In his revision of
estimate, the gap lessens between Judaism and authentic Christianity. It is
important to underscore that when Hegel speaks of authentic Christianity
he is not talking about either biblical Christianity or any form of Christianity before the modern period. Unhappily from Hegel's point of view, no
narrowing of the gap is required between Judaism and many—arguably
most—of the historical forms of Christianity. It is a constant throughout

---

[26] In transliterating Wisdom as *Chokhma* Hegel is both relying on his sources and
following the conventions of the day. Of course, the more common modern transliterations
are *Hokhmah* or *Hokmah*.

[27] For a full discussion of the relation between Hegelian philosophy and the speculative discourse of the Kabbalah, see my "Hegel and Anti-Judaism: Narrative and the Inner
Circulation of the Kabbalah," *The Owl of Minerva* 28 (1997): 141–82, esp.156–72.

Hegel's thought that not only do the earliest forms of Christianity struggle unsuccessfully to liberate themselves from Jewish patterns of thought, but also throughout its history Christianity continually gives in to the temptation to regress to its Jewish origins in its commitment to a God of Law or laws, in its emphasis on the transcendence of God, in the correlative emphasis on the incapacity of knowledge, and in its view of dynamic historical movement devoid of destination.

Without reneging on his view that Judaism constitutionally emphasizes the holiness and transcendence of God (i.e., sublimity), and that this has ontological consequences with respect to the status of the cosmos and existential and epistemological consequences with respect to human being, throughout his discussion in the 1827 Lectures Hegel emphasizes the importance of the role that Wisdom (*Weisheit*) plays in Jewish discourse. Hegel's intent is double: on the one hand, he wishes to underscore that the assertion of the reality of Wisdom compels some rethinking at least of Judaism as a pure monotheistic religion, or purely as a monotheistic religion; at another level, Hegel's intent is a hermeneutical one. He wishes to insist that in addition to the Pentateuch and Prophets, there is a discourse of Wisdom in Jewish literature. Something more specific, indeed decidedly Philonic, comes into view when Hegel claims, "The specific moments of wisdom are goodness and justice" (*LPR* 2:675). Here Hegel seems not only to lexically recall Philo's triad, but also Philo's view that goodness and justice are not other than wisdom but distinct aspects of it. Hegel's account of this revamped form of Judaism matches up with accounts in Philo of goodness and justice (sovereignty) being powers.[28] The correspondence cuts deeper again when Hegel connects the power of goodness explicitly with creation, and the power of justice with the power of ordering. As is well known, in Philo goodness is identified as the creative power (*poitike dynamis*) and the power of judgment or regent power (*basilike dynamis*) with division and arrangement (*Urteil, diachrisis*).

In my rehearsal of Hegel's discussion, citation, and evocation of Philo, I emphasized the narrow range of Hegel's recall, the idiosyncratic way in which he associates key features of Philo's discourse with that of Gnosticism and the Kabbalah, and the way in which a consideration of Philo as the elaborater of the Wisdom strain in Jewish thought helps modify an almost toxic negative view of Judaism that pervades Hegel's mature as well

---

[28] Texts, which especially highlight this aspect of Philo's thought, include *De cherubim*, *De Abrahamo*, and *De opificio mundi*. While Hegel seems to have significant textual range, our sense of his accomplishment is put in perspective when we look at his use of the then current histories of thought.

as early texts. I will return to these issues again in section 2. But it is time to
ask the question what were Hegel's sources, and if there were secondary
sources, did these sources bear in any way on Hegel's construction of
Philo?

Recall Hegel's reference to the 1691 folio edition of Philo in his opening
paragraph to his six page digest in *Lectures on the History of Philosophy* 2.
This might suggest that Hegel has first-hand knowledge of Philo's texts and
is making some independent assessment. As it turns out both the reference
to Pfeiffer and the general characterization of Philo as a Platonic allegorizer
of Jewish scripture are found in the opening paragraph of Jacob Brucker's
brief account of Philo in *Historia critica philosophia*.[29] Logically, this does not
rule out the possibility that Hegel read Philo in the original. Unfortunately,
however, Hegel's reference to an edition of Philo's works cannot be
counted as evidence on its behalf. Brucker, the German Copleston of the
eighteenth century, at the very least seems to provide the frame for Hegel's
discussion. At the same time, Hegel's substantive discussion goes beyond
that supplied by Brucker. In Brucker's brief account, for example, we do not
find the focus on the issue of the divine, our knowledge of the divine, and
the divine's relation to cosmos and human being. Given that these were
Hegel's issues, it is certainly possible that had Hegel read Philo these
would be the points that he would tend to concentrate on. Still, a comparison of Hegel's précis of Philo with an account provided by Johann Gottlieb
Buhle reveals that Hegel follows this second historian of philosophy
extraordinarily closely. In his *Geschichte der neuern Philosophie*,[30] Buhle
underscores the emphasis in Philo on the transcendence of God, about
which Hegel complains, and points out that, for Philo, it is in the Logos that
the divine comes into relation (or the possibility of relation) with nature
(625) and comes to be cognitively accessible also (624, 633). Buhle also
speaks of the Logos as differentiated and articulated by logoi, and as
theologically specified as the Protogenes (625–7) and Primordial Man (633),
thereby associating Philo, on the one hand, with Gnosticism and, on the
other, with the Kabbalah. All of this is repeated by Hegel in the *Lectures on*

---

[29] Leipzig was the place of publication. There were multiple editions of the text,
which spoke to its popularity; the major editions were in 1742–44 and 1766–67. See
especially volume 4. To underscore just how influential this history of philosophy was in
general, see William Enfield, *The History of Philosophy: From the Earliest Periods: Drawn Up
from Bruckers Historia Critica Philosophia* (Bristol: Thoemmes Press, 2001). This is a reprint of
the 1837 edition. There were four other editions, 1791, 1792, 1819, 1839. This speaks
eloquently to its popularity.

[30] All page numbers which follow are from *Geschichte der neuern Philosophie*, Bd. 1
(Göttingen, 1800). Buhle's discussion of Philo covers pages 622–33.

the History of Philosophy. Hegel's elucidation of Philo's elaboration of the divine-world relation also seems more than incidentally close to what is in this history text which struggles to replace the more established Brucker, but in terms that are very much those of Brucker. In Buhle's *Geschichte* there is a also discussion of the *logos prophorikos* and how it relates to matter considered as nothing—the Greek *ouk on* is used (626–28).

A provisional result: The entire six pages on Philo, then, in *Lectures on the History of Philosophy* 2 could be regarded as cobbled together from these two relatively undistinguished sources, with Brucker essentially supplying the historical and ideological frame for the analysis of Philo, and with Buhle providing a synoptic account of the basic religious and philosophical content of Philo's works. While this appears to be an unfortunate result both from the point of view of those interested in Philo as well as Hegel, we might ask ourselves whether Hegel's unoriginal presentation of Philo might not make a deeper point about how eighteenth and nineteenth century Christians of a rationalist temper and humanistic pretension conceived of the religious philosophy of Philo as having something to say to the contemporary Christian world in crisis. It is at least plausibly the case that Hegel's genius lies less in his deep grasp of Philo as an ancient source than in his clear understanding of Philo as a resource for the reconstruction of philosophy, Christianity, and their relation, and his grasp of how Philo can function critically in a contemporary intellectual world marked by Spinozist, Kantian, and Romantic articulations of religious thought.

Consideration of other texts removes the "provisional" status of the above judgment. The references to the Philonic triad of Wisdom, Goodness, and Justice in *Lectures on the Philosophy of Religion* (*LPR* 2:340, 675), which are grist for the mill for Philo's trinitarian contribution, also can ultimately be traced back to Brucker (*Historia*, 399–400). Moreover, the somewhat idiosyncratic connections Hegel makes between discourses that most scholars would likely keep apart for historical and ideological reasons, by and large also represent repetitions. Buhle underscores the inner link between Philo and the Kabbalists regarding their view of Primordial Man or Adam Kadmon (633). Buhle somewhat indeterminately thinks of the production of Kabbalistic texts occurring later than Philo's work, but it is less than clear whether he understands such production to be a discourse of the second or third century of the common era. Brucker certainly does, and is taken in by the literary device of ascribing the *Zohar* to Simeon Ben Jochai, a student of Rabbi Akhiba. From the way he refers to the *Zohar* and *Zetzirah* in the section in *Lectures on the History of Philosophy* 2 (394–95), it is evident that

Hegel is following Brucker incredibly closely,[31] and is probably similarly mistaken about the dating of the Kabbalah, which twentieth century scholarship agrees does not begin until the twelfth century, and whose preeminent text, the *Zohar*, dates from a century later.[32] In addition, Brucker had underscored the "Alexandrian" context of Philo and the Gnostics without specifying precisely what that would mean with respect to method of interpretation, selection of texts to be interpreted, and correspondence of results. By the middle of the eighteenth century it was a considered opinion in German historiography that the discourses of Philo, Gnosticism, and the Kabbalah belonged essentially to the same family. Obviously, of the two linkages that of Philo with Gnosticism has more intellectual gravity and edge. Gravity because Philonic discourse and Gnostic discourses are relatively close historically—whatever date one gives to the emergence of Gnosticism. And the comparison has edge, since, as it was understood in the period, whatever value may be ascribed to Gnosticism, hospitable relations to mainline Christianity, formed essentially from a community reading of the biblical text,[33] is not one of them.

However enlightened Brucker and Buhle are, they are not in the business of recommendation. Neither Philo on his own, nor Philo in concert with other discourses marginal to Christianity and the Western philosophical tradition, are recommended as a cure for what ails Christianity or Christianly influenced philosophical thought in the modern period. Hegel is most certainly in this business. He is unembarrassed about recommending Valentinus, and nonchalant in associating him with Philo in general,

---

[31] Hegel in fact references Brucker's *Historia*, Tom. 2:834–40, 924–27 in his brief account. To be fair to Brucker, however, the view of the ancient nature of the Kabbalah was one that Christians shared with Jews. While there were some Jewish scholars in the eighteenth century who suspected that the *Zohar* did not belong in the earlier centuries, it took the pioneering work of Gershom Scholem in the middle of the twentieth century to persuade that the work was a product of a medieval milieu. Buhle also writes about the Kabbalah and does so with a little more attention to its dissemination in Christianity in the modern period. See *Lehrbuch der Philosophie und einer kritische Literatur* (8 vols.; Göttingen, 1796–1804), 142–73. As was the case with "Wisdom," when it comes to transliterating Hebrew book titles Hegel follows the conventional (Christian) orthography of the eighteenth century. Contemporary scholars more or less uniformly prefer *Yetzirah* to *Zetzirah*.

[32] There is general consensus among scholars of the Kabbalah that the *Zohar* dates from the last decades of the thirteenth century. The editor-translator of selections from the *Zohar* for the Classics in Western Spirituality series, Daniel Chanan Matt, agrees with this dating. See *Zohar: The Book of Enlightenment* (New York: Paulist Press, 1983), 1–39, esp. 3–14.

[33] One can think of Gottfried Arnold and August Neander as providing the late seventeenth and early nineteenth century bookends of his view. Hegel too understands that the relation between Gnosticism and orthodox Christianity is conflictual. See *LHP* 3:20.

particularly as he advises a trinitarian reconstruction of Christianity. Still, with regard both to solidifying the association of Philo and Valentinianism and improving his content knowledge of both, the text of Hegel's period that proved most influential was August Neander's *Genetische Entwicklung der vornehmsten gnostischen Systems* (1818). From this text Hegel supplements what he has learned from Brucker and Buhle about Philo,[34] and found most of what he knew about Valentinus and the Valentinian system of Ptolemy.[35] Here was the text that wove together as a relatively seamless religious philosophy the discourses of Philo, Platonism, Marcionism, and Gnosticism. This meant that one form of thought could interpret the other, and thus prepare the way for interpretations of matter in Philo that more nearly seems to render Gnostic *hylé* than Philo's essentially Platonic appraisal. What Hegel does that Neander does not,[36] is ask the normative question of whether Philo's thought, in association with Gnosticism, can properly correct classical Christianity in terms of its basic ideational frame and thus assist in constructing a viable philosophy. The answer to both questions is yes. Philo and Gnosticism articulate a form of trinitarian religious thought paradoxically more faithful to Christianity's basic inspiration than the historically given forms of Catholic Christianity, as well as the excessive dogmatic forms of Protestantism. And Philo and Gnosticism also shape something like a synthetic narrative philosophy that represents a cure to modern forms of philosophy that have run aground on the rocks of analysis and the constriction of the understanding (*Anstrengung des Begriffs*).[37] In Hegel's highly motivated linkage Philo comes to perform a peculiar Christian service, indeed the service just the opposite to one he performed in the early Church in which he was understood to be a pillar upon which

---

[34] See *Genetische Entwicklung*, 1–22. Here Hegel will find reinforced many of the same points made by Brucker and Buhle about the divine nature of knowing (14–15), although Neander will also point out that there is a strong apophatic element in Philo's thought: the divine as such is graspable only in a form of intuition that transcends concepts (16). More than these other two historians, however, Neander emphasizes the way in which Philo goes against the dominant Rabbinic Judaism of the period (6–7).

[35] See *Genetische Entwicklung*, 92–143, 157–68 respectively. Neander has a thorough knowledge of the heresiological sources and quotes liberally from Irenaeus.

[36] In *Die christliche Gnosis* F. C. Baur, who is Neander's successor in terms of content knowledge, follows Hegel in terms of argument.

[37] The usual translation of *Anstrengung des Begriffs* is "work of the concept." Although this is still a serviceable translation, and captures the ultimate purpose of analysis as a means towards a productive synthesis, I wish (i) to bring out the literal meaning of *Anstrengung* which is that of strain or constriction; (ii) to bring out the ultimate insufficiency of this mode of reasoning to the extent to which it is being recommended as an end rather than a means. Considered as an end, *Verstand*, whether in its non-Kantian or Kantian modalities, is inadequate.

orthodox views of God and creation are built. Instead, Philo deconstructs Christian orthodoxy, which represents the ossification of authentic Christianity and a betrayal of its deepest meaning. He does so before the fact in that he predates the emergence of such orthodoxy, and after the fact in the reading performed by a religious philosopher such as Hegel forced to clean the Augean stables of the historical waste of Christianity.

Philo Expropriated: Repetition Otherwise

When Hegel enlists Philo in his reconstruction of Christian theology and philosophy, he might easily be thought to be involved in a repetition of Christian appropriations of Philo of the earliest centuries. Although his range of appropriation is narrow by contrast with early Christian writers such as Justin Martyr, Clement of Alexandria, Origen, and Gregory of Nyssa, Hegel picks out features of Philo's thought deemed important by early Christian thinkers, for example, Philo's view of Logos as the expression or self-representation of the divine and the locus of intelligibility in the material and historical world. For Hegel, as for Clement and Origen, in particular, the thought of Philo Judaeus is a Wisdom discourse that bears the closest possible relation to the thought of Plato. Dependent on the admittedly very poor scholarship of his day, still Hegel knows enough not to repeat the fictionalizing of the relationship by construing Greek philosophy as a theft from a philosophical Moses. For Hegel Moses is what we presume him to be, a lawgiver (*LPR* 2 n. 685). Hegel assumes that Judaism is older than Platonic philosophy, but by contrast with patristic thinkers such as Clement and Origen, in his view age grants no rights. Hegel clearly regards Platonism and Neoplatonism to be superior to the Bible, because it is these discourses that render the Hebrew texts both intelligible and existentially meaningful.

As I have indicated already, aspects of Philo's thought found important by early Christian theologians, for example, Philo's understanding of law, virtue, and ascetic practice, never come in for discussion in Hegel's brief reportage. Indeed, they are not so much as mentioned. If Hegel is dependent for his knowledge of Philo on secondary sources that themselves are interested only in the architectonic speculative frame of Philo, then lack of mention of these aspects of Philo's thought should come as no surprise. Still, it should be observed that none of these excluded features would have been attractive to Hegel. Law of whatever stripe—interpreted or not interpreted—made him bilious. Law is irredeemably Jewish, and he excoriates it from the beginning of his writing career,[38] either in its biblical form or in the rationalist apologetic form presented by Moses Mendelsohn in *Jerusalem*.[39] And if *virtu* in the Renaissance sense is sanctionable, virtue in the sense of leading one's life according to moral absolutes is self-deceiving. This becomes a major point between Hegel and Kant shortly into Hegel's career and continues to the end. Hegel believes that Kant's *Moralität* is much closer to the divine command view that it would replace than Kant is prepared to admit. Instead of sanctioning the autonomy that Kant desires, it reintroduces heteronomy and reinscribes the alienation that is its consequence. In addition, the textual evidence is overwhelming that it is an axiom for this son of the Reformation that asceticism represents a betrayal of the essential Christian promise to transform the world into the kingdom of God. *Lectures on the Philosophy of Religion* 3 in no wise differs from Hegel's earliest essays in this respect (E 342, G 264–65). Law and ascetic practice represent misunderstandings of the nature of Christianity, indeed, fundamentally contradict it. The contradiction becomes even more glaring in the post-Enlightenment situation where the demand to transform the world is exacerbated. But given Hegel's own very determinate association of the Enlightenment and the Reformation,[40] the only viable option is to encourage forms of life that are anti-legalistic and anti-juridical. Protestantism rests on freedom, not law, self-determination in history rather than appeal to moral absolutes, supports rather than undercuts economic and political activity, and sanctions rather than undermines sexual relations and marriage.[41] The point, I remind, is conditional: knowledge of non-speculative

[38] The two early texts that critique the legal bent of Judaism most severely are "The Positivity of Christianity" and "The Spirit of Christianity and its Fate." For a convenient translation of these texts that date from 1795 and 1795–99 respectively, see *Hegel: Early Theological Writings* (trans. T. M. Knox; Philadelphia: Pennsylvania University Press, 1971; repr.from Chicago: University of Chicago Press, 1948), 67–181, 182–301, esp. 139–40, 189–200, 206–09.

[39] Hegel criticizes Moses Mendelsssohn's *Jerusalem* (1783) in "The Spirit of Christianity and Its Fate" for confounding stipulation and truth. See *Early Theological Writings*, 195–96.

[40] For an account of the relation between the Reformation and the Enlightenment in Hegel's work, see my "The Religious and Theological Relevance of the French Revolution," in *Hegel and the Modern World* (ed. Ardis B. Collins; Albany, N.Y.: SUNY Press, 1995), 29–52.

[41] The most developed presentation of this position is to be found in the third part of Hegel's *Philosophy of Right*. For a convenient English translation of the German text which went under the double title of *Naturrecht und Staatswissenschaft im Grundrisse* and *Grundlinien der Philosophie des Rechts*, see *Hegel's Philosophy of Right* (trans. T. M. Knox; Oxford: Oxford University Press, 1967; repr. from Oxford: of Clarendon, 1952).

aspects of Philo's thought, which early Christians found important, would not have led to more copious adoption, even had Hegel been aware of them. If Hegel was in all likelihood ignorant of these dimensions of Philo's thought, this is not true in either Brucker's or Buhle's cases; both had access to Philo's works. The exclusion here is a bit more telling, because more Christianly or Protestantly typical. While, arguably, those features of Philo's thought not mentioned are less philosophical and less speculative than those features that are, it appears to be no accident that the features not mentioned happen to be both on the wrong side of the Law-Gospel divide and to more nearly rhyme with Catholicism which putatively emphasizes works rather than righteousness. While obviously influenced by the Enlightenment, the historiography of both of these historians of philosophy does not appear to be entirely divorced from their specific confessional tradition.

Nonetheless, Hegel works not only with a Philo cut down to Protestant and Enlightenment size, he actually takes issue with key features of Philo's program endorsed by early Christian writers. He cannot agree with Philo about the authority of Hebrew scriptures—although to be fair he cannot agree with Luther about the authority of scripture in general either.[42] Still, by comparison with the New Testament, not a great deal of Hebrew scriptures is salvageable, certainly not the stories of the patriarchs, nor the law or prophets. With Kant of the *Religion* (Bk. 1), Hegel supposes that the Genesis creation story might—if interpreted correctly—illuminate some truth (*LPR* 3 E 290–94, G 215–18).[43] So also with the story of the fall (*LPR* 3 E 104, G 40–1; E 207–08, G 139–40; E 302–04, G 226–27). And near the end of his writing career, he focuses on Wisdom literature as having value, especially the book of Job (*LPR* 2 E 139–41, G 44–5; E 446–47).[44] Even more obviously, he takes issue with Philo's emphasis on the transcendence of God and of our ultimate inability to name him. For Hegel, what, from the perspective of early Christian appropriation, represent two of Philo's most

---

[42] Although Hegel considers himself a Lutheran, and consistently links the Reformation with both the possibility and actuality of modernity, he does not agree with Luther on the status of the biblical text, although usually he will not make the disagreement pointed. See *LHP* 3:13–16.

[43] As I point out in *The Heterodox Hegel* (pp. 144–51), the caveats are enormous. Proscribed is any view of the world having a temporal beginning, any notion of creation from nothing, and any sense of efficient causality. These points further specify Hegel's discouraging any view of divine lordship. In addition to *LPR3*, *LPR1* has much to say to this topic. See *LPR* 1 E 230, G 139; E 249, G 157).

[44] The first cited passage is especially interesting because Hegel joins Job and Philo together by essentially interpreting Job in light of the Philonic triad of Wisdom, Justice, and Goodness.

fundamental insights, amount to nothing but cowardly reneging on the basic logocentrism of his thought which guarantees a knowable divine and thus supports the most ambitious claims made on behalf of human knowing.

Of course, to be fair to Hegel, Philo himself does make fairly ambitious claims for human knowing of the divine. In *The Life of Moses*, for example, human mind is a fragment of the Logos (2.134). It is this relation that makes possible the ecstatic relation of the human knower to the divine, an ecstasy for which Philo uses the image of Corybantic frenzy,[45] which seems to be echoed in the "bacchanalian revel of thought" in the Preface of the *Phenomenology* (#47). In insisting on ecstasy, as well as suggesting the underlying deep relation between the divine and the human, Philo appears to anticipate Hegel. Hegel insists on ontological commensurability of the divine and the human, and indicates that real knowing involves ecstasy in that it involves a move beyond knowledge understood as ratiocination (*Verstand*). Specifically, it involves a vertical shift in the order of knowing to what Hegel calls *Vernunft*, and which he sees exemplified in the mystical tradition of Christianity. Hegel, then, endorses the mysticism of Philo and thinks that this is precisely what Christianity and philosophy need in the modern age in which confessional Christianity and its rationalist surrogates have both failed. Hegel, however, would have no truck with Philonic qualifiers concerning the status of the knower, namely, the "smallness" of mind that corresponds to the greatness of the divine object. And he would have no truck with Philo's insistence on God's unnamability. The apophatic lexicon of *agentos, adekasastos, akatanomastos, aorastos, aperigraphos, arhetos, asynkritos*,[46] would have been anathema to the religious philosopher who insisted

---

[45] See *De migratione Abrahami*, 34–35. For a good account of Philo's deployment of this classical Greek trope, see David M. Hay, "Philo's View of Himself as an Exegete: Inspired, But not Authoritative," in *Heirs of the Septuagint: Philo, Hellenistic Judaism, and Early Christianity: Festschrift for Earle Hilgert* (= *Studia Philonica Annual* 3 [1991]) (Atlanta: Scholars Press, 1991), 40–52. Now, I am not suggesting a causal relation between Philo and Hegel on this point, nor am I even suggesting that Philo provides the template for Hegel's fairly indeterminate reference in the *Phenomenology*. This is a characterization of philosophy made by Plato and recycled within the Neoplatonic tradition. It is echoed, for example, by Plotinus. My purpose in bringing Philo into the conversation is that in the case of Philo, the ecstasy of which he speaks is religiously as well as philosophically specified. Whatever the ultimate ranking between religion and philosophy in his thought, the fact is that Hegel links them closely. Even if religious ecstasy is not in every circumstance philosophical ecstasy, philosophical ecstasy in Hegel is in important respects "religious."

[46] For this point and the relevant texts in Plato, see David Winston's Introduction to *Philo of Alexandria* (The Classics of Western Spirituality Series; New York: Paulist, 1981), 1–37, esp. 23–24.

that of all misapprehensions of Christianity, the construal of Christianity as a mystery beyond knowledge is the worst.

There are then, significant differences between Hegel's appropriation of Philo and that of the early Christian tradition. But perhaps the major difference occurs in that quarter where there seems to be most overlap, that is, in the casting of Philo as a pre-Christian thinker who adumbrates a trinitarian view of the divine,[47] and thus a witness for the prosecution in the charge brought against Judaism as articulating a less than adequate form of monotheism. In whatever period and for whatever purpose, in casting or recasting Philo in this way, Philo is essentially baptized. His Jewishness becomes mere convention, and possibly grist for the mill of Christian triumphalism. For Hegel, as for early Christians, Philo's articulation of Logos plays the crucial role in his trinitarian enlisting. It is not simply that the Logos is triadically rendered, it is also the case that the Logos is the self-representation of reality as such *(to on)*. And if on the surface this is more binitarian than trinitarian, for Hegel in particular, it is at least implicitly triadic (trinitarian), for the activity of self-representation can and should be attributed to the Spirit. But one can also say that for early Christian thinkers and for Hegel, Philo's trinitarianism is comprehensive. It is not exclusively focused on the properly eternal domain of the divine, it also takes account of the relationship of Logos to the material world and history. Technically put, a Logos theology—at the very least incipiently trinitarian—refers to the economy as its domain of operation. Of course, early Christian adaptations of Philo's *logos prophorikos* turn out to be inadequately trinitarian from the point of view of achieved orthodoxy, since there is not sufficient distinction between Spirit and Son. The latter is not a particular point of contention, however, and is readily taken care of by thinking of Philo under the general auspices of anticipating what is to be fulfilled in Christian theological articulation.

Hegel differentiates the operations of Son and Spirit much more clearly than Philo's early Christian appropriators. This, however, is neither the only nor the most important difference between early Christian trinitarian appropriations of Philo and that of the German philosopher. A number of crucial differences stand out. (i) By contrast with early Christian casting, for Hegel, Philo's trinitarian articulation suggests that the expression of the divine in the physical and historical world is constitutive of who or what the divine is. God depends on the world as the world depends on God. Although early Christian thinkers read Philo in such a way that he endorses divine immanence at a depth that is not apparent throughout Hebrew

---

[47] Winston reserves particular mention for Eusebius. See *Philo of Alexandria*, 35–36.

scripture, nonetheless, they did not think of this as derogating in any way from God's status as sovereign with respect to the world that represents his free expression. Early Christian thinkers took it as an axiom that as a biblical thinker Philo supported the idea of divine self-sufficiency. Not so Hegel, who in *Lectures on the History of Philosophy* reads Philo as articulating a developmental ontology in which the creative divine is dependent on the divine's expression in or as nature and finite spirit for its self-definition. In reading Philo in this way, Hegel by no means suggests that this was Philo's intention. He acknowledges Philo's express commitment to the oneness of God and his distance from the authentic Christian view of Spirit which requires divine articulation (*LHP* 2:390), while suggesting in his description of the Logos that Philo offers an approximation. (ii) Again in *Lectures on the Philosophy of Religion* Philo is enlisted as a thinker who, far from endorsing the classical trinitarian language of substance and person, puts the emphasis on the articulation of a complex dynamic but essentially unitive process. Thus, implicitly Philo represents a critique of trinitarian orthodoxy, which involves an overcoming of Sabellianism. This is not to say that Hegel endorses the kind of Sabellianism of the early centuries, which is based on the static metaphysics that privileges the origin or ground. But it leaves open the question of whether in his embrace of Philo and Neoplatonism Hegel reinscribes Sabellianism while providing it with a developmental inflection.[48] (iii) Hegel thinks that Philo helps to articulate a trinitarian theodicy.[49] The Logos makes the cosmos, history and time completely transparent, even if only in the long run. This is not the view of Christian appropriators of the Logos theory for whom the enactment of the Logos throughout history remains a matter of faith that expresses itself at once in trust and hope that, evidence to the contrary, life and history make sense. The *raison d'être* for Hegel's appropriation is quite different: Hegel thinks that this intelligibility is rationally demonstrable; indeed, he stipulates that the price of intelligibility is rational demonstration. Moreover, he insists that intelligibility can be read off history from a point inside it. The fact that this point is eschatological does not necessarily bring together Hegel with the early Christian writers. For an appropriator of Philo such as Gregory of Nyssa the eschatological is not purely immanent as in the case of Hegel. (iv) Consistently in the work of Hegel, Philo is cast as a trinitarian thinker of the same type as Valentinus. In thinking of Philo as a trinitarian theologian, it was the furthest thing from the mind of thinkers such as Eusebius and

---

[48] For a discussion of this point, see *The Heterodox Hegel*, pp. 139–40.

[49] Hegel uses the term "theodicy" in summing up the contributions of 'Neoplatonism' while he makes the transition to the medieval period. See *LHP* 3:7, *Werke* 19:497.

Jerome that Philo and Valentinianism are discourses of the same type, or that they mutually reinforce each other. Specifically, it was not their view that the mythopoesis of divine perfection, fall and recovery has any intrinsic merit, nor was it their view that Christianity could adopt this form of thought in the same way it could adopt Philo. Nor again was it his view that matter in any way could be associated with Gnostic *hylé*, and thus come to constitute one pole of an antagonism that would take nothing less than the entirety of history to work through, and even then, or only then, to the utter denigration of matter and history. Hegel clearly affirms what early Christian writers reject.

The linkage made between Philo and Valentinianism gives the clue as to the radical shift enacted in Hegel's casting of Philo as a trinitarian thinker. As a trinitarian thinker, Philo is, for Hegel, as well as for Jerome and Eusebius, a Christian thinker. Although Philo's Judaism is officially acknowledged, whether he is inscribed straight up (as he is in Eusebius's fictive historiography in which Philo meets Peter), or inscribed indirectly in that Philo is thought to anticipate (and participate in) Christianity, Philo's Jewishness is essentially erased, although it remains palimpsestically available. This is what is common between the patristic and Hegelian interpretive dispensations. But there is a major difference. In the post-Enlightenment period Hegel inscribes Philo into the Western tradition (defined by classical philosophy and Christianity) as a heterodox rather than orthodox trinitarian thinker. Philo and Valentinus, rather than Athanasius, Gregory of Nanzianzen, and Augustine got the Trinity right, for the Trinity is process: this process is not consigned to the immanent divine realm, but one that moves from the divine through the world back to the divine. Hegel's view exposes the language of "substance" and "person" to be inherently flawed: the Trinity is neither a substance (or substances), nor three persons. Rather the Trinity is a dynamic movement of divine personalization. At the same time, Hegel's reading of Philo and his Valentinian associates essentially subverts the distinction between the immanent and economic Trinity, which was funded heavily by the distinction between the *Logos endiathetos* and *Logos prophorikos*. In the interest of intellectual coherence and adequate intellectual substance, Hegel believes, we can, or should, roll back behind the Catholic period to the time of Philo and Valentinus. But rolling back to that point also means rolling forward to now. In and through the example of the literally dynamic duo of Philo and Valentinus, we have a critical instrument whereby we can put the trinitarian conspectus of Christianity on a new foundation that will support reason and in turn be justified by it. This Trinity will indeed be speculative, and so much the better for that, notwithstanding what the skeptics have said, what the theists have said, and what anti-trinitarians such as Kant and Schleiermacher have said. And most interesting, not withstanding what Spinoza has said, whom Hegel surprisingly takes to be the contrary of the logocentric trinitarianism that he is recommending.

It is worth noting that in *Lectures on the History of Philosophy*, Philo is treated with considerably more admiration than Spinoza, who decisively influences German Idealism, especially in its view of the God-world relation and the reality of a privileged form of knowing beyond discursive knowledge, what in the *Ethics* is variously called "knowledge of the third kind" and "intuitive knowledge" (*scientia intuititiva*). Even more worthy of remarking, however, is that, for Hegel, Spinoza's weaknesses seem to be Philo's strengths. Hegel is doubtful whether Spinoza has either fully thought through the relation between the divine as such and its attributes (Substance and Attributes) (*LHP* 3:264–65) or the relation between divine attributes and finite modes or expressions (*LHP* 3:269–70).[50] In consequence, the finite is not granted genuine independence. In addition, Spinoza is against all teleology both in nature and history, which for Hegel is to forego even the attempt at a justification of God that is necessary in the modern world. At one level, and in one register, Spinoza is faulted as being hopelessly monistic and acosmic. If he is a pantheist, he is a kind of Parmenidean pantheist in which all of physical reality and history is reduced to appearance. The religious, by contrast with the philosophical register for this, is the *Upanishads*.[51] At another level, Hegel thinks of Spinoza's system as a "Jewish" system.[52] Here Hegel seems to think of Spinoza in terms that anticipate the contemporary French reading of Spinoza by Gilles Deleuze.[53] The Logos—or its structural equivalent the divine Attributes—does not, and cannot get a hold in the world. The world is or remains a world of flux; of energies without rhyme or reason.

This latter view, the "Jewish" view, which is in tension with Hegel's monistic reading of Spinoza, presents a parallel to the wandering of Abraham in the desert which early on Hegel thought represented the summary key of Judaism.[54] There has, however, been an important shift in key. In his

[50] Hegel is much more pointed in the *Die Wissenschaft der Logik* (1812). For a convenient English translation, see *Science of Logic* (trans. A. V. Miller; New York: Humanities Press, 1969). (Translation is from the rev. edition of 1832). See especially, 328–29.

[51] See *Encyclopaedia* 3 # 573 for this discussion.

[52] See especially *Encyclopaedia* 1 #151 and *Zusatz*, *LPR* 2 E 124, G 30.

[53] See Gilles Deleuze, *Expression in Philosophy: Spinoza* (trans. Martin Joughin; New York: Zone Books, 1990), esp. 325–54.

[54] For Hegel's account of Abraham, see "The Spirit of Christianity and its Fate," in *Early Theological Writings*, 186–87

early dismissal of Judaism the key of the Abrahamic trope is existential and epistemological, and so it goes with deficiency. Abrahamic nomadism (faith) is servile, alienated, and hopeless, while providing a kind of blueprint for the "unhappy consciousness" of Christianity. In such mature texts as the *Encyclopedia* and *Lectures on the Philosophy of Religion*, however, the key is ontological, and thus deficiency has to do with the fundamental conception of reality. Notwithstanding the critical-rationalist stance Spinoza adopts towards his ancestral religion, in thinking of the material world as expressing the divine (modes and attributes) outside the ordinance of the good, Spinoza's metaphysics represents the functional equivalent of Abrahamic wandering. There is no sense of an ending; no way in which the manifestation of the divine flows back into the divine and constitutes what it is. Also there is no acknowledgment of evil in the world, and what might constitute its objective redemption, other than a recommendation for change in point of view, indeed, a change from the situation of point of view to that of the non-perspectivalism of eternity. In short, there is then in Spinoza, no prospect for thinking a trinitarian narrative of the divine. Only this narrative—of which Philo at least provides a sketch—can account for the vicissitudes of history and human existence. This Jewish nomadism can and should be resisted. Hegel resists it in his own name; but he also has precursors. He has Philo as a precursor. He also has Valentinus. Both are genuinely trinitarian thinkers, thus genuinely Christian thinkers. And this means by Hegelian logic, that both are heterodox Christian thinkers.[55] Philo, the heterodox trinitarian thinker exposes Spinoza's Jewish deficiencies. Spinoza is hoisted on his own critical petard regarding the Jewish tradition, as he is named and maimed as Jew by none other than Philo Judaeus.

But what about Philo's Jewishness? Does not Hegel refer to Philo, after Brucker and Buhle, as Philo Judaeus? More importantly, what about the modification effected on both the description and evaluation of Judaism in the 1827 *Lectures on the Philosophy of Religion*? This presents the most striking evidence in Hegel's texts that Philo is being taken seriously as a specifically Jewish thinker, that is, a thinker who vouchsafes and is continuous with biblical Judaism. Clearly, the Jewishness of Philo functions for the most part in Hegel—and in the historiography upon which he relies—as a simple convention, a means of marking off Philo from other Platonic thinkers of the first few centuries. This is certainly the case in his six page

---

[55] See *LHP* 3:17 where Hegel speaks explicitly of Gnosticism being heterodox, while it offers a "speculative" version of Christianity. In Hegel's language "speculative," while always esoteric, is also always understood positively.

account in *Lectures on the History of Philosophy* 2. There the Philonic triad of wisdom, goodness and justice are now viewed as central to Judaism's view of God and the relation to the world. This means that Judaism can no longer be defined as a religion of pure transcendence and thus as a religion of alienation. Importantly, Hegel realizes that the commitment to this triad, which parses the Logos, does not in itself knock out of action the symbol of creation that emphasizes the separateness of finite from the infinite. Separation can be affirmed, not ontological cleavage. This emphasis, which presumably Philo supported, is necessary if one is to obviate the kind of pantheism that one finds in Indian religion, but also in Spinoza to the extent to which he gravitates toward the pantheist rather than naturalist pole. Needless to say, for Hegel, Judaism will never adequately understand providence, specifically how the Logos functions in the physical world and history. This is an achievement of Christian thought, Christian trinitarian thought in particular.

To the extent to which Philo articulates a logocentric trinitarianism, he necessarily transcends the religion to which he pledges allegiance, and modifies it from within. Essentially outside Judaism, then, Philo can be regarded as conditionally inside. As inside, he functions as a trojan horse: he modifies biblical Judaism in just those ways that Judaism can be seen in its dynamic movement whereby it transcends itself into Christianity. But it turns out Judaism transcends itself not into that form of Christianity that receives its summary in the orthodox rendition of the Trinity in both its immanent and economic aspects. The form of Christianity to which Philo's form of Judaism points is other than orthodox; it is that which orthodox Christianity did not quite reach, or what it either repressed or left behind. Philo with Valentinus is Christian. With Valentinus Philo is a better Christian than, for example, Origen or Augustine. But Philo is so only as he is heterodox. The scouring of orthodox Christianity recommended by Hegel is dependent upon recovering the traces of Philo of Alexandria, who is scoured of his Jewishness only then to scour Judaism and the Jewish remains in Christianity. In an act of Christian repossession of Philo, in Hegel's hands Philo becomes a significant trinitarian Christian heretic who will lead Christianity towards its proper definition.

University of Notre Dame

The Studia Philonica Annual 20 (2008) 129–131

SPECIAL SECTION

PHILO'S *DE ABRAHAMO*

INTRODUCTION

GREGORY E. STERLING

The place of the ancestors (or patriarchs) of Israel presented a challenge for ancient interpreters of Israel's sacred writings. On the one hand, they were Israel's ancestors. For example, Philo called Abraham the "founder of the nation."[1] They were unambiguously part of the story of Israel. On the other hand, they lived long before the law was given through Moses. How did they relate to the law? Philo, like the rabbis after him, offered an intriguing solution: they were embodied law. For Philo the ancestors lived the law before there was a written copy of the law. While the exact relationship between the written code and the unwritten natural law is a subject of some debate,[2] Philo was unambiguous about his understanding that the ancestors were the archetypes of the laws. In this way they demonstrated that the law was in harmony with nature and that it was possible to keep the law without a written copy.[3]

Philo organized the ancestors into two triads. Each ancestor represented a different aspect of virtue. The first triad consisted of Enos who represents "hope," Enoch who represents "repentance," and Noah who represents "perfection" (as well as "rest" and "justice").[4] The Torah exegete had an exegetical basis for each identification. He interpreted Enos as "hope" (ἐλπίς) because the translators of the LXX rendered Gen 4:26 ("then he

---

[1] Philo, *Abr.* 276.

[2] On the relationship between written and natural law or law and nature see the essays in *SPhA* 15 (2003): 1-99. The last full discussion is J. W. Martens, *One God, One Law: Philo of Alexandria on the Mosaic and Greco-Roman Law* (Studies in Philo of Alexandria and Mediterranean Antiquity 2; Leiden: Brill, 2003), esp. 83-130.

[3] Philo, *Abr.* 1-6.

[4] For details see Philo, *Abr.* 7-47 and *Praem.* 7-23.

began to call on the name of the LORD" [MT]) as "he hoped (ἤλπισεν) to call on the name of the LORD God." Similarly, the LXX's version of Gen 5:24 provided a basis for his identification of Enoch with repentance. MT reads: "Enoch walked with God and was no more because God took him." The LXX has: "Enoch pleased God and was not found because God transferred him." Philo reversed the two clauses and understood "transferred" (μετέθηκεν) to refer to repentance (μετάνοια) since "transferred" implies that he turned and changed for the better. Enoch's repentance was thus the basis for his being taken by God. Noah's perfection is stated in the biblical text, "Noah was a just person and was perfect (τέλειος) in his generation" (Gen 6:9). This identification permitted Philo to mark a development from repentance to perfection.

The second triad was fuller and more elaborate. As with the first triad, Philo identified the ancestors with virtues.[5] However, with the second triad he based his interpretation of each ancestor not only on specific biblical statements but on the larger narrative about their life. In keeping with his distinctive allegorical reading of Genesis, he understood each ancestor to be a type of soul. Their lives illuminated the path by which such types of souls could acquire virtue. Abraham represented virtue learned through instruction since he abandoned the polytheism of his ancestors. Isaac represented native virtue, i.e., he was born virtuous. Jacob, the practiser, acquired virtue through practice. Unfortunately, the *bioi* on Isaac[6] and Jacob[7] have been lost. We are, however, fortunate to have the *bios* on Abraham.

Philo's *De Abrahamo* is important for multiple reasons. At the broadest level, it is an invaluable representative of the *bios* tradition in a Jewish setting.[8] More specifically, it is the only life of an ancestor that we have from either of the two triads and permits us to understand how Philo read the Genesis stories of his ancestors. While we also have his *De Iosepho* in the same series and the *De vita Moysis* that serves as an introduction for all of the commentary series, Philo understood the former to be the life of a politician and the latter to be *sui generis*. This puts a premium on the *De Abrahamo* as an example of how Philo related the life of Israel's ancestors to virtue. One of the most intriguing aspects of his reading of the text is his alternation between literal and allegorical readings. Normally we associate

---

[5] For the ancestors as symbols of virtue see *Sobr.* 65; *Congr.* 34-38; *Mut.* 12, 88; *Somn.* 1.168; *Abr.* 52-54; *Ios.* 1; *Mos.* 1.76; *Praem.* 24-51, 57-66.

[6] Philo refers to it in *Sobr.* 9; *Ios.* 1; *Decal.* 1.

[7] Philo refers to it in *Ios.* 1; *Decal.* 1.

[8] For a list of ancient *bioi* see K. Berger, "Hellenistische Gattungen im Neuen Testament," *ANRW* 2.25.2:1232-36.

this technique with the *Quaestiones in Genesin et in Exodum*. The Alexandrian has, however, used the same alternating sequence with good effect in this life.

For these and other reasons, it is important to develop an understanding of the treatise. The following two articles provide important introductory material for an understanding of the treatise. In recent years, the Philo of Alexandria Group of the Society of Biblical Literature has devoted a session to a treatise of Philo on which a member of the group is writing a commentary for the Philo of Alexandria Commentary Series. The papers are intended to provide assistance with aspects of the text that the author of the commentary might find useful. John Dillon is currently working on a commentary on *De Abrahamo*. The two conveners of the Society of Biblical Literature Philo of Alexandria Group, Hindy Najman and David T. Runia, invited a number of scholars to present papers on *De Abrahamo* to assist Professor Dillon. We have selected two of the papers that addressed the Philonic material directly for inclusion in this year's annual. Jim Royse is the leading textual critic on Philo of Alexandria. David Runia, the co-editor of this annual, has been a leading Philonist for the past two decades. Royse points out the need to work beyond the standard critical edition of Cohn-Wendland. Runia explores the place of the treatise in the Exposition of the Law, a topic that deserves more treatment than it has previously received. Together they provide a solid introduction to the treatise and hopefully lay the groundwork for the commentary to follow.

University of Notre Dame

The Studia Philonica Annual 20 (2008) 133–150

THE PLACE OF *DE ABRAHAMO* IN PHILO'S *ŒUVRE*[*]

DAVID T. RUNIA

1. Introduction
2. The place of *De Abrahamo* in editions and translations
3. Formal features of *De Abrahamo*
4. Comparisons between *De opificio mundi* and *De Abrahamo*
5. Thematic connections between *De opificio mundi* and *De Abrahamo*
6. The place of *De Abrahamo* in the Exposition of the Law

1. *Introduction*

Philo's treatise *De Abrahamo* is one of his better known works. As part of the major sequence of treatises called by modern scholars "The Exposition of the Law," it is well attested in the manuscript tradition and is also preserved in a complete Armenian translation.[1] Although apparently relatively little used by the Church fathers,[2] its vivid accounts of the life and virtues of the Patriarch Abraham have found many readers in more recent times. It has been translated into seven modern languages.[3] Ten extracts are included in David Winston's fine anthology of Philonic passages.[4] But regrettably up to now a detailed commentary on the work is lacking.

The object of the present paper is to shed light on the treatise by examining its place in Philo's *œuvre*. I shall first draw attention to the misleading placement it has received in almost all existing editions and

---

[*] My thanks to Ellen Birnbaum and David Winston for reading the version presented at the Conference and their constructive comments.

[1] On the transmission of the work see further the article by J. R. Royse in this volume.

[2] There are only ten references to Patristic works that make reference to *Abr.* in the apparatus of PCW; see the Index in D. T. Runia, *Philo & the Church Fathers: A Collection of Papers* (VCSup 32; Leiden: Brill, 1995), 240–249.

[3] English, French, German, Italian, Spanish, Catalonian and Hebrew; for full details see the references in R-R 417, RRS 381.

[4] D. Winston (ed.), *Philo of Alexandria: The Contemplative Life, The Giants and Selections* (The Classics of Western Spirituality; New York: Paulist Press, 1981), see 163, 178, 198, 221, 222 (2), 235, 245, 246, 262.

translations of Philo's works. Then, as essential background for the remainder of the paper, I shall devote some brief words to the formal features of the treatise. This will allow us to compare the treatise with the work that immediately precedes it in the Exposition of the Law, the *De opificio mundi*, both from the formal and the thematic point of view. Finally the more general subject of the treatise's place in the entire series of writings will be examined.

2. *The place of* De Abrahamo *in editions and translations*

It is a well-known fact that in all the more commonly used complete editions and translations of Philo's works the treatise *De Abrahamo* is placed somewhere in the middle, in contrast to *Opif.* which is always placed at the beginning together with the first treatises of the Allegorical Commentary. In Mangey's great edition it is the first treatise in the second of the two volumes.[5] In Cohn and Wendland's critical edition it is the first treatise in the fourth of the six volumes of text.[6] In the Loeb edition it is the first treatise of the sixth of the ten volumes containing the texts surviving in Greek.[7] In the Revised Yonge single volume English translation it commences on page 411 of 861 pages in total.[8] In the Lyons French translation it is volume 20 of the total of thirty-eight volumes.[9] The only exception is the German translation which was commenced in 1909 and not completed until 1964.[10] In his foreword to the very first volume the founding editor Leopold Cohn gives us valuable information on how he came to deviate from the order adopted in his own critical edition:[11]

---

[5] T. Mangey, ed., *Philonis Judaei opera quae reperiri potuerunt omnia* (2 vols.; London: William Bowyer, 1742), *Abr.* in vol. 2:1–40; cf. *Opif.* in vol. 1:1–42.

[6] L. Cohn and P. Wendland, eds., *Philonis Alexandrini opera quae supersunt* (6 vols.; Berlin: Georg Reimer, 1896–1915), *Abr.* in vol. 4:1–60; cf. *Opif.* in vol. 1:1–60.

[7] F. H. Colson, G. H. Whitaker, J. W. Earp and R. Marcus, eds., *Philo of Alexandria* (10 vols. and two supplementary vols.; Loeb Classical Library; Cambridge, Mass.: Harvard University Press, 1929–62), *Abr.* in vol. 6:1–134; cf. *Opif.* in vol. 1:1–137.

[8] C. D. Yonge, *The Works of Philo Complete and Unabridged, with a Foreword by D. M. Scholer* (Peabody, MA: Hendrickson Publishers, 1993), *Abr.* 411–34; cf. *Opif.* 3–24.

[9] J. Gorez, ed., *De Abrahamo* (Les Œuvres de Philon d'Alexandrie 20; Paris: Éditions du Cerf 1966); cf. R. Arnaldez, *Philon d'Alexandrie De opificio mundi* (Les Œuvres de Philon d'Alexandrie 1; Paris: Éditions du Cerf, 1961).

[10] L. Cohn, I. Heinemann, M. Adler, and W. Theiler, eds., *Philo von Alexandria: Die Werke in Deutscher Übersetzung* (7 vols.; Breslau–Berlin: Marcus Verlag–De Gruyter, 1909–64), *Abr.* in vol. 1:91–152; cf. *Opif.* in vol. 1:23–89.

[11] L. Cohn, *Philo von Alexandria*, vi (my translation of the original German).

In the critical edition of Philo's works it was decided on practical grounds to retain the basic order of the writings as had been customary in the earlier editions since Mangey (London 1742). For the present translation it has been thought appropriate for us to adopt a different order. The various writings which in terms of character and content belong together should be connected up and to the extent possible presented in the order in which the author himself, as far as we can determine from his own statements or from other indications, wrote them. In accordance with this plan we commence with the series of writings in which a systematic presentation of the essential contents of the Pentateuch is given. The present volume contains the book on the Creation, the descriptions of the lives of Abraham and Joseph and the book on the Decalogue.

In this translation, therefore, *Abr.* follows *Opif.* and precedes *Ios.* The only other scholarly work to present the treatises in this sequence is the Hebrew translation, of which only three volumes have appeared so far.[12]

If we examine Cohn's words closely, we should first say that he would be wrong if he implied that it is possible to give a complete chronological order for the entire corpus. All we can do is group the various treatises in the series that Philo appears to have planned and publish them in the internal order of those series. But once this is understood, there can be no doubt whatsoever that his decision was the correct one, at least in relation to the two treatises *Opif.* and *Abr.* Philo makes quite clear that these two treatises form a direct continuity. Twice in *Abr.* he refers to *Opif.* as "the preceding treatise," in the exordium (§2) and then a couple of pages later in a discussion of the number four (§13). Towards the end he makes another reference to the "creation account," which may well have his exposition in *Opif.* in mind (§258). Further evidence is found many treatises later in the exordium of *De praemiis* (§§1–2). Philo describes the structure of the Pentateuch under the headings of the creation account, the historical part and the legislative part, but in so doing it is clear that he also has in mind his own systematic treatment of the biblical text in the earlier treatises. As scholars have recognized, the description of the first two parts corresponds well to the contents of *Opif.* and *Abr.* It may be safely concluded that these two works represent the first two parts of a long sequence of treatises first identified by the nineteenth century scholars Massebieau, Schürer and Cohn, and now generally known under the title Exposition of the Law.[13]

---

[12] S. Daniel-Nataf and Y. Amir, eds., *Philo of Alexandria: Writings* (3 vols. so far; Jerusalem: Bialik Institute and Israel Academy of Sciences and Humanities, 1986–97); *Opif.* and *Abr.* are located in vol. 2 *Exposition of the Law* (1997): the former at 14–62, the latter at 77–120.

[13] On this series see the excellent presentation of J. Morris, "Philo the Jewish Philosopher," in E. Schürer, G. Vermes *et al.*, eds., *The History of the Jewish People in the Age of Jesus*

But we have not yet finished with Cohn's presentation. He continues the quote given above as follows:[14]

> Between the Life of Joseph and the Book on the Decalogue we have interposed the two Books on the Life of Moses. They in fact do not belong to the series of writings mentioned above [i.e. the Exposition of the Law], but in terms of their contents they often present a complement or additions to it.

There has been lively scholarly controversy about the relation of *Mos.* to the Exposition of the Law. Some scholars believe that it does belong to the series, but this view, based primarily on cross-references, cannot be sustained.[15] The two books of this treatise are in fact best seen as introductory to all three major series of treatises that Philo wrote.[16] Cohn recognized that they did not belong to the Exposition of the Law, but nevertheless placed them between *Ios.* and *Decal.* In this he followed the practice of the critical edition, which has in turn been followed by all other editions and translations except one. Perhaps he felt he should compensate for the loss of the two treatises on Isaac and Jacob which were certainly written after *Abr.* and before *Ios.*[17] Nevertheless this was a mistake which detracts from the presentation of the volume. Here the recent Hebrew translation asserts its superiority. Remarkably it is the only edition or translation that presents the treatises of the Exposition of the Law in the sequence that Philo almost certainly wrote them.[18]

I believe that much damage has been done to our understanding of Philo's intentions through the misplacement of these writings, and in particular by the artificial and erroneous separation of two treatises *Opif.* and *Abr.*, written, as far as we can tell, directly the one after the other. Admittedly the damage has been greater for the interpretation of *Opif.* and it has been on this aspect of the problem that most of the scholarly attention has been focused.[19] Nevertheless there are repercussions for our understanding of *Abr.* as well. Part of my aim in this paper will be to try to undo some of

---

Christ (175 B.C. – A.D. 135) (revised and edited by G. Vermes *et al.*, vol. 3 part 2; Edinburgh: T&T Clark, 1987), 840–54 (with further references).

[14] L. Cohn, *Philo von Alexandria*, vi–vii (my translation of the original German).

[15] E.g. V. Nikiprowetzky, *Le commentaire de l'Écriture chez Philon d'Alexandrie: son caractère et sa portée; observations philologiques* (ALGHJ 11; Leiden: Brill, 1977), 195–97; P. Borgen, *Philo of Alexandria: an Exegete for his Time* (NTSup 86; Leiden: Brill, 1997), 46.

[16] As shown by A. C. Geljon, *Philonic Exegesis in Gregory of Nyssa's De vita Moysis* (BJS 333; SPhM 5; Providence, RI: Brown Judaic Studies, 2002), 7–46.

[17] As proven by Philo's statements in *Ios.* 1 and *Decal.* 1.

[18] See above n. 12; *Mos.* is found in vol. 1, *Historical writings, Apologetical writings*.

[19] See the discussion at D. T. Runia, *Philo on the Creation of the Cosmos According to Moses* (PACS 1; Leiden: Brill, 2001), 1–4 (with further references).

the damage by examining in greater detail how the two treatises do relate to each other, both formally and thematically. But before we turn to this subject, we will do well first to look more carefully at the treatise *Abr.* itself.

3. *Formal features of* De Abrahamo

The treatise has a large number of formal features, to six of which I would like to draw attention.

(1) It contains a great number of what we might call "formal markers," phrases and sentences which order and structure its contents and so guide the reader in reading it. Generally these markers serve as passages linking up what precedes to what follows, summarizing the former in a few words and outlining what the next theme will be. A typical example is found at §60:[20]

> So much, then, for what had necessarily to be said first on the three figures in common. Next we must describe in what way each of them individually excelled, taking our start from the first one.

This passage links up the introductory discussion of the three Patriarchs in §§48–59, in which Philo describes various traits that they have in common, with the passage that follows in which Abraham is presented as responding to the divine call and first moving away from Chaldea to Haran, and then from there to the desert. The key term from the formal point of view in this sentence is *hexês*, "next" or "in sequence." It indicates that the treatise is being structured in a logical or systematic way. This is consistent with it being a *suntaxis*, an "ordered composition," the term that Philo regularly uses to describe individual treatises that make up the Exposition of the Law.[21] In §2 he describes *Opif.* as the *protera suntaxis* ("preceding treatise," cf. also §13), by implication giving the same description to *Abr.*[22]

(2) On the basis of these "formal markers" the treatise divides up into a sequence of chapters which mark the progress of the argument. In the following table I set out the division into twenty-three chapters which we

---

[20] Translations of Philonic passages are my own.

[21] Cf. my discussion in *Philo on the Creation of the Cosmos*, 5 and also C. Termini, "The Historical Part of the Pentateuch according to Philo of Alexandria: Biography, Genealogy, and the Philosophical Meaning of the Patriarchal Lives," in *Deuterocanonical and Cognate Literature Yearbook* (eds. N. Calduch-Benages and J. Liesen; Berlin: De Gruyter, 2006), 265 n. 2.

[22] Since the following treatise in the series, *On Isaac*, has gone lost, we do not have a retrospective description of *Abr.* along the same lines.

find in Cohn–Wendland's edition (the number of words for each chapter is added in brackets):[23]

§§1–6	Introduction: subject "living laws" (342 words)	
§§7–16	first triad: Enos = hope (430)	
§§17–26	first triad: Enoch = change of mind (513)	
§§27–46	first triad: Noah = rest or righteous (1059)	
§47	transitional passage: summary of first triad (92)	
§§48–59	introduction of second triad (637)	
§§60–67	Abraham's migrations: literal explanation (476)	
§§68–88	Abraham's migrations: allegorical explanation (1043)	
§§89–98	Abraham's marriage threatened: literal explanation (389)	
§§99–106	Abraham's marriage threatened: allegorical explanation (432)	
§§107–118	Abraham's hospitality: literal explanation (521)	
§§119–132	Abraham's hospitality: allegorical explanation (732)	
§§133–146	Reward and punishment: literal explanation (670)	
§§147–166	Reward and punishment: allegorical explanation (1004)	
§§167–199	Sacrifice of Isaac: literal explanation (1419)	
§§200–207	Sacrifice of Isaac: allegorical explanation (376)	
§§208–216	Abraham's kindness to Lot: literal explanation (444)	
§§217–224	Abraham's kindness to Lot: allegorical explanation (382)	
§§225–235	Abraham's bravery: literal explanation (559)	
§§236–244	Abraham's bravery: allegorical explanation (489)	
§§245–254	excellence of wife shown in Hagar episode (412)	
§§255–261	excellence of sage in response to wife's death (359)	
§§262–276	final encomium of the sage (708)	

It can be seen that with one exception they form acceptable literary units ranging in length from 342 words for the Introduction to 1419 words in the case of the very long chapter on the literal interpretation of the '*Aqedah* (where apologetic concerns are very evident). Exceptionally there is a short passage at §47 which summarizes the first triad of ancestors and is slightly separate from the account of Noah which precedes it. It is perhaps best taken as an independent transitional passage between the introductory and the main parts of the treatise.

(3) Philo, as is now generally agreed, is primarily an interpreter and expositor of scripture and this treatise with its concentration on the biblical figure of Abraham fits in perfectly with such aims. Nevertheless it is striking how little direct reference to scripture it contains. The following table

---

[23] Making 13,488 words in total (based on the TLG text). In *Thesaurus Linguae Graecae: Canon of Greek Authors and Works* (eds. L. Berkowitz and K. A. Squitier; New York–Oxford: Oxford University Press, 1986), 253, the following figures are given: *Abr.* 13,617; *Jos.* 13,088; *Opif.* 13,672. I cannot explain the discrepancy in the number for *Abr.*

lists all the quotations (thirteen), paraphrases (five) and direct allusions (four), amounting to twenty-two in all, that the treatise contains:[24]

§9	Gen 5:1	Q (5 words)	Enos
§13	Lev 19:24	Q (4)	tetrad
§17–19	Gen 5:24	Q (12)	Enoch
§31–36	Gen 6:9	Q (15)	Noah
§51	Ex 3:15	Q (14)	Patriarchs
§56	Ex 19:6	Q (6)	Israel
§67	Gen 11:31, 12:5	P	Abram leaves Chaldea
§77, 80	Gen 12:7	Q (6)	God appears to Abram
§108	Gen 18:6	Q (6)	make three cakes
§112	Gen 18:12	Q (7)	response to Sarah
§131–132	Gen 18:3, 10	Q (12+17)	proof single visitor
§166	Gen 19:20	A	proof fifth city
§173	Gen 22:7	P	Isaac's question
§175	Gen 22:8	P	Abraham's reply
§224	Gen 13:9	A	not living with Lot
§241	Gen 14:10	P	kings in well
§258	Gen 23:3	A	Abraham moves from corpse
§261	Gen 23:6	Q (7)	Abraham king among us
§262	Gen 15:6	Q (3)	Abraham's *pistis*
§270	Gen 24:1	A	Abraham called *presbyteros*
§273	Gen 22:16	Q (3)	God swears oath to friend
§275	Gen 26:5	P	Abraham obeys ordinances

The amount of direct reference to scripture is surely remarkably limited, given that the whole treatise is based on the scriptural narrative. The main function of the quotes seems to be either to highlight some key phrases and terms or to offer proof of a particular interpretation. It should also be noted that there is very little use of secondary biblical texts in the treatise, i.e., scriptural material not directly related to the primary text of Genesis that tells Abraham's story. The only real example is the quote of Lev 19:24 in §13 illustrating Moses' veneration of the tetrad.[25] This is in marked contrast, for example with Philo's method in the Allegorical Commentary.

(4) A further feature of the work that no reader can miss is the alternation of literal and allegorical exegesis which is presented in the sequence of seven twin chapters that forms the main body of the treatise (§§60–244). These can again be very clearly seen in the table of chapters presented

---

[24] Not included are parallels in vocabulary etc. which are inevitable when one is recounting and adapting biblical material.

[25] Also cited in *Plant.* 117, 125, 126, *Somn.* 1.33, 35 (cf. also *Virt.* 159). The quotes from Exodus are directly relevant to the presentation of the ancestors in the first part of the treatise.

above. The scheme is quite simple. The narratives are first explained in terms of Abraham as a wise and God-beloved person, secondly in terms of the virtuous and God-seeking soul. Similarly Sarah represents the ideal woman or wife, or in allegorical terms wisdom. Every time that Philo moves from the literal to the allegorical form of interpretation he makes some transitional comments which give valuable insights into how he sees the essential differences between the two modes of exegesis.[26] Only towards the end does the schema break down. For the account of Sarah's death and Abraham's reaction to it (§§262–267) no allegorical interpretation is given.

(5) Next we should note that the treatise is entitled a *bios*[27] and appears mostly to consist of the retelling of biblical stories, giving Philo ample scope to use his literary talents, but also allowing him to incorporate various traditional elements of the interpretation of Abraham as a biblical figure, whether literal (and midrashic) or allegorical.[28] However, narrative is most certainly not an end in itself. The treatise's structure and method is in fact systematic, with each aspect of or incident in Abraham's life being used to illustrate a particular conceptual point. This is demonstrated by the fact that Philo does not follow the biblical narrative sequentially, but makes jumps backwards and forwards. It is particularly clear in his location of the stories of Lot and Hagar towards the end of the treatise. As Termini has recently pointed out, §208 marks an important point in the systematic development of the treatise, for here Philo moves from stories illustrating Abraham's piety (*eusebeia*) to those that focus on his humanity (*philanthrôpia*). The division thus anticipates the treatment of the two tables of the law in *Decal.*[29] Another important consequence of Philo's systematic approach is the material he leaves out. For example, two themes prominent in Gen 17, the covenant which God promises to Abraham's offspring and the

[26] One of these introductory remarks at *Abr.* 99 formed the basis of Richard Goulet's speculative monograph on pre-Philonic exegesis in Alexandria, *La philosophie de Moïse: essai de reconstruction d'un commentaire philosophique préphilonien du Pentateuque* (Histoire des doctrines de l'Antiquité classique 11; Paris: Librairie Philosophique J. Vrin, 1987).

[27] Even if the title as we have it perhaps was not originally given by Philo, the emphasis on *bios* is clear from the concluding words in §276.

[28] E.g., that Abraham was continent after Hagar conceived; see §253 and Colson's note ad loc. David Winston points out to me that the rabbis in *b. Yoma* 77a note that the Hebrew phrase *watěʿannehā Śarai* in Gen 16:6 means that she prevented Hagar from having sexual relations with Abraham. As proof they cite Gen 31:50 *ʾim těʿanneh ʾet benōtai*, which they translated "if you withhold the conjugal rights of my daughters."

[29] See Termini, "The Historical Part of the Pentateuch according to Philo of Alexandria," 285.

obligation to circumcise males, are simply ignored.[30] It is perhaps no coincidence that these themes are overtly Jewish.

(6) Finally it must be emphasized that the treatise has a strong rhetorical character. The basic tenor is encomiastic. Philo pulls out all the stops to show the excellence of the sage as the embodiment of the divine law. Comparisons are made which work to Abraham's advantage (e.g., on the vicissitudes of emigrating from one's fatherland, §66). Paradoxes are highlighted (e.g., that the stronger person should take the poorer land, §216). In his allegorical exegesis too Philo aims to convince the reader of the validity of his interpretation, using various techniques such as the explanation of names (e.g., the names Abram and Abraham at §§82–83) and the citing of biblical proof texts (e.g., the singular used by Abraham to the group of three cited in §132). Apologetic concerns are closely linked to the encomium and can be seen as the reverse side of the medallion. Instead of the desire to praise there is a perceived need to defend. It is particularly visible in the spirited defence of Abraham's willingness to obey God and sacrifice his son Isaac in Gen 22.[31] The vehemence of Philo's language in §178 and §191 suggests to me that the people making these criticisms might have been rather too close for comfort, i.e., Jewish compatriots who were uncomfortable with a literal reading of the story.[32]

There has been a vast amount of discussion over the years about the intended audience of the Exposition of the Law. The view of Goodenough that it was primarily directed at a gentile audience no longer finds favour with scholars.[33] Philo would certainly have been happy if non-Jews showed interest in these writings. This is perhaps shown by some unusual use of terminology.[34] But educated Jews would have been his chief audience. They were being introduced to the Pentateuch in a well-organized way with a systematic perspective, the main lines of which were not difficult to follow

[30] This point was suggested to me by David Winston.

[31] On Philo's apologetic methods in this passage see the detailed treatment of L. H. Feldman, "Philo's Version of the 'Aqedah'," *SPhA* 14 (2002): 66–86.

[32] As suggested by Goulet, *La philosophie de Moïse*, 542. M. R. Niehoff, *Philo on Jewish Identity and Culture* (TSAJ 86; Tübingen: Mohr Siebeck, 2001), 173, argues for the same view.

[33] Morris, "Philo the Jewish Philosopher," 840 n. 111. The view of M. Böhm, "Abraham und die Erzväter bei Philo: Hermeneutische Überlegungen zur Konzeption der Arbeit am CJHNT," in R. Deines and K.-W. Niebuhr, eds., *Philo und das Neue Testament: Wechselseitige Wahrnehmungen. 1. Internationales Symposium zum Corpus Judaeo-Hellenisticum Novi Testamenti (Eisenach/Jena, Mai 2003)* (WUNT 172; Tübingen: Mohr Siebeck, 2004), 390, that the work is aimed at proselytes is an interesting recent variation of Goodenough's view.

[34] E.g. the use of the term *Chaldaioi* to refer to the Hebrew people and their language; cf. C. K. Wong, "Philo's Use of *Chaldaioi*," *SPhA* 4 (1992): 1–14, esp. 1–4.

and allowed them to gain a theological understanding of the purpose of the Law. The features outlined above fit in well with this understanding of Philo's aims.

4. *Comparisons between* De opificio mundi *and* De Abrahamo

We now turn to a comparison between the two treatises *Opif.* and *Abr.* As was noted at the beginning of our paper, Philo makes it abundantly clear that *Abr.* connects up directly with the preceding treatise *Opif.* The next step will be to compare the formal features of the two treatises before moving on to their thematic similarities and differences. There are at least six points of comparison.

(1) The two works are almost exactly identical in length, a fact somewhat obscured by the marked difference in number of sections (172 for *Opif.*, 276 for *Abr.*), but clearly shown by the fact that both are exactly sixty pages in length in the critical edition and have almost the same number of words.[35]

(2) In the case of *Opif.* too, the work can be divided into chapters, but in fact its structure is much less regular than that of *Abr.* In my commentary I divided it into twenty-five chapters in total, compared with twenty-three in *Abr.*[36] It is striking that one of the chapters in *Opif.*, the long excursus on the number seven in §§89–128, amounts to nearly a quarter of the entire treatise. It also has fewer passages that serve as markers for the reader. The reason for this, as we shall see directly, is that in the first three-quarters of the earlier work Philo follows a rather different method of exegesis.

(3) Direct exegesis of scripture is much more prominent in *Opif.* than in *Abr.*[37] It is true that in the former work too the actual biblical text is quoted or paraphrased relatively sparingly. But for the creation account up to the second creation of humanity in Gen 2:7, Philo follows the biblical text rather closely, adhering to the scheme of the seven days of creation and regularly citing key terms and phrases. Only for the final seven chapters (§§136–172), which deal with the narrative of the events in Paradise, does Philo's method start to resemble more closely what we find in *Abr.* As we shall see, this section also has more thematic resemblances with the main themes of

---

[35] See the statistics cited above in n. 23.

[36] See the analysis in *Philo on the Creation of the Cosmos According to Moses*, 8–10.

[37] Philo's references to scripture in *Opif.* can be followed very closely in my commentary: see *Philo on the Creation of the Cosmos According to Moses*, 11–14 and the footnotes to the translation.

Abr. than the earlier part. As for the use of secondary biblical texts, it is just as infrequent as in *Abr.*, with only two instances (in §84 and §163).[38]

(4) Most of *Opif.*, as is to be expected, follows a literal method of exposition.[39] The first man is the prototype of the sage, until he succumbs to the snares of sexual pleasure. Only in a single important chapter (§§157–166) does Philo distinguish between literal and allegorical interpretation. The stories of the snake and the fruit in the garden of Eden "are not the fabrications of myth ... but indications of character types which invite allegorical interpretation through the explanation of hidden meanings" (§157). Unlike in *Abr.*, however, the allegory of the soul is not prominent in the interpretation he puts forward. There is only a very brief reference to it in §165.

(5) A special feature of *Opif.* is the prominence of number symbolism in the work. forty-nine of the 172 sections are devoted to this theme, which of course relates very directly to the scheme of the seven days of creation.[40] There is less scope for arithmology in *Abr.*, but it is used to explain the generations of the first triad of Patriarchs. Enos is noted as the fourth with a reference to Lev 19:24 (§13), while Noah is marked as the seventh (§28) with a reference to the special role of the hebdomad in the cosmos and in the human being. This is a clear example of continuity between the two treatises. However, other opportunities for exploiting numbers associated with Abraham are not utilized.[41]

(6) Finally, as already noted, *Opif.* follows the sequence of the biblical text much more closely than *Abr.*, which takes great liberties with the narrative order of events in Abraham's life in order to give a systematic presentation of his embodiment as a living law. But this is not to say that the earlier treatise is not marked by the same systematic concerns. These emerge very clearly in the final summary (§§170–72), but also earlier in the work, particularly in the treatment of the first human beings. It is to these themes that we now turn.

---

[38] The former of these instances is not a quotation but an unmistakable allusion.

[39] There is almost no allegorising of Gen 1 in Philo's writings. Only in *Leg.* 2.11–12 is an allegorical interpretation given of Gen 1:24. Goulet, *La philosophie de Moïse*, 139, sees the hint of an allegorical reading of Gen 1:28 in *Opif.* 142.

[40] For the use of number symbolism in *Opif.* see my *Philo on the Creation of the Cosmos According to Moses*, 25–29.

[41] E.g., his 318 men (Gen 14:14), his 86 years (Gen 16:16), 99 years of age (Gen 17:1), the 175 years of his life (Gen 25:7). The final three numbers are explained in *QG* 2.38, 39 and 61, and 151 respectively.

5. *Thematic connections between* De opificio mundi *and* De Abrahamo

Because *Opif.* gives exegesis of the Mosaic creation account, it is usually thought to be a cosmological treatise, but this is in fact not really the case. Just like Plato's *Timaeus*, to which it is so strongly indebted for many of its main insights and themes, it is ultimately more about ethics and how one should live than about science or theology.[42] Philo tells us about this primary purpose of the work right at the outset. The Law of Moses starts off with an account of creation to show that "the cosmos is in harmony with the law and the law with the cosmos, and that the man who observes the law is at once a citizen of the cosmos" (§3). And the summary of the main themes at the end of the treatise emphatically returns to this perspective: the person who learns the main lessons of the creation account "will lead a blessed life of well-being (*eudaimonia*), marked by the doctrines of piety and holiness" (§172). These themes of living in accordance with the law and living the life of excellence (*aretê*) are also the main themes of *Abr.*

Of course one would not wish to deny that there are many thematic continuities between the two treatises in the area of science, philosophy and theology. Four examples can be given. The Chaldeanism that Abraham leaves behind is precisely the misguided theology that Philo warns against at the beginning of *Opif.* before embarking on his exegesis of the six days.[43] The luxuriance of the land of Sodom before it was destroyed recalls the creation of the earth on the third day.[44] Of the five cities in the valley the single one that was not destroyed symbolizes the role of sight and so recalls the importance of light as created on the first and fourth days.[45] Just as the words "let us make" in Gen 1:26 are taken to indicate that God is not responsible for evil, so the plurality of visitors that Abraham receives is interpreted as signifying that the role of punishment is left in the hands of his Powers.[46]

---

[42] The fundamental ethical purpose of the *Timaeus* has been strongly emphasized in recent research. See C. Steel, "The Moral Purpose of the Human Body: A Reading of *Timaeus* 69–72," *Phronesis* 46 (2001): 105–28; T. K. Johansen, *Plato's Natural Philosophy: A Study of the Timaeus-Critias* (New York–Cambridge: Cambridge University Press, 2004); G. R. Carone, *Plato's Cosmology and its Ethical Dimensions* (Cambridge: Cambridge University Press, 2005); and the comments by Julia Annas in her review article in *SPhA* 18 (2006): 126–27. As Johansen makes clear, the link between cosmology and ethics is made via the doctrine of natural teleology.

[43] Compare *Opif.* 7 and *Abr.* 69.

[44] Compare *Opif.* 39 and *Abr.* 134.

[45] Compare *Opif.* 54 and *Abr.* 156–164.

[46] Compare *Opif.* 72–75 and *Abr.* 143.

But the main connection between the two treatises lies elsewhere. Philo sees a significant line of continuity between Adam the first human being, Noah the first representative of a new race after the flood, and Abraham the founder of the race of Israel.[47] Adam was created perfect in body and soul (*Opif.* 136). He obeyed the divine law of the cosmos and reached the peak of human well-being until the creation of a helpmate brings about his downfall (*Opif.* 150–152). Noah was a righteous man, displaying all the excellences and pleasing God, but he was only "perfect in his generation" (Gen 6:9), so worthy of the second prize, not the first prize which will go to others, i.e., the three Patriarchs (*Abr.* 36–38). Like Adam and Noah, Abraham embodies all the *aretai* in his actions and his life, both towards God through his piety and towards human beings through his humanity. The lives of the ancestors, both of the first and of the second triad, are set before the reader in order to show that the ordinances of the law are not inconsistent with nature (cf. *Opif.* 3 cited above) and that the injunction to obey the law is not a heavy task, as shown by the fact that these men were able to carry it out when the laws were not even written down (*Abr.* 5).[48]

It will be one of the tasks of a commentary on *Abr.* to point out and analyse the numerous parallels that Philo sees between Adam and Abraham and the intermediate figures of Noah and two other early Patriarchs. One interesting example can be given. Just as the first man exercised sovereignty by naming all the animals that God led before him (Gen 2:19–20), so scripture states that Abraham was called a king by his neighbours (Gen 23:6), who recognized in him the true kingship of the sage.[49] In both passages Philo exploits the Stoic paradox that only the wise person is the true king and has true knowledge of what things are good and what things are not.[50]

6. *The place of* De Abrahamo *in the Exposition of the Law*

Of the subjects announced at the beginning of my paper only one remains, the question how *Abr.* fits into the grand scheme of the Exposition of the Law in its totality. This is a very large subject and can only be definitively

---

[47] Compare *Opif.* 140–142, *Abr.* 46 and 56.

[48] Cf. Termini, "The Historical Part of the Pentateuch according to Philo of Alexandria," 286, who speaks of a "paradigmatic aspect which characterized the Genesis sages" and an "isomorphism between the Patriarchs' lives and the Mosaic law."

[49] Compare *Opif.* 148–150 (and also earlier 83–88) and *Abr.* 261. Philo does not mention Noah's command to the animals in *Abr.*, but it is briefly mentioned in *Mos.* 2.61.

[50] See *SVF* 3.617, as noted by Colson in his note to *Abr.* 261.

treated if it is preceded by a thorough analysis of the entire series consisting of no less than twelve treatises (two of which have been lost). At this point, however, it will be helpful by way of background to observe that preliminary analysis of Philo's great work, and particularly of the key passages in which he indicates its main contours,[51] shows it to be controlled by four main themes.[52]

The first theme, already presented in *Opif.*, lays out the framework for both the law and the activity of human beings in response to it. When God creates the cosmos, he gives it a normative structure established in the Logos as the intelligible cosmos, then translated into the immanent rational structure of the cosmos identified with the Law of nature.[53] The human being is created as *logikos*, an intellectual and spiritual being endowed with *logos*, and so is able to respond to that structure in his or her life. The first human being resided in the cosmos as his home and used its constitution, the right reason of nature, as the guide for his life.[54]

The second theme, which also already starts in *Opif.*, is that human life is a contest that can lead in two directions, as indicated by a number of fundamental polar opposites, to life or to death, to goodness or to wickedness, to piety or to impiety. Depending on the direction that human beings choose, it can end in well-being (*eudaimonia*) or its opposite, a bad life (*kakodaimonia*). The first human being, on being ensnared in the toils of desire, makes a fateful transition from the one state to the other.[55] The metaphor of the contest recurs time and time again. The devotees of the law are called upon to show what they are worth in the arena of life.[56]

---

[51] Chief among these is the much discussed passage *Praem.* 1–3, composed when most of the work had already been written. Although it is presented as an analysis of the Pentateuch, there is an obvious relation to the structure of Philo's own work, as he himself notes in §3. On this text see further A. Kamesar, "The Literary Genres of the Pentateuch as Seen from the Greek Perspective: The Testimony of Philo of Alexandria," in *Wisdom and Logos: Studies in Jewish Thought in Honor of David Winston* (= *The Studia Philonica Annual 9* [1997]), (eds. D. T. Runia and G. E. Sterling; Brown Judaic Studies 312; Atlanta: Scholars Press, 1997), 143–89.

[52] For what follows I draw on an unpublished paper presented at a conference of the European Association of Jewish Studies in Toledo, Spain, in July 1998. There is a large measure of agreement with Termini, "The Historical Part of the Pentateuch according to Philo of Alexandria," but our research was done independently of each other.

[53] See esp. *Opif.* 3, 16–25.

[54] See esp. *Opif.* 142–144.

[55] See *Opif.* 150–152.

[56] See esp. *Praem.* 4: "They [the citizens of Moses' polity] advanced as if into a sacred contest and revealed the naked choice that they had made for their lives (*proairesis*) as a clearest test of the truth."

The third theme is the observance of the law as given by the great lawgiver Moses. This is central to Philo's concerns and motivates him to set out the Torah in great detail, because he is convinced that the injunctions of the Jewish law embody the right way to live. This occurs at two levels, at the higher level of the contemplative life directed towards God, and at the lower level directed towards life in human society. Observance of the law leads to the practices of the excellences or *aretai*, foremost piety and love of humankind, as summarized in the two tables of the Decalogue, but also of all the others. These are particularly focused on in *De virtutibus*, but also receive much emphasis elsewhere in the Exposition.

The fourth and final theme is that of reward and punishment. Just as in a competition there is a prize for the successful competitor, so God grants rewards to those who succeed in the arena of life, while the reverse happens to those who incline in the wrong direction. If one develops the excellences of character and disposition and becomes pleasing to God, the reward will be a good life. If, however, one chooses the path of self-love and wickedness, punishments and failure will be sure to follow. This theme clearly reaches its climax in *De praemiis*, which sets out the particular rewards and punishments obtained by individuals, families and the nation of Israel. But it is also treated earlier in the account of the events in paradise and the stories of the Patriarchs.[57]

There is much more that needs to be said about this grand scheme, both in terms of detail and by way of evaluation.[58] It is a remarkably ambitious attempt to give a detailed exposition of the entire Torah within a clear systematic framework. This occurs on two levels. The attempt to organize all the commands of the law by means of the ten injunctions of the Decalogue is a remarkable *tour de force*. But Philo goes even further by integrating the entire contents of the Pentateuch, both narrative and law, within his greater scheme. It does not require much insight to observe that this scheme has some quite problematic elements, particularly in its close linkage of excellence and reward, vice and punishment. The occasional remark shows that Philo was not unaware of these problems, particularly in relation to the precarious position of the Jewish people in his own day.[59] It does not deter him, however, in putting forward his bold and forthright

---

[57] See *Opif.* 167–170 (where Philo closes with the theme of divine mercy). *Praem.* 7–51 repeats many of the themes of *Abr.* 7–59 on the two triads of Patriarchs.

[58] See above n. 52. See also the valuable analysis of Borgen, *Philo an Exegete for his Time*, 46–79. He emphasizes, however, the process of "rewriting the Bible" rather than the systematics of the presentation.

[59] See esp. his comment at *Virt.* 120 and the parallel remarks at *Mos.* 2.43–44.

scheme. Let us now end by returning to the treatise that is our focus, *De Abrahamo*.

It is clear that the various elements of Philo's scheme occur in our treatise and that they fulfil an important role in the way it unfolds in the grand sweep from the creation account to the outline of rewards and punishments.

The philosophical, and in particular the cosmological, background is most prominent in the interpretation of Abraham's journey in two stages from Chaldea via Haran to the promised land, the part of his story with which Philo begins his account of the Patriarch's life (*Abr.* 60–88).[60] If one contemplates the cosmos as Abraham did, one does not need spoken or written words in order to learn a law-abiding life (§61). Yet the mistakes of the Chaldeans show that recognition of the creator does not follow as a matter of course. Abraham had to undertake a journey both literally and intellectually, leaving behind astrology and an immanentist view of the world in which there was no room for a transcendent creator. By the end of the account of his journeys Abraham has recognized a higher reality than the physical world, the intelligible order created on "day one" (*Opif.* 15–36) and God who is creator and ruler of both worlds (*Abr.* 88).

As we have already noted above, the entire narrative account of the various incidents in Abraham's life is taken to illustrate his excellence of character and action (*aretê*), falling under the two main heads of piety (*eusebeia*) and humanity (*philanthrôpia*). More specifically the choice between virtue and vice, good and evil, is portrayed in a number of the stories that Philo chooses to elaborate. It already commences with the rather euphemistic account of Abraham and Sarah's journey to Egypt in Gen 12 (§§89–106).[61] Philo introduces the story by saying that the greatness of the friend of God's actions is only apparent to those who have tasted excellence. The hospitality that Abraham shows to the three strangers is in marked contrast to the inhospitality shown by the Egyptians (§107). The deeper spiritual interpretation of the story of the sacrifice of Isaac is that joy belongs to God alone but, being devoid of jealousy, he is willing to share it with one who travels along the path of excellence and good feelings (*eupatheiai*), a path which is blocked to passion and wickedness (§204). The theme of conflict between good and evil returns when Philo discusses the separation of

---

[60] Up to this point the contents of the treatise have been all introductory.

[61] Philo does not distinguish the parts of the narrative before and after the name change in Gen 17. On his selective adaptation of the far from flattering biblical account see further J. Kugel, *Traditions of the Bible: a Guide to the Bible as it was at the Start of the Common Era* (Cambridge Mass., 1998), 254–55.

Abraham and his nephew Lot in Gen 13. Here Lot, as befits a relative of the sage, does not in fact represent vice, but the choice of the lesser goods such as wealth and noble birth, which are not goods in the true sense of the word.[62] There is a natural conflict between these two positions, as symbolized by the strife between their herdsmen, because it is a dispute on what is the most important thing in life, the determination of what are true goods (§222). The man of wisdom and excellence cannot live together with one whose judgment on the true good is erroneous (cf. §224).

The theme of the observance of the law pervades the entire treatise. At the outset we read (§5) that the ancestors were "laws endowed with soul and reason" (*empsuchoi kai logikoi nomoi*), whose example shows that living in accordance with the law is not great trouble (surely an allusion to Deut 30:11). At the end of the treatise we read that the greatest praise which Abraham can be accorded is indicated by scripture when it says, that "this human being performed the divine law and the divine ordinances" (§275, cf. Gen 26:5). He did so by being a "living law," obeying the unwritten law of nature. This is what enables him to be an exemplar of the excellences, as portrayed at great length throughout the various stories of his life, whether read literally or in allegorical terms. Many examples of his humanity are given, e.g., in his treatment of his nephew and various neighbours. But Philo, consistent with his hierarchical view of the *aretai*, places the chief emphasis on Abraham's piety (cf. §60). Abraham (as well as the other ancestors) is not only a lover of God (*philotheos*), but he is also loved by God in return (*theophilês*, cf. §50).

Finally, the rewards that Abraham receives for his piety and excellence are many. They can be summarized in the perfect life of the sage, the good and complete life that is encapsulated in the Greek philosophical term *eudaimonia* (cf. §§268–71).[63] The wise man has a unique place in the world. He is the first-ranked of the human race, like a pilot in a ship or a ruler in a city or a general in war, or like the soul in the body, the mind in the soul, like the heaven in the cosmos and—as grand climax—like God in the heaven (§272). These formulations remind us strongly of the kind of praise that Greek philosophy accords the philosopher and the sage. But Philo also describes Abraham's rewards in more biblical terms. The unexpected birth

---

[62] Note that Philo associates the lesser goods with passions and illnesses in §223. He often takes a hard line on this issue, but is sometimes milder and accepts that they are lesser goods. See further J. M. Dillon, *The Middle Platonists: A Study of Platonism 80 B.C. to A.D. 220* (2d ed; London: Duckworth, 1996), 146–48.

[63] On the importance of this theme in Philo's thought see my article "Eudaimonism in Hellenistic-Jewish Literature," in *Shem in the Tents of Japheth: Essays on the Encounter of Judaism and Hellenism*s (ed. J. L. Kugel; JSJSup 74; Leiden: Brill, 2002), 131–57.

of his son Isaac is a great reward (§254), and through Isaac he will be the progenitor of a great nation, which receives from God the great gift of priesthood and prophecy on behalf of the entire human race (§98).[64] Marvelling at Abraham's faith (*pistis*), God repaid him by confirming with an oath the gifts that he had promised him (§273, citing Gen 22:16).

We see, therefore, that the theme of reward, which brings together the previous themes in the treatise at its end, just as the final treatise *De praemiis* does for the entire Exposition, combines motifs from both Greek philosophy and Jewish scriptural thought. Indeed, the entire treatise is marked by this duality of perspective which all devotees of Philo's writings will recognize. This brief presentation has only been able to scratch the surface of what the treatise has to offer. It needs a detailed commentary to do it full justice.[65] But if my observations have been able to shed a little light on the place of this fascinating treatise in the context of Philo's *œuvre*, particularly in relation to the preceding treatise *Opif.* and the entire series of treatises in the Exposition of Law, I will be more than content.

Queen's College
The University of Melbourne

---

[64] On this striking, in some ways even unique, text in Philo see E. Birnbaum, *The Place of Judaism in Philo's Thought: Israel, Jews, and Proselytes*, (BJS 290; Studia Philonica Monographs 2; Atlanta: Scholars Press, 1996), 179–83.

[65] As being prepared by John Dillon for the Philo of Alexandria Commentary Series.

The Studia Philonica Annual 20 (2008) 151–165

THE TEXT OF PHILO'S *DE ABRAHAMO*[1]

JAMES R. ROYSE

In earlier papers presented to the Philo of Alexandria Group of the Society of Biblical Literature, I have looked at the status of the text of the books *Legum allegoriae* and of *De virtutibus*. In several respects the text of *De Abrahamo* is much more satisfactorily preserved than those works. For one thing, the basic structure of the work has survived perfectly intact in quite a few manuscripts. In this respect, we may contrast it with the structure of *Virt.*, which, as printed in the Cohn-Wendland edition, could be considered a scholarly construct. At any rate, the four sections that are found there appear in the most disparate orders in the various manuscripts. And in fact only one manuscript preserves the order found in PCW; this is the Oxford Selden 12, which is one of the oldest of the medieval manuscripts used by Cohn and Wendland. For *Virt.* it happens, moreover, that the order of the sections found in Selden 12 agrees with the order in which they are used by Clement of Alexandria. It thus appears, as Wendland argued, that Selden 12 has preserved the order found in Clement's manuscript of the work at least. And we can thus conclude that the various other orders of the sections are textual degenerations from that earlier order. But a further complication is the section *De pietate*. The ancient evidence for such a section was sufficient that Cohn postulated a lacuna at *Virt.* 51.[2]

Turning to *Leg.* 1–3, we see that here too the original structure of the works has suffered in transmission. At the beginning of the Allegorical Commentary there were originally (as it seems) four books, of which two have survived and two have been lost:

---

[1] This is a revised version of a paper presented to the Philo of Alexandria Group at the meeting of the Society of Biblical Literature in San Diego, November 20, 2007.

[2] See further my "The Text of Philo's *De virtutibus*," *SPhA* 18 (2006): 73–102. Let me take this opportunity to note that toward the bottom of p. 87, line 29 of the Oxyrhynchus Papyrus fragment should read:

μ]ετρεισθαι παρ ο και δημο

Book 1 = *Leg.* 1–2: Gen 2:1–17 (*Leg.* 1) and 2:18–3:1a (*Leg.* 2).[3]
Book 2 = Lost: Gen 3:1b–8a.
Book 3 = *Leg.* 3: Gen 3:8b–19.
Book 4 = Lost: Gen 3:20–23.[4]

The integrity of *Abr.* is a pleasant change from such difficulties. Moreover, the Greek evidence is more extensive than usual. In contrast to some treatises that have survived in only a few manuscripts, *Abr.* survives in from 11 to 13 (as cited by Cohn). And three of these, BEK, are placed by Cohn among the better manuscripts of Philo. As a result of such comparatively broad attestation, we can be more than usually confident that Philo's Greek is to be found in some witness, and (to put the same point another way) there is less occasion for resorting to conjectural emendation.[5]

Moreover, for *Abr.* as well as for a few other works, we have the valuable witness of the Armenian version, to which we turn.

The Armenian Version of De Abrahamo

Cohn and Wendland were dependent for their knowledge of the Armenian version of *De providentia*, *De animalibus*, the *Quaestiones*, and *De Deo*, on Aucher's Latin translation.[6] But the Armenian version of the other works of Philo (*Contempl.*; *Abr.*; *Leg.* 1–2; *Spec.* 1.79–161; 1.285–345; 3.1–7; *Decal.*; and

---

[3] The division into three books, as presented in the Cohn-Wendland edition, relies on part of the manuscript tradition. However, *Leg.* 1 and *Leg.* 2 are combined into one book in the Armenian version and in one Greek manuscript (and perhaps as well in the Oxyrhynchus Papyrus [see my "The Oxyrhynchus Papyrus of Philo," *BASP* 17 (1980): 159 n 9]), and together they are of roughly the length of *Leg.* 3. See my "The Text of Philo's *Legum Allegoriae*," *SPhA* 12 (2000): 2.

[4] It is likely that some Greek fragments of this work survive; see "The Text of Philo's *Legum Allegoriae*," 2–3. Moreover, at *Sacr.* 51 Philo appears to refer to a discussion in this work; see Jenny Morris, *SJHP*, 3.833 n. 65. On the other hand, Abraham Terian has argued ("The Priority of the *Quaestiones* among Philo's Exegetical Commentaries," in *Both Literal and Allegorical: Studies in Philo of Alexandria's "Questions and Answers on Genesis and Exodus"* [ed. David M. Hay; BJS 232; Atlanta: Scholars Press, 1991], 38–40), that the reference at *Sacr.* 51 to "the earlier books" was to *QG* 1.59 and 2.66. While this is certainly possible, Runia suggests that a more plausible source was the lost fourth book of *Legum Allegoriae*, which discussed Gen 3:20–23; see his "Secondary Texts in Philo's *Quaestiones*," in *Both Literal and Allegorical*, 71–72.

[5] See the comments by Colson, PLCL 6.xviii. Cohn's remarks in PCW 4.xxviii–xxix may be supplemented by his "Beiträge zur Textgeschichte und Kritik der philonischen Schriften," *Hermes* 38 (1903): 498–545.

[6] This is printed facing the Armenian in Aucher 1822 and 1826.

Spec. 3.8–64) was published without Latin translation.[7] As a result Cohn and Wendland depended for their textual citations on information supplied by F. C. Conybeare, whose contribution is described as follows:

> comparationem cum textu graeco instituit et lectiones versionis F. C. Conybeare amicus mihi benignissime commodavit.[8]

From this it is unclear exactly what form this cooperation took. Did Conybeare merely collate the Armenian with some earlier Greek text, and report on differences? Or did he look at some earlier edition (perhaps Mangey's), and report on places where the Armenian supported either a known reading or a reading not found in Greek? Or did Conybeare have some preliminary version of the Cohn-Wendland critical apparatus, so that he could see the range of textual options reported there, and then report on the evidence of the Armenian with respect to those readings? Naturally, the last method would have been preferable, but does not seem quite to be suggested by Cohn's words.

In any case, Cohn continues:

> etenim versio libri *de Abrahamo*, ubicunque codices inter se discrepant, ad textum optimorum codicum BEK proxime accedit, ut lectionum ab iis traditarum probitas auctoritate interpretis Armenii saepe confirmetur.[9]

Cohn then cites twenty-one such places where the Armenian goes with the better manuscripts, BEK. These are:

§4	ὅμοιον	§96	ἐφ᾿ ἡδονήν
§6	ηὐνομήθησαν	§98	ὀλίγων
§78	ἀναβλέψασα	§104	τιτρώσκει
§83	γεγωνοῦ	§122	τύχῃ καθαρθεῖσα
§84	πολλά	§141	μνημεῖον
§91	ἀφορίας	§149	γαστριμαργότατα

---

[7] I follow here the order of the edition, *P'iloni Hebrayec'woy čaṙk'* [The Works of Philo the Jew] (Venice: The Mechitarist Press, 1892). Between *Spec.* 3.1–7 and *Decal.* appears a brief text, which was edited, translated, and discussed by Abraham Terian, "A Philonic Fragment on the Decad," in *Nourished with Peace: Studies in Hellenistic Judaism in Memory of Samuel Sandmel* (ed. Frederick E. Greenspahn, Earle Hilgert, and Burton L. Mack; Chico: Scholars Press, 1984), 173–82. Terian postulates that the fragment is from the lost *De numeris* (Περὶ ἀριθμῶν).

[8] PCW 4.xxi: "Our friend F. C. Conybeare made a comparison with the Greek text and kindly supplied to me the readings of the version."

[9] PCW 4.xxi: "For the version of the book *Abr.*, wherever the [Greek] codices disagree, agrees most closely with the text of the best codices BEK, so that the genuineness of the readings transmitted by them is often confirmed by the authority of the Armenian translator."

§155	χρόνου καὶ βίου	§214	ἐπικυδεστέραν οὖσαν
§159	πελαγῶν	§218	δύο δ᾽ οἱ νυνί
§162	πάθος	§246	καιρόν
§182	πρὸς πολυετίαν ἴσως	§259	ἂν ἄχθοιτο
§193	πράγματος		

But in fact there are other such examples in the apparatus; consider:

§175   σταθερῷ sec. BEKCFG Arm : σταθερωτέρῳ MAHP (v)
§175   ἴσθι BEK Arm ut vid: εἰσὶ ceteri
§184   ἔφασκον BEK Arm : om. F, φασὶ ceteri

It is unclear why Cohn distinguishes the twenty-one places listed in his preface. But in any case, the agreement of the Armenian and the better Greek manuscripts would (presumably, unless we suppose coincidental agreement in error) push a reading back to at least the time of the Armenian translation, i.e., the latter half of the sixth century. Since the Greek manuscripts that contain *Abr.* date from the eleventh century, the confirmation from the Armenian is of prime importance.

 Cohn goes on to state:

> est etiam ubi textus in codicibus depravatus ex Armeniae versionis genuina memoria emendetur.[10]

And Cohn lists five such places. Let us look at these in a little more detail.

 §47 ψυχῆς Arm : ψυχῶν codd. Here the Greek manuscripts have assimilated the number of this word to the number of the following word (τρόπων), although Philo regularly speaks of the "characters of the soul" (see *Abr.* 52, 147, 217).[11] The Armenian indeed has the singular form *ogwoy*.

 §60 γραμμάτων Arm : πραγμάτων codd. The similarity of these two words led to the corruption in Greek. As noted in the PCW apparatus, Mangey had already conjectured γραμμάτων, which certainly fits more smoothly with φωνῆς. The Armenian *gir* regularly corresponds to γράμμα,

---

[10] PCW 4.xxi: "Also the corrupted text in the codices is sometimes to be emended by the genuine testimony of the Armenian version."

[11] The scribes balked at the first occurrence of the singular in *Abr.*, but then accepted it. So this could be seen as an example of the correct reading's finally gaining the victory; see John Wordsworth and Henry Julian White, eds., *Novum Testamentum Domini Nostri Iesu Christi Latine* 1 (Oxford: Clarendon Press, 1889), 727–28.

and we find here *groç*, which is the genitive plural form. (πραγμάτων would be rendered as *iraç*.)

§64 τοὺς σὺν αἰσθήσει Arm : οὓς συναισθήσει ΒΕ, οὐ σὺν αἰσθήσει KFGMAH¹P, σὺν αἰσθήσει H²L(v), ἐν συναισθήσει C. The first three Greek readings seem to derive by omissions from that presupposed by the Armenian. If we ignore the accents and word division (which would not have been present for the first few centuries of transmission), the reading of BE has simply lost a tau, the reading of KFGMAH¹P has then lost one of the two contiguous sigmas, and the reading of H²L(v) has then lost the ου from the second reading or (perhaps more plausibly) has lost the ους from the first reading by a scribal leap (θανατους ους συναισθησει). The Armenian has *ork' handerj zgayowt'eamb*, which indeed corresponds to τοὺς σὺν αἰσθήσει.

§181 προσέσθαι v (Arm) : προέσθαι codd. Here we have a simple lapse, an omission of one of a series of rounded letters (ΠΡΟΣΕΣΘΑΙ). The "v" is the Vulgate edition; presumably the editor corrected to this on his own initiative. The Armenian has *əndownel*, and I have not found a place where this verb renders προσίημι. However, at John 12:48 it renders λαμβάνω in the context of receiving Jesus' words.

§182 πυρὰν νήσαντας Arm : πυρὰν ἀνήσαντας Κ, πυρὰ νήσαντας corr. ex πῦρ ἀνήσαντας Β, πῦρ ἀνήσαντας Ε, πῦρ ἄψαντες C, πῦρ ἄψαντας ceteri (v). Philo here uses two words, ἡ πυρά and νέω, that perhaps were not known to some scribes (they occur four and two times respectively in Philo). In any case, most scribes preferred a form of τὸ πῦρ. The loss of one of the two contiguous nus led to the readings in B (both original and corrected) and the reading in E. The reading of K perhaps derives from one of those found in the related codices BE by the reversion to ἡ πυρά. Most scribes preferred to use a form of ἅπτω, which at least makes sense in the context, while ἀνήσαντας seems not to be construable. The Armenian has *xaroyk kowteal*. That *xaroyk* corresponds to πυρά is shown by the second occurrence in *Abr.* 182 and by Acts 28:2 and 28:3. I have not found an example of a translation of νέω into Armenian, but I see that at Lev 1:7 the verb (ἐπι)στοιβάζω is also rendered by *kowtem* (the same verb as in *Abr.* 182) in the context of placing wood on a fire.

Now, these examples demonstrate the importance of the Armenian version. However, I noticed some different aspects of the version while working through the text with Cohn's apparatus. Perhaps it may be worthwhile to note a few of these very briefly.

As is well known, of course, the translators of Philo belonged to a school of translation that was responsible for rendering the Bible, works of Greek philosophy such as Plato, and works of early Christian writers such as Irenaeus. In general, the translators proceeded literally, even mechanically, and it is thus often possible to reconstruct (as we have seen above) the Greek *Vorlage* with considerable confidence. There are features of Greek that do not find equivalents (μέν is a frequent example), and it is also a feature of the translators that one Greek word is often rendered by two or more Armenian words. So we do not have a one-to-one correspondence. But the Armenian may provide more or less conclusive evidence in favor of one Greek word rather than another (as at *Abr.* 60, as discussed above).

It is thus rather surprising to find that the Armenian version of *Abr.* contains frequent omissions of short bits of the text, and even of longer portions of the text. As far as I can tell, this characteristic has not been discussed by Cohn, although his apparatus duly records the omissions. There would be no point in my listing here what can be found by simply inspecting Cohn's apparatus, but I might call attention to what we see just in the first few pages. The Armenian omits ἣν ἐν ἀρχῇ περιέχει (*Abr.* 1), ἢ λιμὸν καὶ εὐθηνίαν (*Abr.* 1), ἀνατέμνει καὶ (*Abr.* 7), and καὶ ἄρχων Ἀθήνησιν ὁ ἐπώνυμος καὶ τῶν ἐννέα ἀρχόντων ἄριστος ἀφ' οὗ οἱ χρόνοι καταριθμοῦνται (*Abr.* 10). Of these four, it seems possible that the second and third may result from the translators' using a more concise expression (i.e., at *Abr.* 7 for Philo's ἀνατέμνει καὶ ἀνοίγει the translators found an equivalent for ἀνοίγει adequate.) But the first and fourth cannot be so explained. And there are more or less comparable examples throughout the book. Theoretically we might have accidental omission by the translators at the time of translation, but that seems unlikely in view of the literalness of the version. Alternatively, we might postulate accidental omission by the Armenian scribes during several centuries of transmission, or we might suppose deliberate shortening for some reason or other.

Philo's Biblical Quotations in De Abrahamo

Although Philo's discussion of the life of Abraham is closely tied to the text of Genesis, direct citations are in fact relatively infrequent, certainly in comparison with the works of the Allegorical Commentary.[12] Moreover, Philo at several places constructs rather long speeches that he seems to present as quotations (e.g., *Abr.* 71 and 175). But we find about twenty more or less explicit citations, and a few of these merit further attention.[13]

Abr. 13: ἅγιός ἐστι καὶ αἰνετός (Lev 19:24). The Göttingen LXX prints ἅγιος αἰνετός, and cites Philo for the addition of ἐστι καὶ. But it seems unlikely that Philo intended to include those two words as part of an exact quotation; rather the presence of ἐστι καὶ serves merely to complete the syntax. In fact, the crucial words are the first and last, and Philo's text should rather be printed: ὃς σεμνύνων τὸν τέταρτον ἀριθμόν φησιν ὅτι "ἅγιός" ἐστι καὶ "αἰνετός." Philo himself of course did not have quotation marks available, and he and his ancient readers would have had to understand them as required from the context. At *Plant.* 95 and 117 his quotations of this phrase show that he read simply ἅγιος αἰνετός. Lev 19:24 is also referred to at *Plant.* 134 and *Somn.* 1.33.

(In fact, at *Plant.* 95 and 117 the Philonic manuscripts read ἓν ἔτος for αἰνετός, which is basically a simple itacism ε for αι, as noted by Mangey, who restored the correct reading. On the other hand, Markland suggests that Philo and already the LXX had ἄνετος.[14] But that word doesn't occur at all in the LXX, although it is found at Lev 19:24 in F* [where the first hand made the correction], and occurs in Philo at *Leg.* 3.56 and *Virt.* 78 [secl. Cohn]. At *Plant.* 126, where Philo's comment confirms the reading αἰνετός, Markland has no note. However, there Mangey proposes emending χρῆμα ἅγιον to χρῆμα αἰνετόν, "ut ex Contextu liquet." And to this Markland adds "Recte.")

Abr. 17: εὐηρέστησεν Ἐνὼχ τῷ θεῷ καὶ οὐχ ηὑρίσκετο, ὅτι μετέθηκεν αὐτὸν ὁ θεός (Gen 5:24). Here the Armenian of *Abr.* omits Ἐνώχ, supported by the LXX manuscript 125; this must be coincidental agreement in an

---

[12] This feature is noted by David T. Runia, "The Place of *De Abrahamo* in Philo's oeuvre," in this volume 133–150.

[13] Runia, ibid., 133–150, lists thirteen direct quotations, five paraphrases, and four direct allusions. For my brief investigation here I have relied on the volumes of the Göttingen LXX. We find cited there not only the text of Philo, but even readings found in the apparatus of PCW. However, the Armenian translation of the *Quaestiones* seems not to have been utilized.

[14] These notes are in his copy of Mangey's edition, on which see my "Jeremiah Markland's Contribution to the Textual Criticism of Philo," *SPhA* 16 (2004): 50–60.

oversight.[15] Philo cites this verse from οὐχ on at _QG_ 1.86 and at _Praem._ 16, where we find διότι. But I suspect that there we have influence from the New Testament citation of Gen 5:24 at Heb 11:5 (where διοτι is read, and οτι is found only in א*).[16] _Abr._ 17 is much better attested than is _Praem._ 16 (4 manuscripts), and so there seems no reason to doubt that Philo's LXX read ὅτι. The influence of Heb 11:5 has touched quite a few manuscripts at Gen 5:24.

Abr. 31: αὗται αἱ γενέσεις Νῶε· Νῶε ἄνθρωπος δίκαιος, τέλειος ἐν τῇ γενεᾷ αὐτοῦ, τῷ θεῷ εὐηρέστησεν (Gen 6:9). Cohn reports that the second Νῶε is omitted by CFG Arm. Here the Göttingen LXX does not pick up this citation, but reports the omission in two Greek manuscripts and two Ethiopic manuscripts. This is a straightforward haplography that could have occurred independently in the various manuscripts. At _Deus_ 117 Philo has Νῶε· Νῶε.

Abr. 77: ὤφθη δὲ ὁ θεὸς τῷ Ἀβραάμ (Gen 12:7). The LXX has: καὶ ὤφθη κύριος τῷ Ἀβράμ. It would thus appear that Philo has written δέ for καί, substituted ὁ θεός for κύριος, and written Ἀβραάμ for Ἀβράμ. But matters are a little more complex. Consider _Det._ 159, where Philo is allegedly (according to PCW[17]) also citing Gen 12:7: ὤφθη ὁ θεὸς αὐτῷ. We would thus have that Philo, in quoting καὶ ὤφθη κύριος τῷ Ἀβράμ, once writes ὤφθη δὲ ὁ θεὸς τῷ Ἀβραάμ, and once writes ὤφθη ὁ θεὸς αὐτῷ.[18] Such changes find no support among the LXX manuscripts, and such fluctuation would not say much for Philo's accuracy in citing the text of Genesis.[19]

In fact, I would suggest that neither of these should be considered quotations of Gen 12:7. Rather, what Philo seems to have had in mind was

[15] Howover, it io curiouo that the proper name is alsu missing in _QG_ 1.85, where the Armenian corresponds to simply εὐηρέστησε τῷ θεῷ (contrary to the Armenian OT).

[16] That the wording of the New Testament has on occasion entered the manuscript tradition of Philo seems clear. See my "The Text of Philo's _De virtutibus_," 96 and n. 89.

[17] They are followed by the German, English, and French translations, as well as by the _Biblia Patristica, Supplément: Philon d'Alexandrie_ (Paris: Éditions du Centre National de la Recherche Scientifique, 1982), 40.

[18] Although PCW uses quotation marks around ὁ θεὸς ὤφθη at _Abr._ 80, we need not suppose that this is yet a third wording. Philo's point there is simply to emphasize that God is the agent in the appearance.

[19] It is, of course, inevitable that the text of the manuscripts of the LXX used by Philo differed more or less from the text of any extant manuscript and from any printed text. But even if he used two manuscripts of Gen 12:7 at different times, it seems very unlikely that they would have contained such readings.

the wording of Gen 18:1, where the Göttingen LXX reads ὤφθη δὲ αὐτῷ ὁ θεός. This is already closer to the two citations in having ὁ θεός, surely the most notable point (although the MT has יהוה, as at 12:7). However, Philo is not quoting Gen 18:1 very exactly either. At *Det.* 159 he omits δὲ and transposes αὐτῷ ὁ θεός. And at *Abr.* 77 Philo introduces the name Abraham. But if 18:1 is in mind (and incorrectly, or at least anachronistically, referred to an earlier stage in Abraham's career), then it is at least not the *later* name Abraham, as asserted by Peter Katz in his enlightening discussion of the names of Abraham and Sarah in the text of Philo.[20] Furthermore, at 12:7 the only variation among the LXX manuscripts is that κύριος ὁ θεός is read for κύριος by 833 129. And at 18:1 κύριος ὁ θεός is read for ὁ θεός by 376. I would suggest that here we have harmonization between these two verses.[21]

Marcus calls attention to the fact that at *QG* 3.20 (on Gen 16:2) the *quaestio* has "Abraham," although the LXX, MT, and Armenian OT all have "Abram." In fact, though, "Abraham" is read at Gen 16:2 by two minuscules and by Philo at *Congr.* 1 and 12. Similarly, at *QG* 3.41 (on Gen 17:3) the *quaestio* has "Abraham," even though the LXX,[22] MT, and Armenian OT all have "Abram." Here the only evidence for "Abraham" cited in the Göttingen LXX is Philo at *Mut.* 54. Similarly, at Gen 17:1 the only evidence cited for "Abraham" is Philo, who writes the fuller form for the first "Abram" at *Mut.* 1 and for the second "Abram" at *Mut.* 1 and 15. And at Gen 12:1, "Abraham" is read by only 319* and by Philo at *Migr.* 1 and *Her.* 277. Here we see the tendency to insert the later name into contexts where the earlier name would be correct; Katz's discussion indicates that this tendency operated within the textual tradition of the Philonic works, but also even within Philo's original comments.

As a final complication in this passage, let us look at *QG* 4.1, extant in Armenian only. Here we find the quotation of Gen 18:1 as beginning: "And the Lord God appeared to Abraham." This agrees with the citation at *Abr.* 77 except for the addition of "Lord." That addition goes, as Marcus notes, against the LXX and the Armenian version of Genesis. The underlying Greek would seem to have been ὤφθη δὲ κύριος ὁ θεὸς τῷ Ἀβραάμ, and this

---

[20] *Philo's Bible: The Aberrant Text of Bible Quotations in some Philonic Writings and its Place in the Textual History of the Greek Bible* (Cambridge: Cambridge University Press, 1950), 154–57. He notes (156) that *De Abrahamo*, "which addresses a wider public than the Jewish, avoids proper names as far as possible."

[21] That is, at 12:7 833 129 added ὁ θεός from 18:1, and at 18:1 376 added κύριος from 12:7.

[22] But Marcus (PLCL Supp. 1.230 n. e) follows the tendency to introduce "Abraham" for "Abram," and thus cites the LXX as having Ἀβραάμ.

agrees precisely with Eusebius's citation at *Eccl. theol.* 2.21. (On the other hand, at *Dem. ev.* 5.9 Eusebius has ὤφθη δὲ ὁ θεὸς τῷ αὐτῷ.) Clearly we have a complex textual history here, but it seems more reasonable to take the two citations preserved in Greek (i.e., *Abr.* 77 and *Det.* 159) as more authoritative than that found at *QG* 4.1. And there is, it seems, some evidence of a tendency to introduce the phrase "the Lord God" within the *Quaestiones*, although whether this tendency was operative within the transmission of the text in Greek or in Armenian (or both) is unclear to me. See, for example, the following:

> *QG* 3.1 (Gen 15:7): "Lord God," which is read by the Armenian OT (and the Ethiopic), where LXX has "God," as Philo has in *Her.* 96.

> *QG* 3.39 (Gen 17:1): "the Lord God," as found in the Armenian OT and two LXX manuscripts, where "the Lord" is found in the LXX and MT, and in Philo at *Mut.* 1 and 15. Here we may have influence from the latter part of the verse, which reads "God" except for four LXX manuscripts that have "Lord God." Philo's *solutio* refers to the two names of the highest powers, i.e., κύριος and θεός, but these two words occur already (although not together) in the printed text of the LXX of Gen 17:1.

> *QG* 4.215 (Gen 27:28): "the Lord God," although "God" alone is found in the Old Latin version of *QG*,[23] as well as in the LXX[24] and MT, and in Philo at *Migr.* 101.

We could thus see the presence of "Lord God" in the Armenian *quaestio* as a result of this tendency. Moreover, in contrast to *QG* 3.39 Philo at *QG* 4.1 does not emphasize that Scripture refers to the two names of the highest powers; if such an *argumentum e silentio* is of any value, it suggests that Philo had only "God" at *QG* 4.1, thus agreeing with his citation at *Abr.* 77.

Of course, in making any judgment here we must keep in mind that there is much variation concerning the names of God in the textual traditions.[25]

---

[23] See Marcus, PLCL Supp. 1.512 n. f, and Françoise Petit, ed., *L'ancienne version latine des Questions sur la Genèse de Philon d'Alexandrie* (TU 113–14; Berlin: Akademie-Verlag, 1973), 1.84 (text) and 2.126 (commentary).

[24] There is some evidence for "Lord" and for "Lord God."

[25] See further Nathaniel Schmidt, "Yahwe Elohim," *JBL* 33 (1914): 25–47, who gives special attention (28–31) to various problems in Philo's text. Of course, many variations involving the divine names in Hebrew may be found in Kennicott and De Rossi (see Schmidt, 31) that are ignored in *BHS*, just as one will find much greater variation cited in the apparatus of Brooke-McLean or the Göttingen LXX than in the editions of Swete or Rahlfs.

Abr. 112: μὴ ἀδυνατεῖ παρὰ τῷ θεῷ πᾶν ῥῆμα (Gen 18:14) Here we have complications at several levels. There is textual divergence in the tradition of Philo, within the LXX of this verse, and also at its citation at Luke 1:37. Let us look at these in sequence (the MT reads הֲיִפָּלֵא מֵיהוה דָּבָר).

In PCW the apparatus presents two variation units:[26]
τω θεω BEK : θεω MAH² : θεου CFGH¹P
παν BEK : om. ceteri

The Göttingen LXX reads μὴ ἀδυνατεῖ παρὰ τοῦ θεοῦ ῥῆμα, with the following variation units:
αδυνατει : αδυνατησει b 59 : αδυνατηση 108* : αδυνατειση 108ᶜ
παρα του θεου : παρα θεου 961 15-376'-708 55 : παρα τω θεω A M al :
παρα θεω 72' : παρα κυριω 911*ᵛⁱᵈ b : του θεου 16-25-500-761 75 799
ρημα : παν ρημα 833 72' C'' 53'-246 75 74-370 71 31 : om. 15-708 527

Luke 1:37 reads οὐκ ἀδυνατήσει παρὰ τοῦ θεοῦ πᾶν ῥῆμα, with the following variations as found in Greek manuscripts:
παρα του θεου ℵ* B L W Ξ 565 *pc* : παρα τω θεω ℵᶜ A C Θ Ψ *f*³ 33
rell : παρα θεω 1 *l*211 *l*1016 : τω θεω 27 71 788 1194 *l*253* :
παρα κυριου *l*32
παρα του θεου παν ρημα : παν ρημα παρα του θεου D

What can we make of all this? A place to start is with the following analysis by Metzger in support of the reading of ℵ* B L W Ξ 565 *pc* at Luke 1:37:

> Since the word ῥῆμα, reflecting the Hebrew דָּבָר, can mean "thing" as well as "word," in the context the reading παρὰ τοῦ θεοῦ means, "No word [or promise] *from God* will be impossible [will fail]," whereas the reading παρὰ τῷ θεῷ (or simply τῷ θεῷ) means, "*With God* nothing will prove impossible." The former reading, strongly supported by ℵ* B L W Ξ 565, was probably altered to the latter reading, in conformity with the Septuagint text of Gn 18.14, μη ἀδυνατεῖ παρὰ τῷ θεῷ ῥῆμα.[27]

---

[26] Note that the Armenian version of Philo here omits an equivalent of πᾶν. The Armenian (*mi ankar ē aṙaji astowcoy bans*) seems to have been made without any influence from the translation of Gen 18:14 (*mit'ē tkaranayçē aṙ i jastowcoy ban*, in Zohrab's edition), which also omits an equivalent of πᾶν. The three Philonic manuscripts, BEK, in which πᾶν occurs are said by Cohn (PCW 4.xv) to be the best that contain *De Abrahamo*. By the way, Mangey prints the quotation without πᾶν, and with no note.

[27] Bruce M. Metzger, *A Textual Commentary on the Greek New Testament* (1st ed.; London and New York: United Bible Societies, 1971), 130, with Metzger's brackets

Here Metzger perhaps assumes a bit too quickly that the LXX in fact had παρα τω θεω, as found in Rahlfs' edition. Given that the set of readings is similar at both Gen 18:14 and Luke 1:37, it seems perfectly possible to suppose that the LXX had παρα του θεου, and then the harmonization at Luke 1:37 would have proceeded in the opposite direction. (Note, by the way, that the more precise issue with respect to harmonization is not directly what the LXX originally read, but what form of the text was known to the scribes of Luke.) With the text of Philo influences could have come from either the LXX text known to the scribes or from the text of Luke known to the scribes.

But with respect to παν what has happened seems much clearer. This word is unanimously attested in Luke, and I would think that it is more or less certain that it has intruded from there into some of the LXX manuscripts and into three of the Philonic manuscripts.[28] Thus, the word should be relegated to the apparatus at *Abr.* 112. Philo's quotation here would then agree with what we find at *QG* 4.17, which also omits any equivalent of παν.[29]

Whether Philo read τω θεω, θεω, or θεου seems to be a difficult decision. At *Abr.* 112 the Armenian has *aṙaǰi astowcoy*, whereas at *QG* 4.17 it has simply *astowcoy*. The latter does not have an equivalent of παρα, which is unanimously attested by the Greek codices in *Abr.* 112 and would seem to be reasonably represented by *aṙaǰi*. It is thus puzzling that there is no equivalent at *QG* 4.17. On the other hand, note that at *Abr.* 112 BEK, which have harmonized Philo to Luke 1:37 by adding παν, also write the dative, which agrees with the majority text at Luke 1:37. I suggest that just as παν is a harmonization to Luke 1:37, so is τω θεω or θεω, and that Philo's Greek originally had παρα του θεου. Thus Philo's text of Genesis was the text now printed in the Göttingen LXX.

Finally, note that the LXX renders the Tetragrammaton with a form of θεός. Or, at least, this must have been true unless we follow the reading παρα κυριω of 911* b, which is (I suppose) more likely to be either a harmonization to κύριος in vs. 13, or to reflect a scholarly improvement to agree with the Hebrew. But then we also find παρα κυριου in *l*32 at Luke 1:37; did the scribe of that eleventh century lectionary know that the Tetragrammaton was in the Hebrew original of the LXX that was being quoted (not

---

and italics. This variation is not dicussed in the 2d ed. of the *Commentary* (London and New York: United Bible Societies, 1994).

[28] For its intrusion into the LXX tradition see J. W. Wevers, *Notes on the Greek Text of Genesis* (SBLSCS 35; Atlanta: Scholars Press, 1993), 253.

[29] The Armenian reads: *mit'ē tkaranayçē astowcoy ban.* It thus differs from the Armenian translation of Gen 18:14 (see note 26 above) in not having *aṙ i.*

quite precisely [with πᾶν]) at Luke 1:37? Here it certainly seems more likely that harmonization to the context has occurred; that is, the scribe was influenced by vs. 38, which begins: εἶπεν δὲ Μαριάμ· ἰδοὺ ἡ δούλη κυρίου.

Abr. 132: ἐπανιὼν ἥξω πρὸς σὲ κατὰ τὸν καιρὸν τοῦτον εἰς νέωτα, καὶ ἕξει υἱὸν Σάρρα ἡ γυνή σου (Gen 18:10). The phrase εἰς νέωτα is anomalous; the Göttingen LXX cites it only from *Abr.* 132. At *Migr.* 126 Philo has εἰς ὥρας (in all manuscripts), thus showing that his text of Genesis agrees with the LXX.[30] Similarly, at *QG* 4.12 (on Gen 18:10) Philo writes εἰς ὥρας in the *quaestio*,[31] and the *solutio* confirms that reading. On the other hand, νέωτα does not occur in the LXX, and occurs in Philo only at *Abr.* 110 and 132, both referring to Gen 18:10, and *Hypoth.* 7:15. It is thus possible that Philo is not intending to present a direct quotation here, but rather constructs an appropriate statement from Gen 18:10, and feels free to make his points in his own language. Thus, he shifts to the presumably clearer νέωτα, and also introduces the comment with ἐπανιὼν (not found in the LXX manuscripts, but cited from Philo in the Göttingen LXX) rather than ἐπαναστρέφων, as found in the LXX and in Philo at *Migr.* 126.

Note, though, that the Armenian rendering of εἰς νέωτα fluctuates at the two places. At *Abr.* 110, where the phrase occurs apart from the biblical context, the Armenian reads *i miws ews am* (or *ami*), literally "in another year." But at *Abr.* 132, where the larger biblical context is found, the Armenian has *i žams*, literally "in hours," corresponding to the LXX's εἰς ὥρας. This is the same Armenian that is found at *QG* 4.12 and 4.18. But how did this Armenian translation arise? It would hardly be suggested by εἰς νέωτα. And it could not have been influenced by the Armenian OT, which has *i soyn awurs*, literally "in those days" at both Gen 18:10 and 18:14.[32] So, the Armenian rendering at *Abr.* 132 disagrees with both Philo's Greek (as found in the manuscripts) and the Armenian OT, but agrees with the LXX. The most plausible explanation is perhaps that Philo's Greek has been corrupted at *Abr.* 132. That is, Philo originally wrote εἰς ὥρας, as he did at *Migr.* 126, and *QG* 4.12 and 4.18. But some early scribe (or editor) balked at the awkward phrase and decided to replace it with εἰς νέωτα, which had occurred a few pages previously. Of course, we then have the unlikelihood that a scribe who desired to replace εἰς ὥρας would choose a phrase that

---

[30] See Wevers, *Notes*, 250.

[31] The Armenian version of *QG* has the equivalent of "hours" both here and at *QG* 4.18 (quoting Gen 18:14), whereas the Armenian OT has "days" at Gen 18:10 and 18:14. See the notes by Marcus at PLCL Supp. 1.285 n. e, and 1.291 n. f.

[32] See note 31.

occurs rarely in Philo and not at all in the LXX or NT.[33] So we are left with, as it seems to me, a puzzling phenomenon.

In the apparatus Cohn cites the Armenian as having: καὶ ἔσται υἱὸς Σάρρᾳ τῇ γυναικί σου. This is ignored in the Göttingen LXX, presumably being viewed as simply the result of translational freedom. (It reflects the Greek of Gen 18:14.) But there is a curious aspect of the Armenian here: it in fact has *Sarayn*, which is the equivalent of "Sarai" (Σάρᾳ) rather than "Sarah" (Σάρρᾳ).[34]

Abr. 166: διὸ καὶ παγκάλως "μικράν" τε καὶ "οὐ μικρὰν" τὴν πόλιν ταύτην οἱ χρησμοὶ διασυνιστᾶσαν αἰνιττόμενοι τὴν ὅρασιν (Gen 19:20). Philo sees the contradictory predication in his reading of the biblical text as an occasion for allegorical interpretation, just as he does in *QG* 4.47, where (although Philo abbreviates the citation of Gen 19:18–20) it is clear from the *quaestio* and from the discussion that he understood οὐ μικρά ἐστι as an assertion. On the other hand, the usual editions of the LXX present: ἡ πόλις . . . ἥ ἐστιν μικρά, ἐκεῖ σωθήσομαι· οὐ μικρά ἐστιν; (i.e., taking the last clause to be a question). Thus, discussing *Abr.* 166, Colson cites the LXX (. . . οὐ μικρά ἐστι;) and the RV ("Is it not a little one?"), and comments: "Philo either fails to see that the last three words are a question, or more probably thinks that the grammatical possibility of treating them as a statement is a sufficient ground for extracting an allegorical lesson."[35] Similar comments are made by other translators.[36]

These scholars seem to suppose that the punctuation as found in LXX editions is simply *the* punctuation of the LXX. But of course for centuries the LXX was transmitted without punctuation (or accents or breathings or word division), and certainly the manuscript(s) of Genesis that Philo was reading would have had no punctuation. We can reasonably suppose that the LXX translators intended ου μικρα εστι to be a question, if for no other reason than that we can see that the Hebrew *Vorlage* (הלא מצער) contains the interrogative ה.[37] But Philo (as it seems) could not check the Hebrew, and he, like other Hebrew-less readers of the LXX in antiquity, would have had to choose how to read ου μικρα εστι from the Greek alone. And who is

---

[33] Moreover, the LXX scribes had no trouble with the phrase at Gen 18:10 and 18:14.

[34] Σάρᾳ, rather than Σάρρᾳ, is found in two LXX manuscripts.

[35] PLCL 6.84 n. a.

[36] For *Abr.* 166 see PCH 1.131 n.2, and PAPM 20.90 n. 2 (–91). For *QG* 4.47 see PLCL Supp. 1.322 n. k, and PAPM 34B.224–25 n. 1.

[37] Of course, the Hebrew would not have been pointed until much later than our period.

to say that he made an incorrect choice? Indeed, in his *Hom. Gen.* 5.5–6 Origen understands this clause of Gen 19:20 as an assertion, at least according to the Latin version (of the lost Greek) by Rufinus.[38]

Abr. 173: ἰδοὺ τὸ πῦρ, ἔφη, καὶ τὰ ξύλα, πάτερ, ποῦ τὸ ἱερεῖον (Gen 22:7). We can contrast this citation with what we find in *Fug.* 132: ἰδοὺ τὸ πῦρ καὶ τὰ ξύλα, ποῦ τὸ πρόβατον τὸ εἰς ὁλοκάρπωσιν. There we have an exact quotation of the LXX, except for the omission of ἐστιν after ποῦ (contrary to all LXX manuscripts). But at *Abr.* 173 Philo transposes πάτερ from earlier in the verse, and also introduces the word ἱερεῖον, which is not found in the LXX, but occurs fifty-nine times in Philo. So the last four words should be considered as Philo's paraphrase of Isaac's question, rather than a direct citation. And the Göttingen LXX does not refer to Philo's words there.

Conclusion

There are yet further puzzling places, such as *Abr.* 119 and 205. But even with regard to Philo's quotations from the Bible, there are some problems that seem not to be satisfactorily resolved. Nevertheless, the issues raised here may remind us that even in the works of Philo that are well-preserved, there are passages that raise textual questions, others where the Cohn-Wendland text should possibly be altered, and perhaps even some that will remain recalcitrant.

San Francisco

---

[38] See the text in GCS 29.63–64 (ed. W. A. Baehrens, 1920) = SC 7 bis.176 and 180 (ed. and trans. Louis Doutreleau, 1976): "Ciuitas haec pusilla . . . et non est pusilla. . . . ciuitas pusilla et non pusilla," and "cum pusillam et non pusillam ciuitatem Segor." Of course, in writing his Greek text Origen, or his shorthand writers or copyists or girls trained in beautiful writing (Eusebius, *Hist. eccl.* 6.23; see Kim Haines-Eitzen, *Guardians of Letters* [New York: Oxford University Press, 2000], 41–52), also would not have used punctuation. But, unless Rufinus has misrepresented the Greek, the citation and comment entail that Origen took the relevant clause as an assertion rather than a question. Naturally, it is possible that Origen was influenced by Philo here, although he does not seem to utilize Philo's allegorical interpretation. By the way, Mangey (in a note on *Abr.* 166) refers to this work by Origen.

The Studia Philonica Annual 20 (2008) 167–197

BIBLIOGRAPHY SECTION

PHILO OF ALEXANDRIA
AN ANNOTATED BIBLIOGRAPHY 2005

D. T. Runia, E. Birnbaum, K. A. Fox, A. C. Geljon, H. M. Keizer,
J. P. Martín, M. R. Niehoff, J. Riaud, G. Schimanowski, T. Seland

2005[*]

J. A. Arieti, *Philosophy in the Ancient World. An Introduction* (Lanham MD 2005), esp. 299–310.

In this introduction to ancient philosophy a chapter is devoted to Philo, characterizing his thought as a biblical-Platonic mix. The author mainly discusses Philo's view on the Sabbath. He also shows how Philo interprets the creation account in Genesis along Platonic lines of thought. (ACG)

[*] This bibliography has been prepared by the members of the International Philo Bibliography Project, under the leadership of D. T. Runia (Melbourne). The principles on which the annotated bibliography is based have been outlined in *SPhA* 2 (1990) 141–142, and are largely based on those used to compile the 'mother works', R-R and RRS. The division of the work this year has been as follows: material in English (and Dutch) by D. T. Runia (DTR), E. Birnbaum (EB), K. A. Fox (KAF), A. C. Geljon (ACG); in French by J. Riaud (JR); in Italian by H. M. Keizer (HMK); in German by G. Schimanowski (GS); in Spanish and Portuguese by J. P. Martín (JPM); in Scandinavian languages (and by Scandinavian scholars) by T. Seland (TS); in Hebrew (and by Israeli scholars) by Maren Niehoff (MRN). Once again this year much benefit has been derived from the related bibliographical labours of L. Perrone (Bologna) and his team in the journal *Adamantius* (Origen studies). Other scholars not (or formerly) in the team who have given assistance this year are Giovanni Benedetto and Dieter Zeller. My research assistant in Melbourne, Tamar Primoratz, again helped me with various tasks. This year too I am extremely grateful to my former Leiden colleague M. R. J. Hofstede for laying a secure foundation for the bibliography through his extremely thorough electronic searches. However, the bibliography remains inevitably incomplete, because much work on Philo is tucked away in monographs and articles, the titles of which do not mention his name. Scholars are encouraged to get in touch with members of the team if they spot omissions (addresses below in 'Notes on Contributors'). In order to preserve continuity with previous years, the bibliography retains its own customary stylistic conventions and has not changed to those of the Society of Biblical Literature used in the remainder of the Annual.

I. Arnaoutoglou, '«Collegia» in the province of Egypt in the first century A.D.,' *Ancient Society* 35 (2005) 197–216.

It has been argued that the Roman restrictive attitude towards the Collegia, introduced by a Lex Iulia somewhere between 49 and 44 B.C.E. was also introduced in Egypt. The author of this article argues, however, that the evidence adduced for this suggestion does not really support such a view. The evidence from Philo in his *In Flaccum* on the dissolution of the *hetaireiai* and *synodoi* does not support such a conclusion, but is rather to be understood as a temporary response by the Prefect to rising tensions in Alexandria. The other source used as evidence, the *Gnomon of the Idios Logos* §108, is too fragmentary and might only reflect the prohibition by Flaccus the Prefect. Hence, according to the author, the Collegia in Egypt did not suffer from any general prohibition of law. The case of Collegia in Egypt is in fact evidence for the view that the Romans were not suspicious of the collegia as long as they did not challenge the pax Romana. (TS)

H. Attridge, 'Philo and John: Two Riffs on One Logos,' *The Studia Philonica Annual* 17 (2005) 103–117.

This comprehensive comparison of the Logos theologies in the Gospel of John and Philo's Allegorical Commentaries avoids atomistic comparison as is fashionable in commentaries on the Gospel and shows a profound connection between the two. A brief summary of the contours of Philo's treatment of the Logos in *De opificio mundi* is followed by a review of major texts in the Allegorical Commentary against the backdrop of Philo's rhetorical schemes. The Logos as a universal principle of rationality looms large throughout. The rhetorical and conceptual structure of Philo's Logos Theology is precisely that of the Gospel of John. (KAF)

C. Bakhos (ed.), *Ancient Judaism in its Hellenistic Context*, Supplements to the Journal for the Study of Judaism 95 (Leiden–Boston 2005).

This volume of papers presented at a conference held in the UCLA center for Jewish Studies contains a number of papers relevant to the study of Philo and Hellenistic Judaism. See separate entries under the names of J. J. Collins, M. Himmelfarb and G. E. Sterling. (DTR)

C. Batsch, *La guerre et les rites de guerre dans le judaïsme du deuxième Temple* (Leiden–Boston 2005), esp. 151–160, 296–301, 390–393.

The author presents in succession Philonic texts that relate to the 'zeal' of Phineas, the prohibition of combat during the Sabbath and the ties between blood and the soul. (JR)

K. Berthelot, ''Ils jettent au feu leurs fils et leurs filles pour leurs dieux': une justification humaniste du massacre des cananeens dans les textes juifs anciens?,' *Revue Biblique* 112 (2005) 161–191.

Just as is the case for many modern commentators, ancient authors, whether Jews or Christians, felt uncomfortable about the eradication of the Canaanite population during the conquest of Canaan by the Israelites. The author discusses one of the ways in which Jewish authors in antiquity, and in particular Philo, justified these massacres. In *Spec.*

2.167ff. the Alexandrian defends both divine justice and the Israelites who were its agent. He presents the Canaanites as monstrous beings who sacrificed their children to their gods. He also defends the Jewish people against accusations of misanthropy brought against them by Greeks and Egyptians. He turns the tables by accusing them of behaving like the Canaanites when they participate in the Dionysiac cults which accompany human sacrifice or when they expose the newly-born children. These arguments show a certain sensitivity towards humanistic objections against the biblical accounts, even if they do not imply true adherence to humanism on the part of Jewish authors. (JR)

M. Böhm, *Rezeption und Funktion der Vätererzählungen bei Philo von Alexandria. Zum Zusammenhang von Kontext, Hermeneutik und Exegese im frühen Judentum,* Beihefte zur Zeitschrift für die neutestamentliche Wissenschaft und die Kunde der älteren Kirche 128 (Berlin–New York 2005).

This Leipzig *Habilitation* distinguishes between three fundamental parts of the corpus Philonicum: the Exposition of the Law, the Allegorical Commentary on the book Genesis and the *Quaestiones*. The author focuses on the narratives of Abraham, Sarah, Hagar, Ismael, Isaac, Lot, Rebecca, Laban, Esau and Jacob especially in the treatises *De Abrahamo, De Specialibus Legibus, De Praemiis et Poenis* and *De Vita Mosis*. Böhm views the Exposition of the Law as an introduction for interested non-Jews in Alexandria. The 'difficult texts' are skipped, discussions between Jews are not mentioned, Philo seems to decline to work directly with the text of LXX and the biblical text is only paraphrased. The narratives have an ethical orientation and an important focus lies on the dualism of virtue and vice, which originate in God's creation and providence. The second part of Philo's œuvre is a real commentary. The readers are supposed to be familiar with the LXX and they are introduced to a universal meaning of the text. The third part, the *Quaestiones*, is interpreted as an early work of Philo. The main audience for this work also seem to be Jews, to whom a kind of study-book (*Studienbuch*) is offered. In this way the author relates the narratives of the Patriarchs to the different hermeneutical orientations of Philo's writings. This is the reason for the different perspectives, varieties and jumps in content, which are normally attributed to Philo as inconsistencies. But in this hermeneutic Philo is underlined as a contextual theologian and narrator. All in all, the writings of Philo are evaluated as different theological approaches adapted for the task of dealing with the tensions between Egypt, Greek and Jewish inhabitants at an intellectual level. See also the article by the author in the volume of Deines and Niebuhr, summarized at *SPhA* 19 (2007) 147f. (GS)

A. P. Bos, 'Philo van Alexandrië en de Griekse filosofie,' in R. W. Munk (ed.), *Filosofie Jodendom Joodse filosofie,* (Budel, The Netherlands 2005) 9–22.

The author briefly discusses some aspects of Philo's thought, among which we mention God's transcendence, the Logos and the divine powers. He pays also attention to Philo's allegorical exegesis of the figure of Abraham, and the doctrine of the divine pneuma, which, in his view, can be partly labeled as Aristotelian. According to the author, Philo is an exegete who interprets the Bible in service of his Greek philosophical presuppositions. In an appendix Bos offers a Dutch translation of *Her.* 55–57 and 96–99. (ACG)

L. Brisson, *Introduction à la Philosophie du Mythe*. I Sauver les Mythes (Paris 2005), esp. 86–89.

Brief discussion of *Prov.* 2.40–42 in the context of a discussion of the interpretation of the traditional Greek myths in the Platonist and Neopythagorean tradition. (DTR)

F. CALABI, *Filone di Alessandria De Decalogo*, Philosophica 24 (Pisa 2005).

Italian translation—with clarifying notes—of *De Decalogo*, flanked by the Greek text and preceded by an introduction which lucidly exposes the line of argument of the treatise. The translation is in a readable style (Philo's long periods are often divided into separate sentences). There is no indication of what edition of the Greek text has been printed. (HMK)

J. J. COLLINS, *Jewish Cult and Hellenistic Culture: Essays on the Jewish Encounter with Hellenism and Roman Rule* (Leiden–Boston 2005).

This important collection of essays focuses little on Philo specifically, but refers to him frequently as a point of comparison for minor Hellenistic-Jewish authors, particularly in relation to the question of human immortality (Ps.Phocylides 134–135, Wisdom 174–175). For the essay examining whether one should speak of anti-semitism in Alexandria (181–201) see the separate summary below. There is also a brief discussion on Philo's eschatology at 155–156. (DTR)

J. J. COLLINS, 'Anti-Semitism in Antiquity? The Case of Alexandria,' in C. BAKHOS (ed.), *Ancient Judaism in its Hellenistic Context,* Supplements to the Journal for the Study of Judaism 95 (Leiden–Boston 2005) 181–201.

Before the essay examines the main question posed in its title, it discusses the events of 38 C.E. in Alexandria and related incidents, naturally making extensive use of Philo's evidence. There are obvious problems with the use of the term 'anti-semitism'. The central question is whether hostility towards the Jews in antiquity was unique in its own context. The author tends to answer this question in the negative, but he does conclude that their endeavour to maintain a distinct identity and resist assimilation was an essential ingredient in ethnic conflict. The article has been republished in the author's set of collected essays published in the same year (see below). (DTR)

R. R. COX, *By the Same Word: The Intersection of Cosmology and Soteriology in Hellenistic Judaism, Early Christianity and 'Gnosticism' in the Light of Middle Platonic Intermediary Doctrine* (diss. University of Notre Dame 2005).

The dissertation written under the supervision of G. E. Sterling examines the role of the theological intermediary as developed in Middle Platonism and the influence it exerted on theologies founded on a biblical basis. Middle Platonism espoused an intellectual system that would explain how a transcendent supreme principle could relate to the material universe. The central aspect of this system was an intermediary, modeled after the Stoic active principle, which mediated the supreme principle's influence to the material world while preserving its transcendence. Having similar concerns as Middle Platonism, three religious traditions from the turn of the era (Hellenistic Jewish sapientialism, Early Christianity, and 'Gnosticism') appropriated Middle Platonic intermediary doctrine as a means for understanding their relationship to the Deity, to the cosmos, and to themselves. However, each of these traditions varies in their adaptation of this doctrine as a result of their distinctive understanding of creation and humanity's place therein. In particular Hellenistic Jewish sapientialism (Philo of Alexandria and Wisdom of Solomon) espouses a holistic ontology, combining a Platonic appreciation for noetic reality with an ultimately positive view of creation and its place in human fulfillment. Early Christians (those who speak in 1 Cor. 8:6, Col. 1:15–20, Hebr. 1:2–3, and the Johannine prologue) provide an eschatological twist on this ontology when the intermediary figure finds its final expression in the human Jesus Christ. On the other hand, *Poimandres* (*CH* 1) and the *Apocryphon of John*, both associated with the traditional rubric 'Gnosticism,' draw from Platonism to describe how creation is antithetical to human nature and its transcendent source. (DTR; based on DAI-A 66–04, p. 1386)

S. DENNINGMANN, *Die astrologische Lehre der Doryphorie: eine soziomorphe Metapher in der antiken Planetenastrologie*, Beiträge zum Altertumskunde 214 (München–Leipzig 2005), esp. 123–146.

The Münster dissertation examines the metaphor of the 'spear-bearers' (*doruphoroi*) who accompany the king in ancient astrological literature. There are also two philosophical treatises in which the image is used in relation to the sun and the planets, the one in Philo, the other in Proclus. After first setting out the different ancient views on the order of the planets, the author introduces the Philonic text, *Her.* 221–223, in which the sun and the planets as its *doruphoroi* are compared with the Menorah. Noteworthy in this text is Philo's use of the Posidonian order of the planets. Next other Philonic uses of the metaphor are examined: the senses as *doruphoroi* of the mind (cf. *Leg.* 3.115) and God surrounded by his Powers as *doruphoroi* (cf. *Abr.* 121–122). The origin of this use of the metaphor is to be found in Plato *Tim.* 70b, but has been mediated through the Hellenistic philosophical tradition. The author then returns to the presentation of the planets as *doruphoroi* of the sun. The image does not just convey the status of the planets. There is a complex use of analogy involved, which is lucidly set out in a table on p. 143. The monarchic conception of king, assistants and people has been given a theological, cosmological, psychological and an epistemological application. The essential role of the *doruphoroi* in the metaphor is that of mediators. The author suspects that the philosopher Posidonius may have played an important role in developing the metaphor, but this cannot be proven because there is no direct textual evidence. (DTR)

J. DILLON, 'Cosmic Gods and Primordial Chaos in Hellenistic and Roman Philosophy: the Context of Philo's Interpretation of Plato's *Timaeus* and the Book of Genesis,' in G. H. VAN KOOTEN (ed.), *The Creation of Heaven and Earth: Re-interpretations of Genesis 1 in the Context of Judaism, Ancient Philosophy, Christianity, and Modern Physics*, Themes in Biblical Narrative: Jewish and Christian Traditions 8 (Leiden–Boston 2005) 97–108.

The article briefly introduces the controversy generated by Plato's creation account in the *Timaeus*. Dillon is firmly of the view that it should not be taken literally as advocated by Aristotle: there never was a pre-cosmic stage in the cosmos' creation. Rather it reflects a degree of distortion in its material substratum which gives rise to imperfection. After noting some interpretative stages in the Hellenistic period, he then moves on to Philo, who does not follow Stoic ideas, but rather a Pythagoreanized view perhaps mediated by Eudorus. An interpretation in terms of a creation out of nothing is not an option. Philo of course would not openly abandon the conception that God the creator brought the cosmos into existence. Nevertheless his words at *Opif.* 26–29 come close to the original defence of Plato made by Speusippus and Xenocrates. (DTR)

A. C. DINAN, *Fragments in Context: Clement of Alexandria's Use of Quotations from Heraclitus (Philo of Alexandria, Plutarch, Greece)* (diss. Catholic University of Washington 2005).

This dissertation provides the results of an investigation into Clement of Alexandria's use of the pre-Socratic philosopher Heraclitus. The principal means for this investigation is a comparison of those passages in Clement, Plutarch, and Philo of Alexandria which are thought to contain citations of the same Heraclitean fragments. Few conclusions are drawn respecting the source of Clement's Heraclitean citations. Instead the thesis concentrates on Clement's art of citation, his reading of Heraclitus, and the extent to which these had precedent in Philo or Plutarch. The research confirms the lofty esteem in which Clement held Heraclitus, and clarifies the unique way in which Clement invoked the Ephesian philosopher as a prophetic voice within Greek culture. It is also demonstrated that despite Clement's reputation for providing accurate citations, he was not averse to modifying the text of the Heraclitean fragments and even to subverting a standard interpretation. The dissertation contributes to the understanding of the appropriation of Heraclitus in Hellenistic philosophy, adds to our understanding of Clement's penchant for citation, and confers insight into Clement's thought and working methods. For the author's research on Philo see also his article in *SPhA* 19 (2007) 59–80. (DTR; based on DAI-A 65–11, p. 4184)

J.-J. DUHOT, 'Métamorphoses du logos. Du stoïcisme au Nouveau Testament,' in G. ROMEYER DHERBEY and J.-B. GOURINAT (eds.), *Les Stoïciens*, Bibliothèque d'Histoire de la Philosophie (Paris 2005) 453–466.

The author in examining how the transition from the Stoic to the Christian logos took place emphasizes the role played by Philo. Two important texts are the exegesis of the creation account in *Opif.* and the depiction of the role of the Logos in *Her.* 130ff. The Logos is the agent through which God orders the universe, a conception which brings us quite close to the Stoa. There remains, however, an important difference: the logos is the agent, but not God himself. But even if there is no conjunction of the two, as in the Stoa, there does remain an oscillation, just like in the case of the Stoic God, between the two conceptions, i.e. sometimes he is the agent of the divine power, at other times a personified deity. The major problem is the status of the logos as both created and creative. The logos is the first-born of God, the Word which he emits and which effectuates creation, but in achieving this the Word in fact takes on the function of God himself. The logos is thus both Son of God and in his function God himself inasmuch as he creates, orders and maintains the universe. (JR)

A. C. FELLOWS, *Growth of Religion as Affected by Culture: How the Greek and Jewish Diaspora Cultures Preserved in Philo of Alexandria's Writings have Influenced the Development of Christianity* (Boston University 2005).

We have so far not been able to obtain a summary of this thesis prepared for the degree of Master of Sacred Theology. (DTR)

R. B. Finazzi, and P. Pontani, 'Il lessico delle antiche traduzioni armene di testi greci e un nuovo strumento di lavoro,' in R. B. Finazzi (ed.), *Del tradurre: da Occidente verso Oriente come incontro di lingue e culture: atti della giornata di studio su Traduzioni orientali e testi classici: lo stato della ricerca, Brescia, 8 ottobre 2004*, (Milano 2005) 79–173.

Sample (limited to words initiating with alpha) of a comparative Greek-Armenian lexicon based on the Armenian translations of nine Greek texts, included among which are Philo's *De Abrahamo, De specialibus legibus* 1 and 3 (as well as Plato's *Apologia, Minos, Laws*, Aristotle's *Categoriae*, Theon's *Progymnasmata*, and Athanasius' *Epistula ad Epictetum*). The lexicon is printed in ten columns, the first column listing the Greek words and the remaining columns presenting the Armenian renderings—if any—in each of the nine texts (but, in line with the provisory and limited scope of the article, without text references or numbers of occurrences). Introductory observations (79–99) relate to the methods of translation (on a lexical level) used by the Armenian translators. (HMK)

K. Fuglseth, *Johannine Sectarianism in Perspective: a Sociological, Historical, and Comparative Analysis of Temple and Social Relationships in the Gospel of John, Philo, and Qumran*, Novum Testamentum Supplements 119 (Leiden–Boston 2005).

This is a lightly revised version of Fuglseth's doctoral dissertation (Trondheim, Norway) completed in 2002. See further the detailed summary at *SPhA* 17 (2005) 174. (TS)

A. C. Geljon, 'Divine Infinity in Gregory of Nyssa and Philo of Alexandria,' *Vigiliae Christianae* 59 (2005) 152–178.

First, the author deals with the notion of divine infinity in Gregory of Nyssa, and criticizes the thesis of E. Mühlenberg that Gregory was the first to ascribe infinity to God. In the second part Philo's view is discussed. The opinion of Henri Guyot that Philo was the first to introduce divine infinity has to be qualified: there are starting points for the notion of divine infinity in Philo, but Philo never calls God infinite. Philo describes God's blessings and gifts as everlasting and without circumscription, which implies being infinite. God's gifts are too great for human beings to receive fully and they have to be adapted to the capacity of man. In addition, human beings are unable to understand God fully, so the quest of the soul for God is unending. Gregory, who also presents the search for God as without end, was able to connect up with this notion. (ACG)

R. Goulet, 'Allégorisme et anti-allégorisme chez Philon d'Alexandrie,' in G. Dahan and R. Goulet (eds.), *Allégorie des poètes allégorie des philosophes: études sur la poétique et l'herméneutique de l'allégorie de l'Antiquité à la Réforme*, (Paris 2005) 59–87.

Philo is often regarded as the father and example par excellence of Jewish-Christian allegoresis. But it should not be forgotten that he can sometimes express strong hostility towards certain allegories which he reports. An allegory that is too radical in totally and systematically rejecting the literal sense of the text and which denies the historicity of the persons and the incidents recorded in the Bible cannot be accepted by the loyal Jew Philo, who himself adopted a moderate form of allegorization, to be regarded as a pietistic reaction to a far more audacious kind of allegorical enterprise. In his research the author has found traces of this allegorical enterprise in Philo's commentaries. Three valuable appendices presenting the treatises of the Philonic corpus, the structure of the Allegorical Commentary, and a list of etymologies and symbolisms round off the article. See also the review of the collection in which the article is found by Jean Riaud in *SPhA* 18 (2006) 209–212. (JR)

S. GRINDHEIM, *The Crux of Election: Paul's Critique of the Jewish Confidence in the Election of Israel*, Wissenschaftliche Untersuchungen zum Neuem Testament 2.202 (Tübingen 2005), esp. 69–75.

Preliminary to an evaluation of Paul's critique of Jewish confidence in the election of Israel, a review of the motif of election in the literature of Second Temple Judaism is undertaken. The election of Israel does not play a prominent role in the writings of Philo. Even though Israel is a spiritual entity and does not refer to an ethnic group, the concept, which is an honorary title depicting an elite group that attains to seeing God by means of grace, has not been universalized to include gentiles in Israel as seers of God. (KAF)

C. T. R. HAYWARD, *Interpretations of the Name Israel in Ancient Judaism and Some Early Christian Writings: from Victorious Athlete to Heavenly Champion* (Oxford 2005), esp. 156–219.

This survey demonstrates that Jewish exegetes' interpretations of the name 'Israel' reflected their contemporary concerns about what was centrally important to Jewish identity and that some Christians adapted (or may have adapted) Jewish interpretations to suit their own purposes. Chapters cover the Hebrew Bible, the Septuagint, ben Sira, Jubilees, Philo, the Prayer of Joseph, Josephus, Rabbinic texts, the New Testament, and Patristic passages. Philo most consistently understands 'Israel' through the etymology 'one who sees God.' Even though he never uses the LXX to support this understanding, his discussions reflect several LXX themes in relation to Israel such as Jacob's struggle, a link between Jacob's experience at Bethel in Gen. 28 and his change of name in Gen. 32, prophecy and prophetic inspiration, and Israel as a boundary figure between heaven and earth, sometimes turned toward God, sometimes toward the world. This last theme calls to mind the symbol of the high priest, who represents the Jewish people as a whole, though Philo may also have included non-Jews among those who can see God. The Temple is a place where God might be seen, and Israel, 'the one who sees God,' is also the 'suppliant race' that has the Levitical role to serve God. Combining this kind of contemplation and service, the Therapeutae exemplify what it means to be 'Israel.' Hayward further discusses Philo's understanding of 'Israel' in relation to the Prayer of Joseph. Both sources, which have important differences but also similarities, probably drew upon earlier Jewish tradition. (EB)

A. HILHORST, "And Moses Was Instructed in All the Wisdom of the Egyptians' (Acts 7:22),' in A. HILHORST and G. H. VAN KOOTEN (eds.), *The Wisdom of Egypt: Jewish, Early Christian, and Gnostic Essays in Honour of Gerard P. Luttikhuizen*, Ancient Judaism and Early Christianity 59 (Leiden–Boston 2005) 153–176.

Hilhorst deals with the words of Stephen in Acts 7:21–22 that Moses was instructed in all the wisdom of the Egyptians. First, he asks what can be meant by wisdom and what image the author may have had of Egypt. Secondly, he discusses what Hellenistic Jews had to say about Moses' education. It is Philo who gives the most extensive picture of Moses' education (*Mos.* 1.21–24). Moses learns not only subjects belonging to the Greek encyclical education, but also Egyptian hieroglyphs. Because in Acts Moses is only educated in the Egyptian wisdom, but in Philo he also learns typical Greek subjects from Greek teachers, the view that the author of Acts summarizes Philo's portrayal cannot be correct. Finally, Hilhorst refers to patristic readings of Acts 7:22, including Clement's summary of Philo's account on Moses' education at *Str.* 1.153.2–3. (ACG)

M. Himmelfarb, 'The Torah between Athens and Jerusalem: Jewish Difference in Antiquity,' in C. Bakhos (ed.), *Ancient Judaism in its Hellenistic Context*, Supplements to the Journal for the Study of Judaism 95 (Leiden–Boston 2005) 113–129.

Despite other assessments of the challenge to the Jews posed by Hellenization, Himmelfarb, following Elias Bickerman, believes that the Jews were unusually successful in maintaining their distinctness. Whereas Bickerman emphasizes their monotheism, Himmelfarb attributes their success to the Torah, first available in Hebrew and later in Greek. Deuteronomy, with its emphasis on itself as a book but also as oral teaching before a real audience, was especially important for several reasons. As for the role of Torah in the Jews' encounter with Hellenism, Himmelfarb notes that like Greek readers of Homer, Philo allegorized when the Torah presented problems, but he upheld the importance of literal observance. Chaeremon's depiction of priests resembles Philo's portrayal of the Therapeutae but—unlike Chaeremon, whose portrait probably held 'only a rather tenuous connection to reality' (124)—Philo was constricted by a written text and thus could not characterize the priests of Jerusalem as philosophers. Similarly, Josephus too was constrained by the text of Torah, in contrast to Philo of Byblos, who also presented a history of his people. Even though Philo and Josephus used Greek ideas and values to understand the Torah, the distinctly Jewish text anchored their efforts and was central in preserving the distinctiveness of the Jews themselves. (EB)

R. Hirsch-Luipold, 'Der eine Gott bei Philon von Alexandrien und Plutarch,' in R. Hirsch-Luipold (ed.), *Gott und die Götter bei Plutarch. Götterbilder — Gottesbilder — Weltbilder*, Religionsgeschichtliche Versuche und Vorarbeiten 54 (Berlin 2005) 141–168.

The article forms the central paper of a conference volume recording the proceedings of a post-graduate seminar in Göttingen on Plutarch's theology as it relates both to philosophy and to traditional religion. Although there are significant differences between the Delphic priest on the one hand and the exegetically orientated Jew on the other, it also cannot be denied that there are clear convergences between them. The article undertakes to examine them in three specific areas. (1) Both thinkers anchor their philosophy in their respective religious traditions which they fully espouse in their own lives, claiming that their religion gives access to divine truth and then using philosophy to give expression to their reflection on that truth. (2) Both share the hermeneutics of allegory and symbolism in order to interpret their respective religious traditions in terms of a Platonic philosophy. Paradoxically, however, in Philo the God of history is transcendentalized, whereas in Plutarch the transcendent God of Academic tradition is personalized and historicised. (3)

When the content of their theology is examined, it emerges that they have much in common, not only the shared view that God is immaterial and transcendent, but also that he is one and has a personal relation to human beings. In the final section of the article it is argued that the links between the religious philosophy of two thinkers can be explained through their Alexandrian connection, in Philo's case because he lived there all his life, in Plutarch's case through his teacher Ammonius and the pythagoreanizing Platonism that goes back to Eudorus, and also through the attraction that Egyptian myths and rites held for him. See also the review of the collection of articles in *SPhA* 19 (2007) 212–215. (DTR)

S. INOWLOCKI, 'Quelques pistes de réflection au sujet de la mystique de Philon d'Alexandrie,' in A. Dierkens and B. Beyer de Ryke (eds.), *Mystique: la passion de l'Un, de l'Antiquité à nos jours*, Problèmes d'histoire des religions 15 (Brussels 2005) 49–59.

The author presents a valuable and well-documented overview of scholarly views on the subject of Philo's mysticism. She begins with an outline of the main views (esp. Goodenough, Winston) and the main issues. Next, the role of the biblical characters Abraham and Moses and the relevance of the Therapeutae are discussed. A third section focuses on whether Philo was a practising mystic. Finally some brief words are devoted to the Nachleben of Philo's views. Inowlocki concludes that Philo deserves to be ranked among the mystics of antiquity, even if certain nuances remain indispensable. (DTR)

A. KERKESLAGER, 'The Absence of Dionysios, Lampo, and Isidoros from the Violence in Alexandria in 38 C.E.,' *The Studia Philonica Annual* 17 (2005) 49–94.

In this article the author argues against the generally accepted view that three members of the Alexandrian Greek elite known as Dionysios, Lampo and Isidoros were involved in the violence in Alexandria in 38 C.E. In the first section, entitled what Philo does and does not say, the author argues that Philo's texts about the violence do not support the view that the three persons were involved. Kerkeslager bases this position on four arguments. (1) Philo never says that these three persons played a role in plotting the violence. When he mentions their names, he uses them to refer to three categories of people. (2) They are completely absent from Philo's major reports of the riot against the Jews. (3) When their activities as individuals are narrated (*Flacc.* 125–147), they are portrayed not as enemies of the Jews but as hostile towards Flaccus. (4) In *Legat.* Philo pictures Isidoros as anti-Jewish but this passage refers to events which happened in Rome after the summer of 38. The second section deals with the death of Dionysios. Our Dionysios can be identified with the Dionysios that is mentioned in P. Oxy, 8.1089, in which the central theme is a conflict between Dionysios and Flaccus. Isidoros, who was exiled in ca. 33–35, also appears in the papyrus. Kerkeslager suggests that Dionysios was executed by Flaccus as early as 33 and almost certainly before 36. In the third section it is argued that Lampo was not present in Alexandria in 38, because none of his activities in the city can be dated to 38. Highly probably, he was in Rome in 38 because of personal interests. The last section is devoted to Isidoros, and the author claims that his departure from Alexandria described in *Flacc.* 135–145 has to be dated before 38. Isidoros went away from Alexandria into voluntary exile to Rome, where he remained for the entirety of 38. Because of his crimes it was too risky for him to play a leading role in the troubles in Alexandria. In his conclusion Kerkeslager formulates three major implications of his view: (1) Because of the absence of known Greeks from the elite in the violence, it is less probable that civic rights were an issue. (2)

Philo's attribution of blame to the Roman authorities must be taken more seriously. (3) More attention has to paid to the possibility that Flaccus was acting in accordance with Roman policies. P. W. van der Horst responds to some of Kerkeslager's arguments in *SPhA* 18 (2006) 50–55. (ACG)

G. H. VAN KOOTEN, 'The 'True Light which Enlightens Everyone' (John 1:9): John, Genesis, the Platonic Notion of the 'True, Noetic Light,' and the Allegory of the Cave in Plato's *Republic*,' in G. H. VAN KOOTEN (ed.), *The Creation of Heaven and Earth: Re-interpretations of Genesis 1 in the Context of Judaism, Ancient Philosophy, Christianity, and Modern Physics*, Themes in Biblical Narrative: Jewish and Christian Traditions 8 (Leiden–Boston 2005) 149–194, esp. 153–155.

The paper argues at considerable length that the notion of 'true' or 'genuine' light in the Prologue to John's Gospel has a Greek-philosophical background particularly in the Platonic tradition. Philo provides valuable evidence, notably in his connection of intelligible light with the divine Logos. Both Philo and John assume the Platonic differentiation between the intellectual and the visible realms. The idea was not strange because the LXX already offered the basis for this interpretation in its phrasing of Gen. 1:2a, 'but the earth was invisible and unformed.' The author also notes the favourable view that Philo has of Plato (p. 169). (DTR)

E. KOSKENNIEMI, *The Old Testament Miracle-workers in Early Judaism*, Wissenschaftliche Untersuchungen zum Neuen Testament 2.206 (Tübingen 2005), esp. 108–159.

This study investigates the way in which the biblical miracles by the Old Testament figures, such as Moses, Joshua and Elijah, are retold in early Judaism. The following authors and works are discussed: the Wisdom of Ben Sira, the Book of Jubilees, Ezekiel the Tragedian, Artapanus, Philo, the *Lives of the Prophets*, *Liber Antiquitatum Biblicarum*, and Josephus. In *Mos.* Philo retells the miracles that occurred in Egypt and during the Exodus of the people of Israel. He remains faithful to the biblical narrative. But he does add and underline what he regards as important. Philo also interprets the miracles allegorically. A very important theme in his interpretation is the emigration of the soul out of the body and its struggle against desire and pleasure. The Exodus out of Egypt is the symbol of the spiritual emigration. Philo can offer a natural explanation for a miracle, but this is no reason to assume that he explains the miracles rationally. He presents Moses as both a prophet and a miracle-worker, and sometimes ascribes violent miracles to Moses. (ACG)

A. KOVELMAN, *Between Alexandria and Jerusalem: the Dynamic of Jewish and Hellenistic Culture*, The Brill Reference Library of Judaism 21 (Leiden–Boston 2005).

This book seeks to understand the interplay of changes in Jewish and Greco-Roman cultures within the context of various political, social, and economic developments in the larger society. Kovelman sees 'Jewish cultures of the Second Temple and Talmudic periods as stylistic systems,' and key to stylistic changes was 'the collapse of an old literature and the creation of a new one' (xii). In Chapter 1, the author uses Greek papyri from Roman and Byzantine Egypt to understand the transition from the Mishnah to Genesis Rabbah in the fourth and fifth centuries c.e. In the second chapter, he argues that differences between late biblical and early rabbinic literatures reflect 'a general literary revolution ... in the Roman Empire during the first and second centuries c.e.' (xiii). In Chapter 3, he turns to the relationship between Alexandrian exegesis and Rabbinic Midrash. Chapter 4 focuses on the Letter of Aristeas from the perspective of Aggadic Midrash and early Christian literature. In Chapter 5, Kovelman examines the connections between popular mentality and changing literary styles in the early centuries c.e. A discussion of the Philonic evidence is located primarily in Chapter 3, and is based on the author's earlier papers 'Continuity and Change in Hellenistic Jewish Exegesis and in Early Rabbinic Literature' and 'A Clarification of the Hypothesis' (see the summaries of these in *SPhA* 19 (2007) 163 and among the Extra items below). (EB)

R. A. Kraft, 'Philo's Bible Revisited: the 'Aberrant texts' and their Quotations of Moses,' in F. García Martínez and M. Vervenne (eds.), *Interpreting Translation: Studies on the LXX and Ezekiel in Honour of Johan Lust*, Bibliotheca Ephemeridum Theologicarum Lovanisensium 192 (Leuven 2005) 237–253.

This article deals with the so-called 'aberrant' texts in Philo, deviations from the standard LXX text which some manuscripts display. Starting-point is the study by D. Barthélemy (RR 6708), who argues that the 'aberrant' texts of biblical quotations are based on Aquila's version, and that the 'retoucher' was Jewish. Kraft focuses on those passages in which quotation formulae such as 'Moses said' appear in some manuscripts, while others display a more general identification such as 'the sacred word says'. There are ten passages in *Somn.* 1 that show this difference. Because suppression of the formula "Moses said" is not evidenced in other infected treatises apart from *Somn.* 1, Kraft concludes that the changes go back to a time when *Somn.* 1 circulated by itself. The changes, made in the 2nd–3rd century c.e., are probably done by a rabbinically minded Jew, because rabbinic Judaism avoids explicit attributions to Moses. Appendix 1 offers an overview of references in Philo to Moses as scripture-speaker, Appendix 2 to 'lawgiver' as scripture-speaker, while Appendix 3 lists the 'sacred word' references. (ACG)

J. A. Levine, *Philo of Alexandria and Empire: a Study of Philo's Cultural Hybridity in the Context of His Social Location* (MA thesis, Wake Forest University 2005).

We have so far not been able to obtain a summary of this thesis prepared for the degree of Master of Arts at Wake Forest University, Winston-Salem NC. (DTR)

C. Lévy, 'Deux problèmes doxographiques chez Philon d'Alexandrie: Posidonius et Enésidème,' in A. Brancacci (ed.), *Philosophy and Doxography in the Imperial Age*, Accademia Toscana di Scienze e Lettere «La Colombaria» Studi 228 (Florence 2005) 79–102.

Without doubt Philo is a major source of the study of philosophical doxography, but little use has been made of his evidence, partly because historians of philosophy have shown little interest in him, partly because his writings are rather inaccessible. The author does not wish to focus on *De aeternitate mundi*, because it cannot be considered characteristic of the problems posed by the study of doxography in Philo (and its authenticity is still not wholly beyond dispute). Instead he prefers to analyse two other examples. The first concerns the passions of the soul and focuses on the texts *Leg.* 2.99, *Agr.* 14, *Congr.* 81 and *Leg.* 3.116. These texts reveal that Philo does not consider the various passions to be on an equal footing, but regards pleasure as the foundation for the other three. There would appear to be a connection with Posidonius, but it would be wrong to claim that Philo's view of Stoicism was wholly determined by that thinker. Philo respects Stoicism for the way it gives expression to ethical perfection, but is critical of its doctrine of immanence. The second example discussed at greater length relates to the sceptical tropes in *Ebr.* 167–202. Much has been written on this passage, and in particular on its relation to the other sources Sextus Empiricus and Diogenes Laertius. Lévy points out that differences between them could be not just a matter of style or the use of a different source. It is also possible that they point to the incompatibility of the sceptical arguments with Philo's philosophical and religious convictions. He points to at least two interventions on the part of Philo, the omission of the argument that human beings are not truly superior to animals, and the omission of the example of mythology. It is also noted that in Philo's day the tropes may not have had the same fixed form and number that they later acquired. Lévy determines that in Philo only eight of the ten tropes found in Sextus can be identified. He concludes the article by arguing that Philo's evidence in doxographical matters shows that he is 'infinitely better informed about the history and current state of philosophy' than has often been thought (102). He is also interesting because he is not a professional and so gives evidence of the movement of doctrines from the philosophical schools to the cultured public. (DTR)

R. LIONG-SENG PHUA, *Idolatry and Authority. A Study of 1 Corinthians 8.1–11.1 in the Light of the Jewish Diaspora,* Library of New Testament Studies 299 (London 2005), esp. 57–68.

In this study on idolatry in 1 Cor 8:1–11:1, the author discusses the issue of idolatry in some Diaspora Jewish works in Chapter 3. Works and authors discussed are: Wisdom of Solomon 11–13; Philo; Josephus, Joseph and Asenath; and the *Sibylline Oracles* (50–89). More specifically in his section on Philo (57–68), he deals with the issue of idolatry in texts such as *Opif.* 170–172; *Decal.* 52–81; *Spec.* 1.12–31; *Contempl.* 3–8 and some aspects of *Legatio ad Gaium.* The author suggests that Philo sees idolatry as having different grades of seriousness, from worship of the elements, of demigods, of actual idols of wood and stones, to the worst: Egyptian animal worship. He finds some similarities between Philo and Wisdom of Solomon, but not enough to suggest a common tradition. In the rest of this study, the texts of Philo play no central role in the author's discussions of 1 Corinthians. (TS)

M. F. MACH, 'Lerntraditionen im hellenistischen Judentum unter besonderer Berücksichtigung Philons von Alexandrien,' in B. EGO and H. MERKEL (eds.), *Religiöses Lernen in der biblischen, frühjüdischen und frühchristlichen Überlieferung,* Wissenschaftliche Untersuchungen zum Neuen Testament 180 (Tübingen 2005) 117–139.

The article investigates whether exegetical traditions in Ancient Judaism can be institutionally identified. The author offers a detailed introduction discussing the problems of studying Hellenistic Judaism in comparison to Palestinian Judaism, stressing that many sources have been lost and many of those extant cannot be located with any degree of certainty. Concerning Philo, the author argues hesitantly against the current consensus that assumes organised Torah study in Alexandria with which Philo was familiar. Following Dillon, the author rather stresses Philo's individual synthesis of Greek traditions with the Biblical text. (MRN)

S. Mancini Lombardi, 'L'antica versione armena del *Legum Allegoriae* di Filone Alessandrino: riflessioni sulle modalità di traduzione,' in R. B. Finazzi (ed.), *Del tradurre: da Occidente verso Oriente come incontro di lingue e culture : atti della giornata di studio su Traduzioni orientali e testi classici: lo stato della ricerca, Brescia, 8 ottobre 2004,* (Milano 2005) 175–187.

The Armenian translation of *Legum Allegoriae*, attributed to the 'Hellenizing school of translation' (5th or 6th century), is characterized by a strong textual correspondence between the Greek source text and its Armenian rendering. Starting with a few concrete examples, the author proceeds with analytical reflections on the process of translation in general. The article concludes with the observation that the 'Hellenizing school' and the translation of Philo's works have contributed to both the lexical and the syntactical development of the Armenian language. (HMK)

M. Marin, 'La forza di persuasione della logica aristotelica: Filone di Alessandria e l'eternità del mondo,' *Salesianum* 67 (2005) 213–232.

Philo, notwithstanding his biblical belief in a Creator God, in *De aeternitate mundi* defends the Aristotelian thesis of the eternity of the world (ungenerated and incorruptible). The article first reviews the 'crisis of the Platonists and Stoics' (who saw the material world as generated and possibly perishable) as an effect of Aristotle's arguments. It then discusses how Philo in *Aet.* dismantles objections against the corruptibility of the world, and how he presents arguments in favour of this thesis (the most important: Providence has willed the world to be unperishable). There follows a discussion of the 'riddle' represented by the end of *Aet.* (the reference to a counter-argumentation in a lost second part). The article concludes with the allegorical solution regarding the eternity of creation exposed by Philo in his exegetical treatises, where he attributes incorruptibility to the intelligible world (in the logos) as distinct from the material world. (HMK)

J. P. Martín, 'Teoría, técnica y práctica de la hermenéutica en Filón,' in A. J. Levoratti (ed.), *Comentario Bíblico Latinoamericano, Antiguo Testamento I,* (Estella 2005) 95–104.

The article considers a hermeneutic theory, in which the biblical text and the organization of the world and its history correspond to the same creative Logos, with human beings having an intermediate place that allows them to understand these languages and to be comprehended by them. The article also presents a hermeneutic technique according to which the whole text of the Pentateuch has a finished coherence for the communication of truth if it is read through the norms of Greek exegesis. Finally, it presents a hermeneutic praxis in the sense that the Pentateuch is the crucial factor for the ethical and political formation of the Jewish community, especially in diaspora. (JPM)

J. P. MARTÍN, 'Corrientes hermenéuticas de la época patrística,' in A. J. LEVORATTI (ed.), *Comentario Bíblico Latinoamericano, Antiguo Testamento I*, (Estella 2005) 105–127.

Presents the development of primitive Christianity as a progressive interpretation of texts, first of the writings with Hebrew origins, later also of the proper Christian books. For this hermeneutical core Philo had made some important preparations, like the concept of 'typos' applied to Adam and a double dimension of the sense of the Torah, comparable to the relation between body and soul. (JPM)

E. F. MASON, *The Concept of the Priestly Messiah in Hebrews and Second Temple Judaism* (diss. Notre Dame 2005).

The dissertation examines whether prior traditions have influenced the presentation of Jesus as messianic high priest in Hebrews. The evidence from Qumran has dealt a blow to the theory that the letter's author may have been indebted to the Middle Platonism of Philo of Alexandria. (DTR; based on author's summary in DAI-A 66–02, p. 630)

L. MIRALLES MACIÁ, "'Thíasoi' y 'syssítia' esenios: la perspectiva helenística de Filón de Alejandría acerca de la organización esenia," *Miscelánea de estudios árabes y hebraicos* 54, Sección de Hebreo (2005) 27–42.

Considers the two terms, *thiasos* and *syssition*, which Philo uses to describe the Essenes as brotherhoods and affiliations, cf. *Hypoth.* 11.5. Although Philo does not explain the meaning of these terms, they must have been understandable for his readership. They probably refer to small communities that held table and house in common. This agrees with the information we have about Qumran. (JPM)

M. R. NIEHOFF, 'Response to Daniel S. Schwartz,' *The Studia Philonica Annual* 17 (2005) 99–101.

The author gives a brief response to Daniel S. Schwartz's article 'Did the Jews Practice Infant Exposure and Infanticide in Antiquity?' in *SPhA* 16 (2004) 61–95 (summarized in *SPhA* 19 (2007) 180), arguing that some of the arguments relating to child sacrifice in her monograph *Philo and Jewish Identity and Culture* (summarized in *SPhA* 19 (2007) 186) which Schwartz attacked were misunderstood and misrepresented. (DTR)

M. R. NIEHOFF, 'New Garments for Biblical Joseph,' in C. HELMER and T. G. PETREY (eds.), *Biblical Interpretation. History, Context, and Reality*, Society of Biblical Literature Symposium Series 26 (Atlanta 2005) 33–56.

The author compares Philo's and Josephus' interpretations of the biblical figure of Joseph, asking whether the personality or historical situation of the interpreter is reflected in his exegesis. Both interpreters are shown to offer topical interpretations. The figure of Joseph enables Philo to reflect on the issue of Jewish existence in Egypt, showing in the literal interpretation how an ideal leader maintains his Jewish identity in mental separation from the environment, while the allegory takes into account the reality of Jewish assimilation to Egypt which Philo frowned upon. (MRN)

E. F. Osborn, *Clement of Alexandria* (Cambridge 2005), esp. 81–105.

In his final monograph the author returns one more time to the subject of Clement's debt to Philo in a chapter full of rich insight entitled 'Philo and Clement: from Divine Oracle to True Philosophy.' A rational reconstruction of the thought of the two writers reveals common ground in their essential monotheism. Philo moves from divine oracle to true philosophy with a central focus on Moses and the Law. Clement makes the same move with a central focus on Jesus and the Gospel. The decisive difference between them lies in the relation of logos to God. For Philo the powers under God unite in the Logos. For Clement there is reciprocity of God and logos, father and son. In addition Clement's view of the role of the Jewish people differs from Philo's. It is more complex and also more abstract, because he did not have direct contact with Jews. The chapter proceeds to examine the main passages where Clement makes use of Philo, first the four short sequences, then the four longer passages. Some reflections are appended on literary issues and the problem of why Clement gives so little acknowledgement of his debt to Philo. Osborn concludes that Philo anticipates parts of Clement's 'true dialectic,' but lacks his redefinition in terms of prophecy and economy. Both Philo and Clement are audacious in their thought, but Philo lacks Clement's gift for argument. Clement did not see Philo as a rival, but as one of the many predecessors who had said something well. The concluding words are worth quoting: 'Clement found in Philo the wonder of the elusive God and the richness of the history of Moses. Wonder was for Clement the beginning of knowledge and, time and again, Philo pointed to the wonder of scripture (105).' (DTR)

M. Pesthy, "Mulier est instrumentum diaboli': Women and the Desert Fathers,' in A. Hilhorst and G. H. van Kooten (eds.), *The Wisdom of Egypt: Jewish, Early Christian, and Gnostic Essays in Honour of Gerard P. Luttikhuizen,* Ancient Judaism and Early Christianity 59 (Leiden–Boston 2005) 351–362, esp. 357–359.

In this article focusing on the ideas of the Egyptian Desert Fathers about women a few pages are devoted to Philo who is said to display 'misogynous tendencies.' It is noted that in his reading of Gen. 3 Philo interprets women as sense perception, which caused the fall of man/intellect. Pesthy quotes from *Opif.* 165–166 and *Hypoth.* 11.14–15, 17. (ACG)

Γ. Philip, *The Origins of Pauline Pneumatology: The Eschatological Bestowal of the Spirit upon Gentiles in Judaism and the Early Development of Paul's Theology,* Wissenschaftliche Untersuchungen zum Neuem Testament 2.194 (Tübingen 2005), esp. 100–119.

Pneuma has an extensive range of meaning in Philo. Philo's lack of interest in prophetic eschatology indicates that for him divine Spirit is not something to be anticipated in the future. As the principle of life and reason Philo does not think divine Spirit has been withdrawn from Israel. The Spirit and gift of prophecy are presently available to all, depending on one's moral status and not limited to a few good wise men within Judaism. The Spirit is the source of charismatic revelation, wisdom, and knowledge, as well as skills and abilities. Abraham's experience of the Spirit at *Virt.* 212–219 is a model for all proselytes to be open to the indwelling of the Spirit. (KAF)

M. Pucci Ben Zeev, *Diaspora Judaism in Turmoil, 116/117 CE: Ancient Sources and Modern Insights,* Interdisciplinary Studies in Ancient Culture and Religion 6 (Leuven–Dudley, MA 2005).

A collection of texts related to the revolt in 116–117 c.e., followed by a series of analytic chapters on the revolt, with special attention to chronology and regional developments in Egypt, Mesopotamia, and Judaea. The author presents several compelling arguments to demonstrate that the beginning of the revolt can no longer be dated to 115 c.e. Philo's *In Flaccum* is cited in a discussion of the mime tradition in Egypt (140). While the transmission of Philo's works is not addressed in the book, its argument that the revolt brought 'the very end of the Jewish presence' in Egypt (p. 264) will need to be addressed in future research on this issue. Although Philo is mentioned only once, Philonic scholars may be interested in this important sourcebook on and analysis of this crucial event in Alexandrian Jewish history. (EB; adapted from a summary supplied by A. Kerkeslager)

R. Radice, 'La funzione teologica del *logos* nel giudaismo alessandrino e i suoi possibili sviluppi: una linea di ricerca,' *Humanitas (Brescia)* N. S. 60 (2005) 844–858.

There is no other concept in Philo's thought as complex (and seemingly confused) as that of the *logos*. It is argued in this article that the reason for this lies in the fact that for Philo the same doctrine can be expressed both in philosophical and in biblical terms (and in Philo's eyes the latter option is the better of the two). Philo represents an important step in Jewish Hellenistic thought: from a physical conception of God's workings (Aristobulus: *dynamis*) to a metaphysical one, for which Philo (maybe surprisingly so) makes use of the Stoic concept of *logos* as well as of the Demiurge in Plato's *Timaeus*. The influence of Philo's *logos* theory was not limited to Jewish Hellenistic thought, but reached Middle-Platonism, Gnosticism, the Prologue of the Gospel of John, and Plotinus. (HMK)

J. R. Royse, 'Three More Spurious Fragments of Philo,' *The Studia Philonica Annual* 17 (2005) 95–98.

In an earlier article (in *SPhA* 5 (1993) 156–179, see summary in RRS 3214) the author had listed 124 unidentifiable texts attributed to Philo in one source or another. Through the aid of the TLG database of Greek texts he has now identified another three of these texts as spurious (i.e. non-Philonic). They are not to be attributed to Gregory Thaumaturgus, Theophylactus Simocatta, and John Chrysostom respectively. The article ends with some comments on the remaining corpus of 121 fragments. The use of the rare word μονωτικός in two of them (nos. 43 & 56) is intriguing because it only occurs elsewhere in Aristotle (twice) and Philo (seven times). It is surely evidence of the authenticity of the ascription. (DTR).

D. T. Runia, 'A Conference on Philo in Germany,' *The Studia Philonica Annual* 17 (2005) 141–152.

The review article focuses on the collection of papers edited by R. Deines and K.-W. Niebuhr, *Philo und das Neue Testament*, published in 2004 (see summary at *SPhA* 19 (2007) 153). Philonic studies owe an enormous amount to German scholarship, but since the Second World War the scholarly output has declined. It was thus an event of great significance that in 2003 a conference was held in Eisenach which was largely devoted to Philo, organized by the Corpus Judaeo-Hellenisticum Novi Testamenti project. The aim was not only to see what New Testament studies could learn from Philo, but also the reverse, what Philonic studies could learn from New Testament scholarship. The volume under review is based on the papers of the conference, which divide into four parts: three survey articles, twelve articles in six pairs by a Philonist and a New Testament specialist looking at the same theme, two further articles on separate themes, and three detailed readings of Philonic texts (*Opif.* 15–25, *Mos.* 1.60–62, *Spec.* 2.39–48). The article summarizes all the contributions and concludes that the volume is 'warmly to be recommended to all scholars interested in the relation between Philo and ... the New Testament' (151). (DTR)

D. T. RUNIA, E. BIRNBAUM, K. A. FOX, A. C. GELJON, H. M. KEIZER, J. P. MARTÍN, R. RADICE, J. RIAUD, D. SATRAN, G. SCHIMANOWSKI, and T. SELAND, 'Philo of Alexandria: an Annotated Bibliography 2002,' *The Studia Philonica Annual* 17 (2005) 161–214.

The yearly annotated bibliography of Philonic studies prepared by the members of the International Philo Bibliography Project primarily covers the year 2002 (99 items), with addenda for the years 1998–2001 (11 items), and provisional lists for the years 2003–05. (DTR)

D. T. RUNIA, and G. E. STERLING (eds.), *The Studia Philonica Annual*, Vol. 17, Brown Judaic Studies 344 (Providence, RI 2005).

This volume in the journal dedicated to the thought of Philo contains five general articles, a special section entitled Philo and the Tradition of Logos Theology with an introduction and two articles, two review articles, the usual bibliography section (see summary above), and nine book reviews. In addition there is the annual News and Notes section. The various articles are summarized elsewhere in this bibliography. This volume was the last to be published in the series Brown Judaic Studies. (DTR)

K.-G. SANDELIN, 'Philo and Paul on Alien Religion: A Comparison,' in A. MUSTAKALLIO (ed.), *Lux Humana, Lux Aeterna. Essays on Biblical and Related Themes in Honour of Lars Aejmelaeus*, Publications of the Finnish Exegetical Society 89 (Helsinki–Göttingen 2005) 213–246.

After a sketch of the social situations of Philo and Paul, the author discusses their treatment of various aspects of alien religion under headings such as 'The Evaluation of alien Gods,' 'Participation in alien religious activities,' 'Arguments from the Bible,' 'Conversion and apostasy,' and 'The rescue from polytheism and idolatry.' The main text of Paul investigated here is 1 Corinthians 8:1–11:1. From Philo he draws on a wider set of texts. He emphasizes that Philo considers polytheism a strong evil force, and he may attribute it both to ignorance and to an evil aim in the minds of those who have introduced polytheism. Furthermore, Philo apparently considers club-meetings as a dangerous arena of polytheism, and he uses the episode of the golden calf in the desert as a warning example. Finally, in Philo's view the rejection of polytheism cannot be achieved by human beings through their own powers, but they are in need of God's help. The author's main conclusion is that the way Paul handles what he sees as idolatry demonstrates that he is an heir of the same Jewish tradition which Philo represents. (TS)

K. Schenck, *A Brief Guide to Philo* (Louisville–Kentucky 2005).

This book serves as a helpful introduction to Philo and his writings. Chapter one summarizes scholarly portraits of Philo and discusses Philo as a biblical interpreter, philosopher, and mystic. Chapter two provides an overview of scholarly consensus on Philo's family, education, and political involvement, and of how scholars categorize Philo's writings. Chapter three traces the fine line Philo walked between loyalty to Judaism and love of Hellenism. Chapter four presents Philo's relationship to Jewish interpretive traditions in Alexandria and to Greek philosophical traditions. Philo's views of God, the Logos, creation, humanity, truth, ethics, society, and women are summarized. Chapter five sketches a common Jewish Hellenistic milieu in which Philo and certain New Testament writers moved. Many similarities between Philo's writings and the Book of Hebrews and the Letters of Paul (1 Cor 15:39–49; Col 1:15–20) suggest the authors lived in a similar linguistic universe. John's use of Logos at John 1:1–14 is compared with Philo. Chapter six provides a brief summary of each Philonic treatise. The book concludes with Chapter seven presenting a useful topical index to the Philonic corpus. (KAF)

G. Schöllgen (ed.), *Reallexikon für Antike und Christentum Lieferungen* 164–166 (Stuttgart 2005).

A. Lumpe, art. Kontemplation, 485–498, esp. 490–492 (Contemplation; includes section on Therapeutae); W. Speyer, art. Kopf, 509–535, esp. 524–525 (Head); D. Wyrwa, art. Kosmos, 614–761, esp. 652–661 (Cosmos);

T. Seland, *Strangers in the Light: Philonic Perspectives on Christian Identity in 1 Peter*, Biblical Interpretation Series 76 (Leiden–Boston 2005).

This is a collection of five articles, three of which have been previously published. The first chapter is entitled 'The Making of 1 Peter in Light of Ancient Graeco-Roman Letter Writing and Distribution' (9–37), and argues *inter alia* that Silvanus (1 Pet 5.12) probably is to be understood as the writer/secretary of the letter, not the carrier. The next chapter, entitled 'Paroikos kai parepidemos: Proselyte Characterizations in 1 Peter?' (39–78), was published in 2001 (see *SPhA* 16 (2004) 255). The third, on 'The 'Common Priesthood' of Philo and 1 Peter' (79–115), published in 1995 (RRS 9573), is a 'Philonic reading' of 1 Pet 2:5 & 9. The two last chapters deal with 1 Pet 2:11–12, both drawing on Philo's work in the interpretation of these verses. Chapter four, 'The Moderate Life of the Christian paroikoi: a Philonic Reading of 1 Pet 2:11' (117–145) was published in 2004 (cf. *SPhA* 19 (2007) 181). The last chapter (147–189), dealing with assimilation and acculturation in 1 Peter, is published here for the first time. (TS)

R. Sgarbi, 'Acquisizioni filologico-linguistiche in margine all'esperienza traduttiva armena della «Scuola ellenistica»,' in R. B. Finazzi (ed.), *Del tradurre: da Occidente verso Oriente come incontro di lingue e culture: atti della giornata di studio su Traduzioni orientali e testi classici: lo stato della ricerca, Brescia, 8 ottobre 2004,* (Milano 2005) 211–218.

This article presents two passages from Philo, *Spec.* 1.304, 5.73.17–20 C-W, and *Contempl.* 61, 6.62.4–9 (as well as passages from Porphyrius and Dionysius Thrax) in Greek and

Armenian (both versions with Italian renderings). On the basis of the Armenian translations observations are made on probable readings of the Greek original. (HMK)

F. Shaw, 'The Emperor Gaius' Employment of the Divine Name,' *The Studia Philonica Annual* 17 (2005) 33–48.

The article focuses on Philo's account of the words of the Emperor Gaius to the Embassy of Alexandrian Jews (of which Philo himself was the leader) in *Legat*. 353. Two main problems are discussed. First, how are Gaius' words to be interpreted? Shaw discusses the two different understandings of the words (i.e. the adjective ἀκατόνμαστος refers to God or to the Emperor himself) and concludes that Philo might have wished to convey both interpretations that have been made by modern scholars. The second question is the divine name that Gaius most likely uttered. It is argued that it would have been a Greek name and that it was most likely Ιαω. In an Appendix Shaw discusses evidence for the knowledge of a Hebrew divine name among Romans. A brief response to the article was published by P. W. van der Horst in *SPhA* 18 (2006) 49–50. (DTR)

R. Skarsten, P. Borgen, and K. Fuglseth, *The Complete Works of Philo of Alexandria: A Key-Word-In-Context Concordance*, 8 vols. (Piscataway NJ 2005).

This printed Key-Word-In-Context Concordance is a result of The Norwegian Philo Concordance Project. The text database has been published in various ways, e.g. in *The Philo Index* (Eerdmans/Brill, 2000, cf. *SPhA* 15 (2003) 112, and *SPhA* 12 (2000) 205–206) and in different electronic versions included in PC programs like Libronix™, BibleWorks™ and Accordance™. This edition, printed as a Key-Words-in-Context (KWIC) version, is a concordance containing every occurrence of all the Greek words present in Philo's works. It is a monumental achievement, consisting of eight volumes with a total number of 7,556 pages. The database consists of 437,433 tokens (text forms) and more than 14,000 different lemmas (the chosen entry forms), and is built on four major text editions of Philo (Cohn-Wendland, Colson, Petit, and Paramelle). Each lemma is alphabetically ordered and presented within its context and thus designed to give optimal aid to research on Philo of Alexandria's writings. (TS)

G. E. Sterling, '"The Jewish Philosophy": the Presence of Hellenistic Philosophy in Jewish Exegesis in the Second Temple Period,' in C. Bakhos (ed.), *Ancient Judaism in its Hellenistic Context*, Supplements to the Journal for the Study of Judaism 95 (Leiden–Boston 2005) 131–153.

The author deals with the question of the extent to which Hellenistic philosophy was popular among Second Temple Jews. To examine this issue Sterling discusses three areas in which both Hellenistic philosophy and Jewish thought are interested: theology, creation, and ethics. In this discussion frequent references are made to Philo. His conception of the transcendent God, for instance, is influenced by Hellenistic thought. He offers a Platonizing exegesis of the creation account in Genesis. Concerning ethics, Jewish writers identify Mosaic legislation with natural law. Sterling concludes that there were exegetical traditions influenced by Hellenistic philosophy that enjoyed wide circulation. As a consequence we should take the influence of Hellenistic philosophy on Greek-speaking Judaism seriously. (ACG)

G. E. Sterling, "Day One': Platonizing Exegetical Traditions of Genesis 1:1–5 in John and Jewish Authors,' *The Studia Philonica Annual* 17 (2005) 118–140.

The author first affirms that the Prologue of the Gospel of John is based on Gen. 1:1–5, and then argues that there are points of contact between the Prologue and the Platonist tradition. Four Platonizing features are discussed: (1) the world of being versus the world of becoming; (2) the Logos; (3) prepositional metaphysics (4) light versus darkness. Other Platonizing exegetical traditions of Gen. 1:1–5 can be found in Philo and in 2 Enoch. In his discussion about Philo's creation account in *Opif.* Sterling deals with the same Platonizing topics found in John. Regarding the treatment of Gen. 1:1–5 in John, Philo and 2 Enoch the author concludes that all three texts identify 'day one' with the eternal, intelligible, or invisible world. The differences suggest that they made independent use of a common tradition. The transmission was transmitted to later Christians (Clement, Origen, Eusebius) largely, although not exclusively, through the works of Philo. (ACG)

C. Termini, 'Tipologías de filiación en Filón de Alejandría,' in J. J. A. Calvo, P. de N. Benlloch and M. A. Esnaola (eds.), *Filiación: Cultura pagana, religión de Israel, orígenes del cristianismo. Actas de las I y II Jornadas de Estudio «La filiación en los inicios de la reflexión cristiana»*, Colección Estructuras y Procesos: Serie Religión (Madrid 2005) 73–88.

The article presents a philological and ideological study of terms in Philo that mean paternity, filiation, adoption and related terms. It first analyses the natural relation of parents and children, treated specially in *Decal.* 106–120 and *Spec.* 2.223–248. In the author's view this relation has the following characteristics: it is hierarchic, asymmetric—because the children will not be able to repay the received gifts—, contains reciprocity and affection, and includes a promise of immortality by the fact of having children. The semantics of filiation extends to other hermeneutical fields: the filiation of the world in respect to God and the Logos as first-born. Considering specially *Conf.* 144–146 the article analyses the distinction of degrees in the filiation of those who have a human being, the Logos, or God as father. Philo develops the Greek idea of virtue caused by divine seed but denies that this topic has any mythological implications. The mother of the God's son is not Rachel but Leah, not a woman but a virgin. The author credits the Greek sources that Philo uses, especially those with a Platonic background, but she argues that Philo uses these sources to give original readings of biblical texts. The result is not far from a New Testament idea, namely that true sonship does not occur by ties of blood but derives from a gift of God. (JPM)

L. Troiani, 'Ambascerie e ambasciatori nella «Legatio ad Gaium» di Filone Alessandrino,' in E. T. Pagola and J. S. Yanguas (eds.), *Diplomacia y autorrepresentación en la Roma antigua*, Serie Acta 6 (Vitoria 2005) 77–85.

In the context of a discussion about practices and procedures of the embassies coming from the entire Empire to the court of Rome during the Julio-Claudian Dynasty, the author presents a report based on *Legat.* 178–193 and related passages to describe two embassies that came to Rome about the year 40 c.e., one headed by Apion representing the Egyptians, the other headed by Philo and representing the Jews, in response to the anti-Jewish disturbances of the year 38 c.e. (JPM)

C. VASANTHARAO, 'The Right to Life in Human Discourse: Emphasis on Animal Life,' *Religion and Society* 50 (2005) 13–30.

For guidance about the role of humans in relation to animals and to God, the author considers the law of not boiling a kid in its mother's milk, especially in Deut. 14:21b. Philo and others view this law, whose significance is obscure, as relating partly to the pain that the suckling mother would feel if she could not express milk to her young. The law must also, however, be seen in the larger context of the mother-offspring bond. Here too, Philo —followed by later Jewish and Christian exegetes—provides evidence that this and other biblical laws regarding animal mothers and offspring were meant to show kindness to animals. Another possible explanation, found in *Virt.* 143, is the separation of the forces of life (represented by the mother's milk) and death (represented by cooking), a theme also found elsewhere in biblical laws pertaining to animals. This explanation and others aid Vasantharao in understanding why the rabbis greatly developed the prohibition of boiling a kid in its mother's milk to extend to the separation between milk and meat products and utensils. (EB)

S. VIDAL, *Filón de Alejandría, Los terapeutas, De vita contemplativa, Texto griego con introducción, traducción y notas* (Salamanca 2005).

This book represents the first bilingual edition with Spanish translation of Philo's *De vita contemplativa*. The Greek text, although it does not discuss Paola Graffigna's edition of 1992 (RRS 2452), is correctly presented and generally follows the edition of Daumes (R-R 2210). The translation is valuable, staying close to the original text but in good Spanish. The notes deal with the main questions of terminology, with the relation of text to other writings of Philo and Greco-Roman Literature, and with references to the socio-historical context of Roman Alexandria. The subjects broached in the Introduction will interest all students of Judaism, Christianity or Hellenism who wish to gain access to the difficult questions posed by Philo's work: the place of *Contempl.* in the Philonic corpus, the genre and structure of the treatise, the historicity of the group of Therapeutae in the Alexandrian context, the history of the confusion between Christian monks and Jewish Therapeutae, and the authenticity of the work established first by the literary criticism in the 19th century. (JPM)

J. P. WARE, *The Mission of the Church in Paul's Letter to the Philippians in the Context of Ancient Judaism*, Supplements to Novum Testamentum 120 (Leiden–Boston 2005), esp. 131–143.

This volume represents an extensive study of the role Paul's churches played in his view of mission commitment, asking: what role did Paul envision his churches having in the advancement of the Gospel? Concerning the background of the missionary consciousness of Paul, Ware rejects the possibility of relevant figures in Hellenistic philosophy or religion as models, and focuses instead on Paul's Jewish background. Chapter One deals with 'The Problem of Jewish Mission' (23–55). Did the missionary consciousness of the early Christians have its origins in Judaism? And if so, in what ways? Ware here deals with the much discussed questions of Jewish missionaries, the number of converts, and the nature of the 'God-fearers.' His conclusions are that there is little evidence that converts were actively sought by Jews, and that there is no evidence of missionaries and/or missionary preaching to gentiles. Chapter Three deals with 'Conversion of Gentiles and Interpretation of Isaiah in Second Temple Judaism' (93–155). The main question here is: 'to what extent were Jewish attitudes toward gentiles in the second temple period related to the Old Testament, especially the book of Isaiah?' Ware here deals with the relevant texts from Isaiah in the LXX version, with Targum Isaiah, Sibylline Oracles, Wisdom of Salomon, the parables of Enoch, Philo of Alexandria, Romans 2:17–29, as well as the *Testament of Levi* and some related Qumran texts. In his analysis of Philo (esp. *Virt.* 175–186; *Spec.* 2.162–167; *Mos.* 1.149 and 2.43–44; *Abr.* 98), he finds that Philo did understand the Jewish people to have a priestly and mediatorial role for the gentiles, but there is no concern for a mission for their conversion. He welcomed present-day proselytes as a foreshadowing of the coming eschatological coming. Summarizing the results of his investigation of these Jewish texts, Ware finds that there existed a widespread interest in an eschatological conversion of gentiles, but not all shared the same interest in the present conversion of gentiles, and there is no evidence to be found of a concern for mission. (TS)

E. WASSERMAN, *The Death of the Soul in Romans 7: Sin, Death, and the Law in Light of Hellenistic Moral Psychology* (diss. Yale University 2005).

This dissertation argues that Rom 7:7–25 should be understood as a dramatic depiction of the death of the soul, a moral-psychological condition ascribed to extremely immoral persons. In Chapter 2 the author discusses Hellenistic discussions of extreme immorality and focuses on Philo of Alexandria who often uses death analogies to describe the mind which has been completely overwhelmed by the passions. It is argued that Paul represents such an extreme type of wickedness in Rom 7:7–25 and that he similarly uses death and dying as moral-psychological metaphors to describe the mind's total domination by passions and vices. (DTR; based on author's summary in DAI-A 66/11, p. 4056)

S. WEITZMAN, *Surviving Sacrilege: Cultural Persistence in Jewish Antiquity* (Cambridge Mass. 2005), esp. 58–75.

Weitzman studies the tactics that Jews used to preserve their culture, particularly in times when the Temple and/or Jewish ritual were endangered. He thus considers the Babylonian destruction of the First Temple, the threat against Jewish religious practices by Antiochus IV in the time of the Maccabees, Caligula's attempt to install a statue of himself in the Temple, and the Roman destruction of the Second Temple. Philo is discussed most prominently in the chapter on the crisis with Caligula, based on Philo's account of the Embassy (55–78). Weitzman focuses on Agrippa's approach to the Emperor and analyzes it in terms of notions that were nearly contemporary with Philo about friendship and flattery. Recognizing that Philo's account of Agrippa and his letter to Caligula is a rhetorical device, Weitzman then considers Philo's own tactics and concludes that he presents Jewish culture and imperial rule as having an important affinity, but one that is not quite complete because of the Jews' commitment to preserving their ancestral beliefs and practices. After Caligula's assassination, Claudius acted favorably to the Jews because of the friendship that he had with Agrippa and Herod and the friendship that the Jews had shown to the Romans. In relation to the Caligula episode and its immediate aftermath, therefore, the Jews managed to preserve their culture by having 'Friends in High Places' (which is the title of this chapter). (EB)

W. T. WILSON, 'Pious Soldiers, Gender Deviants, and the Ideology of Actium: Courage and Warfare in Philo's *De Fortitudine*,' *The Studia Philonica Annual* 17 (2005) 1–32.

Plato's understanding of courage (ἀνδρεία) in the *Republic* provides a gateway to a thoroughgoing comparison of Cicero and Philo with respect to their philosophical understandings of courage, as understood in relation to other virtues deemed essential for personal, civic, and military life. Both Cicero and Philo work out their treatments in the context of participating in public life. A systematic commentary on Philo's treatment of courage, found in *De fortitudine* (= *De virtutibus* 1–50), presupposes realities specific to Philo's situation in Roman Egypt and his political desire to construct an image of Judaism congenial to the ideology of the Roman ruling classes, as reflected in the propaganda of the Augustan principate. (KAF)

K. S. WINSLOW, *Early Jewish and Christian Memories of Moses' Wives: Exogamist Marriage and Ethnic Identity,* Studies in the Bible and Early Christianity 66 (Lewiston, NY 2005), esp. chapters 5 and 6.

The accounts of Moses' Midianite wife, Zipporah, in Exodus 2, 4, and 18 and his unnamed Cushite wife in Numbers 12 give rise to several exegetical motifs that include Moses' exogamous marriage(s), Zipporah's act of circumcision, and Moses' later celibacy. Winslow examines how these accounts and motifs are treated in the Hebrew Bible, later Jewish sources—including the LXX, Artapanus, Demetrius, Ezekiel the Tragedian, Jubilees, Philo, Josephus, Targums, and Rabbinic literature—and Christian sources—including Origen, Tertullian, Aphrahat, Ephrem the Syrian, Jerome, and Gregory of Nyssa. Philo does not appear to be bothered by Moses' marriage to a Gentile, but he does not refer to Zipporah's act of circumcision in any of his writings. This omission may reflect Philo's general tendency to avoid portraying women as taking initiative or having the ability to influence Israel's history. In *Mos.* 2, Philo mentions Moses' marriage and children (from Exodus) without referring to Zipporah by name. She is named, however, in *Mut., Post.,* and *Cher.,* in which she is allegorized, as is Moses' Ethiopian wife (from Numbers 12) in *Leg.* 2. Both wives represent qualities that advance Moses' character development. Philo is the first Jew we know of to claim that Moses renounced sex in order to be prepared to hear God's words (*Mos.* 2.68–69). This claim appears to be influenced not by exegetical concerns, as in some other sources, but by 'Philo's fundamental assumptions about the incompatibility of the 'female' with the attainment to knowledge of the divine' (272). (E.B.)

D. WINSTON, 'A Century of Research on the Book of Wisdom,' in A. PASSARO and G. BELLIA (eds.), *The Book of Wisdom in Modern Research,* Deuterocanonical and Cognate Literature Yearbook (Berlin–New York 2005) 1–18.

As the title promises, this article surveys scholarship on the Book of Wisdom (Wis) over the past century. A central, puzzling issue is the Book's combination of an apocalyptic outlook and philosophical sophistication. Winston discusses examples of the conjoining of wisdom and apocalyptic in other literature and mentions Philo in passing to illustrate the theme that unmediated understanding given by God is superior to mediated learning acquired through a teacher. In Wis, wisdom is understood as 'immanent divine causality' (10), which is not explicitly identified with Torah. Relevant in this context is Philo's understanding of natural law and of the patriarchs as its living embodiments. One can also discern similar tensions between apocalyptic and philosophy in Philo, whose 'quasi-apocalyptic messianic vision' (14), restricted to only a few passages, seems to conflict with his notion of divine providence. Winston suggests that both sources were written during the period of severe persecution of the Jews in Alexandria and that both authors were motivated 'by the need to fuse Jewish tradition with Greek philosophy in an attempt to defend its integrity both in the face of persecution and the intellectual changes of pagan culture' (15–16). Biblical exegesis, therefore, is only secondary to this aim. (EB)

J. WOYKE, *Götter, ,Götzen', Götterbilder. Aspekte einer paulinischen ,Theologie der Religionen'*, Beihefte zur Zeitschrift für die neutestamentliche Wissenschaft 132 (Berlin–New York 2005).

Discussions on aspects of Philo's theology occur at various points in this Tübingen dissertation. On p. 90–94 there is an extensive excursus on the terminology used for foreign gods in which Philo's use of the terms *eidola, theoplastein, theoi* is also investigated. It is only against the background of a Platonic world-view that the term *eidolon* can have the double signification of 'a divine image' and 'phantom.' The designation of the stars as *theoi aisthetoi* however is conventional and does not imply veneration. On p. 123–126 Philo's concept of faith is outlined: it comprises knowledge of God, trust in God, and conversion as well. On p. 133–138 F. Siegert's thesis that QE 2.2 betrays the existence of polytheistic sympathizers of the hellenistic synagogue is contested. Jethro, however, could be the symbol of such an exterior circle of adherents. Further references to Philo's doctrine of monotheism are found on p. 174–176 and 397–401. The author observes a tendency to abstract from God's activity in history; in contrast to Stoicism, Philo confines the knowledge of a Creator's existence to the intellectual inference of philosophers. (DZ)

A. T. WRIGHT, *The Origin of Evil Spirits: The Reception of Genesis 6.1–4 in Early Jewish Literature*, Wissenschaftliche Untersuchungen zum Neuem Testament 2.198 (Tübingen 2005), esp. 191–219.

The monograph is a revision of his 2004 dissertation submitted to the faculty at the University of Durham. In order to understand Philo's place in Early Judaism and his approach to Genesis 6:1–4, Philo's role as an exegete, his audience, and his view of the soul, and in particular its immortality, are discussed. Philo's interpretation of the text offers an alternative approach to the responsibility for human suffering to the tradition set forth in 1 Enoch 1–36. The Watcher tradition describes the 'angels of God' as rebellious angels who entered the human realm to fornicate with women. Philo interprets them as 'souls' that descend to earth to take on a human body. For Philo, the giants are neither physical nor spiritual entities. They are irrational vices born as a result of being drawn into the torrents of the flesh. Despite differences, the giants of the Watcher tradition and the giants of *De gigantibus* threaten the survival of humanity, although one is external and the other internal to the person. Philo may have been writing a corrective to Watcher tradition and its view that evil spirits are the cause of human sufferings. (KAF)

A. T. WRIGHT, 'Some Observations on Philo's *De Gigantibus* and Evil Spirits in Second Temple Judaism,' *Journal for the Study of Judaism* 36 (2005) 471–488.

This article is taken almost *verbatim* from the monograph summarized above. (KAF)

Extra items from before 2005

M. Brinkschröder, 'Die Karriere des Homosexualitätsverbots im Diasporajudentum: Ehebruch und Päderastie zwischen Heiligkeitsgesetz und Dekalog,' in B. Heininger (ed.), *Geschlechterdifferenz in religiösen Symbolsystemen*, (Münster 2003) 158–169.

This short study gives a general presentation of adultery and pederasty in essential texts of Hellenistic Judaism (Sibylline Oraces, Ps-Phocylides, Philo and Josephus). Philonic texts cited are *Hypoth.* 7.1; *Decal.* 51 and *Spec.* 3. The confrontation of the Jews in Alexandria with the city's Hellenistic milieu could explain the frequency of the subject of pederasty and must be seen as playing a role in the background. Philo's significance lies in his framing of the question within the exegesis of the sixth commandment. In this way the prohibition of homosexuality is diverted into the paranetic sequences of the Decalogue as understood in Hellenistic Judaism. (GS)

J. Byron, *Slavery Metaphors in Early Judaism and Pauline Christianity: A Traditio-Historical and Exegetical Examination*, Wissenschaftliche Untersuchungen zum Neuen Testament 2.Reihe 162 (Tübingen 2003), esp. 33–35, 102–116.

This study, the published version of a Durham dissertation, examines the Jewish background to Paul's statements that he is a 'slave of Christ' and other uses of slave terminology and metaphor. In a preliminary discussion of terminology, Byron notes that slavery language is extremely common in Philo (more than 800 instances). There seems a preference for the term δοῦλος above that of θεράπων, but the term διάκονος is quite rare. Philo uses slavery language mainly in philosophical and exegetical contexts, and not with reference to historical situations as in Josephus. These insights are further developed in chapter 6 entitled 'Responses to Slavery in the Writings of Philo.' The author argues that participation in the Alexandrian Jewish diaspora community seems to have shaped Philo's views on slavery. The Jews could accept their situation because they had the freedom to worship God. Philo recasts Judaism in philosophical terms with as most important marker: 'his tenacious adherence to monolatry and the belief that God is sovereign over all creation' (100). Both the themes of covenant and exile are largely absent in Philo's thought, allowing him to blur the outsider/insider ideology of enslavement to God found in other Jewish writers. Philo's approach to slavery is further investigated through an analysis of his writings in two stages: (a) *Prob.* illustrates his views from the philosophical (esp. Stoic) perspective; (b) his exegetical writings offer a more theological perspective. Slavery and freedom are most often interpreted in terms of the moral qualities of the soul. Esau is a prime example of the slave, because he is enslaved to his passions. His example shows that it can be beneficial to be physically enslaved. The last part of the discussion focuses on slavery to God. According to Philo God has sovereign control over creation and humanity's response should be one of obedience and loyalty, coupled with the rejection of self-rule. This is typified by the reponse of Abraham, whom the visitors (Gen. 18) call a 'fellow slave' of God (*Abr.* 116). Philo's view is perhaps best summarized by his statement that 'of all things slavery to God is best' (*Somn.* 2.100). (DTR)

H. Dijkhuis, *Kaïns kinderen: Over Kaïn en de oorsprong van het kwaad* (Amsterdam 1999), esp. 21–56.

In this study on the interpretations of the story of Cain and Abel by philosophers through history, the first chapter deals with Philo's exegesis. Dijkhuis offers an overview of Philo's interpretation. Cain is generated by Eve, symbol of sense perception, and Adam, who symbolizes the mind. The name Cain means possession and he thinks that all things are his own possession, not regarding God as creator. He is placed opposite to Abel, who refers all things to God. Protagoras, who thinks that man is the measure of all things, is an offspring of Cain's madness. Because Cain regards himself as his own possession he is also a self-lover, whereas Abel is a lover of God. Characterizing Cain as self-loving Philo is inspired by Plato (*Laws* 731d–e). Cain challenges Abel for a dispute in order to master him with sophistical tricks. He kills his brother but Philo explains that in reality Cain kills himself: he loses the virtuous life; Abel continues to live the happy life in God. Cain builds a city, that means he constructs his own world view. Philo's interpretation influenced Christian thought: both Ambrose and Augustine follow Philo's exegesis of the two brothers. (ACG)

E. Filler, 'Notes on the Concept of Woman and Marriage in Philo,' *Iyyun* 53 (2004) 395–408.

This short article contains rich material contesting Daniel Boyarin's conclusion that Philo was a misogynist, rejecting women both as a symbol of the senses and as partners in marriage. Filler argues that passages such as *Cher.* 60 show that Philo regarded the mind without the senses as incomplete and that *Opif.* 151ff and *Gig.* 29 suggest the importance of partnership between husband and wife as well as Philo's general acceptance of sexuality. Filler stresses that Philo did not recommend abstinence and was thus closer to the rabbis than to certain Greek thinkers. Moreover, the Therapeutae are identified as a group of elderly philosophers, who abstained from marital life only towards the end of their lives, after establishing a family. Finally, Filler explains Philo's famous insistence on the separate place of women in the house as an expression of his concern that homosexuality may spread if the essential difference between man and woman is not upheld. (MRN)

R. Goldenberg, *The Nations That Know Thee Not: Ancient Jewish Attitudes toward Other Religions* (Sheffield 1997), esp. 51–56, 65–69.

Material from Philo is extensively used in this study of ancient Jewish attitudes towards other peoples and other religions. The chapter entitled 'Judaism at War (II)', which treats Jewish literary polemic, commences with Philo's strictures against polytheism in Decal. and uses it to structure the discussion. In the following chapter entitled 'Judaism at Peace,' Philo, though called 'the philosophical scourge of polytheism,' is interpreted as providing evidence of a softer view of pagan religions. This chapter also includes a discussion of Philo's exegesis of the LXX rendering of Ex. 22:27. (DTR)

G. Hasan-Rokem, 'Genre Dynamics in Historical Context: The Rabbis as Greco-Roman Jewish Authors,' *Review of Rabbinic Judaism* 7 (2004) 152–161.

In this response to A. Kovelman ('Continuity and Change in Hellenistic Jewish Exegesis and in Early Rabbinic Literature,' *Review of Rabbinic Judaism* 7 (2004) 123–145; see *SPhA* 19 (2007) 163), the author argues against Kovelman's claim that Alexandrian exegesis was a missing link in the evolution from biblical epic to rabbinic *spoudogeloion*, or serio-comical literature. Questioning this characterization of the evolution altogether, the author maintains that 'the admission of humor' into the rabbinic corpus reflected an internal change in Jewish literature—but not a change in genre—and that this change came about 'in dialogue and community with the Greco-Roman' literatures (155). To counter Kovelman's argument that the Rabbis were influenced by Philo's treatment, she also discusses rabbinic interpretations of Eve's creation and rabbinic use of the androgynous human creation myth. (EB)

A. KOVELMAN, 'A Clarification of the Hypothesis,' *Review of Rabbinic Judaism* 7 (2004) 162–168.

Kovelman responds to two commentators on his article 'Continuity and Change in Hellenistic Jewish Exegesis and in Early Rabbinic Literature' (see summaries under Kovelman in *SPhA* 19 (2007) 163; M. Niehoff in *ibid.*, 171; and G. Hasan-Rokem, summarized above). Here he clarifies his understanding of *spoudogeloion*, or serio-comical literature, as a combination of academic and farcical elements, defends the use of 'epic' to describe Scripture, and continues to argue that certain rabbinic interpretations of the androgynous creation myth in relation to the biblical creation stories came from Alexandria. Rejecting the literal meaning of aspects of the biblical creation stories, Philo presented his philosophical understanding. The rabbis, however, accepting the literal meaning, 'went so far as to use it for parody and travesty' (165). The rabbis 'rejected the seriousness and didactic tone of the Second Temple literature (Rewritten Bible, Alexandrian exegesis), changed the style, while standing on the shoulders of this literature' (167). Kovelman emphasizes that to understand the developments in Jewish culture specifically, one must understand general developments in the larger context regarding 'the style of exposition from one period to another' (168). (EB)

L. KUNDERT, *Die Opferung/Bindung Isaaks. Vol. 1: Gen 22,1–19 im Alten Testament, im Frühjudentum und im Neuen Testament; Vol. 2: Gen 22,1–19 in frühen rabbinischen Texten,* Wissenschaftliche Monographien zum Alten und Neuen Testament 78–79 (Neukirchen-Vluyn 1998), esp. 1.107–163.

This research work under the supervision of Prof. Wolfgang Stegemann was accepted as a dissertation in Basel in 1997. Philo's writings are analyzed together with the Book of Jubilees, the texts of Qumran, Josephus' *Antiquities*, 4 Macc and the Pseudo-Philonic *Biblical Antiquities*. In the long chapter on Philo a brief introduction discusses Philo's education and his allegorical method. The research method outlined here dates back to the early nineties. Different exegetical tendencies of Philo's writings are not mentioned and hermeneutical questions are not strongly prioritised. The account of the sacrifice of Isaac in the book *De Abrahamo* is central. Material relating to the New Testament (the letters of Paul, Hebrews, but also James) is emphasized. Parallels to Jewish traditions are give more consideration than the Greek philosophical background. The author distinguishes between 'Alexandria' for Hellenistic traditions and 'Jerusalem' for Palestinian traditions. In addition, other texts of Philo are discussed, for example the offering of Isaac as parable to the behaviour of the wise (*Fug.* 132ff.). In *Fug.* 166ff. Isaac is the symbol of the man who receives the gift of wisdom. In *Cher* 106 Isaac is exemplified as the soul which loves virtue, bearing fruit through Divine powers. All in all, two different interpretations are offered for the writings of Philo. First, in the allegorical interpretation the wise man (Abraham) discovers the enjoyment (Isaac) as the embodiment of otherworldly life. Second, the offering is viewed from the point of the son Isaac himself: the willingness of the wise man (here Isaac) is symbolised as offering God his own spirit. Apparently Philo has drawn on the wisdom tradition of Early Judaism. Links to the Christology of John (for example John 8.36–38) on the basis of this Wisdom-literature are postulated. This also applies to the question of the Logos' pre-existence. (GS)

M. F. MACH, 'Choices for Changing Frontiers?: The Apologetics of Philo of Alexandria,' in Y. SCHWARTZ and V. KRECH (eds.), *Religious Apologetics – Philosophical Argumentation*, Religion in Philosophy and Theology 10 (Tübingen 2004) 319–333.

The author calls for a new appreciation of the inconsistencies in Philo's writings, which cannot be harmonized, but need to be appreciated in light of the changing circumstances in Alexandria. While Philo before the riots was a 'humanistic,' cosmopolitan philosopher, he was later forced to withdraw to the Jewish community and to defend his tradition vis-à-vis outsiders. While the author does not offer a chronological analysis of all Philonic writings, he suggests that the Allegorical Commentary must be seen as the clearest expression of his state of mind prior to the riots. *De Somniis*, on the other hand, reflects the tension in the city. (MRN)

L. NASRALLAH, *An Ecstasy of Folly: Prophecy and Authority in Early Christianity*, Harvard Theological Studies 52 (Cambridge MA 2003), esp. 36–46.

The author examines a range of sources to show that discussions about prophecy and ecstasy are less concerned to understand these experiences in themselves than to set limits on who can have access to divine knowledge, to establish the authority of one's own group, and to define community identity. Although she focuses mainly on early Christian debates (especially as reflected in Paul, Tertullian, and Epiphanius), the author also considers Artemidorus, Plato, and Philo. The discussion of Philo (36–46) centers on his treatise *Her.* Using Dionysian cultic language and a fourfold taxonomy of ecstasy similar to Plato's, he highlights the abandonment of body, sense perception and logos to allow for 'the rising of the divine mind' (44) during a state of 'ecstasy and inspired possession and madness' (*Her.* 264). In Philo's account, when one leaves behind the shallow, human realms of knowledge, one can receive the 'truly rich inheritance' of divine knowledge (44). (EB)

H. TIROSH-SAMUELSON, *Happiness in Premodern Judaism: Virtue, Knowledge, and Well-Being*, Monographs of the Hebrew Union College 29 (Cincinnati 2003), esp. 81–99.

The author commences this extensive monograph on happiness in pre-modern Judaism by arguing that it is wrong to think that the question of happiness is not relevant to Jewish religion. She believes that through the ages Jews have been deeply convinced that their tradition was the best path to a happy life and thus secured their happiness. There is thus no irreconcilable conflict between Judaism and the tradition of Aristotelian ethics in which happiness plays such a crucial role. The absorption of Aristotelian ethics by the Jewish tradition in fact begins with Philo. She begins her section on Philo by citing with approval Wolfson's claim that medieval Jewish philosophy is a continuation of Philonic thought. Philo agrees with the Greek philosophers that only a life lived in accordance with reason will lead to human happiness. She then delineates Philo's views by first examining his views on God, the Logos and the nature of the human being. God is the origin of human happiness. Humans have been created in such a way that in order to attain the ultimate end of human life they must devote themselves to virtue. A long section follows on Philo's views on the virtues, which departs from the views of his Greek teachers in placing a strong emphasis on religious and social virtues. The Laws instituted by Moses are an aid to human beings because he could use audio-visual aids to convey his conceptual message. But the main task of the educated reader is to penetrate to the deeper meaning of the Law through allegorical interpretation. The final part of the section discusses the goal of happiness for Philo as 'being loved by God,' which is a relational concept. The zenith of happiness is thus reached in an individual, ecstatic, unmediated coming to know the transcendent God. It is not clear, however, whether such a mystical state can be attained in this life. Certainly, however, the Therapeutae are the people who in Philo's view are able to attain the happiest way of life. (DTR)

D. Vigne, 'Origene et l'exégèse juive: l'Homélie II sur la Genèse,' *Bulletin de littérature ecclésiastique* 105 (2004) 105–146.

The author finds in this homily direct and personal reminiscences of Philonic exegesis. Origen cites in particular QG Book 2 in relation to the plan of the Ark, its tripartite structure which is an image of the human body, and its window compared to the faculty of sight which opens up the first path to philosophy. Also mentioned are the texts concerning Noah the righteous man, whom Philo presents as 'heir of the divine essence' and as the 'true and faithful covenant,' and texts which deal with the difference between the order of entry into the ark and departure in terms of the difference between separation of the sexes and mixing, i.e. the obligation of continence and that of procreation. (JR)

D. Winston, 'Un secolo di ricerca sul libro della Sapienza,' in B. G. and P. A. (eds.), *Il Libro della Sapienza: tradizione, redazione, teologi* (Rome 2004) 13–31.

In the twentieth century a *communis opinio* was formed on the book of Wisdom that it was the work of a single author who wrote in Greek. Research since then has concentrated on a central question, to the understanding of which John Collins has given an important contribution: how to reconcile the book's philosophical vision (Wisdom, as world order, permeating the world) with its apocalyptic views (Wisdom or order having retreated from the world)? Winston argues that the friction between these two visions has an analogy in Philo. The analogy can be found in Philo's ambivalence with regard to the unique position of the people of Israel and to the prophesied messianic era, given his views on the world as involved in an 'ahistorical' process guided by the *logos* and on the Torah as representing natural law. Winston states that Philo and the author of Wisdom share the need to reconcile two opposed concepts of divine providence, and that both probably wrote in a situation of heavy persecution. Another point both authors have in common is that for them biblcial exegesis is never an end in itself. The key to understanding Philo's intentions is recognising the midrashic-allegorical character of his exegesis. It is misleading to see Philo primarily as an exegete of Scripture, and the same holds true for the author of Wisdom. Both are driven by the need to fuse Jewish tradition and Greek philosophy in an attempt to defend their own integrity in the face of persecution and pagan cultural changes. (HMK)

M. YTTERBRINK, *The Third Gospel for the First Time. Luke within the Context of Ancient Biography* (diss. Lund 2004), esp. 94–103.

This study is the author's 2004 dissertation from Lund University, Sweden (advisor Prof. Birger Olsson). The book is a kind of narrative analysis of the Gospel of Luke. The reader is invited to accompany the first readers or hearers of the gospel and to experience the narrative alongside them. It utilizes W. Iser's theory about reading and readers and focuses on gaps and vacancies in the texts. It is also suggested that the readers would probably have been acquainted with comparables stories, and this is where Philo come into focus. Ytterbrink presents aspects of biographical works of Isocrates, Xenophon, Plutarch, Philo and some others. Of Philo's biographies she presents *De vita Mosis*, *De Abrahamo* and *De Josepho* (94–103). It is probably too much to say that Philo's works are prominent in the rest of this study, but some further comparative remarks occur. Commenting on the Narrator, the author suggests that, when compared to Philo, Isocrates, Xenophon, and many others, the author of the Third Gospel takes a much more obtrusive role, more like that of an editor than of a real author. It was most probably possible for the contemporary audience to apprehend the differences (229). (TS)

SUPPLEMENT

A Provisional Bibliography 2006–2008

The user of this supplementary Bibliography of very recent articles on Philo is
once again reminded that it will doubtless contain inaccuracies and red herrings,
because it is not in all cases based on autopsy. It is merely meant as a service to the
reader. Scholars who are disappointed by omissions or are keen to have their own
work on Philo listed are strongly encouraged to contact the Bibliography's com-
pilers (addresses in the section Notes on Contributors).

2006

AA.vv., *Le Décalogue au miroir des Pères*, Cahiers de Biblia Patristica
(Turnhout 2006).

J. Annas, 'Recent Work on Plato's *Timaeus*,' *The Studia Philonica Annual* 18
(2006) 125–142.

A. Birkan-Shear, '"Does a Serpent Give Life?" Understanding The Brazen
Serpent According to Philo and Early Rabbinic Literature,' in I. H.
Henderson and G. S. Oegema (eds.), *The Changing Face of Judaism, Chris-
tianity, and Other Greco-Roman Religions in Antiquity (= FS Charlesworth)*,
Studien zu den Jüdischen Schriften aus hellenistisch-römischer Zeit Band
2 (Gütersloh 2006) 416–426.

E. Birnbaum, 'Two Millennia Later: General Resources and Particular Perspectives on Philo the Jew,' *Currents in Biblical Research* 4 (2006) 241–276.

P. Borgen, 'Crucified for His Own Sins—Crucified for Our Sins: Observations on a Pauline Perspective,' in J. Fotopoulos (ed.), *The New Testament
and Early Christian Literature in Greco-Roman Context: Studies in Honor of
David E. Aune*, Novum Testamentum Supplements 122 (Leiden–Boston
2006) 17–36.

P. R. Bosman, 'Conscience and Free Speech in Philo,' *The Studia Philonica
Annual* 18 (2006) 33–47.

M. Broze, 'Les Enseignement de Sylvanos et la parole tranchante. Jeux de
mots et assonances plurilinguistiques,' *Apocrypha* 17 (2006) 79–86.

C. Carlier, *La Cité de Moïse*, Monothéismes et Philosophie (Turnhout 2006).

N. G. Cohen, 'La dimensión judía del judaísmo de Filón. Una elucidación
de *De Spec. Leg.* IV 132–150,' *Revista Bíblica* 68 (2006) 215–240.

S. Di Mattei, 'Moses' Physiologia and the Meaning and Use of *Physikôs* in
Philo of Alexandria's Exegetical Method,' *The Studia Philonica Annual* 18
(2006) 3–32.

S. Di MATTEI, 'Paul's Allegory of Two Covenants (Gal. 4.21–31) in Light of First-Century Hellenistic Rhetoric and Jewish Hermeneutic,' *New Testament Studies* 52 (2006) 102–122.

L. H. FELDMAN, *Judaism and Hellenism Reconsidered* (Leiden–Boston 2006).

M. FRENSCHKOWSKI, 'Studien zur Geschichte der Bibliothek von Cäsarea,' in T. J. KRAUS and T. NICKLAS (eds.), *New Testament Manuscripts: Their Texts and Their World* (Leiden–Boston 2006) 53–104.

K. FUGLSETH, 'The Reception of Aristotelian Features in Philo and the Authorship Problem of Philo's *De Aeternitate Mundi*,' in D. BRAKKE, A.-C. JACOBSEN and J. ULRICH (eds.), *Beyond Reception. Mutual Influences between Antique Religion, Judaism, and Early Christianity*, Early Christianity in the Context of Antiquity 1 (Frankfurt 2006) 57–67.

M. E. FULLER, *The Restoration of Israel: Israel's Re-gathering and the Fate of the Nations in Early Jewish Literature and Luke-Acts*, Beihefte zur Zeitschrift für die neutestamentliche Wissenschaft und die Kunde der älteren Kirche 138 (Berlin 2006), esp. 82–102.

A. C. GELJON, 'Philo en de kerkvaders,' *Schrift* no. 223 (2006) 26–30.

A. C. GELJON, 'Philo of Alexandria and Gregory of Nyssa on Moses at the Burning Bush,' in G. H. VAN KOOTEN (ed.), *The Revelation of the Name YHWH to Moses*, Themes in Biblical Narrative, 9 (Leiden–Boston 2006) 225–236.

A. GRAFTON and M. WILLIAMS, *Christianity and the Transformation of the Book: Origen, Eusebius, and the Library of Caesarea* (Cambridge Mass. 2006).

M. HADAS-LEBEL, *Jerusalem against Rome*, Interdiscipinary Studies in Ancient Culture and Religion 7 (Leuven 2006).

G. HATA, *Nottoraretta Seisho* (Kyoto 2006), esp. 128–134.

P. HEGER, 'Sabbath Offerings according to the Damascus Document — Scholarly Opinions and a New Hypothesis,' *Zeitschrift für die Alttestamentliche Wissenschaft* 118 (2006) 62–81.

P. W. VAN DER HORST, 'Two Short Notes on Philo,' *The Studia Philonica Annual* 18 (2006) 49–55.

S. INOWLOCKI, *Eusebius and the Jewish Authors: His Citation Technique in an Apologetic Context*, Ancient Judaism and Early Christianity 64 (Leiden–Boston 2006).

A. P. JOHNSON, 'Philonic Allusions in Eusebius, *PE* 7.7–8,' *Classical Quarterly* 56 (2006) 239–248.

H. M. KEIZER, 'Philo en het Nieuwe Testament,' *Schrift* no. 223 (2006) 21–25.

A. KERKESLAGER, 'Agrippa and the Mourning Rites for Drusilla in Alexandria,' *Journal for the Study of Judaism* 37 (2006) 367–400.

A. KERKESLAGER, 'Jews in Egypt and Cyrenaica 66-c. 235 CE' in S. T. KATZ (ed.), *Cambridge History of Judaism, Volume 4: The Late Roman Period* (Cambridge 2006) 53–68.

D. KONSTAN, 'Philo's *De virtutibus* in the Perspective of Classical Greek Philosophy,' *The Studia Philonica Annual* 18 (2006) 59–72.

G. H. VAN KOOTEN, *The Revelation of the Name YHWH to Moses: Perspectives from Judaism, the Pagan Graeco-Roman World, and Early Christianity,* Themes in Biblical Narrative: Jewish and Christian Traditions 9 (Leiden–Boston 2006).

A. LE BOULLUEC, *Alexandrie antique et chrétienne. Clément et Origène,* Collections des Études Augustiniennes Série Antiquité 178 (Paris 2006).

C. LÉVY, 'Philon et les passions,' in L. CICCOLINI (ed.), *Receptions antiques: Etudes de littérature ancienne* (Paris 2006) 27–41.

G. P. LUTTIKHUIZEN, *Gnostic Revisions of Genesis Stories and Early Jesus Traditions,* Nag Hammadi and Manichaean Studies 58 (Leiden–Boston 2006).

M. R. NIEHOFF, 'Philo's Contribution to Contemporary Alexandrian Metaphysics,' in D. BRAKKE, A.-C. JACOBSEN and J. ULRICH (eds.), *Beyond Reception. Mutual Influences between Antique Religion, Judaism, and Early Christianity,* Early Christianity in the Context of Antiquity 1 (Frankfurt 2006) 35–55.

C. O'BRIEN, 'Platonism and the Tools of God,' *Trinity College Dublin Journal of Postgraduate Research* 6 (2006) 60–72.

P. K. POHJALA, *Similaries of Redation of the Gospel according to Matthew with Texts of Philo of Alexandrinus* (Liskeard, Cornwall 2006).

I. RAMELLI *Il basileus come nomos empsychos tra diritto naturale e diritto divino. Spunti platonici del concetto e sviluppi di età imperiale e tardo-antica,* Memorie dell'Istituto Italiano per gli studi filosofici 34 (Naples 2006), esp. 89–91.

D. G. ROBERTSON, 'Mind and Language in Philo,' *Journal of the History of Ideas* 67 (2006) 423–442.

J. R. ROYSE, 'The Text of Philo's *De virtutibus,*' *The Studia Philonica Annual* 18 (2006) 73–101.

D. T. RUNIA, 'Philo – een introductie,' *Schrift* no. 223 (2006) 3–11.

D. T. RUNIA, E. BIRNBAUM, K. A. FOX, A. C. GELJON, H. M. KEIZER, J. P. MARTÍN, R. RADICE, J. RIAUD, D. SATRAN, G. SCHIMANOWSKI, and T. SELAND, 'Philo of Alexandria: an Annotated Bibliography 2003,' *The Studia Philonica Annual* 18 (2006) 143–204.

D. T. RUNIA and G. E. STERLING (eds.), *The Studia Philonica Annual,* Vol. 18, Society of Biblical Literature (Atlanta 2006).

K. O. SANDNES, 'Markus – en allegorisk biografi?' *Dansk Teologisk Tidsskrift* 69 (2006) 275–297.

B. SCHLIESSER, *Abraham's Faith in Romans 4: Genesis 15:6 and its History of Reception in Second Temple Judaism and Paul. A Contribution to the Pauline Concept of Faith (Saint Paul the Apostle)* (diss. Fuller Theological Seminary 2006).

T. SELAND, 'Philo, Magic and Balaam: Neglected Aspects of Philo's Exposition of the Balaam Story,' in J. FOTOPOULOS (ed.), *The New Testament and Early Christian Literature in Greco-Roman Context: Studies in Honor of David E. Aune,* Novum Testamentum Supplements 122 (Leiden–Boston 2006) 333–346.

P. D. STEIGER, *Theological Anthropology in the Commentary 'On Genesis' by Didymus the Blind (Egypt)* (diss. Catholic University of America 2006).

G. E. STERLING, '"The Queen of the Virtues": Piety in Philo of Alexandria,' *The Studia Philonica Annual* 18 (2006) 103–123.

G. J. STEYN, 'Torah Quotations Common to Philo, Hebrews, Clemens Romanus and Justin Martyr: What is the Common Denominator?,' in C. BREYTENBACH, J. C. THOM and J. PUNT (eds.), *The New Testament Interpreted: Essays in Honour of Bernard C. Lategan,* Supplements to Novum Testamentum 124 (Leiden–Boston 2006) 135–151.

H. P. THYSSEN, 'Philosophical Christology in the New Testament,' *Numen: International Review for the History of Religions* 53 (2006) 133–176.

J. L. TINKLENBERG DE VEGA, *'A Man who Fears God':* Constructions of Masculinity in Hellenistic Jewish interpretations of the Story of Joseph (Josephus, Philo) (diss. Florida State University 2006).

T. H. TOBIN S.J., 'The World of Thought in the Philippians Hymn (Philippians 2:6–11),' in J. FOTOPOULOS (ed.), *The New Testament and Early Christian Literature in Greco-Roman Context. Studies in Honor of David E. Aune,* Novum Testamentum Supplements 122 (Leiden–Boston 2006) 93–104.

H. TRONIER, 'Markus – en allegorisk komposition om Jesu vej,' *Dansk Teologisk Tidsskrift* 69 (2006) 298–306.

G. VELTRI, *Libraries, Translations, and 'Canonic' Texts: The Septuagint, Aquila and Ben Sira in the Jewish and Christian Traditions,* Supplements to the Journal for the Study of Judaism 109 (Leiden-Boston 2006).

U. VOLP, *Die Würde des Menschen. Ein Beitrag zur Anthropologie in der Alten Kirche,* Supplements to Vigiliae Christianae 81 (Leiden–Boston 2006), esp. 77–81.

2007

AA.vv., *Lun Moxi de sheng ping [On the Life of Moses]* (Beijing 2007).

M. ALESSO, 'Qué es una madre judía según Filón,' *Circe* 11 (2007) 11–25.

M. ALEXANDRE, 'Les études philoniennes et le renouveau patristique,' in Y.-M. BLANCHARD *et al.* (eds.), *"De commencement en commencement." Le renouveau patristique dans la théologie contemporaine* (Paris 2007) 141–179.

S. BADILITA, *Recherches sur la prophétie chez Philon d'Alexandrie* (diss. Université de Paris IV–Sorbonne 2007).

J. M. G. BARCLAY, *Flavius Josephus: Translation and Commentary, Volume 10 Against Apion: Translation and Commentary* (Leiden–Boston 2007).

C. T. BEGG, 'Josephus' and Philo's Retelling of Numbers 31 Compared,' *Ephemerides theologicae Lovanienses* 83 (2007) 81–106.

P. J. BEKKEN, *The Word is Near You. A Study of Deuteronomy 30:12–14 in Paul's Letter to the Romans in a Jewish Context*, Beihefte zur Zeitschrift für die neutestamentliche Wissenschaft und die Kunde der älteren Kirche 144 (Berlin–New York 2007).

K. BERTHELOT, 'Philo of Alexandria and the Conquest of Canaan,' *Journal for the study of Judaism in the Persian, Hellenistic and Roman period* 38 (2007) 39–56.

K. BERTHELOT, 'Zeal for God and Divine Law in Philo and the Dead Sea Scrolls,' *The Studia Philonica Annual* 19 (2007) 113–129.

P. BILDE, 'Filon som polemiker og politisk apologet,' in A. K. PETERSEN and K. S. FUGLSETH (eds.), *Perspektiver på jødisk apologetik*, Antikken og kristendommen 4 (København 2007) 155–180.

M. BONAZZI, C. LÉVY, and C. STEEL, *A Platonic Pythagoras. Platonism and Pythagoreanism in the Imperial Age*, Monothéismes et Philosophie 10 (Turnhout 2007).

A. P. Bos, 'Is God 'Maker' of 'Vader' van de kosmos? Het debat tussen Plato en Aristoteles en de voortzetting ervan bij Philo,' in K. SPRONK and R. ROUKEMA (eds.), *Over God*, (Zoetermeer, Netherlands 2007) 47–71, 188–191.

D. BOYARIN, 'Philo, Origen, and the Rabbis on Divine Speech and Interpretation,' in J. E. GOEHRING and J. TIMBIE (eds.), *The World of Early Egyptian Christianity: Language, Literature, and Social Context: Essays in Honor of David W. Johnson* (Washington DC 2007).

F. CALABI, 'Tra Atene e Gerusalemme: Anima e parola in Filone di Alessandria,' in R. BRUSCHI (ed.), *Gli irraggiungibili confini. Percorsi della psyche nell'età della Grecia classica* (Pisa 2007) 217–236.

F. CALABI, 'Filone di Alessandria e Ecfanto. Un confronto possible' in M. BONAZZI, C. LÉVY and C. STEEL (eds.), *A Platonic Pythagoras. Platonism and Pythagoreanism in the Imperial Age*, Monothéismes et Philosophie 10 (Turnhout 2007) 11–28.

J. CHERIAN, *Toward a Commonwealth of Grace: A Plutocritical Reading of Grace and Equality in Second Corinthians 8:1–15* (diss. Princeton Theological Seminary 2007).

H. CLIFFORD, 'Moses as Philosopher-sage in Philo,' in A. GRAUPNER and M. WOLTER (eds.), *Moses in Biblical and Extra-biblical Traditions* (Berlin–New York 2007) 151–167.

N. G. COHEN, *Philo's Scriptures: Citations from the Prophets and Writings: Evidence for a Haftarah Cycle in Second Temple Judaism*, Supplements to the Journal for the Study of Judaism 123 (Leiden–Boston 2007).

J. J. COLLINS, 'Philo and the Dead Sea Scrolls: Introduction,' *The Studia Philonica Annual* 19 (2007) 81–83.

R. COX, *By the Same Word: Creation and Salvation in Hellenistic Judaism and Early Christianity*, Beihefte zur Zeitschrift für die neutestamentliche Wissenschaft und die Kunde der älteren Kirche 145 (Berlin–New York 2007).

M. R. D'ANGELO, 'Gender and Geopolitics in the Work of Philo of Alexandria: Jewish Piety and Imperial Family Values,' in T. PENNER and C. VANDER STICHELE (eds.), *Mapping Gender in Ancient Religious Discourses*, Biblical Interpretation Series 84 (Leiden–Boston 2007) 63–88.

S. DI MATTEI, 'Quelques précisions sur la φυσιολογία et l'emploi de φυσικῶς dans la méthode exégétique de Philon d'Alexandrie,' *Revue des Études Juives* 166 (2007) 45–74.

A. DINAN, 'The Mystery of Play: Clement of Alexandria's Appropriation of Philo in the *Paedagogus* (1.5.21.3–22.1),' *The Studia Philonica Annual* 19 (2007) 59–80.

T. L. DONALDSON, *Judaism and the Gentiles: Jewish Patterns of Universalism (to 135 CE)* (Waco TX 2007), esp. 217–278.

M. EBNER, 'Mahl und Gruppenidentität. Philos Schrift De Vita Contemplativa als Paradigma,' in M. EBNER (ed.), *Herrenmahl und Gruppenidentität*, Quaestiones disputatae 221 (Freiburg 2007) 64–90.

L. H. FELDMAN, 'Moses the General and the Battle Against Midian in Philo,' *Jewish Studies Quarterly* 14 (2007) 1–18.

L. H. FELDMAN, *Philo's Portrayal of Moses in the Context of Ancient Judaism* (Notre Dame IN 2007).

L. H. FELDMAN, 'The Case of the Blasphemer (Lev. 24:10-16) according to Philo and Josephus,' in L. LIDONNICI and A. LIEBER (eds.), *Heavenly Tablets: Interpretation, Identity and Tradition in Ancient Judaism*,

Supplements to the Journal for the Study of Judaism 119 (Leiden 2007) 213–226.

P. Frick, 'The Means and Mode of Salvation: A Hermeneutical Proposal for Clarifying Pauline Soteriology,' *Horizons in Biblical Theology* 29 (2007) 203–222.

E. Früchtel, 'Philon und die Vorbereitung der christlichen Paideia und Seelenleitung,' in F. R. Prostmeier (ed.), *Frühchristentum und Kultur*, Kommentar zu frühchristlichen Apologeten. Ergänzungsband 2 (Freiburg 2007) 19–33.

K. S. Fuglseth, 'Filons forhold til tempelet i Jerusalem i eit apologetisk perspektiv,' in A. Klostergaard Petersen *et al.* (eds.), *Perspektiver på jødisk apologetik*, Antikken og kristendommen 4 (København 2007) 263–82.

S. Gambetti, 'A Brief Note on Agrippa I's Trip to Alexandria in the Summer of 38 CE,' *Journal of Jewish Studies* 58 (2007) 33–38.

F. García Martínez, 'Divine Sonship at Qumran and in Philo,' *The Studia Philonica Annual* 19 (2007) 85–99.

A. C. Geljon, 'Didymus the Blind's use of Philo in his exegesis of Cain and Abel,' *Vigiliae Christianae* 61 (2007) 282–312.

A. C. Geljon, 'God in de duisternis: een Alexandijnse uitleg van Exodus 20:21,' *Hermeneus* 79, no. 4 (2007) 184–190.

M. E. Gordley, *The Colossian Hymn in Context: An Exegesis in Light of Jewish and Greco-Roman Hymnic and Epistolary Conventions*, Wissenschaftliche Untersuchungen zum Neuen Testament 2.Reihe 228 (Tübingen 2007), esp. 105–108.

G. Holtz, *Damit Gott sei alles in allem: Studien zum paulinischen und frühjüdischen Universalismus* (Berlin–New York 2007), esp. 139–167.

R. A. Horsley, *Wisdom and Spiritual Transcendence at Corinth: Studies in First Corinthians* (Eugene 2007).

J. Hyldahl, 'Mellem ny og gammel kultur: Allegori i apologetisk perspektiv i aleksandrinsk jødedom,' in A. Klostergaard Petersen *et al.* (eds.), *Perspektiver på Jødisk Apologetik*, Antikken og kristendommen 4 (København 2007) 181–206.

O. Kaiser, *Des Menschen Glück und Gottes Gerechtigkeit. Studien zur biblischen Überlieferung im Kontext hellenistischer Philosophie* (Tübingen 2007), esp. 209ff.

M. B. Kartzow, *Gossip and Gender: Othering of Speech in the Pastoral Epistles* (diss. University of Oslo 2007), esp. 112–114.

A. Kovelman, 'Jeremiah 9:22-23 in Philo and Paul,' *Review of Rabbinic Judaism* 10 (2007) 162–175.

S. Krauter, 'Die Beteiligung von Nicht-juden am Jerusalemer Tempelkult,' in J. Frey, D. R. Schwartz and S. Gripentrog (eds.), *Jewish Identity in the Greco-Roman World*, Ancient Judaism and Early Christianity 71 (Leiden–Boston 2007) 55–74.

M. LANDFESTER and B. EGGER (eds.), *Geschichte der antiken Texte. Autoren– und Werklexicon*, Der Neue Pauly Supplemente Band 2 (Stuttgart 2007), esp. 456–459.

P. LANFRANCHI, 'Reminiscences of Ezekiel's *Exagoge* in Philo's *De vita Mosis*,' in A. GRAUPNER and M. WOLTER (eds.), *Moses in Biblical and Extra-biblical Traditions* (Berlin–New York 2007) 144–150.

K. D. LAVERY, *Abraham's Dialogue with God over the Destruction of Sodom: Chapters in the History of the Interpretation of Genesis 18* (diss. Harvard University 2007).

J. LEONHARDT-BALZER, 'Jewish Worship and Universal Identity in Philo of Alexandria' in J. FREY, D. R. SCHWARTZ and S. GRIPENTROG (eds.), *Jewish Identity in the Greco-Roman World*, Ancient Judaism and Early Christianity 71 (Leiden–Boston 2007) 29–54.

C. LÉVY, 'La question de la dyade chez Philon d'Alexandrie,' in M. BONAZZI, C. LÉVY and C. STEEL (eds.), *A Platonic Pythagoras. Platonism and Pythagoreanism in the Imperial Age*, Monothéismes et Philosophie 10 (Turnhout 2007) 11–28.

A. LIEBER, 'Between Motherland and Fatherland: Diaspora, Pilgrimage and Spiritualization of Sacrifice in Philo of Alexandria,' in L. LI DONNICI and A. LIEBER (eds.), *Heavenly Tablets: Interpretation, Identity and Tradition in Ancient Judaism*, Supplements to the Journal for the Study of Judaism 119 (Leiden 2007) 193–210.

N. E. LIVESEY, *Circumcision as a Malleable Symbol: Treatments of Circumcision in Philo, Paul, and Justin Martyr* (diss. Southern Methodist University 2007).

J. P. LOTZ, *Ignatius and Concord: the Background and Use of the Language of Concord in the Letters of Ignatius of Antioch*, Patristic Studies 8 (New York 2007).

S. D. MACKIE, *Eschatology and Exhortation in the Epistle to the Hebrews*, Wissenschaftliche Untersuchungen zum Neuen Testament 2. Reihe 223 (Tübingen 2007), esp. 108–111, 117–122.

J. P. MARTÍN, 'Il primo convegno italiano su Filone di Alessandria,' *Adamantius* 13 (2007) 276–281.

L. H. MILLS, *Zaratoustra, Philo, the Achaemenids and Israel, Part II : Being a Treatise Upon the Antiquity and Influence of the Avesta* (Whitefish MT 2007).

H. NAJMAN, 'Philosophical Contemplation and Revelatory Inspiration in Ancient Judean Traditions,' *The Studia Philonica Annual* 19 (2007) 101–111.

M. R. Niehoff, 'Homeric Scholarship and Bible Exegesis in Ancient Alexandria: Evidence from Philo's 'Quarrelsome' Colleagues,' *Classical Quarterly* 57, no. 1 (2007) 166–182.

M. R. Niehoff, 'Did the *Timaeus* Create a Textual Community?,' *Greek, Roman, and Byzantine Studies* 47 (2007) 161–191, esp. 170–177.

F. Oertelt, 'Vom Nutzen der Musik. Ein Blick auf die Funktion der musikalischen Ausbildung bei Philo von Alexandrien,' in A. Standhartinger, H. Schwebel and F. Oertelt (eds.), *Kunst der Deutung — Deutung der Kunst: Beiträge zu Bibel, Antike und Gegenwartsliteratur. FS Sieghild von Blumenthal* (Münster 2007) 51–62.

M. Osmanski, *Filona z Aleksandrii: etyke upodabniania sie do Boga* (Lublin 2007).

S. J. K. Pearce, *The Land of the Body: Studies in Philo's Representation of Egypt*, Wissenschaftliche Untersuchungen zum Neuem Testament 204 (Tübingen 2007).

S. K. Pearce, 'Philo on the Nile,' in J. Frey, D. R. Schwartz and S. Gripentrog (eds.), *Jewish Identity in the Greco-Roman World*, Ancient Judaism and Early Christianity 71 (Leiden–Boston 2007) 137–157.

B. Pearson, 'Earliest Christianity in Egypt: Further Observations,' in J. E. Goehring and J. Timbie (eds.), *The World of Early Egyptian Christianity: Language, Literature, and Social Context: Essays in Honor of David W. Johnson* (Washington DC 2007).

A. K. Petersen, 'Filon som apologet – en læsning af De migratione Abrahami,' in *Perspektiver på Jødisk Apologetik*, Antikken og kristendommen 4 (København 2007) 233–262.

A. Piñero, *Literatura judía de época helenística en lengua griega. Desde la versión de la biblia al griego hasta el Nuevo Testamento* (Madrid 2007).

P. K. Pohjala, *Divination by Bowls in Bible, Septuagint, Qumran Texts, Philo and Matthew 13:1–12: Magnified Visions from Glass Bowls in Bible Interpretation* (London 2007).

D. Robertson, *Word and Meaning in Ancient Alexandria: Theories of Language from Philo to Plotinus* (Aldershot 2007).

D. T. Runia, 'Philo in the Reformational Tradition,' in R. Sweetman (ed.), *In the Phrygian Mode: Neocalvinism, Antiquity and the Lamentations of Reformed Philosophy*, Christian Perspectives Today (Lanham etc. 2007) 195–212.

D. T. Runia, 'The Rehabilitation of the Jackdaw: Philo of Alexandria and Ancient Philosophy,' in R. Sorabji and R. W. Sharples (eds.), *Greek and Roman Philosophy 100 BC–200 AD*, (London 2007) 483–500.

D. T. Runia, E. Birnbaum, K. A. Fox, A. C. Geljon, H. M. Keizer, J. P. Martín, R. Radice, J. Riaud, D. Satran, G. Schimanowski, and

T. SELAND, 'Philo of Alexandria: an Annotated Bibliography 2004,' *The Studia Philonica Annual* 19 (2007) 143–204.

D. T. RUNIA and G. E. STERLING (eds.), *The Studia Philonica Annual*, Vol. 19 (Atlanta 2007).

L. SAUDELLI, 'La *hodos anô kai katô* d'Héraclite (Fragment 22 B 60 DK/33 M) dans le *De Aeternitate Mundi* de Philon d'Alexandrie,' *The Studia Philonica Annual* 19 (2007) 29–58.

G. SCHÖLLGEN (ed.), *Reallexikon für Antike und Christentum Lieferungen 170* (Stuttgart 2007).

L. T. STUCKENBRUCK, 'To What Extent Did Philo's Treatment of Enoch and the Giants Presuppose a Knowledge of the Enochic and Other Sources Preserved in the Dead Sea Scrolls?,' *The Studia Philonica Annual* 19 (2007) 131–142.

J. E. TAYLOR, 'Philo of Alexandria on the Essenes: A Case Study on the Use of Classical Sources in Discussions of the Qumran-Essene Hypothesis,' *The Studia Philonica Annual* 19 (2007) 1–28.

C. TERMINI, 'La Scrittura nei tre grandi commenti di Filone di Alessandria: forme e metodi esegetici,' *Ricerche Storico-Bibliche* 19 (2007) 47–73.

C. TIBBS, *Religious Experience of the Pneuma: Communication with the Spirit World in 1 Corinthians 12 and 14*, Wissenschaftliche Untersuchungen zum Neuen Testament 2.Reihe 230 (Tübingen 2007), esp. 125–131.

R. M. VICTOR, *Colonial Education and Class Formation in Early Judaism: A Postcolonial Reading* (diss. Texas Christian University 2007).

D. WINSTON, 'Philo of Alexandria on the Rational and Irrational Emotions,' in J. T. FITZGERALD (ed.), *Passions and Moral Progress in Greco-Roman Thought* (London–New York 2007) 327–364.

2008

F. ALESSE (ed.), *Philo of Alexandria and Post-Aristotelian Philosophy*, Studies on Philo of Alexandria 5 (Leiden–Boston 2008).

J. S. ALLEN, *The Despoliation of Egypt in Pre-Rabbinic, Rabbinic and Patristic Traditions*, Supplements to Vigiliae Christianae 92 (Leiden–Boston 2008), esp. 91–117 and passim.

M. A. BADER, *Tracing the Evidence: Dinah in Post-Hebrew Bible Literature*, Studies in Biblical Literature 162 (New York 2008).

R. M. VAN DEN BERG, *Proclus' Commentary on the Cratylus in Context: Ancient Theories of Language and Naming*, Philosophia Antiqua 112 (Leiden–Boston 2008), esp. 52–56.

M. BONAZZI, 'Towards Transcendence: Philo and the Renewal of Platonism in the Early Imperial Age,' in F. ALESSE (ed.), *Philo of Alexandria and*

Post-Aristotelian Philosophy, Studies on Philo of Alexandria 5 (Leiden–Boston 2008) 13–52.

F. Calabi, *God's Acting, Man's Acting: Tradition and Philosophy in Philo of Alexandria*, Studies in Philo of Alexandria 4 (Leiden–Boston 2008).

C. Carlier, *La Cité de Moïse*, Monothéismes et Philosophie 11 (Turnhout 2008).

J. Dillon, 'Philo and Hellenistic Platonism,' in F. Alesse (ed.), *Philo of Alexandria and Post-Aristotelian Philosophy*, Studies on Philo of Alexandria 5 (Leiden–Boston 2008) 223–232.

M. Graver, 'Philo of Alexandria and the Origins of the Stoic ΠΡΟΠΑΘΕΙΑΙ,' in F. Alesse (ed.), *Philo of Alexandria and Post-Aristotelian Philosophy*, Studies on Philo of Alexandria 5 (Leiden–Boston 2008) 197–221.

C. Lévy, *Les Scepticismes*, Bibliographie thématique «Que sais-je» 2829 (Paris 2008), esp. 84–87.

C. Lévy, 'La conversion du scepticisme chez Philon d'Alexandrie,' in F. Alesse (ed.), *Philo of Alexandria and Post-Aristotelian Philosophy*, Studies on Philo of Alexandria 5 (Leiden–Boston 2008) 103–120.

A. A. Long, 'Philo and Stoic Physics,' in F. Alesse (ed.), *Philo of Alexandria and Post-Aristotelian Philosophy*, Studies on Philo of Alexandria 5 (Leiden–Boston 2008) 121–140.

M. W. Martin, 'Progymnastic Topic Lists: A Compositional Template for Luke and Other Bioi,' *New Testament Studies* 54 (2008) 18–41.

E. F. Mason, *'You are a Priest Forever': Second Temple Jewish Messianism and the Priestly Christology of the Epistle to the Hebrews*, Studies on the Texts of the Desert of Judah 74 (Leiden–Boston 2008).

E. Muehlberger, 'The Representation of Theatricality in Philo's Embassy to Gaius,' *Journal for the Study of Judaism* 39 (2008) 46–67.

M. R. Niehoff, 'Questions and Answers in Philo and *Genesis Rabbah*', *Journal for the Study of Judaism* 39 (2008) 337–366.

R. Radice, 'Philo and Stoic Ethics. Reflections on the Idea of Freedom,' in F. Alesse (ed.), *Philo of Alexandria and Post-Aristotelian Philosophy*, Studies on Philo of Alexandria 5 (Leiden–Boston 2008) 141–167.

G. Ranocchia, 'Moses against the Egyptian: the Anti-Epicurean Polemic in Philo,' in F. Alesse (ed.), *Philo of Alexandria and Post-Aristotelian Philosophy*, Studies on Philo of Alexandria 5 (Leiden–Boston 2008) 75–102.

G. Reydams-Schils, 'Philo of Alexandria on Stoic and Platonist Psycho-Physiology: the Socratic Higher Ground,' in F. Alesse (ed.), *Philo of Alexandria and Post-Aristotelian Philosophy*, Studies on Philo of Alexandria 5 (Leiden–Boston 2008) 169–195.

A. RUNESSON, D. D. BINDER, and B. OLSSON (eds.), *The Ancient Synagogue from its Origins to 200 C.E.: A Source Book* (Leiden–Boston 2008).

D. T. RUNIA, 'Worshipping the Visible Gods: Conflict and Accommodation in Hellenism, Hellenistic Judaism and Early Christianity,' in A. HOUTMAN, A. D. JONG and M. MISSET-VAN DE WEG (eds.), *Empsychoi Logoi — Religious Innovations in Antiquity. Studies in Honour of Pieter Willem van der Horst*, Ancient Judaism and Early Christianity 73 (Leiden–Boston 2008).

D. T. RUNIA, 'Philo and Hellenistic Doxography,' in F. ALESSE (ed.), *Philo of Alexandria and Post-Aristotelian Philosophy*, Studies on Philo of Alexandria 5 (Leiden–Boston 2008) 13–52.

R. W. SHARPLES, 'Philo and post-Aristotelian Peripatetics,' in F. ALESSE (ed.), *Philo of Alexandria and Post-Aristotelian Philosophy*, Studies on Philo of Alexandria 5 (Leiden–Boston 2008) 55–73.

J. WOYKE, 'Nochmals zu den 'schwachen und unfähigen Elementen' (Gal. 4.9): Paulus, Philo und die στοιχεῖα τοῦ κόσμου,' *New Testament Studies* 54 (2008) 221–234.

D. ZELLER, 'Schöpfungsglaube und fremde Religion bei Philo von Alexandrien,' in L. BORMANN (ed.), *Schöpfung, Monotheismus und fremde Religionen*, Biblisch-Theologische Studien 95 (Neukirchen-Vluyn 2008) 125–148.

BOOK REVIEW SECTION

George W. E. NICKELSBURG, *Jewish Literature Between the Bible and the Mishnah: A Historical and Literary Introduction*, 2nd ed. Minneapolis: Fortress Press, 2005. xxiii + 445 pages. ISBN 0-80063-7682. Price $45.00 (hardcover), $29 (paperback).

For a quarter century, the first edition of this masterful work was unsurpassed as a guidebook to much of the extra-biblical literature of pre-rabbinic Judaism. It provided an invaluable first introduction for informed non-specialists as well as an engaging analysis for those who knew the material well. Now, an updated and expanded edition equips yet another generation with a helpful guide to an even broader selection of ancient Jewish literature.

Of special interest to Philonists is the addition of a brief introduction to Philo of Alexandria in this new edition. Here one finds the same learned discussion that typifies the treatment of other authors and sources, although in this case Nickelsburg departs from his usual literary focus. Because much is known about Philo himself, and because the Philonic corpus is so large, Nickelsburg concentrates on Philo's life and thought, describing only the broad contours of Philo's literary *œuvre* and discussing parts of only one Philonic text (*On Joseph*). Introductions to Flavius Josephus and the Septuagint have also been added, as have discussions of several Qumran texts that were either unavailable or inadequately understood in 1981 when the first edition was published (the *Halakhic Letter* [4QMMT], the *Rule of the Congregation* [1QSa], the *Songs of the Sabbath Sacrifice*, the *Aramaic Levi Document*, the *Psalms Scroll*, *Sapiental Work A* [4QInstruction], and the *New Jerusalem* text). The few "Apocryphal" works not treated in the first edition (the *Prayer of Manasseh*, the *Tale of the Bodyguards* [1 Esdras 3–4], and Psalm 151) are likewise included now.

In addition to expanding the contents, Nickelsburg has improved the arrangement. The Qumran scrolls and related texts are now assembled in a single chapter. Other writings are arranged more consistently by historical period rather than by genre or supposed provenance; thus the chapter on "The Exposition of Israel's Scriptures" has been eliminated and its contents dispersed among other chapters. Whatever the heading, Nickelsburg is careful to contextualize each document in time and place insofar as the evidence will allow. His historical inferences are consistently judicious and his perception of how theological ideas and literary patterns relate to historical circumstances always insightful.

Three works included in the first edition have been omitted in the second (the *Martyrdom of Isaiah*, the Greek Apocalypse of Baruch [3 *Baruch*], and the Paraleipomena of Jeremiah [4 *Baruch*]) because of doubts about whether non-Christian Jewish forms of these texts can be recovered, and indeed whether such ever existed. For the same reason, a new chapter on "Texts of Disputed Provenance" collects several works that were scattered among other chapters in the previous edition but whose origin in non-Christian Judaism is now considered doubtful enough that they should no longer be used to reconstruct a picture of early Judaism (the *Testaments of the Twelve Patriarchs*, the *Testament of Job*, the *Testament of Abraham*, the *Life of Adam and Eve*, *Joseph and Aseneth*, and the *Prayer of Manasseh*). This shift reflects a growing emphasis on the well-known fact that many works long considered Jewish were preserved and transmitted by Christians. Robert Kraft, among others, has insisted that the Christian setting of these texts is the given, the starting point for studying them and perhaps even the best evidence for who produced them. Nickelsburg is absolutely correct that "[o]ne must begin with what is given, namely the Christian provenance of the manuscripts" (301), and his relegation of texts with dubious Jewish origin to a chapter on "texts of disputed provenance" is probably wise. Certainly Harnack's default canon that "whatever is not clearly Christian is Jewish" is untenable. However, Nickelsburg's inverse view (following Kraft) that the Christian origin of a text preserved by Christians is the proper "default position," and that the burden of proof rests on those who argue for its Jewish origin, is also problematic. The Christian transmission of a work shows that at some point the work was meaningful to Christians, but it affords no evidence of its Christian *origin*, as many works preserved by Christians but known to have been composed by Jews (*e.g.*, *Jubilees*, most of *1 Enoch*, and the writings of Philo and Josephus) demonstrate. Saying that Christians *preserved* a work because they found parts of it useful is a far cry from saying that a Christian could or would have *composed* the entire work. The time has come to dispense with any "default position" and recognize that the burden of proof rests on *any*one making *any* claim about the origin of a work, whether Jewish, Christian, or other. No proposal should be saddled with a greater burden of proof, or privileged with a lesser burden of proof, than any other.

Nickelsburg does not deny that early Jewish sources and traditions, and perhaps even entire Jewish works, lie embedded in works that are Christianized in their preserved forms. Indeed, he favors such a conclusion in several cases. He simply insists that such conclusions need to be argued rather than assumed, and he is more skeptical than before of our ability to extract the non-Christian elements with such surgical precision that they provide reliable witnesses to earlier, even pre-Christian forms of Judaism. This methodological caution is laudable, even if there is room for disagreement about which works belong in the "disputed" category.

Another commendable feature of Nickelsburg's work is his remarkable mastery of the secondary literature, which has grown exponentially in the quarter century between the two editions. Whatever the ancient text under discussion, the reader finds both the seasoned judgment of a leading specialist in the field and the best insights from up-to-date research by others. Further enhancing the utility of the new edition is the inclusion of a CD-ROM with the searchable text of the book, dozens of images to help bring the historical settings of the literature to life, and a Study Guide with chapter summaries, study questions, and links to useful web sites.

Nickelsburg's revision makes an already outstanding book even better. Whether as an introduction to early Jewish literature for the beginner or a stimulating fresh analysis for the expert, this book remains without equal. Students of early Judaism and early Christianity are indebted to Nickelsburg for updating and expanding the 1981 original to provide a state-of-the art guidebook that will serve well for another quarter century and beyond.

Randall D. Chesnutt
Pepperdine University

Terence L. DONALDSON, *Judaism and the Gentiles: Jewish Patterns of Universalism (to 135 C.E.).* Waco, Texas: Baylor University Press, 2007. xvi + 563 pages. ISBN 1-60258-025-1. Price $69.95.

This examination of Jewish stances toward Gentiles from the beginning of the Hellenistic period to 135 c.e. is a major contribution to scholarship on Second Temple Judaism. Despite its focus on a specific era in the past, the book also raises important issues that extend into the present. Similarly, as the author makes clear, our present dispositions have ramifications for the way we interpret evidence from this time long ago. Lest readers remain oblivious to these contemporary implications and influences, Terence L. Donaldson frames his study with two telling remarks. On page 1, he notes that earlier, mainly Christian, scholars had depicted Second Temple Judaism pejoratively as "particularistic" in contrast to Christianity, which they viewed positively as "universalistic." At the very end of his study, Donaldson observes that in our current environment "the 'religious other' has become a more immediate fact of human life" than ever before, and it is thus "imperative that persons of faith learn how to create theological space for the other even as they remain true to their own identity and vision" (513). In the over 500 pages between these remarks, Donaldson examines more than 200 instances of evidence—from early Jewish, Christian, and other texts and from inscriptions—that offer, as he suggests, instructive models for today. His aim is to show that "[d]uring this period Judaism was in its own ways just as 'universalistic' as was Christianity—indeed, in some ways even more so" (1). In achieving this aim, Donaldson amply succeeds. As I progressed through his work, though, ironically I became more and more convinced that we should avoid—or at least seriously rethink—our use of the term "universalism." Since the focus of the book, however, is on universalistic aspects of Jews and Judaism during the Second Temple period, let us give due attention to these features from the past before turning to our use of the term in the present.

In a brief and stimulating Introduction, Donaldson discusses various Jewish approaches to the religious status of non-Jews and sets forth his intention to study those expressions of the position that "the Gentiles are able, in one way or another, to relate positively to the God of Israel and to share somehow in Israel's ultimate destiny" (4). The "portion of the spectrum" that expresses these positive attitudes toward non-Jews Donaldson calls "universalistic," and he further identifies four Jewish "patterns of universalism." *Sympathization* describes the involvement of non-Jews in activities—such as worship at the Jerusalem Temple, adoption of some Jewish practices, or association with the Jewish community—that imply a sympathetic attitude toward Jews and Judaism. *Conversion* refers to a Gentile's complete adoption of the Jewish way of life and incorporation into the Jewish community. *Ethical monotheism* reflects the presentation of the Torah as "a particular expression of a natural law accessible to everyone through reason" and the construal of "Torah religion and Greek philosophy as parallel paths to the same goal—namely, a vision of one universal deity and a life of virtue...." (11). Finally, *eschatological participation* indicates the participation of Gentiles in benefits accrued to Israel at the end of time through, for example, Gentiles' turning to worship of Israel's God or sharing in Israel's blessings. Besides these "patterns," Donaldson also mentions related questions, debated by scholars, that are of secondary concern. These questions include whether Judaism was a missionary religion, whether the audience for Jewish apologetic literature was Jewish or Gentile, whether a formal class of Gentile sympathizers existed, what the relationship was between textual image and social reality, and whether Judaism should be seen as a unity or as "a set of distinct socio-religious entities" (8)—i.e., as Judaism or Judaisms.

Having laid this groundwork, Donaldson now turns to the evidence itself in Part One ("Texts and Commentary"), which comprises eight chapters and some 450 pages. Here in admirable detail he considers an extensive collection of texts in chapters devoted to Scripture, Septuagint, and Apocrypha (fifty-nine pages); Pseudepigrapha (117 pages); Qumran (twenty-one pages); Philo (sixty-two pages); Josephus (eighty-three pages); Greco-Roman literature (forty-seven pages); early Christian literature (twenty-five pages); and inscriptions (thirty pages). For each numbered "principal text," he provides a translation and analysis, preceded by a list indicating the edition, translation, date, provenance, original language, relevant bibliography, and category assignment(s) according to the four patterns of universalism. In Part Two ("Patterns of Universalism"), which includes one chapter apiece on each pattern and a conclusion, Donaldson synthesizes his findings and addresses the secondary questions raised in his introduction. Finally, the volume is capped by a Works Cited section and three indices: Principal Texts According to Category, Ancient Sources, and Modern Authors. I noted with interest that texts describing sympathization numbered 112; conversion, eighty-four; ethical monotheism, thirty-two; and eschatological participation, twenty-nine (some of the 222 texts in total are assigned to more than one category).

The sheer breadth of evidence that Donaldson examines commands deep admiration. His analyses, moreover, are judicious, careful, and nuanced, and he recognizes and respects the complexity of both the material and the topic. Readers will undoubtedly also gain fresh insights from his presentations. In addition, while offering his own opinions, Donaldson also provides those of others so that readers can consider the sources from different positions and judge for themselves. One can smile at Donaldson's occasional quips related to circumcision, but he demonstrates a notable sensitivity to Jewish perspectives in his use of such terms as Second Temple Judaism (in contrast, e.g., to Intertestamental Judaism); in the very framing of his study as a response to earlier, Christian views; and in his grasp that Jews were (and can be) open to others in their own ways. Below I will address Donaldson's approach in general, his treatment of Philo in specific, and briefly some larger issues raised by his study.

Perhaps Donaldson's most important contribution to the discussion of Jews and Gentiles in antiquity is his insistence that universalism might manifest itself *in several different ways* or patterns. The patterns he sets forth are extremely helpful. The categories of sympathization and conversion are fairly straightforward and easy to understand; ethical monotheism and eschatological participation, however, require some fine-tuning. The label "ethical monotheism," for example, is somewhat imprecise. This category encompasses not one but *two* somewhat different notions: 1) the presentation of *Jewish* teachings in universal terms, and 2) the recognition in *Gentile* teachings of religious parallels to Jewish teachings. In the *Letter of Aristeas* (16), for example, the declaration that Jews and Gentiles worship the same God, albeit with a different name, expresses the position that Gentiles' belief in God parallels Jewish belief, while the *Sibylline Oracles'* (3:624–631) call to the "devious mortal" to propitiate God reflects the presentation of Jewish beliefs in universal terms. A source that presents Jewish teachings in universal terms, however, may simply see these teachings as universally applicable and not *necessarily* as a kind of generic ethical monotheism shorn of Jewishness. In addition, "ethical monotheism" refers to both ethics and monotheism, but some passages assigned to this category speak only about belief in and/or worship of God and say nothing about ethics. Moreover, in one instance (Artapanus, fr. 3, *P.E.* 9.27.4), as Donaldson himself acknowledges, a passage is henotheistic rather than strictly monotheistic (97–100). Finally, while each of the other categories refers to an activity—e.g., Gentiles sympathize, convert, and/or participate —"ethical monotheism" is somewhat inconsistent in that it does not connote an activity.

The category of eschatological participation requires slight refinement for a different reason, namely, the ambiguous understanding of "eschatological." In some texts that fall into this category it is not clear whether the time envisioned is simply an ideal era in the future or the very end of days, as "eschatological" denotes. If an ideal era in the future is envisioned, the expectation may be that this will not necessarily be the end of time and history but rather a continuation of life under much improved conditions.[1] Thus this category might be more precisely labeled "eschatological or ideal-future participation." Somewhat related is that Donaldson occasionally refers to what he calls the "eschatological pilgrimage tradition," a notion based on biblical prophecies that he takes for granted and explains only in passing until the penultimate chapter. Because this tradition is important for some of his interpretations, it would have been helpful had he described it more fully and explicitly in the Introduction.

---

[1] The distinction pertains to whether realization of a vision is expected within history or beyond it; see, e.g., P. D. Hanson, *The Dawn of Apocalyptic* (rev. ed.; Philadelphia: Fortress Press, 1979), 1–31. Donaldson himself makes a similar distinction; see, e.g., 118–19 and 209.

As with any exercise that depends somewhat on subjective judgments, one may not always agree with Donaldson's selection and classification of evidence. At times, for example, one wonders why certain relevant passages are not officially included as "principal texts" (e.g., 3 Macc. 3.8–10 on the sympathetic Greeks [68–74]). By contrast, Donaldson usefully discusses as principal texts some questionable passages that he later concludes do not fit his categories. This is either because on closer inspection a passage may be understood differently (e.g., 1 Enoch 108:11) or because when considered within the larger context of a source that emphasizes particularistic elements, individual passages may lose their universalistic sense (e.g., Wisdom of Solomon 1:1–2 and 6:9–11). This last observation raises a key, challenging question: to what extent can or do individual passages represent an entire source or, even more, Second Temple Jews and Judaism as a whole? We will come back to this question further below.

Many of these general remarks are illustrated specifically in Donaldson's extended discussion of Philo. According to Donaldson, as "a devoted servant of two masters, Plato and Moses," Philo strives to show that they said the same thing (218–19). These "masters" share three points of connection: the attainment of virtue; the notion of a constitution, or *politeia*; and the vision of one, true God. As Donaldson observes, Philo "attempts to chart a course both from a starting point in Moses moving outwards towards Plato, and from Plato back towards Moses, but the two courses are not well aligned, and his navigational deficiencies become apparent precisely at those points at which they should join up with each other" (221). The course that begins with Moses features Jewish law as the best path to virtue and as the best constitution and inclines Philo logically to emphasize proselytism. The course that begins with Plato focuses on the quest to see God—a quest undertaken by Jewish ancestors like Abraham and Moses but potentially open to all philosophers—and puts into question the relevance of becoming a Jew. How, Donaldson wonders, does Philo view the relationship between the proselyte and the "one who sees God"?

Before answering this question, Donaldson analyzes twenty-three principal texts, and he assigns some texts to more than one category. Thus, sixteen are classified as conversion; five as sympathization; four as ethical monotheism; and one as eschatological participation. Here as elsewhere, Donaldson offers noteworthy insights. Especially perceptive is his observation that Philo couples remarks about proselytes and apostates together both near the beginning of his discussion of the special laws (*Spec.* 1.51–59) and near the end of the Exposition (*Praem.* 152). Donaldson views these coupled remarks as an *inclusio* for the Exposition as a whole and sees them as a key to Philo's purpose in writing this series, namely, to underscore "what is at stake—blessings for those who follow the path of virtue laid out in the law and curses for those who do not" and to show that "these outcomes are dependent not on circumstances of birth but on human response" (237). These lessons, however, are but part of several emphases in Philo's Exposition. Moreover, one can hardly consider these coupled remarks as an *inclusio* for the entire Exposition when they are preceded by several other important treatises: *De Opificio Mundi*, *De Abrahamo*, two lost treatises on Isaac and Jacob, *De Iosepho*, and *De Decalogo*. Nonetheless Donaldson's valuable observation merits attention and should stimulate further thought.

Most of my comments on the analysis of Philonic texts can be grouped according to conversion, ethical monotheism, and eschatological participation. Donaldson's consideration of each Philonic passage about conversion allows him ably to highlight its theological, ethical, and social dimensions. Questioning whether Philo thinks that circumcision is required of proselytes, Donaldson finds it significant that Philo does not mention Abraham's circumcision in *Virt.* 212–19, in which Philo calls Abraham "the most ancient member of the Jewish nation" and "the standard of nobility for all proselytes." As Donaldson recognizes, for Philo the defining features of Abraham's conversion are his leaving Chaldea and Haran and his seeing and believing in God (based on Gen. 11:31; 12:1, 7; 15:6). All these events occur, however, before God and Abraham make a covenant whose sign is circumcision (Gen. 17). Philo's Abraham, then, becomes a proselyte *before* he is circumcised. Because he may therefore be an exceptional case and especially because the passage emphasizes Abraham's overcoming the circumstances of his birth, I do not regard Philo's omission of his circumcision to be significant. I would otherwise agree with Donaldson, however, that Philo probably does see circumcision and the full adoption of Jewish laws as essential to conversion, even though he does not provide enough information for us to determine the matter with certainty. Finally, I would question the categorization of *QG* 3.62 as conversion since the reference to Abraham's circumcision of foreigners (*allogeneis*) simply reflects the biblical language in Gen. 17:27.

As for ethical monotheism, it is interesting and perhaps surprising that all the Philonic passages assigned to this category acknowledge Gentile parallels to Jewish teachings but none reflect the presentation of Jewish teachings in universal terms. Two passages, *Virt.* 65 and *Spec.* 2.165, would appear to be strong examples of Philo's recognition that Gentiles can attain the same knowledge of God as the Jews by following the parallel route of philosophy. However, although Donaldson does mention these passages (e.g., 274), for some reason he does not include them among his principal texts.

Donaldson's only Philonic example of eschatological participation, *Mos.* 2.44, is debatable. Here Philo appears to look toward an ideal time in the future—not necessarily the end of days—when all Gentiles will honor Jewish laws exclusively. Donaldson, however, draws a questionable link between this passage and Philo's eschatological vision in *Praem.* 162–72 and related passages. In addition, Donaldson refers to the Gentiles in *Mos.* 2.44 as "end–time converts" (235). Philo's point, however, seems to be that the Gentiles *as Gentiles* will embrace the laws.[2] Since the theme of the larger section is Gentile admiration for Jewish laws in the past (*Mos.* 2.25–40) and present (*Mos.* 2.17–24), Philo's expectation of Gentile acceptance of these laws in the future fits in quite well. According to Donaldson's categories, then, I would view this passage as an example of sympathization, albeit in the future. If the category "eschatological participation" were modified to encompass an ideal future era, then I would agree with this classification as well.

In his concluding remarks, Donaldson notes that Philo "presents us with two quite distinct patterns of universalism—one by means of proselytism and the law of Moses, the other by means of philosophy and reason" (275). At different points, Philo can claim either that the path according to Mosaic law is superior to philosophy or that the paths of law and philosophy are equal. Accordingly, Donaldson declares—very wisely, in my view—that "the tension between these two patterns of universalism must be allowed to stand" (276). How difficult it is, though, to do this! In fact Donaldson goes on to speculate that Philo would advise a sympathetic Gentile to become a proselyte rather than follow the path of philosophy as a Gentile. Donaldson does not view Philo as an *active* proselytizer, however, but instead as someone who understands "Israel as having a positive role to play in making the glories of the law accessible to the wider world," in the past, present, and future (278).

Whether or not he would have advised a Gentile to become a proselyte—and Donaldson may be right that he would have—Philo clearly shows positive regard for others by allowing for conversion and welcoming proselytes, recognizing and appreciating sympathization, and acknowledging that Gentiles can achieve ethical monotheism without becoming Jews. Can we therefore characterize his thought as universalistic according to

---

[2] It is interesting that in an earlier article, which Donaldson does not mention here, he himself argues that these Gentiles were not converts ("Proselytes or 'Righteous Gentiles'? The Status of Gentiles in Eschatological Pilgrimage Patterns of Thought" (*JSP* 7 [1990]: 16).

Donaldson's understanding? Philo surely does express openness to Gentiles, especially philosophers. At the same time, however, he deplores polytheism, atheism, and idolatry; denounces the beliefs and practices of various groups, especially Egyptians; and scorns the sensual excesses and certain values of Greeks and others (e.g., *Decal.* 52–81, *Spec.* 1. 327–44, and *Contempl.* 40–64). Interwoven with Philo's universalistic tendencies, then, are others that are unmistakably particularistic.

This intertwining of universalism and particularism in Philo's thought suggests issues about universalism, alluded to earlier, that go well beyond Donaldson's book. As he is quite aware, universalism has long been defined in various ways that all favor Christianity. Despite its difficulties, however, Donaldson uses this term precisely because it "has been used in the past to compare Judaism unfavorably with Christianity," and he wishes to contribute "to a discussion in which the term is already well established" (4). He also recognizes that conversion may not quite fit the definition of universalism because the active endeavor to spread one's beliefs to encompass everyone is now often viewed as particularistic and "distasteful." Within the context of antiquity, however, Donaldson explains that this endeavor actually "represented a striking step in a universalistic direction" (4–6). He concludes nonetheless that although Jews allowed for conversion and welcomed proselytes, they did not actively seek proselytes. Indeed, reading through this massive collection of evidence, one may be struck by a certain passivity on the part of Jews about incorporating others into their fold. To be sure, sympathization—the largest category, to which about half the passages are assigned—mainly demonstrates Gentile interest but not Jewish solicitation of this interest.

Someone accustomed to equating universalism with active proselytization may be puzzled that universalism might also be understood as the passive acceptance of proselytes and recognition of outside interest. By introducing several patterns, however, Donaldson expands the definition of universalism. Indeed, his insistence that Judaism accommodates Gentiles in a *variety* of ways and can therefore be seen as universalistic is, from my perspective, his most significant contribution. Now that he has accomplished this, however, it is time for us to rethink our use of "universalism" for several reasons. Because the term has historically favored Christianity, expanding and/or changing its definition as Donaldson has done is an important step. Nonetheless, that different people can bring such different associations to universalism suggests that this term may no longer be effective. Perhaps most compelling—as I have shown with Philo—is that even Donaldson's expanded definition does not encompass the whole picture, whether of a single source or of Jews and Judaism as a whole. This is because, regardless of the source—whether Jewish or Christian—particularistic elements are necessarily interwoven with universalistic ones.[3] No matter how we define universalism, it cannot embrace those inevitable aspects that define boundaries and therefore do not display openness toward *all* others. By his own declaration, Donaldson has focused on only one side of the Jewish spectrum. Without due attention to the other side, however, we will have only a partial sense of the universalism of each source or of all the sources put together.

In showing that Judaism can be brought under the "universalistic umbrella," Donaldson has, with insight and sensitivity, significantly advanced the conversation about religious stances towards others, whether in the past or present. Obvious yet implicit in his effort is that universalism is to be valued positively and particularism is not. To understand why this is so will require similarly nuanced assessments of what constitutes particularism and why it is regarded negatively.[4] That his study leads us to pose these questions is one of its salient accomplishments. This is an impressive book. It deserves our careful attention and its author, our considerable gratitude.

Ellen Birnbaum
Cambridge, Massachusetts

Naomi G. COHEN, *Philo's Scriptures. Citations from the Prophets and Writings: Evidence for a* Haftarah *Cycle in Second Temple Judaism.* Supplements to the Journal for the Study of Judaism 123. Leiden: Brill, 2007. xvii + 278 pages. ISBN 90-04-16312-6. Price €99, $142.

The book contains two revised versions of previously published articles combined with new chapters on the topic of Philo's quotations of the Bible. The first chapter presents the author's view on Philo in his historical

---

[3] On this point, see A. Runesson, "Particularistic Judaism and Universalistic Christianity? Some Critical Remarks on Terminology and Theology," *ST* 54 (2000): 55–75; J. D. Levenson, "The Universal Horizon of Biblical Particularism," in *Ethnicity and the Bible* (ed. M. G. Brett; Boston-Leiden: Brill, 2002), 143–69; and A. F. Segal, "Universalism in Judaism and Christianity," in *Paul in his Hellenistic Context* (ed. T. Engberg-Pedersen; Minneapolis: Fortress Press, 1995), 1–29. See also Donaldson's apt comments (476–79) about the "whole woven pattern" of biblical material, which combines threads of universalism and particularism. Because Donaldson focuses on Judaism and Christianity, I restrict my comments to these two traditions.

[4] For a recent example, see J. S. Kaminsky, *Yet I Loved Jacob: Reclaiming the Biblical Concept of Election* (Nashville: Abingdon Press, 2007).

setting. Then the main part begins with the two already published articles: one on Philo's quotations of the Pentateuch and one on evidence for a Haftarah cycle in Philo's quotations of the prophets, both first published in 1997. The fourth chapter takes up the article on the Haftarah and studies Philo's citations of the latter prophets in greater detail. The fifth chapter expands this theory with regard to Philo's quotations of the former pro- phets and Chronicles. The sixth chapter addresses Philo's psalm quotations, and chapter seven rounds out the topic of Philo's non-pentateuchal quota- tions by studying his references to the books of Proverbs and Job. The final chapter presents the hypothesis of an "allegorical circle of Moses" based on the way Philo introduces the quotations of the Psalms and prophets. The book concludes with a number of endnotes and two appendices.

Cohen begins with the question of why Philo's references to books outside the Pentateuch are so much rarer than those to the Torah. Her answer is that Philo limits his references to those texts familiar to his readers from their worship (1). Thus the reason, for her, lies in the context of Philo's writings, not in his ignorance of the non-pentateuchal biblical books (6–7). Cohen's answer, however, still does not explain why an exegete like Philo chose not to interpret any non-pentateuchal book; her statement that the non-pentateuchal references are ancillary to the inter- pretation of the Pentateuch in Philo because Philo only wrote commentaries on the Pentateuch (10) is a tautology. The conclusion that in Philo's time the other books may not have had the same standing as the Torah itself is studiously avoided by Cohen. Still, her theory that in his use of non- pentateuchal writings Philo restricted himself to texts familiar to his readers through their worship offers a good basis for her further study of the evidence in the remainder of the book.

Chapter 2, while useful, does not fit into the topic of the book: it deals neither with non-pentateuchal quotations nor their worship setting. Instead it offers a critical review of the traditional theories of Philo's references to the titles of the books of the Pentateuch and a new study of the Philonic passages.

The main body of the book consists of chapters 3–5, the evidence for Cohen's theory of a relation between Philo's non-pentateuchal quotations and the worship activities of his readers. She compares Philo's quotations of the former and the latter prophets with the Haftarot between the seventeenth of Tammuz and after the Day of Atonement. Chapter three mainly provides a list of Philo's quotations of the latter prophets compared with the Haftarot of the said time span—in the order of the biblical books as well as that of the Loeb Classical Library (PLCL). Chapter four examines the quotations in greater detail. Cohen compares once again the Philonic reference with the Haftarot and examines the introduction of each quotation. After excluding passages such as *Leg.* 1.69 on Isa 6:9 (76–77) and changing the text referred to in *Mut.* 169 from Isa 48:22 to Isa 57:21 (79), her conclusion is that all of Philo's Isaiah quotations are part of one of the Haftarot, except for Isa 5:7 in *Som.* 2.172ff, which she claims—in spite of a complete lack of evidence—must have been a Haftarah omitted later because of the Christian usurpation of the parable of the vineyard (74–76). Cohen not only parallels Philo's quotations to the Haftarot, she also compares them with the LXX text. Through this she identifies a set of non-pentateuchal quotations in *Conf.* 39–62 which are not all dependent on the LXX text but seem closer to the Hebrew (92–96) and which she considers are based on a "midrashic source that has been translated from Hebrew / Aramaic" (96). The LXX-based quotations imply to her "a different source, one whose point of departure must have been the Septuagint text" (102). The question remains, however, why Philo could not have produced the LXX-based interpretation himself. The fifth chapter with its study of the former prophets and Chronicles also deals with Philo's sources. Cohen focuses on the accuracy of the identified quotation. She concludes that Philo's interpretation frequently is based on the peculiarities of the LXX text, and she identifies further sources of Philo's exegesis: an "allegorical source" for his exegesis of the Haftarot, a scriptural concordance, and a homiletical lexicon of proper names, all of which appear to be translations from Hebrew or Aramaic into Greek.

Chapter six on the book of Psalms is almost entirely a list of the quotations and their introductions, again quoting the Hebrew rather than the LXX text. Cohen does not find any relationship between Philo's psalm quotations and modern liturgical practices but regards it as likely that they indicate their use in the synagogues of Philo's time (154, 156). The chapter on Proverbs and Job differs from the previous chapter in that it provides a more detailed interpretation of the Philonic passages.

The final chapter is based on Philo's introduction of quotations studied so far. On the basis of guild terminology in Philo's introductions, Cohen postulates the existence of a "group of *scholars, teachers, students and disciples,* who engaged in esoteric philosophical allegorization of the Pentateuch with a special branch devoted to Scripture as a whole" (175), to which Philo was close at one time. She does not see that the synagogues were described in Hellenistic times not only as schools but also in terms of Hellenistic clubs and religious associations. The terminology that she bases her conclusions on merely refers to the Jews of the synagogue as an ideal group of disciples of Moses, not to a particular group. Cohen observes a change in reference to these groups in Philo's Halakhic works (189) and sees this as sign of Philo's later estrangement from that group—she does not take into account that Philo might be using different language for the same thing depending on the genre, be that allegorical interpretation or Halakhah. Altogether, the story of Philo's adherence to and estrangement from this group of allegorists relies too much on visualisation and imagination to fill the gaps in the evidence.

There are some comments to be made about the book as a whole. The author bases her studies on the Loeb Classical edition and not the critical text of Cohn–Wendland and she treats the order of the books in the Loeb edition as if they were the order of the historical production of the writings. She adds the PLCL volume number to every Philonic reference, produces lists in the order of the PLCL as well as in that of the biblical books, and suggests that this is not only for convenience but also relevant for their interpretation (cf. 60, 194). Modern research, however, has been unable to provide definite evidence for the historical order in which Philo's writings were written. By contrast it has been found that their genre—e.g. allegorical commentary, interpretation of the laws—provides a more relevant frame of reference, though genre is largely ignored by Cohen. There is also an inconsistency in Cohen's use of the Hebrew text of the Haftarot in chapter three as a point of comparison, since she vehemently argues that it is the LXX that Philo uses (60). With regard to her use of indices, she takes Philo's biblical quotations from Colson and Earp (e.g. 72, 103), but neither the old Index from Leisegang (1926) nor the one of the *Biblia Patristica* (1982) are referred to in the text, although the latter appears in her bibliography. The bibliography itself has its focus on earlier literature: except for a few articles by Cohen herself, there are only two titles published after the year 2000.

Altogether, the book is very disparate in its content and in its procedure, sometimes offering full interpretations of the texts, at other times merely listing them. Its strength lies in providing evidence for the link between Philo's scriptural quotations and their setting in the worship of his time. A study of Philo's references to non-pentateuchal biblical books has long been overdue, and this book provides a basis for filling this gap.

Jutta Leonhardt-Balzer
University of Aberdeen

Francesca CALABI, *God's Acting, Man's Acting: Tradition and Philosophy in Philo of Alexandria.* Studies in Philo of Alexandria 4. Leiden: Brill, 2007. xiv + 265 pages. ISBN 90-04-16270-9. Price €119, $169.

This book is a study of God's essential nature and of His mode of interaction with the world, as well as of man's efforts to assimilate himself to God, in the philosophy of Philo. It is divided into three parts: I) The Nature of God (3–69), consisting of three chapters, plus an appendix; II) The Mediation Activity (71–152), consisting of three chapters; and III) God as Model (153–232), consisting of one (long) chapter, and two appendices.

An odd feature of the book is that all of the chapters except two, and the appendices, have been published before (in Italian), and of those two chapters, one (ch. 2) has been delivered before as a separate paper, so that the book is really a connected series of independent essays. There is nothing wrong with this, of course, and it is most welcome to have these works collected together in English (and excellent English it is!), but it does make for a certain amount of repetition.

In Part I, for example, the three chapters ("Plato and the Bible: Ontology and Theology in Philo," "Simplicity and Absence of Qualities in God," and "Unknowability of God") all concern in one way or another the problem of the tension between Philo's anxiety to preserve the total transcendence and otherness of God and his activity as creator and preserver of the universe. In the first of these, Calabi approaches the topic from the point of view of Philo's attempt to reconcile the Greek (Pythagorean-Platonic) philosophical tradition with Jewish religious beliefs. The traditional themes of one and many, intelligible and sensible reality, form and matter, God as transcendent first principle and God as creator, have to be projected onto the biblical text. She illustrates well how this is done, and in the process, raises a number of themes which are explored further in subsequent chapters, notably the role of the Logos and the Powers. On one question I would take issue with her: on the matter of the origin of the concept of the Forms as thoughts of God (6), she seems too inclined to go along with Roberto Radice in the improbable notion that this might be an original doctrine of Philo's. I have argued elsewhere of the unlikelihood of this, proposing even Xenocrates in the Old Academy. But the fact of the allegorization of Minerva (Athena) as the Forms springing from the brow of Jupiter (Zeus) by Antiochus of Ascalon's partisan Varro should put paid to Radice's proposal.

In the second chapter, which also concerns God's uniqueness and simplicity, Calabi starts from a consideration of *Deus* 107–110 (an exegesis of Gen. 6:8: "Noah found favour (*charis*) in the eyes of the Lord") as a way of exploring the contradiction between God as simple and immutable and God as benefactor and disciplinarian of the whole of creation and, primarily, man (indeed, the traditional Jahweh). She shows well how Philo wrestles with the contradictions involved. As regards Noah finding *charis,* this for Philo has to be taken as a discovery by Noah, not as evidence of some change in attitude on the part of God. In this connection, she has a good discussion of God's unknowability, and the role of the Logos and the powers as providing views of God that we humans can latch onto.

The Logos and the Powers come to the fore again in Ch. 3, on God's unknowability. On the question of God's unnameability, I doubt there is much in the distinction between God's not having a name and His name not being revealed to us (42ff.), even though Philo speaks of both possibilities. I would have thought that, for Philo (influenced as he would be, immediately or mediately, by Plato's *Parm.* 142a), God simply has no name, i.e. He is *akatonomastos.*

There follows as the first of three "appendices" a helpful comparison of Origen's use of light imagery with that of Philo. In both cases, they are ultimately dependent, as Calabi notes, on Plato's *Republic,* but they both place more emphasis on the *blinding* nature of the divine light for human eyes, or minds.

In the first essay of Part II (Ch. 4: "The Powers of God"), she takes her start from a passage of the (possibly spurious) *De Deo* (6), which oddly (for Philo) adduces Isaiah 6 as an example of ecstatic vision, where Isaiah sees the Lord upon a high throne, flanked by seraphim. This leads into a comprehensive discussion of the role and status of the Powers in general, including the Logos, which I found sound and useful. How far they should be hypostatized is indeed a delicate question.

In Ch. 5, "Roles and Figures of Mediation", she turns to the question of the role of daemons and angels in Philo's system, on which once again she is very sound. Angels as such are no threat to God's omnipotence; the only problem would arise from the existence of "wicked angels" *(angeloi ponêroi)* such as seem to be referred to in *Gig.* 17–18, but Nikiprowetzky is probably right that the reference is really to souls that descend into incarnation and consort with the passions. Punitive angels are another matter, of course.

Ch. 6, "The Snake and the Horseman" (the reference is to Dan as the serpent who bites the horse's heel, Gen. 49:16–18), turns to the topic of human action, the relation between intellect and sensation (symbolized by Adam and Eve) and the tension between pleasure and self-control, using the Snake as a major Philonic image. Once again we have a most useful and sophisticated treatment.

The third part of the work consists of one chapter, "Happiness and Contemplation: The Contemplative Life," which sets out Philo's views on the theoretical and practical modes of life, and contains a good discussion of the role and nature of the Therapeutae. Philo, despite his philosophical bent, was no world-negating ascetic, and is mindful of his civic duties as a prominent member of the Alexandrian Jewish community. He has little patience with those who "drop out," and his approval of the Theraputae rests on the fact that, in his view, they have done their bit earlier in life.

The book is rounded off with two further appendices, in either case separate articles, but both of interest: "Philo of Alexandria and Ecphantus' *Peri Basileias*," and "Galen and Moses." The former speculates on the relation between Philo's political philosophy and various Pythagorean pseudepigrapha; the latter discusses the possibility of Galen's having Philo in his sights when he criticises the Jews.

All in all, this is a fine product of current Italian scholarship on Philo and Hellenistic Judaism, and very good to have in a (faultlessly idiomatic) Anglophone format.

John Dillon
Trinity College, Dublin

Ronald Cox, *By the Same Word: Creation and Salvation in Hellenistic Judaism and Early Christianity*. Beihefte zur Zeitschrift für die neutestamentliche Wissenschaft 145. Berlin: Walter de Gruyter, 2007. xiv + 392 pages. ISBN 3-11-019342-8. Price € 98, $157.

This book is a revised version of a dissertation completed at the University of Notre Dame and directed by Gregory E. Sterling. Cox proposes in Chapter One that a characteristic Middle Platonic doctrine of an intermediate reality between the transcendent supreme principle and the material world serves as a crucial source, "a surviving mythic form," for the development of similar intermediary figures in Hellenistic Jewish sapiential writings such as the Wisdom of Solomon and Philo of Alexandria's biblical commentaries, in New Testament texts such as 1 Cor 8:6, Col 1:15–20, Heb 1:1–4, and John 1:1–18, and in disparate texts such as the *Poimandres* and the "Sethian" Gnostic *Apoocryphon of John*.

In Chapter Two Cox deals with the character of Middle Platonism in general but concentrates on what we know of this intermediate reality between the supreme principle and the material world so characteristic of the Platonic tradition from its revival in the first century B.C.E. to the beginnings of Neoplatonism in the beginning of the third century C.E. Using what we know of Eudorus of Alexandria and such writers as Plutarch, Alcinous, Numenius, Seneca, and others, Cox describes a variety of ways in which Middle Platonic thinkers conceived of an intermediate reality between the transcendent supreme principle and the material world. Although quite varied, Middle Platonists consistently affirmed two characteristics of this reality. It shared in the supreme principle's transcendent, noetic character, and it mediated that character to the material world. More specifically, the intermediate principle was often conceived of as a copy or paradigm of the first principle and at the same time as an image or *exemplar* for the material world. This figure also played a significant role in Middle Platonic anthropology in the sense that it was often taken as an object for human contemplation or, more actively, as an anagogue of the human soul on its journey from the material world and toward its transcendent source.

In Chapter Three, after brief remarks about the Jewish writer Aristobulus, Cox turns his attention to the Wisdom of Solomon and the writings of Philo of Alexandria (Hellenistic Jewish sapientialism) and how these two appropriated in different ways the intermediate figure of Middle Platonism. Cox places the Wisdom of Solomon at the turn of the era and argues that underlying the author's notion of Sophia is a "thought-out (though not erudite) Middle Platonic framework (59)." Although dealing with the whole of the book, Cox concentrates on Wisdom 6–10. Sophia is an intermediate figure which is a reflection of or an emanation from the Deity and it is through this intermediate figure that the Deity both creates and administers the cosmos. At the same time Sophia also plays a soteriological role in the sense that it makes human beings "friends of God."

Cox then turns to the works of Philo of Alexandria. He begins on a cautionary note. Because Philo's primary interest in his allegorical commentary is on the advancement of the soul, his treatment of a divine intermediary's role in either cosmology or anthropological fulfillment is rather infrequent and certainly unsystematic. With this caution in mind, however, Cox explores the figure of the Logos in Philo in which he appropriates and turns to his own purposes the intermediary figure of Middle Platonism. Cox begins with an analysis of *Sacr.* 8, a passage he thinks of as emblematic of Philo's understanding of the Logos. The emphasis is especially on the anagogic role of the Logos in leading the human mind to God. But in that context Philo also explains the cosmological role of the Logos. The same anagogic emphasis runs throughout Philo's treatment of the Logos elsewhere in his works. The Logos is certainly an intermediary figure between God and the created world. In this role the Logos is understood in different ways, not all of which can be smoothly integrated together. The Logos is that entity between God and matter which brings the divine image to bear on matter and so produces, orders, and sustains the sense-perceptible world. It is both transcendent as the reality closest to God and at the same time immanent in that it fills all things and orders them. More important, however, for Philo is its anthropological role in which the Logos brings the human mind into existence, provides it with its own intellectual nature and guides it beyond the material world back to God.

Chapter Four is devoted to four New Testament texts: 1 Cor 8:6, Col 1:15–20, Heb 1:1–4, and John 1:1–18. Here of course the issues are somewhat different since Cox is not dealing with complete texts but in each case with traditional material (usually creedal or hymnic in character) embedded in larger texts. What Cox tries to show is how all four texts exhibit in different ways a combination of Platonized Jewish traditions and Christian eschatological convictions. What the Platonized Jewish traditions contribute is a fairly uniform cosmological perspective and terminology in which we see a divinely related intermediary reality (*eikôn, apaugasma, charactêr, logos, theos*) quite similar to such figures in the Wisdom of Solomon and in the works of Philo responsible for creating and sustaining the existence of all things. This is combined with and transformed by Christian eschatological convictions about the significance of Jesus Christ. He is the Lord whose sacrifice redefines human perfection (1 Cor), or the Son who pacifies and reconciles rebellious creation (Col), or the exalted heir who has made purification for sins (Heb), or finally the Logos who has become flesh (John). In each case Christ serves as a reality-changing historical moment. The intermediary figure of these Platonized Jewish traditions becomes a concrete historical figure.

In the fifth and last chapter Cox turns to two different and rather disparate texts: the *Poimandres* from the *Corpus Hermeticum* and the *Apocryphon of John* from the Nag Hammadi codices. Here again he does not try to analyze the whole of these texts. Rather he is interested in the cosmological and soteriological roles played by intermediary figures. While the *Poimandres* (which Cox locates in first century C.E. Alexandria) has been influenced by Middle Platonism and Hellenistic Jewish sapientialism, it is not itself either a Middle Platonic or a Jewish text but a religious text devoted to Hermes Trismegistus. Its very lack of any sustained philosophical interest, however, contributes to the difficulties in interpreting the text. But Cox does show how there are multiple intermediary figures (at the pre-creation level, at the level of cosmology, and of anthropology) whose relationship is anything but clear. These intermediary figures (the *Logos Hagios,* the *Dêmiourgos Nous,* and the *Anthrôpos*) are all influenced by both Middle Platonism and Hellenistic Jewish sapientialism.

The final text that Cox analyzes is the *Apocryphon of John.* This is a text originally in Greek, perhaps from the latter half of the second century C.E. We now have it, however, only in four Coptic manuscripts, three of which are from the codices found at Nag Hammadi. The text itself is an example of "Sethian" Gnosticism. In addition, although the text is Christian in its present form, Sethian Gnosticism may well go back to a Jewish matrix independent of Christianity. The *Apocryphon of John* is filled with a dizzying array of intermediary figures of various sorts as it explains first the origins of the heavenly world from a first principle (the Monad) and then the origins of the earthly world, and finally an anthropogony/soteriology of the race of Seth, Adam's son. But what Cox concentrates on is the Platonized Judaism that lies behind, on the one hand, the origins of the heavenly world through the intermediary role of a female figure Barbêlo, and, on the other hand, the anthropogony/soteriology of the race of Seth through the guidance of Barbêlo/Epinoia. This latter is a parody or reversal of what is contained in Gen 1–6.

This is a very well done analysis of some very difficult texts, difficult in each case for different reasons, but still all difficult. Without trying to cram them into some rigid structure, Cox manages to show how all of these texts used and transformed Middle Platonic views of an intermediary figure that has both cosmological and soteriological functions in four quite different traditions, Hellenistic Jewish sapientialism, early Christianity, religious devotion to Hermes, and Gnosticism. He also succeeds in showing how the three latter traditions were working with an already existing combination of Middle Platonism and Hellenistic Jewish wisdom sapientialism. Another value to Cox's study is that it can serve an important platform for further research. Here I am thinking in particular of the relationship between Hellenistic Jewish sapientialism, especially that found in the works of Philo, and the Sethian Gnosticism found in works such as the *Apocryphon of John*. It may be unfashionable to raise the issue of the "origins" of the Gnostic mythology in such texts, but Cox's work has shown that the issue deserves a good deal more attention.

Thomas H. Tobin, S.J.
Loyola University, Chicago

Torrey SELAND, *Strangers in the Light: Philonic Perspectives on Christian Identity in 1 Peter*. Biblical Interpretation Series 76. Leiden: Brill, 2005. x + 216 pages. ISBN 90-04-14491-9. Price €83, $124.

This book represents about ten years of work that Torrey Seland has done at the intersection of 1 Peter and Philo. Four of the five chapters were either published or presented previously in other contexts. Seland suggests three unifying features of the collection beyond the fact that they are all work he has done in relation to 1 Peter (8). First, they attempt to appropriate social scientific study of the Greco-Roman world in relation to 1 Peter. Secondly, they focus on insights drawn from the Jewish Diaspora. Finally, three of the five essays draw significantly on Philo's writings in these pursuits.

The title, *Strangers in the Light*, reflects two verses of keen interest in the book: 1 Pet 2:9 and 11. The latter describes the audience as παροίκους καὶ παρεπιδήμους, while the former verse speaks of how God had called the audience "out of darkness into marvelous light." Although Seland only engages with 2:11 in chapters 2 and 4, he clearly considers his perspective on this verse his signature contribution. The premise of his title is that "the author of 1 Peter considers his readers ... living a life influenced by social circumstances very much comparable to those experienced in the Diaspora by proselytes to Judaism" (2).

The two chapters that do not engage significantly with Philo are the first and fifth. The first chapter is the only one that Seland has written strictly for the publication of the book. It is an appropriate starting point for a collection of essays concerned significantly with the social location of the audience, for it focuses on the concrete process by which 1 Peter was likely written and delivered. Seland rightly questions those who insist that the phrase διὰ Σιλουανοῦ in 1 Pet 5:12 must mean that Silvanus/Silas was the letter carrier (22–28). Rather, he believes it more likely that he served as the letter's amanuensis. He considers it implausible that a solitary individual delivered the letter to such a vast area. Rather, several copying processes were likely involved with several carriers over an extended period of time before all the intended audience was reached (36–37).

Chapter 5 deals with issues of acculturation and assimilation in 1 Peter. Insightfully, Seland suggests that the issue of assimilation is not primarily the relationship of the audience to Greco-Roman culture but its assimilation "to the (still developing) Christian system of cult, beliefs, ethos, and symbols" (168). Since the audience likely consisted primarily of Gentile converts in the first place, it was the host Greco-Roman culture that they had *left*. The question was thus one of how much of that culture *to retain* rather than assimilate (173). Seland finds much secondary literature on the topic imprecise in its use of terms like *assimilation* and *acculturation*, in part because it does not engage with scholarship in the social sciences (149–56). After reviewing some of this literature and applying it to 1 Peter, he implies (although curiously he never states this conclusion explicitly) that the author aims at "integration" with the host culture, in which positive relationships are desired with the Greco-Roman environment while maintaining a distinct identity from it (173–89).

It is in chapters 2–4 that Seland interacts significantly with Philo, especially chapters 3 and 4. Chapter 2 is the signature chapter of the book, the one in which Seland argues most extensively that the social world of Jewish proselytism served as the source domain for language that 1 Peter then applied metaphorically to its audience as target domain (40). Here and in chapter 4, he briefly considers Philo's use of the words πάροικος, παρεπίδημος, as well as προσήλυτος. In general, Philo prefers terms like ἔπηλυς, ἐπηλύτης and ἐπήλυτος in his discussions of proselytes. Nevertheless, Seland finds a foothold for a connection in Philo between the term πάροικος and proselytism in Philo's work on Abraham. The Septuagint of Gen 23:4 refers to Abraham as a πάροικος καὶ παρεπίδημος, using the same words found in 1 Pet 2:11. Meanwhile, Philo uses Abraham as the paradigmatic proselyte who abandoned the idols of Chaldea to serve the one God (e.g., *Virt.* 219).

Unfortunately, however, neither Philo nor the Septuagint will bear the load Seland wants to put on them. Philo never uses the word πάροικος or παροικέω in connection with proselytism. When Philo refers to Abraham as a πάροικος, it is always used in the sense of a sojourner rather than a proselyte (e.g., *Conf.* 79; *Her.* 267). As polyvalent as the biblical text is for Philo, it is precarious in the least to connect one allegorical interpretation to another, let alone to a literal interpretation in a different biblical passage. Seland rightly sees the primary audience of 1 Peter as proselytes to the Christian movement, but he cannot establish a connection between this fact and the terms πάροικος and παρεπίδημος, which are certainly not from Philo.

In chapters 3 and 4, Seland engages in a reader-response approach to 1 Peter of a unique kind. He assumes the perspective of a "Philonic reader" addressing the text of 1 Peter. This hypothetical reader is "a Jewish reader who is well versed in Philo's works" and "would know the symbolic universe laid out in Philo's works just as well as Philo, if not better" (79). The fundamental question of chapter 3 is how such a Philonic reader might read 1 Pet 2:5 and 9. Chapter 4 then asks how this reader would understand 1 Pet 2:11. In both chapters Seland's approach is the same. First he explores relevant concepts in Philo's writings to set the stage for the interpretive issues of the relevant verses. Then he proceeds through those issues first with a brief summary of biblical scholarship, finally bringing in his Philonic reader for his or her perspective.

With regard to 1 Pet 2:5, our Philonic reader would likely take οἰκοδομεῖσθε as an indicative rather than an imperative, for the Jewish nation was already a house for the Lord, not a house to build (94–95). Seland strongly disagrees with John H. Elliott's understanding of Philo in *Abr.* 56. Elliott distances any focus on Israel as a nation of priests from this text and, thus, from the relevant verses in 1 Peter (101–3). Seland rightly points out that *Abr.* 98 speaks of Israel receiving the priesthood for all humankind and thus that Elliott cannot so quickly dismiss the corporate priesthood of Israel from Philo's interpretation of Ex 19:6 (LXX 23:22), which 1 Pet 2:9 echoes. So he concludes, drawing also on *Sobr.* 66, that a Philonic reader would understand βασίλειον ἱεράτευμα as two distinct nouns, "the King's House" and "priesthood," with βασίλειον referring to the temple. Another significant suggestion in the chapter is that ἐξαγγείλητε be understood, not as missionary proclamation, but as praise to God (107–13). Seland argues that a Philonic reader would certainly understand the verb in this way, while likely hinting that the author of 1 Peter understood it in this way as well.

The Philonic reader of chapter 4 tackles the interpretation of 2:11, the focal verse of chapter 2, as well. We have already encountered Seland's interpretation of παροίκους καὶ παρεπιδήμους as a metaphor of proselytism. Nevertheless, he is forced to admit that a Philonic reader would more likely see these words in reference to the soul's sojourn in the body (144–45). Four times in the chapter Seland quotes Eduard Schweizer's claim that this verse is "the most strongly Hellenized ψυχή passage in the NT" (e.g., 137). Seland does not find anything in the verse that would problematize a straight-forward Philonic reading of it (145). He references Philo's somewhat Aristotelian interpretation of Deut 23:13 in *Leg.* 3.153, where reason is like a shovel that must follow passion around to keep it from dominating (140). The idea that desire is at war with the soul, whose dominant part for Philo is the mind (e.g., *Leg.* 1.39), would resonate with a Philonic reader.

These two chapters are an interesting hermeneutical exercise, although they will leave many biblical scholars wondering whether Seland had any hidden purposes for them beyond a novel reader-response approach to a biblical text. Indeed, most of the material in these chapters is contextual in nature, engaging particularly with matters of a socio-cultural sort. In each case, we seem to be watching a historical-cultural plane moving down a historical-cultural runway. Then just as the plane is about to take off, the camera cuts to a different, Philonic plane taking off. This dynamic does not undermine the integrity of Seland's work here, although it possibly will leave traditional biblical scholars a little frustrated. Nevertheless, Seland's book as a whole advances a number of discussions in relation to 1 Peter, and it highlights the often untapped potential of Philo's writings in relation to our understanding of the New Testament and its world.

Kenneth L. Schenck
Indiana Wesleyan University

William LOADER, *The Septuagint, Sexuality, and the New Testament: Case Studies on the Impact of the LXX in Philo and the New Testament.* Grand Rapids, Mich.: Eerdmans, 2004. x + 163 pages. ISBN 0-8028-2756-2. Price $20.

New Testament scholars have long recognized Philo's importance for understanding aspects of the New Testament (NT). For instance, one of the greatest commentators on Hebrews, C. Spicq, found the similarities between Philo and Hebrews so close that he suggested that the author of Hebrews went to Philo's lectures. Owen Chadwick has said, "of all non-Christian writers of the first century A.D., Philo is the one from whom the historian of emergent Christianity has the most to learn." Typically NT studies that turn to Philo do so for comparison. In such cases correct interpretation of Philo becomes essential for understanding particulars of a NT text. One of the more influential cases of such comparison in recent times is R. A. Horsley's article "Spiritual Marriage with Sophia," (1979) in which he argued that the principles and ideas of the Corinthians are similar to those found in Philo's writings.

In Loader's work, Philo is also used for comparison. However, rather than using Philo as a comparative example in order to understand a particular NT passage, Loader studies a theme common to Philo and the NT—the theme of sexuality—in comparison with the Septuagint on the same theme. His work proceeds on the basis of levels of comparisons. First Loader compares LXX passages having to do with sexuality to the relevant Hebrew passages. The pay-off of this comparison is Loader's determination of distinctive LXX emphases in regards to sexuality.

Loader chooses three sets of texts directly related to the matter of sexuality: the Decalogue, the creation stories and the Deut 24 passage on divorce (respectively, Exod 20:2–17; Deut 5:6–21; Genesis 1–3, especially 1.26–28, 2.18–25, 3.16–19 and 5:1–3; and Deut 24:1–4). His work on the Decalogue allows him to note, for instance, that the LXX of Exod 20:1–17 and Deut 5:6–21 differ from most Hebrew manuscripts in the ordering of the commandments. While in the vast majority of Hebrew texts the prohibition against adultery is seventh in the list, in the LXX it is in the sixth position, and so the first in the second table. He also finds in the LXX , unlike the Hebrew, an emphasis placed on desiring one's neighbor's wife. Loader's third comparative observation about the Decalogue is that the translation in both Exodus and Deuteronomy of לא תחמד as οὐκ ἐπιθυμήσεις in the LXX's tenth commandment lends itself to a negative evaluation of sexual passion itself and "provides a link to value systems which portray passions negatively" (11).

Loader then asks how the LXX versions of the Decalogue might have influenced Philo in regard to sexuality. Studying *De decalogo* and *De specialibus legibus* 1–4 Loader notes that Philo interprets the placement of the prohibition against adultery as indicative that God "begins with adultery" (*Decal.* 121; cited from Loader, p. 12) because it is the greatest transgression (see also *Spec.* 3.8). Philo, Loader proposes, is aided in his denigration of sexual passion by the LXX translation οὐκ ἐπιθυμήσεις. While Philo understands every passion to be blameworthy—whether passions of pleasure, pain, fear or desire—he gives particular prominence to passion in connection with sexuality. And so, perhaps under the influence of the LXX, Philo thinks that sexual pleasure even with one's wife is dangerous, for any excessive or superfluous pleasure distracts from growth in virtue (*Spec.* 1.9).

Loader then explores in the NT the three elements of the LXX texts of the Decalogue which he studied in Philo: the prominence given to adultery, the prominence given to lusting after one's neighbour's wife, and the translation "you shall not desire" in that prohibition. Loader casts his net widely as he explores these elements in the NT, commenting on most of the relevant NT texts.

In a similar vein Loader studies the creation stories and the Deut 24:1–24 passage on divorce in their LXX versions relative to their Hebrew precursors. He then proceeds to ask whether there is evidence for influence of the LXX on Philo's and the NT's use of these LXX passages in relation to sexuality. Here he also discusses the Gospel of Thomas.

The conclusion of Loader's study is inconclusive in regards to the main question he asks: what is the impact of the LXX on Philo and the NT in regards to the topic of sexuality? Loader opines that the views on sexuality found in Philo and the NT reflect the mores of Hellenistic Judaism, which typically highlighted sexual sins and expressed severe reservation about sexual passion. His opinion that the LXX was already affected by this cultural attitude means in effect that he admits that his operating question is largely unanswerable.

Furthermore, the conclusion is disappointing in regards to what many readers might hope for—a study which sheds new light on the views of Philo and the NT about sexuality. There is little of interest in that regard here.

This is a short book (155 pages, including bibliography) which tries to do a great deal. We find responsible, albeit brief, analysis of particular passages in the three sets of texts to which Loader turns: LXX, Philo and the NT. Loader's reference to other scholars is adequate but not extensive.

Some discussion of methodological issues would have made this a stronger work. The reader would have benefited from Loader's sharing some of the guideposts he used in answering the question at the heart of his book: how a text (the LXX) "enabled itself to be read" (2). This is an interesting question, but Loader offers us no structure to read along with him as he seeks to answer it. We are in effect asked simply to trust his insights and observations. Lack of a methodological discussion, and, it would seem, of methodological clarity on Loader's part, leads to some confusing statements. For instance, Loader distinguishes between the influence of the LXX and its interpretation (p. 115). It is unclear to this reader how the LXX's influence could result from anything other than its interpretation.

Perhaps one of the chief contributions of this work is the question Loader brings to the discussion of the theme of sexuality in Philo and the NT: how did the LXX influence both sets of texts? This is a question worth further exploration and we should be grateful to Loader for raising it and making some valuable observations.

L. Ann Jervis
Wycliffe and Trinity Colleges,
University of Toronto

John BARCLAY, *Against Apion*. Flavius Josephus, Translation and Commentary 10. Leiden: Brill, 2007. lxxi + 430 pages. ISBN 90-04-11791-1. Price €144, $215.

Ancient historians made the claim to be the first to write on a period or area a trope: Polybius,[1] Dionysius of Halicarnassus,[2] and Eusebius[3] all made the claim for their major histories. Josephus modified the claim and, with characteristic modesty, merely claimed that he and he alone was capable of writing *The Jewish Antiquities*.[4] These historians did, however, have predecessors: Polybius had Ephorus; Dionysius had Hieronymus of Cardia, Timaeus of Tauromenium, and Polybius; Josephus had the Hellenistic Jewish historians; and Eusebius had Luke-Acts. The trope functioned to set their works off from the more partial and incomplete works of their predecessors. Like these ancient historians, John Barclay can lay claim to be a first. He has an older German predecessor in J. G. Müller,[5] a limited

---

[1] Polybius 1.4.2. See also 9.1.2–3.

[2] Dionysius, *Rom. ant.* 1.5.4.

[3] Eusebius, *Hist. eccl.* 1.1.5.

[4] Josephus, *A.J.* 20.262.

[5] J. G. Müller, *Des Flavius Josephus Schrift gegen den Apioni: Text und Erklärung* (eds. C. J. Riggenbach and C. von Orelli; Basel: Bahnmeier, 1877).

Italian predecessor in Lucio Troiani,[6] a thorough but less critical Hebrew predecessor in Aryeh Kasher,[7] and a still incomplete German predecessor in Dagmar Labow.[8] He does not, however, have any significant predecessor in English. He may therefore rightly claim to be the first to write a full scale commentary on *Contra Apionem* in English.

As the first, he has done a remarkable job of interpreting a complex text. The commentary is an erudite work that combines industry and learning with sober judgment and creative insights. The scale of the commentary is formidable: there are four hundred and forty large, double columned pages of introduction, notes, and appendices (not counting the indices). More specifically, there are 2,267 notes on 616 sections of text or an average of a little more than three and a half comments on each Niese section.[9] The length of the commentary is due in part to the nature of the text. As is well known, the work is a small library of ancient works dealing with Jews. It is the largest single source of information for the early Greek material in Menahem Stern's *Greek and Latin Authors on Jews and Judaism.*[10] Of the ca. 197 fragments from Greek authors up through the end of the first century C.E., fifty-one or 26% are from *Contra Apionem*[11] while another twenty-seven or 14% are from the *Antiquitates Judaicae.*[12] If we restrict our survey to the earliest material, twenty-four of the first fifty fragments or 48% are from *Contra Apionem*. Barclay works through each author, each text, each event with care.

The commentary is, however, far more than an update of Stern. Its greatest strength is the analysis of Josephus' argumentation. This extends from an analysis of the structure of the work and its major parts to the analyses of specific arguments on individual authors. Barclay divides the work into two parts: 1.6–218, the Antiquity of the Jews; and 1.219–2.286, Refutation of

---

[6] L. Troiani, *Commento storico al 'Contra Apione' di Giuseppe: Introduzione, Commento storico, tradzione e indici* (Pisa: Giardini, 1977).

[7] A. Kasher, *Contra Apionem, Flavius Josephus* (2 vols.; Jerusalem: Merkaz Zalman, 1996).

[8] D. Labow, *Flavius Josephus Contra Apionem Buch 1: Einleitung, Text, Textkritischer Apparat, Übersetzung und Kommentar* (Beiträge zur Wissenschaft vom Alten und Neuen Testament 167; Stuttgart: W. Kolhammer, 2005).

[9] 3.68 to be precise.

[10] M. Stern, *Greek and Latin Authors on Jews and Judaism* (3 vols.; Jerusalem: The Israel Academy of Sciences and Humanities, 1974).

[11] ##5, 12, 13, 15, 16, 17, 19, 20, 21, 24, 25, 27, 28, 30a, 33, 34, 35, 36, 38, 44, 47, 48, 49, 50, 77, 80, 87, 98, 144, 158, 159, 160, 161, 162, 164, 165, 166, 167, 168, 169, 170, 171, 172, 173, 174, 175, 176, 177, 178, 198, 199.

[12] ##30b, 32, 76, 79, 81, 82, 83, 84, 85, 86, 88, 89, 90, 91, 92, 93, 99, 100, 101, 102, 103, 104, 105, 106, 107, 108, 132.

Slanders. This analysis gives the work a tighter unity than others might allow. 2.145–286 is often thought of as a third part since it is primarily cast as an encomium on the law rather than a direct response to critics. There is even a more radical possibility. If we separate 2.145–286 into a third part, it is possible to understand it as a later addition. The preface in 1.1–5 announces the treatment of the antiquity of the Jews and the refutation of the slanders; it does not mention the encomium on the laws. The two major parts each have transitional phrases: 1.219 opens part two with "There is still one major topic set out in the beginning of my work." 2.144 ends with "let this then be the end of my argument." While I am not prepared to claim that 2.145–86 was a later addition, the possibility deserves serious consideration.[13] I mention it as a possibility for future work and to register the fact that I found the commentary provocative in a number of surprising ways. In this case, the commentary made me think through the structure of the text with more care than I had previously.

Barclay argues that *Contra Apionem* is an ἀπολογία. He maintains that an apology must meet two requirements: it must be a direct response to explicit accusations and it must be directed toward an outside audience. He offers a nuanced and creative interpretation of the audiences and functions of the work. He distinguishes among the *declared audience*, the *implied audience*, and the *intended audience*. The declared audience is addressed twice by Josephus: it consists of non-*Ioudaioi*.[14] The implied audience is very similar to the declared audience: it is a relatively well informed audience of non-*Ioudaioi* who are curious about the *Ioudaioi*. The intended audience incorporates readers who are not explicitly addressed or implied, but fit the basic profile of the implied audience and may have been a targeted audience. In this case the *intended* audience may include *Ioudaioi* who shared Josephus' social and intellectual status, e.g., members of the Herodian family or individuals like Flavius Clemens, the emperor's cousin, and his wife, Flavia Domitilla, who converted to Judaism.[15] There is some tension between the generic analysis and the analysis of audience. If an apology must be directed *ad extra*, how can the *intended* audience be *ad intra*? The tension is more apparent than real, but it might be helpful to rethink the narrow definition of apology. Similarly, as someone who has doubts about the cogency of E. D. Hirsch's *Validity in Interpretation*,[16] I would prefer to

---

[13] Apparently, D. Schwartz communicated the same possibility to Barclay in a private letter. See Barclay, *Against Apion*, 242 n. 523.

[14] Josephus, *CA* 2.147, 287.

[15] Suetonius, *Domitian* 15.1; Cassius Dio 67.14.1–2; Eusebius, *Hist. eccl.* 3.19–20.

[16] E. D. Hirsch, Jr., *Validity in Interpretation* (New Haven–London: Yale University Press, 1967).

avoid the term *intended* since authorial intention is slippery at best. If it is necessary to move beyond *implied* and *real* audiences, perhaps a less loaded term like *potential* would be preferable.

Barclay's analysis of the complex audience leads him to think about reading the text in different ways. Before each major section, he offers a series of reading options that work through the thrust of the text for a Roman audience, a Jewish audience, an early Christian audience (since they preserved the work), a Western scholarly audience (since we are the contemporary readers), and his own reading. The placement of the Roman audience first is not accidental. He—rightly in my judgment—emphasizes this perspective throughout his commentary. His own perspective is shaped by a postcolonial reading. In particular, he draws on the concept of "hybridity" or "in-betweenness," developed by Homi Bhabha.[17] "Hybridity" refers to the destabilizing and paradoxical position of a new culture that neither fully continues a native culture nor fully embraces the hegemonic culture. For Barclay, hybridity helps to explicate Josephus' ambiguous position as someone who lived in an elite Roman setting and was, at the same time, a defender of his ancestral traditions.

With these presuppositions Barclay works painstakingly through the text. I would like to address his analysis of two major portions of the text. Barclay, like Shaye Cohen before him,[18] recognizes the importance of the historiographical essay that opens the work in 1.6–56. What he does not address, at least not at any length, is the question of whether Josephus argued for the existence of a distinct Eastern historiographical tradition. Interestingly, Tertullian referred to some of the same authors and others whom Josephus did not mention as witnesses to the antiquity of the *Ioudaioi*.[19] While Tertullian knew Josephus, he appears to have known the Eastern tradition independently. Josephus only gave us a sample. The basic principle for selection was a reference to the *Ioudaioi*. So, for example, we know of eleven authors of Egyptian antiquities;[20] Josephus only cited four. Similarly, we know of five Phoenician writers who wrote along similar

---

[17] H. K. Bhabha, *The Location of Culture* (London: Routledge, 1994).

[18] S. J. D. Cohen, "History and Historiography in the *Against Apion* of Josephus," *History and Theory* 27 (1988): 1–11; reprinted in A. Rapoport-Albert, ed., *Essays in Jewish Historiography* (South Florida Studies in the History of Judaism 15; Atlanta: Scholars Press, 1991).

[19] Tertullian, *Apol.* 19.6.

[20] Manetho (*FGrH* 609), Ptolemy of Mendes (*FGrH* 611), Chaeremon (*FGrH* 618 TT 5, 10; F 1), whose works are relatively well known. Others wrote Αἰγυπτιακά: Lysimachus (?) (*FGrH* 621 F 1), Apion (*FGrH* 616), Mosmes (*FGrH* 614), Lysias of Naucratis (*FGrH* 613), Asclepiades of Mendes (*FGrH* 617 F 1), and Thrasyllus of Mendes (*FGrH* 622 F 1). Others wrote Περὶ τῶν Αἰγυπτιῶν: Hermaeus (*FGrH* 620) and Demetrius (*FGrH* 643 F 1).

lines, including Philo of Byblos.[21] Josephus did not mention any of these in *Contra Apionem*. Among the Babylonians we only know of Berossus whom Josephus cites.[22] These authors probably made a case for their civilizations that was similar to the one that Josephus made for the *Ioudaioi* in his *Antiquities*. Is this defense of Eastern historiography a defense of the historiography of the *Jewish Antiquities*? Does it point to a historiographical tradition? The question should be addressed.

The second section is the third part of the work or the addition of 2.145–286. This second has a significant number of striking similarities to the *Hypothetica* attributed by Eusebius to Philo of Alexandria and to the maxims in Pseudo-Phocylides. Barclay challenges the authenticity of the *Hypothetica*. While it is an unusual text, I am not convinced by his arguments against authenticity. There are two major arguments for its authenticity. One, Eusebius had relatively good access to Philo's corpus. Sometime prior to the destruction of the Alexandrian community in 115–117 C.E., Philo's corpus and the writings of other Jewish authors must have passed into Christian hands or they would have perished with the community.[23] Origen carried a number of these texts to Caesarea when he moved north to escape an overbearing bishop. Eusebius of Caesarea knew Philo's works[24] and referred to the *Hypothetica* on two occasions, although once he called it Περὶ Ἰουδαίων.[25] If it were spurious, the forgery would probably have needed to take place within fifty years of Philo's death. The window of opportunity for pseudonymity was not great. Further, Eusebius did not credit Philo with a work that we know to be spurious. While this is not an air-tight argument, it should caution us against rejecting the tradition too quickly. Two, the specifics of the comments on the laws largely agree with what Philo says elsewhere in his corpus. Although there are variations, this is hardly a surprise in the Philonic corpus.[26] It is easier for me to explain the unique features of the work as a result of the specific context than to

---

[21] Laetus (*FGrH* 784 T 1), Hestiaeus (*FGrH* 786), Hieronymus (*FGrH* 787), Claudius Iolaus (*FGrH* 788), and Philo of Byblos (*FGrH* 790).

[22] *FGrH* 680.

[23] On this point see G. E. Sterling, "'The School of Sacred Laws': The Social Setting of Philo's Treatises," *VC* 53 (1999): 148–64, especially 160–63.

[24] On the transmission of the Philonica corpus via Origen and Eusebius see D. T. Runia, *Philo in Early Christian Literature: A Survey* (CRINT III.3; Assen: Van Gorcum–Minneapolis: Fortress, 1993), 16–24.

[25] Eusebius, *Hist. eccl.* 2.18.6. Cf. *Praep. ev.* 8.5.11 where he uses ὑποθετικά and 8.10.19 where he uses ὑπὲρ Ἰουδαίων ἀπολογία.

[26] See G. E. Sterling, "Philo and the Logic of Apologetics: An Analysis of the *Hypothetica*," *SBLSP* 29 (1990): 412–30, esp. 413, 416–17, 423. A good example of this is his treatment of the Sabbath.

attribute the fragments to another author. It is worth remembering that while Cohn and Wendland did not print it in their *editio major*, they did print it as an appendix in their *editio minor*. It was from the *editio minor* that it passed to the Loeb Classical Library edition.

Barclay follows the majority of scholars who argue that Philo, Pseudo-Phocylides, and Josephus all drew from a common tradition rather than from one another. I concur. If I may be forgiven a self reference, I have recently tried to advance this discussion by arguing that there are nine clusters of laws that the three share in common: sexual offenses, violations of person and property, *Haustafel*, property rights, care for others (laws of Buzyges), burial practices (laws of Buzyges), human reproduction, economic honesty, and the treatment of animals. These clusters probably represent areas of ethical instruction in Jewish houses of prayer or synagogues. Barclay did not know these essays since they are relatively recent.[27]

It would be possible to continue to add similar observations. I suspect that virtually all of us will find things with which we disagree given the scope of the coverage. At the same time, it would be a mistake to emphasize these and not express a deep sense of appreciation for Barclay's accomplishment. It is a first rate work of scholarship. I suspect that the commentary will be used principally as a reference work. It can be so used with profit. Each section is full enough to stand on its own. It will also reward those who spend the time to work through the whole. It is worth the time and effort to do so.

We are fortunate that some scholars in Second Temple Judaism and Early Christianity are writing commentaries on non-biblical texts. We have more than enough commentaries on the biblical texts and too few on the non-biblical texts. I do not anticipate another English commentary on *Contra Apionem* for many years. Thankfully, we will not need one. Barclay's commentary will serve us well for many years. To quote Josephus: this is its "most just defense."[28]

Gregory E. Sterling
University of Notre Dame

---

[27] G. E. Sterling, "Universalizing the Particular: Natural Law in Second Temple Jewish Ethics," *SPhA* 15 (2003): 64–80 and idem, "Was there a Common Ethic in Second Temple Judaism?," in *Sapiential Perspectives: Wisdom Literature in Light of the Dead Sea Scrolls. Proceedings of the Sixth International Symposium of the Orion Center, 20–22 May, 2001* (ed. J. J. Collins, G. E. Sterling, and R. A. Clements; STDJ 51; Leiden–Boston: Brill, 2004), 171–94.

[28] Josephus, *CA* 2.147.

M. Bonazzi, C. Lévy, and C. Steel (eds.), *A Platonic Pythagoras: Platonism and Pythagoreanism in the Imperial Age.* Monothéismes et Philosophie 10; Diatribai Colloquia in Ancient Philosophy 3. Turnhout: Brepols, 2007. ISBN 2-502-51915-9. Price €45.

The volume under review contains papers presented at a colloquium on the subject of 'Platonismo e pitagorismo in età imperiale' (i.e. the book's subtitle) held at Gargnano (Lake Garda, Italy) on 14–16 April 2005. The conference was organized by scholars from three universities, the State University of Milan, the University of Paris IV (Sorbonne) and the Catholic University of Leuven. The volume contains nine papers by scholars all working on the European continent. Although the title, the Introduction and three of the papers are in English, it is very much a European (i.e. non-Anglo-American) product. The language best represented is Italian with four papers, reflecting the location of the conference. The remaining two papers are in French.

The importance of the conference's theme is considerable from a historical point of view. Pythagoreanism as a school of thought (*hairesis*) never became wholly extinct in the Hellenistic period, but the revival that took place in the first centuries B.C.E. and C.E. was essential to its fortunes. From that time on until the end of antiquity it was a constant presence in the shadow of Platonism. It was often a part of the Platonic tradition, but was not always fully to be identified with it. The papers are fairly evenly divided between the period of Middle Platonism (the first four) and that of Neoplatonism (the last four), with a paper on Nicomachus as a fitting bridge between the two periods (he was active in the early second century but his writings were extensively commented on by later Neoplatonists).

The opening two papers both mention Philo in their titles. The first by Carlos Lévy is on "the question of the dyad in Philo of Alexandria." The formulation of the title is no doubt deliberate, because the author wishes to emphasize that it is not easy to determine the exact role that the dyad plays in Philo's writings (not to speak of his thought) and that the subject has been quite controversial in Philonic scholarship. Lévy first discusses the overt presence of Pythagoreanism in Philo's writings which is quite considerable, certainly in comparison with other schools, especially if his fondness for arithmology is taken into account. But when the specific role of dyad is examined, he argues that there is a danger that it is treated too systematically. It is important to note not only when Philo uses the concept, but also when he does not use it. In Pythagorean thought, and also in strands of Platonism that take over Pythagorean ideas, there is a clear connection between the indefinite dyad and the status of matter as a principle. Philo shows little hesitation in associating God with the monad, but he is very clearly uncomfortable with the association of the dyad as principle with matter. This is shown in an important discussion of the key text *Opif.* 8 (where the dyad is in fact not explicitly mentioned). Lévy makes quite clear his indebtedness to the paradigm shift introduced into Philonic studies by the late Valentin Nikiprowetzky. When philosophical ideas are used to explain the meaning of scripture, Philo is quite prepared to be flexible in their application, but sometimes there are limits and the concept of the dyad is a good example. The final words of the paper are worth quoting: "Même avec toutes les modluations auxquelles it était soumis par Philon, le concept de dyade restait suffisamment difficile, embarrassant pour que le traitement de la matière de la Création soit apparue à l'Alexandrin bien plus problématique que celui du Créateur (28)." I strongly recommend this essay to all Philonists.

The second essay is by the Italian Philonic scholar Francesca Calabi, who engages in an extensive comparison between the four extracts from a Pythagorean treatise "On kingship" attributed to the Pythagorean Ecphantus which have been preserved in Stobaeus and the writings of Philo. Arguing against the classic treatment of Delatte, she argues that the resemblances can shed light on various obscure points in Ecphantus' text and point to a shared Middle Platonist background. A fluent English translation of her paper can be found as an Appendix (185–215) in the monograph by the same author reviewed by John Dillon elsewhere in this Annual (see 224–227).

The two articles on Plutarch's position as a Platonist between the sceptical Academy and dogmatic Pythagoreanism by Daniel Babut and Pierluigi Donini will also be of interest to scholars working in the Philonic field, not only because of the extensive comparative work being done on the two thinkers at present (see the review of the volume edited by Rainier Hirsch-Luipold in last year's Annual [212–15]), but also in light of the surprising strand of scepticism found from time to time in the Alexandrian. Similarly Christoph Helmig's analysis of the relationship between Forms and numbers in Nicomachus' *Introduction to arithmetic* is relevant to Philonic studies because the scheme of cosmic creation involving a demiurgic *paradeigma* presented in the introductory part of the work shows some remarkable resemblances to what we find in Philo's exegesis of day one of creation in *Opif.*, including use of the term *logos*. Helmig argues that Nicomachus does not make a clear-cut distinction between Forms and numbers, and that in the demiurgic paradigm the former are replaced by the latter.

One of the best-known yet most enigmatic Pythagorean doctrines is the harmony of the spheres. The music produced by the whirling heavenly bodies is supposed to be of overwhelming beauty, yet we are unable to hear it. Dominic O'Meara devotes a stimulating essay to this theme, dedicated to the memory of Jean Pépin. He focuses on two aspects, (1) Neoplatonist responses to Aristotle's sceptical critique, and (2) Neoplatonist views on the value that hearing the harmony of the spheres might have for human beings, if only they could hear it. According to Porphyry and Iamblichus, Pythagoras was the only human being who was actually able to hear the music. In an interesting footnote (150 n. 8) O'Meara, who was indebted to Francesca Calabi on this point, notes that Pythagoras was reported to be outside his body when this happened, and that the same is said by Philo of Moses in *Somn.* 1.36. This would seem to be another example of Philonic one-up-manship.

Essays on Pythagoreanism and dialectical method in Proclus and on Pythagorean and Platonist perspectives in the same author by Elena Gritti and Alessandro Linguiti respectively follow. The final paper is a brilliant essay by Carlos Steel on Pythagorean geometrical theology, which ranges widely in order to help us understand how Pythagoreanizing philosophers could associate geometrical figures such as triangles and circles with divine beings, "a strange combination of mathematical rationalism and esoteric beliefs and magical rituals," but perhaps inherent in this philosophical and religious movement from the beginning (242).

If the truth be told, this book is not more than the sum of its parts. The overview of its theme in the brief Introduction is perfunctory and no overall thesis is pursued. But the parts certainly make attractive reading, and there is no doubting the importance of its subject, as I said at the outset of my review.

David T. Runia
Queen's College
The University of Melbourne

NEWS AND NOTES[1]

Philo of Alexandria Group of the Society of Biblical Literature

The Philo of Alexandria Group of the Society of Biblical Literature convened for two sessions on November 18–19 2007 in San Diego, California, during the Annual Meetings of the Society of Biblical Literature and the American Academy of Religion.

The theme of the first session was "Philo in Context" and was presided over by Hindy Najman. Speakers were Julia Annas (University of Arizona), "Philo and Plato's Laws"; Robert A. Kraft (University of Pennsylvania), "Looking for Abraham in all the Wrong Places"; Allen Kerkeslager (St. Joseph's University), "Rome as an Alternative to Alexandria in the Early Transmission of Philo's Works and Philonism"; Robert Hayward (University of Durham), "Philo, Jerome and Jewish Exegesis of Genesis 49:14–15."

The second session followed the customary format of concentrating on a Philonic treatise and was presided over by Annewies van den Hoek (Harvard Divinity School). The choice this year fell on *De Abrahamo*. First John Dillon (Trinity College, Dublin), who is preparing a treatment of this work in the Philo of Alexandria Commentary Series, presented a sample translation and commentary on *Abr.* 119–132. Responses were given by Erich Gruen (UC Berkeley) and Ellen Birnbaum (Cambridge, MA). David Runia then presented a paper on "The Place of *De Abrahamo* in Philo's *œuvre*," followed by James Royse (Berkeley), who spoke on "The Text of Philo's *De Abrahamo*" (these two papers have now been published in this year's Annual).

After a lively discussion a business meeting was held. It was decided that Hindy Najman would continue as chair and would be joined in that role by Sarah Pearce (University of Southampton). A steering committee was also chosen to assist them in their task.

The next meeting of the Philo of Alexandria group will be at the Annual meeting of the Society of Biblical Literature in Boston on November 21–25 2008. There are three sessions planned. The first will be on The Formation of the Soul in Hellenistic Judaism and James (together with the Letters of

---

[1] Items of general interest to Philo scholars to be included in this section can be sent to the editor, David Runia (contact details in Notes on Contributors below).

James, Peter and Jude section). The second will focus on the treatise *De vita contemplativa*. In the third, various papers of subjects related to Philo's writings and thought will be presented.

Hindy Najman, University of Toronto
David T. Runia, Queen's College, Melbourne

In Memoriam John Strugnell (1930-2007)

John Strugnell, Professor of Christian Origins Emeritus at Harvard Divinity School, who passed away on November 30, 2007, played an important role in fostering and advancing the study of Philo. Although he is known primarily for his work on the Dead Sea Scrolls, Professor Strugnell greatly contributed to Philonic studies as a teacher. In his Advanced Greek course, he trained many HDS students to read Philo in the original Greek and thus introduced them to Philo's thought and exegesis. Strugnell also did much to further knowledge about Judaism in the Hellenistic period. In 1970, he conducted a seminar on then little-known fragmentary Jewish writings in Greek; several students from this seminar later published introductions to and annotated translations of these writings in *The Old Testament Pseudepigrapha*, edited by James H. Charlesworth. By calling attention to these sources, Strugnell helped to illuminate Philo's cultural background and the traditions that may have influenced him. More directly, Strugnell offered guidance on and encouraged the publication of several doctoral theses that prominently featured Philo, including three that he supervised in which Philo was the central topic: "The Creation of Man: Philo and the History of Interpretation," by Thomas H. Tobin, S.J.; "The *Quaestiones et Solutiones in Genesim et in Exodum* of Philo Judaeus: A Synoptic Analysis," by Sze-kar Wan; and my own study, "The Place of Judaism in Philo's Thought: Israel, Jews, and Proselytes." Strugnell devoted many hours and much care to reading and reviewing his students' work and to discussing it with them. He was gracious in helping not only his students at Harvard but also others, including myself, from beyond Harvard and around the world. Students, colleagues, and friends will remember him for his remarkable generosity, keen wit, and enormous erudition.

Strugnell was born on May 25, 1930, in Barnet, England. He began to learn Greek at the age of six, later attended St. Paul's School as a scholarship student, and studied Classics and Semitic languages at Oxford, where he earned a B.A. and was later granted an M.A. While at Oxford in 1954, Strugnell was selected to become a member of the international team in Jerusalem assigned to prepare the Dead Sea Scrolls for publication, and he

dedicated much of his scholarly career to this project. Besides his appointments in Jerusalem and at Harvard Divinity School, where he began
teaching in 1966, Strugnell also held positions at the University of Chicago
and Duke University. With his combined training and extraordinary exper-
tise in classical and Semitic languages and literatures, he had a panoramic
understanding of history, thought, and religion in antiquity, particularly in
the centuries from Alexander the Great through Constantine. Strugnell is
survived by a sister, his former wife, five children, and five grandchildren.

During his retirement, when he was no longer able to attend annual
meetings of the Society of Biblical Literature, Strugnell would ask me to
buy him the latest issue of *The Studia Philonica Annual* and any new volume
from the Studia Philonica Monographs subseries. He wanted, he said, to
support the study of Philo. How well he succeeded!

Requiescat in pace.

Ellen Birnbaum
Cambridge, Massachusetts

Torrey Seland's blog activities restructured

For the past four years our Norwegian colleague has done a marvelous job
keeping us informed about his Philo studies via the philoblogger blog (see
the announcement in this Annual, vol. 16 (2004) 322). A little while ago
Torrey informed me that he is unable to keep three different blogs going
(Philo, I Peter, Biblical resources) and so will now concentrate his blog
activity on the last-named. See his announcement on April 26 at philo-
blogger.blogspot.com/. The Philo blog will not be taken down, so it can be
consulted for the foreseeable future. The remaining blog is called R P B S
(Resource pages for biblical studies) Blog, to be found at:

www.biblicalresources.wordpress.com.

It will continue to provide material on Philo studies, but much less than in
the past. All Philo scholars will join me in expressing my appreciation for
the labor of love that Torrey has performed for all of us over the past four
years. It has kept us well informed, not only about Philo, but also about our
friend Torrey. It will be missed.

David T. Runia, Queen's College, Melbourne

The Studia Philonica Annual 20 (2008) 248–251

NOTES ON CONTRIBUTORS

ELLEN BIRNBAUM has taught at several Boston-area institutions, including Boston University, Brandeis, and Harvard. Her postal address is 78 Porter Road, Cambridge, MA 02140, USA; her electronic address is ebirnbaum@comcast.net.

RANDALL D. CHESNUTT is the William S. Banowsky Chair of Religion and chairman of the Religion Division at Pepperdine University. His postal address is Religion Division, Pepperdine University, Malibu, CA 90263-4352, USA; his electronic address is randall.chesnutt@pepperdine. edu.

RONALD R. COX is Assistant Professor and Seaver Fellow in the Religion Division, Pepperdine University. His postal address is Religion Division, Pepperdine University, Malibu, CA 90263-4352, USA; his electronic address is Ronald.Cox@pepperdine.edu.

JOHN DILLON is Regius Professor of Greek (Emeritus) at Trinity College, Dublin. His postal address is: School of Classics, Arts Building, Trinity College, Dublin 2, IRELAND; his electronic address: dillonj@tcd.ie

KENNETH A. FOX has been Associate Professor of New Testament at the Canadian Theological Seminary in Toronto. His postal address is Canadian Theological Seminary, 30 Carrier Drive, Toronto ON M9W 5T7, CANADA; his electronic address is kennethafox@yahoo.ca.

ALBERT C. GELJON teaches classical languages at the Christelijke Gymnasium in Utrecht. His postal address is Gazellestraat 138, 3523 SZ Utrecht, THE NETHERLANDS; his electronic address is geljon@ixs.nl.

L. ANN JERVIS is Professor of New Testament at Wycliffe College at the University of Toronto. Her postal address is Wycliffe College, 5 Hos-kin Ave., Toronto, Ontario, M5S 1H7 CANADA; her electronic address is a.jervis@utoronto.ca.

HELEEN M. KEIZER is Dean of Academic Affairs at the Istituto Superiore di Osteopatia in Milan, Italy. Her postal address is Via Guerrazzi 3, 20052 Monza (Mi), ITALY; her electronic address is h.m.keizer@virgilio.it.

JOHN S KLOPPENBORG is Professor and Chair of the Department for the Study of Religion and the Centre for the Study of Religion at the University of Toronto. His postal address is Trinity College, 6 Hoskin Avenue, Toronto M5S1H8, CANADA; his electronic address is john.kloppenborg@utoronto.ca

JUTTA LEONHARDT-BALZER is Lecturer in New Testament at the University of Aberdeen. Her postal address is School of Divinity and Religious Studies, King's College, University of Aberdeen, Aberdeen AB24 3UB, UNITED KINGDOM; her electronic address is j.leonhardt-balzer@abdn.ac.uk.

BURTON L. MACK is Emeritus Professor of New Testament, Claremont School of Theology. His postal address is 608 W 9th St., Claremont, CA 91711, U.S.A.; his email address is burton.mack@uai.net.

JOSÉ PABLO MARTÍN is Director of Studies at the Universidad Nacional de General Sarmiento, San Miguel, Argentina, and Senior Research fellow of the Argentinian Research Organization (CONICET). His postal address is Azcuenaga 1090, 1663 San Miguel, ARGENTINA; his electronic address is fmk@ciudad.com.ar.

MAREN S. NIEHOFF is Senior Lecturer in the Department of Jewish Thought at the Hebrew University, Jerusalem. Her postal address is Department of Jewish Thought, Hebrew University, Mt. Scopus, Jerusalem 91905, ISRAEL; her electronic address is msmaren@mscc.huji.ac.il.

CYRIL O'REGAN is the Huisking Professor of Theology, Department of Theology, University of Notre Dame. His postal address is Department of Theology, University of Notre Dame, Notre Dame IN 46556, USA; his electronic address is coregan@nd.edu.

ROBERTO RADICE is Professor of Ancient Philosophy at the Sacred Heart University, Milan. His postal address is Via XXV Aprile 4, 21016 Luino, ITALY; his electronic address is rradice@iol.it.

ILARIA L. E. RAMELLI is Assistant in Ancient Philosophy at the Catholic University of the Sacred Heart, Milan, Department of Philosophy. Her postal address is Via Faustini 6, 29010 San Nicolò, Piacenza, ITALY; her electronic address is ilaria.ramelli@virgilio.it.

JEAN RIAUD is Professor in the Institut de Lettres et Histoire, Université Catholique de l'Ouest, Angers. His postal address is 24, rue du 8 mai 1945, Saint Barthélemy d'Anjou, FRANCE; his electronic address is jean.riaud@wanadoo.fr.

DAVID T. RUNIA is Master of Queen's College and Professorial Fellow in the School of Historical Studies at the University of Melbourne. His postal address is Queen's College, 1–17 College Crescent, Parkville 3052, AUSTRALIA; his electronic address is runia@queens.unimelb.edu.au.

KENNETH L. SCHENCK is Professor in the Division of Religion and Philosophy, Indiana Wesleyan University. His postal address is Division of Religion and Philosophy, Indiana Wesleyan University, Marion, IN 46953, USA; his electronic address is ken.schenck@indwes.edu.

GOTTFRIED SCHIMANOWSKI is Research Fellow at the Institutum Judaicum Delitzschianum in Münster, Germany. He also works as Schulreferent in the Saarland region of Germany. His postal address is Mittelstaedter Strasse 19, 72124 Pliezhausen, GERMANY; his electronic address is gschimanow@ gmx.de.

JAMES M. SCOTT is Professor of Religious Studies at Trinity Western University. His postal address is Department of Religious Studies, Trinity Western University, 7600 Glover Road, Langley, B.C. V2Y 1Y1, CANADA; his electronic address is scott@twu.ca.

TORREY SELAND is Professor of New Testament, School of Missions and Theology, Stavanger, Norway. His postal adress is School of Missions and Theology, Misjonsveien 34, 4024 Stavanger, NORWAY; his electronic address is torrey@gmail.com.

GREGORY E. STERLING is Dean of the Graduate School and Professor of New Testament and Christian Origins in the Department of Theology, University of Notre Dame. His postal address is 408 Main Building, University of Notre Dame, Notre Dame IN 46556, USA; his electronic address is sterling.1@nd.edu.

THOMAS H. TOBIN, S.J. is Professor of New Testament and Early Christianity at Loyola University Chicago. His postal address is Department of Theology, Loyola University Chicago, 6525 N. Sheridan Road, Chicago, IL 60626, USA; his electronic address is ttobin@luc.edu.

STEVEN WEITZMAN is Irving M. Glazer Chair of Jewish Studies, Professor of Religious Studies, and Director of the Robert A. and Sandra S. Borns Jewish Studies Program at Indiana University, Bloomington. His postal address is Borns Jewish Studies Program, 326 Goodbody Hall, Indiana University, Bloomington, IN 47405, USA; his electronic address is sweitzma@indiana.edu

DAVID WINSTON is Emeritus Professor of Hellenistic and Jewish Studies, Graduate Theological Union, Berkeley. His postal address is 1220 Grizzly Peak, Berkeley, CA 94708, USA; his electronic address is davidswinston@comcast.net.

The Studia Philonica Annual 20 (2008) 252–258

INSTRUCTIONS TO CONTRIBUTORS

Articles and Book reviews can only be considered for publication in *The Studia Philonica Annual* if they rigorously conform to the guidelines established by the editorial board. For further information see also the website of the Annual:

http://www.nd.edu/~philojud

1. *The Studia Philonica Annual* accepts articles for publication in the area of Hellenistic Judaism, with special emphasis on Philo and his *Umwelt*. Articles on Josephus will be given consideration if they focus on his relation to Judaism and classical culture (and not on primarily historical subjects). The languages in which the articles may be published are English, French and German. Translations from Italian or Dutch into English can be arranged at a modest cost to the author.

2. Articles and reviews are to be sent to the editors in electronic form as email attachments. The preferred word-processor is Microsoft Word. Users of Nota Bene or Word Perfect are requested to submit a copy exported in a format compatible with Word. Manuscripts should be double-spaced, including the notes. Words should be italicized when required, not underlined. Quotes five lines or longer should be indented and may be single-spaced. Preferred Greek and Hebrew fonts are the GreekKeys system (American Philological Association), Linguists Software fonts (Greek and Hebrew), or the fonts developed by 3DL. Unicode systems are strongly to be encouraged for ease of conversion. In all cases it is **imperative** that authors give **full details** about the word processor (if it is not Word) and foreign language fonts used. Moreover, if the manuscript contains Greek or Hebrew material, a pdf version of the document must be sent together with the word processing file. If this proves difficult, a hard copy can be sent by mail or by fax. No handwritten Greek or Hebrew can be accepted. Authors are requested not to vocalize their Hebrew (except when necessary) and to keep their use of this language to a reasonable minimum. It should always be borne in mind that not all readers of the Annual can be expected to read Greek or Hebrew. Transliteration is encouraged for incidental terms.

3. Authors are encouraged to use inclusive language wherever possible, avoiding terms such as "man" and "mankind" when referring to humanity in general.

4. For the preparation of articles and book reviews the Annual follows the guidelines of *The SBL Handbook of Style for Ancient Near Eastern, Biblical, and Early Christian Studies*, Hendrickson: Peabody Mass., 1999. A downloadable pdf version of this guide is available on the SBL website, www.sbl-site.org. Here are examples of how a monograph, a monograph in a series, an edited volume, an article in an edited volume and a journal article are to be cited in notes (different conventions apply for bibliographies):

Joan E. Taylor, *Jewish Women Philosophers of First-Century Alexandria—Philo's 'Therapeutae' Reconsidered* (Oxford: Oxford University Press, 2003), 123.

Ellen Birnbaum, *The Place of Judaism in Philo's Thought: Israel, Jews, and Proselytes* (BJS 290; SPhM 2; Atlanta: Scholars Press, 1996), 134.

Gerard P. Luttikhuizen, ed., *Eve's Children. The Biblical Stories Retold and Interpreted in Jewish and Christian Traditions* (Themes in Biblical Narrative 5; Leiden: Brill, 2003), 145.

Gregory E. Sterling, "The Bond of Humanity: Friendship in Philo of Alexandria," in *Greco-Roman Perspectives on Friendship*, (ed. John T. Fitzgerald; SBLRBS 34; Atlanta: Scholars Press, 1997), 203–23.

James R. Royse, "Jeremiah Markland's Contribution to the Textual Criticism of Philo." *SPhA* 16 (2004): 50–60. (Note that abbreviations are used in the notes, but not in a bibliography.)

Note that, when joining up numbers in all textual and bibliographical references the n-dash should be used and not the hyphen, i.e. 50–60, not 50-60. For publishing houses only the first location is given. Submissions which do not conform to these guidelines will be returned to the authors.

5. The following abbreviations are to be used in both articles and book reviews.

(a) Philonic treatises are to be abbreviated according to the following list. Numbering follows the edition of Cohn and Wendland, using Arabic numbers only and full stops rather than colons (e.g. *Spec.* 4.123). Note that *De Providentia* should be cited according to Aucher's edition, and not the LCL translation of the fragments by F. H. Colson.

Abr.	*De Abrahamo*
Aet.	*De aeternitate mundi*
Agr.	*De agricultura*
Anim.	*De animalibus*
Cher.	*De Cherubim*
Contempl.	*De vita contemplativa*
Conf.	*De confusione linguarum*
Congr.	*De congressu eruditionis gratia*
Decal.	*De Decalogo*
Deo	*De Deo*
Det.	*Quod deterius potiori insidiari soleat*
Deus	*Quod Deus sit immutabilis*
Ebr.	*De ebrietate*

Flacc.	*In Flaccum*
Fug.	*De fuga et inventione*
Gig.	*De gigantibus*
Her.	*Quis rerum divinarum heres sit*
Hypoth.	*Hypothetica*
Ios.	*De Iosepho*
Leg. 1–3	*Legum allegoriae* I, II, III
Legat.	*Legatio ad Gaium*
Migr.	*De migratione Abrahami*
Mos. 1–2	*De vita Moysis* I, II
Mut.	*De mutatione nominum*
Opif.	*De opificio mundi*
Plant.	*De plantatione*
Post.	*De posteritate Caini*
Praem.	*De praemiis et poenis, De exsecrationibus*
Prob.	*Quod omnis probus liber sit*
Prov. 1–2	*De Providentia* I, II
QE 1–2	*Quaestiones et solutiones in Exodum* I, II
QG 1–4	*Quaestiones et solutiones in Genesim* I, II, III, IV
Sacr.	*De sacrificiis Abelis et Caini*
Sobr.	*De sobrietate*
Somn. 1–2	*De somniis* I, II
Spec. 1–4	*De specialibus legibus* I, II, III, IV
Virt.	*De virtutibus*

(b) Standard works of Philonic scholarship are abbreviated as follows:

G-G Howard L. Goodhart and Erwin R. Goodenough, "A General Bibliography of Philo Judaeus." In *The Politics of Philo Judaeus: Practice and Theory* (ed. Erwin R. Goodenough; New Haven: Yale University Press, 1938; repr. Georg Olms: Hildesheim, 1967), 125–321.

PCH *Philo von Alexandria: die Werke in deutscher Übersetzung*, ed. Leopold Cohn, Isaac Heinemann *et al.*, 7 vols. (Breslau: M & H Marcus Verlag, Berlin: Walter de Gruyter, 1909–64).

PCW *Philonis Alexandrini opera quae supersunt*, ed. Leopoldus Cohn, Paulus Wendland et Sigismundus Reiter, 6 vols. (Berlin: Georg Reimer, 1896–1915).

PLCL *Philo in Ten Volumes (and Two Supplementary Volumes)*, English translation by F. H. Colson, G. H. Whitaker (and R. Marcus), 12 vols. (Loeb Classical Library; London: William Heinemann, Cambridge, Mass.: Harvard University Press, 1929–62).

PAPM *Les œuvres de Philon d'Alexandrie*, French translation under the general editorship of Roger Arnaldez, Jean Pouilloux, and Claude Mondésert (Paris: Cerf, 1961–92).

R-R Roberto Radice and David T. Runia, *Philo of Alexandria: an Annotated Bibliography 1937–1986* (VCSup 8; Leiden etc.: Brill 1988).

RRS	David T. Runia, *Philo of Alexandria: an Annotated Bibliography 1987–1996* (VCSup 57; Leiden etc.: Brill 2000).
SPh	*Studia Philonica*
SPhA	*The Studia Philonica Annual*
SPhM	Studia Philonica Monographs
PACS	Philo of Alexandria Commentary Series

(c) References to biblical authors and texts and to ancient authors and writings are to be abbreviated as recommended in the *SBL Handbook of Style* §8.2–3. Note that biblical books are not italicized and that between chapter and verse a colon is placed (but for non-biblical references colons should not be used). Abbreviations should be used for biblical books when they are followed by chapter or chapter and verse unless the book is the first word in a sentence. Authors writing in German or French should follow their own conventions for biblical citations.

(d) For giving dates the abbreviations B.C.E. and C.E. are preferred and should be printed in small caps.

(e) Journals, monograph series, source collections and standard reference works are to be be abbreviated in accordance with the recommendations listed in *The SBL Handbook of Style* §8.4. The following list contains a selection of the more important abbreviations, along with a few abbreviations of classical and philosophical journals and standard reference books not furnished in the list.

ABD	*The Anchor Bible Dictionary*, 6 vols. New York etc. 1992.
AC	*L'Antiquité Classique*
ACW	Ancient Christian Writers
AGJU	Arbeiten zur Geschichte des antiken Judentums und des Urchristentums
AJPh	*American Journal of Philology*
AJSL	*American Journal of Semitic Languages*
ALGHJ	Arbeiten zur Literatur und Geschichte des hellenistischen Judentums
ANRW	*Aufstieg und Niedergang der römischen Welt*
APh	*L'Année Philologique*
BDAG	Bauer, W., F. W. Danker, W. F. Arndt, and F. W. Gingrich. *A Greek-English Lexicon of the New Testament and other Early Christian literature.* 3^d ed. Chicago: University of Chicago Press, 1999.
BibOr	Bibliotheca Orientalis
BJRL	*Bulletin of the John Rylands Library*
BJS	Brown Judaic Studies
BMCR	*Bryn Mawr Classical Review* (electronic)
BZAW	Beihefte zur Zeitschrift für die alttestamentliche Wissenschaft
BZNW	Beihefte zur Zeitschrift für die neutestamentliche Wissenschaft
BZRGG	Beihefte zur Zeitschrift für Religions- und Geistesgeschichte
CBQ	*The Catholic Biblical Quarterly*

CBQMS	The Catholic Biblical Quarterly. Monograph Series
CC	Corpus Christianorum, Turnhout
CIG	*Corpus Inscriptionum Graecarum*. Edited by A. Boeckh, 4 vols. in 8. Berlin 1828–77.
CIJ	*Corpus Inscriptionum Judaicarum*. Edited by J. B. Frey, 2 vols. Rome 1936–52.
CIL	*Corpus Inscriptionum Latinarum*. Berlin 1862–.
CIS	*Corpus Inscriptionum Semiticarum*. Paris 1881–1962.
CPh	*Classical Philology*
CPJ	*Corpus Papyrorum Judaicarum*. Edited by V. Tcherikover and A. Fuks, 3 vols. Cambrige Mass. 1957–64.
CQ	*The Classical Quarterly*
CR	*The Classical Review*
CRINT	Compendia Rerum Iudaicarum ad Novum Testamentum
CPG	*Clavis Patrum Graecorum*. Edited by M. Geerard, 5 vols. and suppl. vol. Turnhout 1974–98.
CPL	*Clavis Patrum Latinorum*. Edited by E. Dekkers. 3rd ed. Turnhout 1995.
CSCO	Corpus Scriptorum Christianorum Orientalium
DA	Dissertation Abstracts
DBSup	*Dictionnaire de la Bible*, Supplément. Paris 1928–.
DSpir	*Dictionnaire de Spiritualité*, 17 vols. Paris 1932–95.
EncJud	*Encyclopaedia Judaica*, 16 vols. Jerusalem 1972.
EPRO	Études préliminaires aux religions orientales dans l'Empire romain
FrGH	*Fragmente der Griechische Historiker*, Edited by F. Jacoby et al. Leiden 1954–.
GCS	Die griechischen christlichen Schriftsteller, Leipzig
GLAJJ	M. Stern, *Greek and Latin authors on Jews and Judaism*, 3 vols. Jerusalem 1974–84.
GRBS	*Greek, Roman and Byzantine Studies*
HKNT	Handkommentar zum Neuen Testament, Tübingen
HNT	Handbuch zum Neuen Testament, Tübingen
HR	*History of Religions*
HThR	*Harvard Theological Review*
HUCA	*Hebrew Union College Annual*
JAAR	*Journal of the American Academy of Religion*
JAOS	*Journal of the American Oriental Society*
JAC	*Jahrbuch für Antike und Christentum*
JBL	*Journal of Biblical Literature*
JHI	*Journal of the History of Ideas*
JHS	*The Journal of Hellenic Studies*
JJS	*The Journal of Jewish Studies*
JQR	*The Jewish Quarterly Review*
JR	*The Journal of Religion*
JRS	*The Journal of Roman Studies*
JSHRZ	Jüdische Schriften aus hellenistisch-römischer Zeit
JSJ	*Journal for the Study of Judaism in the Persian, Hellenistic and Roman Periods*
JSJSup	Supplements to the Journal for the Study of Judaism
JSNT	*Journal for the Study of the New Testament*
JSNTSup	Journal for the Study of the New Testament. Supplement Series
JSOT	*Journal for the Study of the Old Testament*

JSOTSup	Journal for the Study of the Old Testament. Supplement Series
JSP	*Journal for the Study of the Pseudepigrapha and Related Literature*
JSSt	*Journal of Semitic Studies*
JThS	*The Journal of Theological Studies*
KBL	L. Koehler and W. Baumgartner, *Lexicon in Veteris Testamenti libros*, 3 vols. 3rd ed. Leiden 1967–83.
KJ	*Kirjath Sepher*
LCL	Loeb Classical Library
LSJ	*A Greek-English Lexicon*. Edited by H. G. Liddell, R. Scott, H. S. Jones. 9th ed. with revised suppl. Oxford, 1996.
MGWJ	*Monatsschrift für Geschichte und Wissenschaft des Judentums*
Mnem	*Mnemosyne*
NCE	*New Catholic Encyclopedia*, 15 vols. New York 1967.
NHS	Nag Hammadi Studies
NT	*Novum Testamentum*
NTSup	Supplements to Novum Testamentum
NTA	*New Testament Abstracts*
NTOA	Novum Testamentum et Orbis Antiquus
NTS	*New Testament Studies*
OLD	*The Oxford Latin Dictionary*. Edited by P. G. W. Glare. Oxford, 1982.
OTP	*The Old Testament Pseudepigrapha*. Edited by J. H. Charlesworth. 2 vols. New York–London, 1983–85.
PAAJR	*Proceedings of the American Academy for Jewish Research*
PAL	*Philon d'Alexandrie: Lyon 11–15 Septembre 1966*. Éditions du CNRS, Paris 1967.
P G	Patrologiae cursus completus: series Graeca. Edited by J. P. Migne. 162 vols. Paris, 1857–1912.
PGL	*A Patristic Greek Lexicon*. Edited by G. W. H. Lampe. Oxford 1961.
PhilAnt	Philosophia Antiqua
P L	Patrologiae cursus completus: series Latina. Edited by J. P. Migne. 221 vols. Paris, 1844–64.
PW	Pauly-Wissowa-Kroll, *Real-Encyclopaedie der classischen Altertumswissenschaft*. 49 vols. Munich, 1980.
PWSup	Supplement to PW
RAC	*Reallexikon für Antike und Christentum*
RB	*Revue Biblique*
REA	*Revue des Études Anciennes*
REArm	*Revue des Études Arméniennes*
REAug	*Revue des Études Augustiniennes*
REG	*Revue des Études Grecques*
REJ	*Revue des Études Juives*
REL	*Revue des Études Latines*
RGG	*Die Religion in Geschichte und Gegenwart*, 7 vols. 3rd edition Tübingen, 1957–65.
RhM	*Rheinisches Museum für Philologie*
RQ	*Revue de Qumran*
RSR	*Revue des Sciences Religieuses*

Str-B	H. L. Strack and P. Billerbeck, *Kommentar zum Neuen Testament aus Talmud und Midrasch*, 6 vols. Munich 1922–61.
SBLDS	Society of Biblical Literature Dissertation Series
SBLMS	Society of Biblical Literature Monograph Series
SBLSPS	Society of Biblical Literature Seminar Papers Series
SC	Sources Chrétiennes
Sem	*Semitica*
SHJP	E. Schürer, *The History of the Jewish People in the Age of Jesus Christ*. Revised edition, 3 vols. in 4. Edinburgh 1973–87.
SJLA	Studies in Judaism in Late Antiquity
SNTSMS	Society for New Testament Studies. Monograph Series
SR	*Studies in Religion*
SUNT	Studien zur Umwelt des Neuen Testaments
SVF	*Stoicorum veterum fragmenta*. Edited by J. von Arnim. 4 vols. Leipzig, 1903–24.
TDNT	*Theological Dictionary of the New Testament*. 10 vols. Grand Rapids 1964–76.
THKNT	Theologischer Handkommentar zum Neuen Testament, Berlin
TRE	*Theologische Realenzyklopädie*, Berlin
TSAJ	Texte und Studien zum Antike Judentum
TU	Texte und Untersuchungen zur Geschichte der altchristlichen Literatur, Berlin
TWNT	*Theologisches Wörterbuch zum Neuen Testament*, 10 vols. Stuttgart 1933–79.
VC	*Vigiliae Christianae*
VCSup	Supplements to Vigiliae Christianae
VT	*Vetus Testamentum*
WMANT	Wissenschaftliche Monographien zum Alten und Neuen Testament
WUNT	Wissenschaftliche Untersuchungen zum Neuen Testament
ZAW	*Zeitschrift für die alttestamentliche Wissenschaft*
ZKG	*Zeitschrift für Kirchengeschichte*
ZKTh	*Zeitschrift für Katholische Theologie*
ZNW	*Zeitschrift für die neutestamentliche Wissenschaft*
ZRGG	*Zeitschrift für Religions- und Geistesgeschichte*

www.ingramcontent.com/pod-product-compliance
Lightning Source LLC
Chambersburg PA
CBHW020403100426
42812CB00001B/173